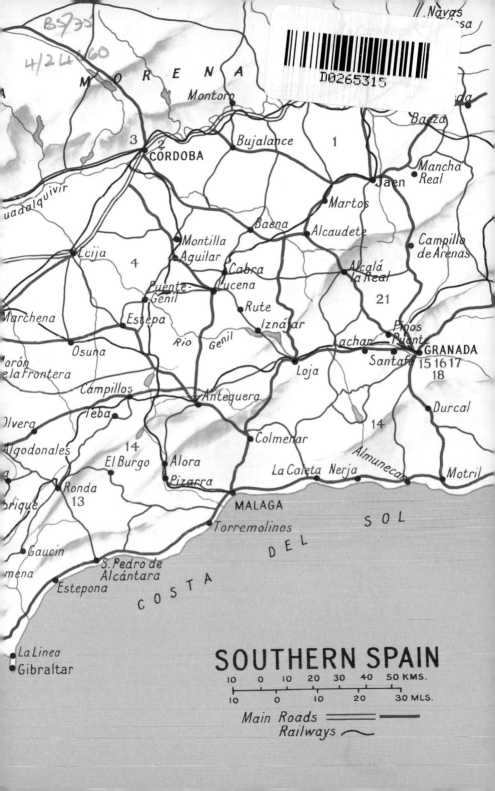

SOUTHERN SPAIN

10 0 10 20 30 40 50 KMS.

10 0 10 20 30 MLS.

Main Roads
Railways

THE COMPANION GUIDE TO
The South of Spain

THE COMPANION GUIDES

GENERAL EDITOR: VINCENT CRONIN

It is the aim of these Guides to provide a Companion, in the person of the author, who knows intimately the places and people of whom he writes, and is able to communicate this knowledge and affection to his readers. It is hoped that the text and pictures will aid them in their preparations and in their travels and will help them to remember on their return.

THE COMPANION GUIDE TO

The South of Spain

ALFONSO LOWE

Correspondent of the Royal
Academy of Córdoba

COLLINS
ST JAMES'S PLACE, LONDON 1973

Maps by Charles Green

© Alfonso Lowe, 1973

ISBN 0 00 211138 1

Printed in Great Britain
Collins Clear-Type Press
London and Glasgow

Contents

❧

Photographs

❧

Except where otherwise indicated photographs are by the author

Introduction

✦

The territory I have described uses the natural boundary of the Sierra Morena on the north; this is prolonged eastward by an imaginary line to the Cabo de la Nao. It is therefore a purely geographical division, including Andalucía, Murcia and the greater part of the Province of Alicante. The inhabitants, as well as the styles of architecture, may therefore be expected to vary considerably, and even in Andalucía there are noticeable differences between city and country dwellers, and from one province to another. The visitor must rid himself of one fallacy for a start; the Andalucian is not an idle hedonist, dividing his time between rolling cigarettes and strumming on the guitar. Life is still hard here and the borderline between poverty and famine is easily crossed. The Spaniard, generally speaking, has to work hard for small rewards and the traditional Spanish gaiety is obvious only at the *fiesta* or when supplied commercially, often by gypsies.

The route I have chosen makes a rough figure of eight, with the crossing at Granada. It enables the visitor to see nearly all the coast as well as every place of interest inland. There are also optional excursions from the main centres to enable lesser known towns to be seen, often with great enjoyment by those who have previously seen the showplaces in a hurried, organised tour. The route is planned primarily for a motor car tour, but it can be adequately covered by public transport. Towns, whenever possible, should be seen on foot, and one should remember to look upwards from time to time; only a part of the interesting features is at eye level.

Package tours are a wonderful invention—for the participants. Relieved of all responsibility, shepherded through famous buildings by competent guides, told what to eat and when, visitors can give their full attention to a study of the country, confident that a hotel bedroom awaits them. Other travellers, however, find their pleasure diminished by the preferential treatment given to the package tour; too often hotel accommodation is found only after a tiring search and the repeated, 'Sorry, but we have three *grupos* coming.' It has thus become essential to book ahead at many towns, especially Granada, and it is as well to choose a first-class or de luxe pension, too small to accommodate a *grupo*. A regrettable and world-wide consequence of this state of affairs is a falling off in the quality of accommodation in hotels that make their living out of package tours; the complaints of one or two individual tourists have very little effect.

Except in July and August Southern Spain can have cold spells and rain, though rarely. In winter the usual clothes for northern latitudes can be taken, with a change of lighter ones for the frequent sunny days. The unshepherded tourist may find the following accessories useful: a pocket compass and torch, opera glasses, a detailed map—the Mapa Oficial de Carreteras (250 pesetas) is the best—and visiting cards. The last make life much smoother, for they imply a *caballerismo* that is respected; this has nothing to do with snobbishness, for the bootblack expects to be treated as a *caballero* and Spain, apart from a few profiteers and civil servants drunk with their recent rise to authority, is a democratic country. Among my treasured souvenirs is the visiting card of a young man who did me a service and to whom I had handed my card. His read 'Miguel Fulano de Tal, Car Park Attendant in the Plaza Mayor'.

Visiting hours at places of interest are apt to change, and in smaller towns may not exist. They can usually be obtained from the hotel, or from the local tourist office, a useful place to find at the beginning of a visit. Official guides are always useful and have passed examinations; they prefer taking a guided tour, but if they have the time will accompany you for a pre-arranged sum. In small towns the services of a small boy are often useful and ten pesetas for a morning's walk will be gratefully received. It should be enough to indicate the next place you wish to visit, and the boy will do the rest, but it is essential that you should say the names correctly, particularly with the stress on the proper syllables. So it is useless to ask the way to 'Jane' as I heard one traveller pronounce it, when you want to go to HaEN (Jaén). If a church is closed, provided it is not between the hours of 1 pm and 4, your boy will find the keys and whoever brings them will also expect a tip.

Arabic names have been given in the simplest possible way, ignoring the precise transliteration of the Royal Asian Society. There are twenty-six Arab consonants in place of twenty English ('p' being a later, Persian addition), but the difference between 'k' and 'q', two 't's, two 'd's, two 'z's and so on are of interest only to the orientalist.

Of the various periods and styles found in Southern Spain, it is as well to remember that many Spaniards confuse Mozarabic and Mudéjar. The former signifies Christians who remained true to their faith under Moslem rule, and finally fled to the North when persecution began under the Moorish invasions. Thus their epoch extends from the eighth to the thirteenth centuries. The Mudéjars were Moslems living under Christian rule and their work and influence extends from the thirteenth to the seventeenth centuries.

Similarly, Visigothic and Gothic are often used without definition. In this book the former will refer to the Germanic tribe that entered Spain in the fifth century and ruled until the eighth. Gothic refers only to a period of art, especially architecture, which made its appearance in the thirteenth century and persisted, in a specially modified form, until well into the sixteenth, when it became blended with the lately arrived Renaissance style.

I should like to acknowledge the help of the Dirección General de Promoción del Turismo and all their Provincial Chiefs of Delegation, which was essential in compiling this book. Individual names are left out as transfers between posts are so frequent. Of the foreign staff, however, I should like to thank Don Jesús Aramendi, in Johannesburg, for his efficient and never-failing interest. The Directors of almost all the museums described put their knowledge at my disposal. Special thanks are gladly offered to Don Luis Mapelli and Don Anastasio Pérez Dorado of Córdoba; to Don José Molina of Baeza; to Don Vicente Martínez Morellá of Alicante; and to an old friend, teacher and antiquarian, the Reverend Don Cristóbal Cantero Lorente of Úbeda.

CHAPTER ONE

Introducing Andalucía: The Road to Córdoba

✤

Despeñaperros—Bailén—Andújar—Cañete de las Torres—
Bujalance—Montoro—Alcolea

The road from Madrid climbs gradually and the cars crawl like ants trying to escape from the giant saucer of the central Spanish plateau. Almost imperceptibly the landscape becomes hilly, the earth dull and barren; then the rocks break through their sparse cover and quite suddenly you arrive at the **Pass of Despeñaperros** from which, as if from the saucer's rim, you see the fertile plains of Andalucía. This is the Sierra Morena, running east and west and forming a natural boundary to Southern Spain, wild country fit for wild men and dark deeds, a home for brigands from Roman days until our own. In these mountains Don Quixote met the priests carrying the mysterious body from Baeza to Segovia, now believed to have been the stolen remains of St. John of the Cross, whose body was actually smuggled from Úbeda, only 9 km. from Baeza; and when he had liberated the galley slaves, Don Quixote retired to the Sierra Morena to avoid the *Santa Hermandad*, the Holy Brotherhood, ancestor of the Civil Guard.

The fine road through the Puerto de Despeñaperros was built as recently as 1779 by Le Maur, a French engineer in the service of Charles III; before that the Highway ran through Ciudad Real to the west. There are parking places and view-points from which you can see the crags and scree above, studded with ever-green oaks and stone pines and the domestic olive which, like the Catalans, seems to extract a living from the stones. Below are precipitous slopes that never quite meet, for between the opposing sides runs a tributary of the Guadalimar, destined to join the Guadalquivir, the Great River, and to flow with its majestic stream through Córdoba and Seville, through fertile plains and lonely marshes to the Atlantic. Beside it is the railway line on which a toy train, hundreds of feet below, winds in and out of its seven tunnels.

To the east an almost vertical stratification, witness of an

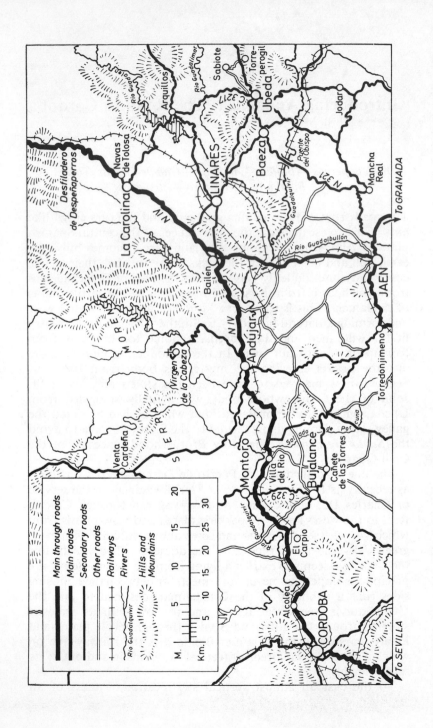

upheaval far back in geological time, has earned the title of **Los Órganos** and indeed the sharp spurs, yellow-green with lichen, bear some resemblance to an organ. Further on **El Salto del Fraile** is marked by twin pinnacles, but local memory has long forgotten who the monk was, or why he jumped; the inhabitants seem satisfied with the fact that he tumbled to his death. The name Despeñaperros is puzzling: literally it means 'throwing down of the dogs' and the facile change to 'overthrow', commemorating the battle of Las Navas de Tolosa, is a bold assumption. There is another Despeñaperros, by the way, inside the city of Tarragona, and no history of any victory near by. To stand between these crags and precipices is to understand the desperation of the Spanish and their allies in 1212 when they found all the passes guarded by the Almohads who, under the command of An-Nasir, were marching north in a holy war or *jehad*, while the Christians, with Pope Innocent III's blessing, were performing the same exercise in a southward direction. The kings of Castile, Aragón and Navarre had for once united; they were supported by 60,000 foreigners, mainly French; most of these, however, turned back home in disgust when they were not allowed to butcher the Moslem prisoners captured in Calatrava or the Jews of the allied city of Toledo.

Alfonso VIII of Castile, entitled the Noble, had been disgracefully defeated at Alarcos in 1195 and had vowed never to ride a horse or know a woman again until the defeat had been avenged. As he marched south in the hot summer of 1212 we can understand his eagerness to get to grips with the enemy, for walking must have been tiring. The Almohads were Moroccans, to whom Moslem Spain was only a dependency, but in less than a century they had established themselves as formidable fighters, ruthless fanatics and enlightened engineers. Had they but known, the coming battle was to be the turning point of Moslem fortunes in Spain; this time marked the beginning of the Christians' ascendancy and Spanish Islam was shortly to become a vassal state, existing precariously until its final obliteration. When the Christians found no way through the Sierra, Alfonso commended his cause to God, who sent him a humble shepherd, they say from Cuenca, accustomed to driving his flocks over the Sierra Morena every winter; this was still done each year until it was found more convenient (within living memory) to move the sheep by train. Thanks to the shepherd's local knowledge the Christian host was able to fall on the Moslems and inflict a decisive defeat, with the result that only the kingdom of Granada survived for a few more centuries. It is understandable that the *pastorcito*, the little shepherd, should have become semi-divine in an age when that side won which could chalk up most miracles; there was therefore no question about his supernatural origin, the only arguable point being his identification with St. Isidore of Seville, St. Isidro the patron of Madrid, or St. James of Compostela.

Fifteen kilometres farther is the tiny village of **Las Navas de Tolosa**, to the left of the highway, an uninspiring introduction to the South, where a hundred more attractive ones will be seen. There is no monument to mark the scene of a great victory; this, they tell you, is to be found farther on at **La Carolina**, 2½ kilometres ahead. This, too, is an undistinguished town on the west side of the road, but has had its hour in the days when a determined effort was made under Charles III to stamp out the lawlessness of the Sierra Morena. One measure, as we have seen, was the construction of the great highway, now the arterial N IV; another was the foundation of a number of settlements in the depopulated, bandit-infested area, with La Carolina as their capital. Many of the smaller villages were also named after members of the royal family—Isabela and Fernandina are only a few miles away on the left. The idea was that of Pablo Olavide, a royal minister, who had come from Peru; the settlements were occupied by thrifty and hardworking colonists, recruited chiefly from Switzerland and Germany, who became acclimatised so rapidly that when Borrow passèd through, just two generations later, they no longer spoke German. Olavide was later seized by the Inquisition, incarcerated for a year and then sentenced to eight years' detention in a monastery for impiety and immorality; he managed to escape to France but the Inquisition's main object had been achieved, for they had seized his wealth and property. The moral of the tale is that one should leave vested interests well alone; it was the monks of the Sierra who reported Olavide in revenge for his interference with their established practice of sharing the bandits' booty. If you are still thinking of the great battle you will search in vain for the monument; it was knocked over by a lorry in 1966 and its remains removed later by the town council, though the news has not yet reached Las Navas de Tolosa.

But all these are a mere prelude to 'our divine Andalucía', as García Gómez calls it. As the road descends, the great plain of the Guadalquivir unfolds and one sees some of the hundred and fifty million olive trees of this province of Jaén, planted in

exact rows that converge in the distance, looking rather like
expanses of corduroy. The Phoenicians took its minerals, the
Romans its grain and horses; the Vandals stayed here for a short
time and then moved on to North Africa because of famine,
leaving their name to become the Moslem's Al-Andalus, applied
to every part of Spain that came under their rule. No one treasured
this beautiful land more than the Arabs and Africans and none
enriched it more with intelligent agriculture and the importations
of new crops; they changed its face with irrigation and the cultivation of rice, sugar-cane, carobs, citrus fruits and a dozen other
products of which the Christian West had barely heard. Secure
in this fertile paradise they also cultivated science and the arts,
transmitting the knowledge of ancient Greece and the Orient to
European scholars so that their influence can be detected in every
literary and scientific achievement, in the songs of the trouba-
dours, the poems of Dante and the discoveries of Copernicus.

The plain is dotted with white farmhouses where villages are
far apart, self-contained units called *cortijos*, their main entrance
crowned with a religious image in ceramic, for everything goes
better under sacred patronage. Garages and filling stations may
have some such name as 'The Five Wounds', and a ramshackle
lorry may crawl thundering up a hill, belching dense black
clouds from behind and carrying above the windscreen the
boldly painted and somehow appropriate name *Nuestra Señora
de los Dolores*. The *cortijo* is built as a rectangle round a spacious
courtyard; one side is taken up by the family's living-quarters,
and the rest accommodates the servants and field workers, the
stables, cowshed, grain-stores, hayloft, chicken-house and frequently an oil-press and *bodega* for home-produced wine. Up to
the end of last century the labourer wore the Berber breeches
called *zaragüelles*, short jacket, red sash and leather gaiters; they
still wear the *calañés*, a wide straw hat with upturned brim. The
women in many parts of the South wear a similar hat over a coif
that covers all except the eyes, nose and mouth, long detachable
sleeves with flaps for the backs of the hands and trousers beneath
the skirts; 'Arab', say the writers who see them for the first time,
not knowing that working class women regard a sun-tan as a
social stigma and covet veins that show 'blue blood' through a
white skin.

The Andalucian is supposed to have certain characteristics
that distinguish him from other Spaniards; certainly his language
does so, for his dialect changes 'c' and 'z' to 's' and drops the
's', often along with a syllable or two, at the end of a word.

Books have been written about his temperament, his *duende* or ebullient spirit, his (or her) propensity for breaking into song and dance at the drop of a hat, his panache and wit. The truth is that one can generalise as little about the Andalucian as one can about the Spaniard—or man himself. Sometimes, during a *romería*, or local pilgrimage and Bank Holiday combined, he is gay and his gaiety expresses itself in music and dancing; usually he is serious, for life is hard where many are poor; in one district, such as that of Álora, he is *cerrado*, 'shut in', unapproachable by the stranger, even by an Andalucian from elsewhere; in Jaén Province there is a large number of blond and blue-eyed Andalucians, descendants of Castilian conquerors, while in the southern part of Granada Province a whole family may look North African. Generally speaking, the countryman is conservative, the population of seaports liberal: Cádiz saw the birth of the first attempt at a modern constitution, that of 1812; Málaga has a reputation for resistance to authoritarian rule, and José Antonio Primo de Rivera, founder of the Falange, was shot at Alicante. But Andalucía is unique, if not in its population, in another important sphere—food and wine. Everyone knows *gazpacho*, the mixture of oil, vinegar and vegetable pulps that workmen take to the fields as such and convert into a cold soup with water from a porous jar that has been hung from the branch of a tree, subsequently adding dry bread; even the hotels that cater for package tours dare not omit it from their summer menu. But how many know *ajo blanco*, an equally delightful cold soup of garlic? Or the omelet made with wild mountain asparagus, or the *rabo de toro*, a seasoned ox-tail stew, allegedly bulls' tail, just as we are never served duck or mutton but always duckling and lamb? For some reason the soil of Andalucía produces little or no table wine, so that even the humblest *venta* stocks the red wine of La Mancha, but she more than atones for this by the excellence of her heavier offerings from Jerez, Montilla, Málaga and the Alpujarras.

At **Bailén**, 24 kilometres farther on, the Albergue de Carretera —one of the smaller hotels run by the D.G.T., the Government Department of Tourism, who also control the bigger and equally good Paradors—is noteworthy in that it conscientiously implements the policy of the Department, to provide at least one local dish on each meal's menu. One of these is *guiñapos*, a strong soup flavoured with tomato and a few drops of the local olive oil, in which there is a soft and very light variety of noodle, so light as to be almost foamy, in contrast to Italian *pasta*. Another is a rice dish, *arroz caldoso*, which resembles a more liquid *paella* without saffron (or yellow dye, which is more usual today) and contains a similarly wide variety of items—meat, chicken and shellfish in harmonious combination with asparagus and a dozen other unidentified ingredients. *Pipirana*, too, sounds interesting but turns out to be a pedestrian, ungarnished mixture of chopped-up cucumber, tomato, green pepper and onion; in short a salad with the lettuce left out.

Bailén is one of the least interesting towns in Spain and has but two claims on our memories: that it lies on the intersection of the main Madrid to Granada highway and that from Jaén to Córdoba, and that a battle of the greatest importance to Europe was fought here. The church is a late Gothic pile of dark red masonry with a Baroque south doorway, dedicated to the Virgin of the Incarnation. The half dome of the final chapel of the left aisle[1] has an interesting fresco of the Virgin of the Rosary with male and female saints duly separated on either side. Otherwise there is a great deal of limewash, the curse of Andalucian church interiors, and the tomb of Francisco Javier Castaños y Arragori, victor of Bailén. Over the tomb is a good marble bas-relief of his profile: he looks surprisingly like the Duke of Wellington.

The Battle of Bailén was the immediate result of Napoleon's fixed idea that bullying was the best form of leadership. Three years earlier he had forced Villeneuve to sail from Cádiz with a combined French and Spanish fleet, to be largely destroyed off Cape Trafalgar; the surviving ships of that disaster had lain in Cádiz harbour ever since. Secondly, his 'continental system' of blockading Britain had little chance of success and necessitated the despatch of an expeditionary force to Portugal, using Spain as a friendly corridor. The friendship became strained when Napoleon began interfering in the internal affairs of the Spanish royal family, and the Spanish people, like any other nation most attached to its worst rulers, erupted in the celebrated *Dos de Mayo*, the rising of the people of Madrid on the 2nd May, 1808. Though the revolt was put down in Madrid with the greatest brutality, it rapidly spread throughout Spain which, with Portugal, became the one corner of continental Europe that was not even temporarily servile. It was to save the French warships

---

1. When facing the high altar, the side on your left is that of the Gospel, that to your right of the Epistle, from the position of the priest during these two parts of the Mass. It is necessary to define here what is meant by 'left' and 'right'; they will be taken throughout as 'Gospel' and 'Epistle' respectively.

in Cádiz, therefore, that Masséna sent General Dupont with nearly 23,000 troops marching into Andalucía, quite unaware that the ships had been handed over to the patriots as soon as news of the revolt had reached Cádiz.

Dupont's army contained a large number of inexperienced conscripts, and his own hesitant command contributed to the general lack of organisation and low morale among the troops. For some time he lingered indecisively in the plain of Andújar, and made the fatal mistake of sending his second-in-command Vedel ahead, with 10,000 of his troops, to reconnoitre the country. Taking advantage of this, the 30,000 strong army of Andalucian peasants, under their general Castaños, swept upon the town of Bailén, which lay between the two divisions of the French army. Castaños left 17,000 men and 16 guns here to split the French, and with the remainder attacked the main French army in the rear. Dupont was trapped, his men's morale shaken and Vedel unable to come to the rescue. After several days, during which Dupont hoped vainly for help, the French capitulated in a cloud of ignominy and 18,000 conscripts were taken prisoner. An army of apparently disorganised and untrained peasants had defeated 23,000 French troops. Europe was astounded.

The importance of Bailén lay in the fact that it was the first major defeat suffered by one of Napoleon's armies and it was followed a month later by Junot's defeat at Vimeiro by Sir Arthur Wellesley. Napoleon, on hearing the news of Bailén, flew into one of his rages, shouting 'a rabble of peasants led by a rabble of priests!' But the legend of France's invincibility on land was forever discredited, Spain became the running sore that drained her of men and money, and the news of Bailén and Vimeiro filtered through subject Europe like spring rain through the thirsty soil.

Castaños later fought at Wellington's side at Salamanca and Vitoria, and received many decorations, the dukedom of Bailén and the rare honour of commendation from Wellington, who had no high opinion of Spanish generals as a class. Both died in the year 1852, Castaños at the age of 94, Wellington a comparative youth of 83. In the sacristy of the Bailén church a display cabinet holds parts of Castaños' uniform and decorations with a bullet-torn standard that went through the battle. The Albergue has reproductions of paintings and prints that illustrate the battle and the uniforms of the opposing armies.

Joining N IV again we reach **Andújar** after 27 kilometres. The

one church that should be visited is Santa María, but it is gener
ally known as the Parroquia, or parish church. It was built on
the site of a mosque, as happened so frequently in the South, and
is mainly Gothic; the façade however is Plateresque, a style involving surface ornamentation of otherwise severe Renaissance
and so called because of its resemblance to the intricate work of
the silversmith (*platero*). In every respect the outside is a mixture,
of styles as well as materials; the stone looks old enough to
have been Romanesque and much of the brickwork has the
geometric patterns typical of the Mudéjars, Moslems living
under Christian rule who were usually skilled artisans and trans-
mitters of Oriental styles. The altar lies at the west end, a rare
arrangement and one that seems to be found only in churches
that have replaced mosques. The second chapel on the left contains El Greco's *Oración*, showing Peter, James and John asleep
in the sombre foreground with an unearthly light illuminating the
angel and the praying Saviour in his rose-red robe. The *reja*, or
grille, of this chapel is a fine example of an art that is peculiarly
Spanish, and whose origins go back to the thirteenth century.
The sixteenth was the century of its full flowering and its acknow-
ledged master Bartholomew of Jaén, who constructed this
example; one should note that the figures produced in repoussé
are built up from two mirror images placed back to back. There
is also an unimpressive *Assumption* by Pacheco, teacher and
father-in-law of Velázquez; some late Gothic groining and a
frescoed sixteenth-century dome over the chancel. The clock
and bell tower stands apart, like the minarets of many mosques,
and it is probable that this was its origin, though the parts of old
wall that join it suggest that it may have been one of the square
towers of the city wall, of which there are still some lengths to
be seen.

Andújar is usually described as a gloomy town, though without
much reason today. It differs from others only in its pottery, for
here are manufactured *alcarrazas*, porous jars that keep water
cool and are found in every part of Spain. Till recently every
house had its jar cooling on the balcony or, in the case of inns,
beside the door; hence the *copla* so applicable to this town:

Alcarraza de tu casa, chiquilla, quisiera ser
Para besarte los labios cuando fueras a beber.
Your house's *alcarraza* I would that I might be,
To kiss your lips, my darling, when you came to drink from
    me.

The Countess D'Aulnoy, whose account of a journey through
Spain in 1679–1681 is a mine of shrewd observation and Gallic
wit, had left France rather hurriedly after weathering several
criminal charges, including treason and the administration of
poison to the Chevalier de la Motte. The clay from which
Andújar pottery is made aroused her interest, and she had
probably heard of the ceramic rosaries of Talavera, to whose clay
a scent had been added 'which excites women who thus eat their
beads and give great trouble to their confessors. . . .' At all
events, referring to the Andújar brand, she wrote of 'the longing
many women feel to chew this clay which often obstructs their
stomachs'. She tried a mouthful but said she would rather eat a
grindstone. Of the *búcaro*, a vessel that gives off an agreeable
odour when filled, she wrote, 'I possess one which spoils the taste
of wine but greatly improves water', and, 'they claim that it
betrays the presence of poison'. She should have known. Some
of the best products of this town are on view—in the Victoria
and Albert Museum, London.

The cattle-drovers of Andújar, like the *piqueros* or bull-herders
of Jerez, are said to have routed a French detachment with the
cold steel of their goads during the operations that preceded the
battle of Bailén; moreover Andújar saw the signing of the Convention of Bailén, with the surrender of 18,000 French soldiers on
honourable terms subsequently broken, so that only 3,000 eventually returned home from the hulks and the desert island of
Cabrera. Fifteen years later the restored Bourbon Ferdinand
VII, unpopular with the liberals for breaking *his* word to them,
called on the aid of his cousin of France, the Duke of Angoulême,
who led the hundred thousand 'sons of St. Louis', as they called
themselves, to his rescue and at Andújar issued the proclamation
that all Spanish authorities were to be subordinated to the
French.

The bridge across the Guadalquivir is said to be Roman. It
has been restored a good deal, but the foundations of the piers
may be original.

The only excursion from Andújar is to the **Sanctuary of
Nuestra Señora de la Cabeza,** 33 kilometres to the north. A heroic
defence by a small detachment of the Guardia Civil during the
1936–39 war involved the complete destruction of the mediaeval
buildings so that the journey is only of scenic interest, unless it
happens to coincide with one of the picturesque *romerías*. There
is, however, a Parador Nacional of the D.G.T. that makes the
journey worth while.

Andújar was also the home of an Arab tribe, even after the reconquest, who voluntarily embraced Christianity and allied themselves to the Catholic Monarchs when many of their chiefs were treacherously murdered in the Alhambra of Granada by the Moslem ruler. Their descendants were still the aristocracy of the town in 1690 when it was visited by the Moroccan ambassador. The name of the tribe was Banu Sarraj, recognisable in the Hall of the Abencerrajes of the Alhambra, where the massacre is thought to have taken place.

Twenty kilometres farther along N IV and just before the town of Villa del Rio, which need not detain us, we cross the Salado de Porcuna (many rivers in Andalucía are called salty); upstream, on the right, is a Roman bridge of three arches which presumably carried the main road to Cádiz; the passing of twenty centuries has buried its piers in silt, but the tiny arches are still above ground. A by-pass takes us south before leaving Villa del Rio and a road that is pleasantly rustic after the hustle of the broad highways brings us after 18 kilometres to **Cañete de las Torres**. In the Plaza Mayor one handsome tower remains of the great castle and though the portal with its horseshoe arch is whitewashed and represents only the entrance to a delightful private house, it still evokes something of those bloody days that made castles a necessity. The lower courses are probably original and would thus date back to the year AD 899, when Awsacha Ibn Jali parted from his chief Omar Ben Hafsun and resumed his allegiance to the Emir of Córdoba. The *ajimez* window, consisting of twin arches separated by a slender column, gives the authentic touch of Arabic with its square frame or *alfiz*. The almost incredible tale of Ben Hafsun must be postponed until we visit his headquarters at Bobastro.

To **Bujalance** it is only 7 kilometres. The town is so ancient that it precedes written records, its earliest documentation being an Iberian stone lion now in the Archaeological Museum of Córdoba. Its oldest known name is Bursabolis, which is probably Greek; it was called Vogia by the Romans and the present name dates only from the Arab domination. Abderrahman III, first caliph of Córdoba, built a great castle here in 935 and one can see its celebrated seven towers on the city's crest. Of the castle itself, which was surrounded by an outer wall with seven towers there are only negligible remains at the top of the hill.

The Ayuntamiento or town hall preserves the standard of the volunteer battalion of mounted herdsmen or *garracheros* who—need I say?—fought at Bailén. At least they introduced a varia-

tion into this hoary tale, for by changing their *garrachos* or goads
to the left hand they so confused the French that the battle was
won. Hearing of this sinister manoeuvre the British adopted the
same tactic and that is why we drive on the left today—or so they
say in Bujalance. On the walls of the Ayuntamiento are many of
the paintings of a local artist called Benítez Mellado; they are
not only agreeable to the eye but instructive too, for their portrayal of local types is sensitive and accurate.

From Bujalance north along C329 is **Montoro**, an attractive
town astride the Guadalquivir. The northern half, or *ciudad* (city)
is the more picturesque and is entered over the fourteenth-century
bridge; the white houses cluster along the steep north bank, the
contrast of their black, shadowed doors and windows reminding
one of a handful of dice tumbled along the slope. From nearer,
you can see the beige tiled roofs and even portions of the ancient
walls that have been incorporated into the buildings and, of
course, whitewashed. The local rose-coloured stone can be seen
untouched in the parish Church of San Bartolomé as well as on
the façade of the Ayuntamiento.

The Church of San Bartolomé is a late Gothic building with
a Baroque bell tower in the same ruddy sandstone relieved by
the mat of grass which grows out between the roof tiles. The
parish priest is an enthusiast and gladly takes visitors round,
omitting no detail. The ceiling gives us our first glimpse of an
artesonado, so-called because it is shaped like an inverted trough
(*artesón*); many are decorated with elaborate geometric patterns
of interlacing strips of carved wood, painted or inlaid with ivory
or mother-of-pearl, as in this instance, and the word has come
to be applied to all ceilings thus decorated, irrespective of
their shape. The purist will continue to employ the word
alfarje (Arabic *al-farx*, carpet) for those that are not trough-
shaped.

This is the first pretty town we have visited and also the first
which feels typically Andalucian, with its narrow streets, iron
balconies with their trailing flowers, street-lamps that are decorative but dignified (as everywhere in Spain) and the *rejas* or window
grilles, that would appear unnecessary in such an honest country.
They may however have been fixed there originally not so much
to prevent men from getting in, as girls from getting out. At the
very top, after a steep climb on foot, is the site of the Church of
Santa María, one of the oldest in Southern Spain. The Civil War,
or the disturbances before it, left it in ruins now said to be in
process of restoration. At present you can only peer through the

hoarding which encircles it and see a few of the famous columns with their Romanesque capitals, so rare in these latitudes.

Continuing westward N IV leaves El Carpio with its privately-owned palace and castle on the left and then crosses over to the right bank on the famous **Bridge of Alcolea**. Two battles were fought for its possession: the first, between the French and Spanish, was just another episode in the short campaign that ended at Bailén; the second was far more important, for the rebellion of the liberal generals under Prim in 1868—they were marching up from Cádiz under General Serrano—met its only loyalist opposition here and defeated it, thus causing the abdication of Isabel II. Peter de Polnay tells of John Rutledge, the Northumbrian engineer, 'who ran down from Cordova on his engine by the line that crossed the battlefield and, taking no notice of cannon balls and bullets, tended the wounded and the dying. On the next day Serrano started for Madrid with his victorious troops. Before he left he decorated Rutledge with the Order of Isabel la Católica.' The railway line is still there and so is a small shrine in the fields, commemorating the battle; the bridge of twenty arches is an almost black reminder of it and the only excuse for stopping at the village of Alcolea.

Córdoba is now only 12 kilometres farther on and the traveller cannot but feel a breath of excitement at the prospect of arriving at this once fabulous city. The name is said, though without much evidence, to derive from the Punic *karta-tuba*, an important city, but from Roman times its history is well known. Under them and their successors the Visigoths it was a provincial capital; after the Moslem invasion of 711 it was the seat of the emirs appointed by the Caliph of Damascus, heir to the Prophet Mohamed and ruler of the Faithful. But the Omayyad caliphs had rivals and the revolt of the Abbasids succeeded in establishing another line of religious and political dictators which was to include the well-known Caliph Haroun Al-Rashid. No believer in half-measures, the first of the new line had all the Omayyads butchered, a carpet spread over the fresh corpses and supper served. One Omayyad, however, escaped by swimming the Euphrates and after a succession of adventures arrived in Morocco; from here he was invited to Spain by officials who had been appointed by the Omayyads and were afraid of being superseded by favourites of the new dynasty.

Thus it happened that in 756 Abderrahman landed at Almuñécar and became Emir of Moslem Spain (756–788). For almost three centuries he and his successors ruled from Córdoba, enlarging, enriching and beautifying it; its chief mosque became a centre of pilgrimage, rivalling Mecca, its university attracted the finest brains of Islam and Jewry, its libraries became the world's most complete, and its wealth and importance so great that Abderrahman III (912–961) took the title of Caliph. Córdoba's decline can be dated roughly from the year 1000 and the ensuing century saw the end of the short-lived caliphate. The resulting splinter-states or *taifas* fought among themselves and Moslem Spain fell under successive waves of Berber reformers, the Almoravids and Almohads until, as we have seen, the latter were decisively defeated at Las Navas de Tolosa. The earliest Moslem remains are those of Córdoba; Seville and Granada represent subsequent epochs, and it is in this order that we shall visit them.

CHAPTER TWO

Córdoba and the Great Mosque

✧

*The Calahorra—San Jacinto—The Mezquita—Patio de los
Naranjos—The Chapels—The Mihrab—The Cathedral—The
Alcázar Real*
>   . . . *Oh siempre gloriosa patria mia*
>   *Tanto por plumas cuanto por espadas* . . .

Córdoba lies along the north bank of the Guadalquivir and owes
its existence to the Roman bridge that carried the Via Augusta
on its way from Gaul to Cádiz. The bridge, though frequently
restored, preserves its original piers and all its old grandeur and
still carries traffic bound for Seville and the Atlantic over its
sixteen arches, mirrored in the quiet river. The southern end is
guarded by a castle, the **Calahorra**; it is reasonable to believe
that a Moslem fort must have stood at this vital spot, but documented history takes us back no further than 1369. Additions
and reconstructions were ordered in that year by Henry of
Trastamara, after the abortive siege by his legitimate half-
brother, Pedro the Cruel, had exposed the weakness of Córdoba's
defences. A horseshoe arch, now blocked up, gives no assistance
to the historian, for it might equally have been built by Moslems
under Christian rule. The ground plan is peculiar in that it
traces a stumpy letter 'T' with the angles filled by a quarter
circle of tower. It is now a historical museum. On the first floor
are relics of Gonzalo de Córdoba, *El Gran Capitán*, Spain's
greatest warrior, and on the second of Góngora, author of a
famous sonnet from which the lines above are taken; intensely
patriotic, as his *Ode to the Invincible Armada* shows, his deepest
affection was still for his birthplace, its towers and river, plain
and sierra, 'fatherland, flower of Spain'.

From the battlements of La Calahorra, which thus enshrines
the memory of both the sword and pen for which Córdoba is
famous, you look over the river; though it flows sluggishly for
most of the year, downstream to the left the water is collected by
a zigzag bar and directed into four channels. The first three
supplied power to the Arab water-mills whose ruins still stand
in the river-bed; the fourth, against the embankment on the
far side, propelled the paddles of the giant wooden *noria*, the

water-wheel whose circumference was fitted with clay jars that filled up below the surface and emptied into an aqueduct next to the top of the wheel. The *noria* has been built again, though it lies idle, and you can still see the beginning of the aqueduct which used to conduct the water across what is now the Ronda de Isasa, the northern embankment, into the gardens of the Alcázar. Arab writers from before the reconquest—Córdoba fell to St. Ferdinand in 1236—mentioned the noise of the groaning wheel that kept them awake and Ferdinand the Catholic ordered its demolition because Queen Isabel made the same complaint during their stay in the New Alcázar at the end of the fifteenth century. Wooden *norias* survived elsewhere until recently; one is mentioned in connection with the Battle of Bailén in 1808 and Dumas, describing his journey from Paris to Cádiz in 1846, writes of '. . . an inhuman noise . . . the long cry of a man whose throat is being cut' at his first introduction to a *noria*.

Behind the *noria* and extending westward are the remains of the old town wall, punctuated by the bases of towers whose tops have long since disappeared, and one octagonal survivor that rises above the riverside drive. Straight ahead, over the end of the bridge, is the low, tawny stretch of the Great Mosque with the higher Christian addition projecting from its centre and the Baroque bell tower behind it. On either side are the plains and behind the city is the line of the low sierra, so that Góngora's sonnet is fully illustrated; and yet the view does nothing to prepare one for the enchantment of Córdoba, the spell that it weaves only around those embraced by its walls.

There is nothing impressive about the view, nor anything to remind one of the glorious days of the caliphate, when it set itself up as the rival of Mohamed's successors in Baghdad. Where are the twelve royal palaces, with their exotic names—'The Flower', 'The Diadem', 'The Joyful'—the thousand mosques, the 700 public baths, the libraries and colleges, the three thousand country villas and the botanical gardens filled with exotic plants? Quarrels among the Moslems, and civil wars, gradually wore down this proud city, so ostentatious that it even had paved streets, and dispersed its half million inhabitants; then came the destruction of the Christian reconquest and further decline over the centuries. Apart from the Great Mosque only the spirit lingers on, so that even today the Cordoban is noted for his distinguished manners, amiability and good taste, just as he was in the days of El-Idrisi, the geographer, who lived at the court of the Norman kings of Sicily.

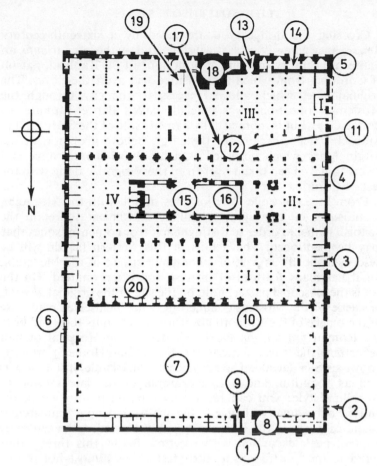

PLAN OF MEZQUITA, CÓRDOBA

I   Original building of Abderrahaman I
II Addition by Abderrahamen II
III Addition by Al-Hakam II
IV Addition of Almansor

1. Puerta del Perdón
2. Postigo de la Leche
3. Puerta de San Esteban
4. Puerta de San Miguel
5. Closed Sabat passage
6. Puerta de Santa Catalina
7. Patio de los Naranjos
8. Minaret and bell tower
9. Entrance to No. 8
10. Arco de las Palmas
11. Chapel of Villaviciosa

12. Capilla Real
13. Mihrab
14. Pasadizo
15. "Cathedral"
16. Coro
17. Capilla de San Pablo
18. Capilla de Santa Teresa and Treasury
19. Capilla de la Santa Cena
20. Capilla de las Animas, "of the Inca"

Crossing the bridge, you are faced by a sixteenth-century Renaissance gateway in classical style, and on the left a *triunfo*, an eighteenth-century monument in honour of St. Raphael, patron of Córdoba, from which the sensitive will avert their eyes. The original gate, which allowed access to the city through the Moslem fortifications, was officially called Bab el-Kantara, or Bridge Gate, but is more usually named Gate of the Statue in the Arab chronicles, because of the effigy, believe it or not, of the Virgin Mary which occupied a niche above the entrance and seems to have been taken over from the Visigoths along with the rest of Córdoba.

From here the Calle Torrijos goes uphill, with the Mezquita, or mosque, on the right; it will be convenient to retain the Spanish name, in order to distinguish it from other mosques that may be mentioned. The details of this western façade will be described shortly as part of a complete circuit of the Mezquita, for it has many features of interest, too often omitted. On the left is the episcopal palace, built on the site of the original *alcázar*, or castle of the Moslem conquerors, who themselves made use of the palace of the Visigoth governor which in its turn had been the Roman *praetorium*. Next to it is the old Hospital of San Sebastián, the *Cuna* (cradle) or Foundling Home, popularly known as **San Jacinto**. The entrance is remarkable, instructive as well as beautiful, and a fine example of the late Gothic or Isabelline style; you can see the two patterns into which the Gothic ogive finally changed: the main arch now semicircular again, as it was in the Romanesque, but topped in the centre by a small peak decorated with rosettes. Below this three saints stand in the lunette and at their feet is the almost horizontal, slightly lobulated portal which is the last reminder of the cusped lancet. Here too is an example of a constant feature of Moslem and later Spanish and South American architecture, the *alfiz*, a rectangular frame round a portal or window, which is now so much a national characteristic that it is used in modern buildings. We saw one example in Cañete de las Torres; in this one the uprights are typically Gothic, while the *enjutas*, or upper corners, are filled with geometric designs in relief, another harmonious echo of Saracen art.

The site of the **Mezquita** has been used for worship uninterruptedly since Roman days. A Christian church succeeded the Roman temple of Janus and under the Visigoths was dedicated to St. Vincent. When the Moslems came, in 711, they appropriated half the church and about 70 years later Abderrahman I, last of the Omayyads of Damascus and first of those of Spain, bought the remaining half, pulled down the building and constructed the first part of the present one.

Relatively few Arabs and Berbers conquered almost the whole peninsula; most of the Hispano-Romans and all the Jews welcomed them, for the Visigothic aristocracy had made itself unpopular. Even among the masters there was treachery; Roderick, the last king, was betrayed by the partisans of Witiza's heirs, who, in many cases were allowed to retain their estates. Abdul Aziz, son of the conqueror, Musa, married Roderick's widow and one Sara, a granddaughter of Witiza, was twice married to Arabs. The result was that after a few generations the 'Arabs' of Spain were largely of Spanish blood, many of them being blond or red-headed. Many Moslems spoke only Romance, the parent of modern Spanish, while their knowledge of Arabic was limited to the Koran, which they had learned by heart without understanding the words. The remaining Christians, penalised only by having to pay a poll tax, gradually became Arabic in clothing and customs and, more to the point, had themselves circumcised, much to the horror of Johann von Görtz, ambassador of the Emperor Otto I in 954. Here we are inevitably faced with the problem of names; are we to call the invaders Arabs, Berbers or Moors? The last, and most popular, term is insufficiently defined for regular use; Arabs were prominent, as were Persians and Syrians, only in the early centuries of the occupation. On the whole, then, it seems more accurate to use the words Moslem and Berber for occasions when people of that religion or race are indicated. 'Moors' and 'Moorish' are applicable to men or things from Morocco; it is a pity that a dark skin is so often taken for granted, for the Berbers are white when not descended from black wives and concubines.

The north wall of the Mezquita contains the main entrance to the patio, the Puerta del Perdón, or Penitents' Gate, a Mudéjar work of the fourteenth century, modelled on the gate of the same name at Seville. The arch is a pointed horseshoe and the *alfiz* is completely filled with *ataurique*, a relief of stylised leaf designs which still leave room for shields with crests in the *enjutas*. The doors are massively built of wood and faced with bronze sheets beaten into a design of small ovals resembling the ancient Egyptian cartouches; on these are engraved alternate sentences in Gothic and Arabic script, while another inscription in Gothic lettering runs round the archivolt, stating that the gate was raised for Henry II of Castile in 1377. It is quite possible that there was a previous Islamic Penitents' Gate, for we are told that the philosopher Averröes, incurring the displeasure of the religious fanatics and the Almohad ruler, was sentenced to stand in the gate for a day while the True Believers, entering and leaving, spat upon him. The interior of the gate house has an ugly and quite unnecessary Baroque ceiling, but beautiful knockers on the doors themselves. Above the *alfiz* is a blind arcade of three cusped or lobulated arches and others are seen in the walls at the sides. Traces of later fresco painting survive in some of these but there is every indication that they will soon be completely washed away.

Following the wall in an anti-clockwise direction we turn the corner into the **Calle Torrijos**, where much of the primitive masonry remains, though the golden stone has suffered greatly from the erosion of wind and rain. The first door is the Postigo de la Leche, or Milk Postern, so-called from its original use as a place for depositing unwanted babies

The third door, the **Puerta de San Esteban** (St. Stephen's Door), still shows the features of the eighth-century building executed by Abderrahman I, although an inscription on the arch gives the date of its completion as 855. It may be studied as typically Cordoban before the advent of Christian styles; the door has a plain horizontal lintel and the horseshoe arch in the *alfiz* is purely a relieving one, whose function is to divert weight from the lintel. The arch has alternate brick and stone voussoirs, giving a pleasing colour contrast, and the latter are embellished with arabesques in relief. On either side are lattice windows of stone over partly obliterated carved decorations, and over all are the saw-toothed merlons which are being reproduced by builders in Córdoba and elsewhere to this day; these are Syrian in origin, evidence of homesickness in Abderrahman I.

Next comes the **Puerta de San Miguel**, with a somewhat closed horseshoe and a geometric design of brick and stone in the lunette, a design which has been used again and again in later additions. Of the next two doors the first and third have been so extensively restored in the present century that experts shudder while sightseers rejoice; perhaps a more authentic reconstruction would have been preferable but most of us are happy to see something both complete and picturesque between the crumbling buttresses of the façade. Finally there is the most interesting of all, a simple oblong door, now walled up, about twelve feet up the wall; this is the *sabat*, an entrance which was reached by a bridge from the old Alcázar, that is the present episcopal palace, and which enabled the emir and his entourage to attend the Friday service in their private pew, protected by lattice work and invisible to the vulgar gaze.

Round the corner, on the south side, you can see the row of windows that used to light the *sabat* passage. There are other windows and balconies that date from the time of the Catholic Sovereigns and a single item of interest, a large marble plaque on which is engraved the shape of a custodial, a reminder of the previous one which disappeared at the time of the French occupation in Napoleon's day.

The east wall, while authentically Islamic, must be somewhat later as it was built at the time of the fourth and last extension of the Mezquita at the end of the tenth century. There is much restoration here, too, though the main fabric is intact. Two columns on the pavement mark the Renaissance **Puerta de Santa Catalina**, quite out of keeping with the rest of the wall but preserving a valuable pictorial record, for on the shields of the *enjutas* are carvings that show how the minaret used to look before its conversion to the present bell tower. And now you can have a pleasant change from what is perhaps becoming a monotonous succession of doorways. On the other side of the street is the Plaza Catalina with the Calle de Martínez Rücker leading from it; follow this to the Plazuela de la Concha and then turn left into the Calleja de los Rincones de Oro, which for all its grand name quickly narrows to less than three feet. Honeysuckle tumbles down the walls and the alley finishes in a minute, shady patio, where the neat doors of the canons' houses, with their shining brass, open to face a weathered caliphal column and capital.

Going back to the Mezquita and turning the corner, we come upon an exterior chapel, which is nothing more than an elaborate shrine, called the **Virgen de los Faroles**; Spain likes surrounding its outdoor images with street-lamps, just as candles are used in churches and on processional floats. The old painting of the Assumption which it contained was destroyed in 1928 and a new one by Córdoba's favourite painter, Julio Romero de Torres, substituted. At this point another short digression north along the Calle de Velázquez Bosco passes, on the left, the sole complete survivor of the hundreds of Arab public baths; they are now permanently closed but are not comparable, in size or preservation, with others that can be seen elsewhere in Andalucía. Returning to the shrine of the Virgen de los Faroles and passing one more Renaissance portal, we arrive back at the Puerta del Perdón and enter the **Patio de los Naranjos**.

The outer court was an essential part of the mosque, both because it almost always contained facilities for ritual washing and because it was usual for all inhabitants to attend the principal mosque on a Friday and the overflow could therefore be accommodated in the courtyard. The north wall of the Mezquita that faces the visitor entering through the Puerta del Perdón was built after the Reconquest; previously the side of the building was open and the courtyard could therefore be regarded as an extension of the praying area. The bell tower is on the right of the entrance, though the way to the stairs is on the left; over half-way up it is quite astonishing to find that you are winding round the outside of another stone tower which is, in fact, the original minaret.

Descending and again entering the patio, there is a ground plan on the right showing the outline of another minaret, built during the reign of Hixem I (788–796). On the left is a Baroque fountain with a gnarled old olive tree at one corner; the feeder pipe at this corner is called the Caño del Olivo and a legend has it that a spinster drinking from this pipe will be married within the year. There are four more fountains, of which three may well be replacements of those once used ritually, so evenly are they spaced. Around are the walls of the courtyard, displaying surviving timbers from the original ceiling of the Mezquita with their geometric carving. From mid-April to mid-May a lazy inspection of these and of the uninspiring north wall of the Mezquita itself is made still more agreeable by the pervading scent of orange blossom.

The entrance to the Mezquita itself is through the Arco de las Palmas, directly opposite the Puerta del Perdón, and is an unsuccessful attempt at combining eastern and western styles; on either side stands a Roman milestone, with a badly fitting Corinthian capital giving the distance to the Temple of Juno by the sea as 28 miles and therefore obviously brought from elsewhere.

Once inside, the visitor stands and gazes with awe at the forest of columns and the vista of striped arches that dwindle into the distance without, at first sight, any apparent order. To appreciate this marvel fully it is essential to realise that it was being built, in various stages, for two and a half centuries. The development of Hispano-Arab architecture can be followed from the first simple building of Abderrahman I, with its borrowed decoration; through the gradual enrichment of the next two centuries, culminating in the great *mihrab*; and on to the reaction of an almost Puritan simplicity in the last addition by Almansor. You can even see the path taken by the Mudéjars in this branch of art, after the Christian reconquest. Every writer who has entered this remarkable building has felt the urge to describe it, and as the centuries pass they have had more and more difficulty in finding something original to say.

Let us begin by dispelling some fallacies. Many descriptions convey the impression that the vast size and sombre limits of the building were planned with the object of inspiring reverence through the dim half-light, surely unnecessary in a community that prays five times a day and has even the natural functions governed by regulations and restrictions. They forget that the Mezquita includes three additions to the original building, each necessitated by the growing number of Moslems in the expanding metropolis, and that the first and second phases together were not large enough to have dark corners; that the north wall was not yet built and that much of the Mezquita was consequently flooded with daylight; that even when the building was complete the further part was lighted by a profusion of lamps; and that in any case there was enough light for the building to be used as a university for the study of theology, philosophy and the sciences on six days a week.

The second suspect belief is that the architect planned the double row of arches, horseshoe below and semicircular above, for its effect; it is more reasonable to agree with those who point out that the average height of the Roman columns, which were brought to the site from many, sometimes distant parts, was too small to allow a roof to be placed directly above them. That the columns were not produced specifically for the Mezquita is obvious from the fact that they are of different heights, so that some were bedded below pavement level and others had bases of different heights placed beneath them. Tiers of arches were, of course, nothing new in Roman architecture and must have been familiar to the Moslem conquerors before they ever came to Spain, for North Africa had numerous examples of Roman aqueducts. But that the builders were inspired by the aqueduct of Mérida (which has alternate series of red brick and grey stone) in having the arches striped with alternate brick and stone is equally absurd; the interpolation of brick courses was well known in the Near East, where it is still said to diminish the damage caused by earthquake shocks, and the Dome of the

Rock in Jerusalem had striped arches some years before the Mezquita was built.

The first object that meets the eye is a beautiful Visigothic carved pedestal and stoup, one of the finest relics of the strange Teuton domination of the sixth and seventh centuries; many of the capitals and some marble lattice work in this part of the mosque are of similar origin. One may identify the boundaries of the original mosque of Abderrahman I, built in 785–786, according to some, though it is not thought that the work could have been completed in a year as was once believed; the extent can be accurately followed by the fact that the floor on the south and east sides slopes down to it in a gentle ramp, a few inches high. All the columns and their capitals are Roman or Visigothic, many of them being superb examples of the Corinthian order; this is the only part of the Mezquita in which the columns have bases. One of the Visigothic capitals, against the north wall, has a defaced area, where a cross was chipped out by the Moslems. There are ten files of columns leading, with interruptions, to the southern extremity of the Mezquita; in the ninth from the right, or west, the second column has achieved notoriety. As far back as 1772 Jean Peyron wrote of a column which gave off a foetid smell if it was rubbed with iron; today the column is half rubbed through and even as you are looking at this black, spiral Roman shaft someone will come and rub it with a key, simultaneously bending his head so as not to miss the bouquet of sulphur. The Moslems were more sensible for they are said to have used 140 pounds of incense a year, mostly aloes and ambergris.

The second part of the Mezquita, built by Abderrahman II, extends southward for the distance covered by the next seven columns and their arches. It ends at a row of stone piers, where the original cathedral of the fifteenth century stood. In the left, or east half of this portion is the present choir of the sixteenth-century cathedral, constructed by the Chapter against the wishes of the City Council but at the orders of the young Emperor Charles V. When he saw what had been done to the Mezquita on his first visit three years later he said—the story is inevitable and has to be retold in every book—'You have built here what could have been built anywhere and you have destroyed what was unique.' This fine sentiment loses some of its force when we remember that the same monarch, three years later, had a Renaissance structure built into the Palace of the Alhambra and after that constructed a breakwater at Porto Empedocle in Sicily by pulling down the Greek Temple of Heracles and carting off much of the ruins of the Temple of Olympian Zeus. Dozens of writers have castigated the clergy for building the choir and high altar of the Cathedral inside the Mezquita; but has anyone asked himself what would have happened to this wonderful building had they not done so? We are bound to admit that if it had survived intact up to the present day, it would be the only Islamic religious building in Spain to have done so; it is inconceivable that it could have stood for seven centuries, immune from pilfering and decay, without the protection of Christian consecration. This argument, valid for Rome's Pantheon, is equally applicable to the Mezquita.

Near the northern end of this second part there is a pair of Roman alabaster columns, spirally carved and very rare, and then comes the final portion at this west side, the addition of Al-Hakam II. This superb creation is as large as the original mosque of Abderrahman I and was added in the latter half of the tenth century, after the failure of awnings in the patio to provide shade for the ever-growing number of worshippers. In line with the Puerta de las Palmas, through which we entered the Mezquita, we pass the *trascoro* or western boundary of the Christian addition and enter the **Chapel of Villaviciosa.** As this has only one wall, on the east, we may take the opportunity of gaining a general impression of the area. First it will be seen that the capitals of the columns are of a simple type throughout, Corinthian reduced to its barest essentials with three rows of stylised leaves no longer recognisable as acanthus. Secondly, the columns of the naves are now arranged so that different colours and patterns of marble, jasper and porphyry are in an ordered sequence; thirdly, the upper rows of arches are now supported largely by columns engaged in the rectangular supports; fourthly, light is admitted by four lanterns with important roof detail; and finally, the simple striped arches change to highly ornate, lobulated ones of a type that originated in Mesopotamia, richly decorated with designs recalling chased silver that extend through the intrados, while the arches themselves cross in intricate patterns. But with all their exotic curves and delicate designs one senses an economy of weight that allows the superstructure, elaborate as it is, to rest safely and harmoniously on its elegant columns.

The Chapel of Villaviciosa is remarkable chiefly for the ceiling, which is the original covering of the *Mihrab* of the first extension of the Mezquita, the contribution of Abderrahman II. The crossed stone ribs of the vault were built in the first half of the ninth century: Christian churches, first the Romanesque and later the Gothic, took another two centuries to appreciate and copy the idea. In this chapel we may be looking at the first example of the solution of an architectural problem of the greatest importance: how best to cover a building with an arched roof. The chapel's single wall, on the east side, is actually the west wall of the Royal Chapel (*Capilla Real*), and on it are a crucifix and several inscribed stone tablets, some in Gothic lettering and dating from after the Reconquest, while three others are in Arabic, one of them beginning 'In the name of Allah . . .' This wall formed the retablo or reredos of the original Christian cathedral that was placed inside the Mezquita in the fifteenth century, the Chapel of Villaviciosa therefore representing the sanctuary.

The **Capilla Real** has to be seen from the south side and has obviously been altered by the building of a 'crypt', which in this case is above ground. One can tell that this alteration is later by the fact that the original stout supporting columns with their caliphal capitals are half-buried in the new addition. The 'crypt' simply consists of a floor built about eight feet above ground level, resting on three pointed arches and two columns that have odd capitals. At a glance this must be a post-Reconquest addition, for the Moslem builders would be quite incapable of such a solecism. Here were kept the bodies of two kings of Castile, Ferdinand IV and Alfonso XI, whom we shall meet again in the Church of San Hipólito.

Even if there were no documentary evidence, we could be quite sure that the decoration of this beautiful chapel dates from after the Reconquest, for in its profusion, intricacy and variety it most nearly approaches the Palace of the Alhambra at Granada, most of which dates from the fourteenth century. Access is usually forbidden, so the visitor misses the mosaic tile-work of the lower walls, but the upper parts of the walls can be seen easily and you can verify that there is not a square inch free from elegant stucco decoration. The Christian conquerors wisely entrusted much building and decoration to their Moslem subjects, the Mudéjars, and in 1263 Alfonso X, the Learned, decreed that every Moslem artisan in Córdoba should work for two days in the Mezquita, in order that the necessary maintenance should not be neglected. Furthermore he ordered that four Moslems, two masons and two carpenters, should be exempt from taxes while they worked in this building. It is not so surprising, therefore, to find a chapel erected after the Reconquest in Oriental style, whose stucco work of arabesques is relieved by the royal arms, the towers of Castile and the lion of Léon. The interior of the dome could only be the handiwork of Moslem craftsmen; the crossed ribs are here repeated in wood carved with transverse rolls, and above them the hollow is filled with the stalactites that are so abundant in the fourteenth-century works at Seville and Granada.

The south wall of the second addition to the Mezquita, that of Hakam II in the tenth century, contains the culmination of the beauty which was so lavishly bestowed on this building by the Moslem princes, but while approaching the **mihrab** you should not miss the more refined arrangement of the naves, with columns of alternate colours, each type with its own style of capital. The purpose of a *mihrab* is to show the *kibla*, or direction of Mecca, in which the worshipper has to prostrate himself during prayer. The *mihrab*, which was originally a simple shallow niche, is said to have been for the benefit of the blind who could thus orientate themselves after feeling their way round the walls. Here and in other parts of Spain and in Morocco the simple niche, sometimes adorned with the design of a lamp, gave way to an elaborate chamber in which the worshipper could make seven circuits on his knees, in imitation of the ritual circuits round the Kaaba at Mecca.

When Córdoba became the most enlightened city of Europe it was made a centre of pilgrimage, both to save the Moslems of the West the hazardous journey to Mecca and no doubt for financial reasons as well. A foot bone, allegedly of Mohammed, was obtained and the chapel where it was kept called 'The House of Purification' or *zeca*, according to Ford. As an aspiring pilgrimage centre Córdoba had to put on some outward show and it is not surprising to find the richest and most artistic decoration in and around the *mihrab*. It is however startling to find the *mihrab* pointing to Timbuktu instead of Mecca. The reason seems to be that the whole Mezquita is based on the orientation of the Church of St. Vincent, which it first shared and then replaced, and that possibly only the south wall was available for a *mihrab*, that is, supposing the east end was still occupied by the Christian altar. Successive editions, by simply extending the lines of columns, only moved the *mihrab* further south without changing its orientation.

It is without doubt the mosaics that set the Mezquita apart from all other mosques, with the possible exception of the Great Mosque of Damascus; the reason is simple, for the eastern Caliph had asked the Byzantine Emperor to send artists to decorate the mosques of Jerusalem, Damascus and Medina with mosaics. Al-Hakam II, determined to be second in nothing else, sent an embassy to the Emperor Nicephoros Phocas at Constantinople with the same request. It is an indication of Córdoba's importance that the Emperor not only sent a specialist in mosaic work but about 16 tons of stone and glass cubes with which he was to work.

The *mihrab* is a small octagonal chamber with a shell-patterned roof worked from a single block of marble that has cusped blind arches on each side; it is quite possible that some of these were once windows covered with lattice-work through which the ruler could listen to and join in the Friday prayers. The entrance is a horseshoe arch surmounted by a blind arcade and the roof above the antechamber has another rib-vaulted dome. Each of these features, the voussoirs, the *alfiz*, the arcade and even the dome, are decorated with enchanting mosaics of leaf pattern with every refinement of invention in which green, yellow and purple stand out, not in contrast but in harmony with the black, white and gold. The only Islamic note in this artistic production is provided by the friezes of Cufic script in the *alfiz*, in which the transliteration *fusaifisa* of the Greek word for polychrome cubes can be made out. Above the *alfiz* of the *mihrab* is a blind arcade consisting of seven trilobed arches in whose recesses gleam more rich mosaics. It has been thought that this example may be the origin of the blind arcading of Durham and Norwich Cathedrals, dating respectively from 1093 and 1119, and that the Normans later took it to their new kingdom of Sicily. The open area in front of the *mihrab*, called the Chapel of San Pedro or of the *Zancarrón*, introduces another innovation in the shape of intersecting arches which also found their way into Norman architecture.

Arches decorated with mosaic also stand on either side of the *mihrab*, but are plainly of inferior quality. That on the right as you face the *mihrab* allowed the caliph to issue from the *pasadizo*, the passage that led from the *sabat* door that we saw from outside; its mosaics were made by pupils of the Byzantine artist and those of the left arch are complete reconstructions by Valencian artists of the last century. The *pasadizo* still exists but has been transformed into lavatories. The function of the lateral arches is not known for certain but they are believed to have been subsidiary *mihrabs*, a concept difficult to explain but at least one that was copied in several western mosques. The one on the left also housed sacred vessels and a precious copy of the Koran, with four pages written by the Caliph Othman, drops of whose blood were visible on the parchment. This recalls the fate of Mohamed's secretary so well described by Gibbon: 'Forsaken by those who had abused his simplicity, the helpless and venerable caliph expected the approach of death: the brother of Ayesha marched at the head of the assassins; and Othman with the Koran in his lap, was pierced with a multitude of wounds.' It is a reasonable guess that the *maksura* or 'lattice'—the private enclosure where the members of the royal court could pray in privacy—was either in or in front of the western recess, which communicated through the *pasadizo* with the *sabat* entrance.

The Capilla Real is similarly believed to occupy the site of an earlier, raised *maksura* adjoining the *mihrab* of the second mosque, of Abderrahman II. Among the many treasures that have disappeared is the movable pulpit, or *mimbar*, which was composed of numerous rare woods with inlays of ivory and mother-of-pearl. Gorgeous as is the effect of this end of the Mezquita today, it must be a pale ghost of its former glory, with panelled and painted ceilings, rugs and hangings, its 2,400 lamps and the candelabras that were brought out on the penultimate day of Ramadan, all glittering with brass, silver and gold. The space in front of the *mihrab* and the lateral arches, formerly covered with retablos, is called the Chapel of St. Peter, or vulgarly *del Alcorán* or *del Zancarrón*. The former name is self-explanatory; the latter suggests that it was here that the bone of Mohamed's foot was kept in Moslem days, when Córdoba rivalled Mecca as a place of pilgrimage and so had to have a sacred relic to attract the customers.

The last portion of the Mezquita is the addition of Almansor, the prime minister and general of that nonentity, Caliph Hisham II. With his army of Berbers, who came in large numbers from North Africa to be recruited, and of Christian mercenaries, Almansor found time to make annual expeditions into Christian territory, never, it is said, suffering defeat until the doubtful outcome of the questionable battle of Calatañazor in 1002. The word 'questionable' is used because confirmatory evidence in Islamic documents has been discovered only recently; there are still die-hards who have not been convinced. Abi Amir Mohamed, self-styled Al-Mansur or Almansor, the Victorious, entered every Christian capital in the peninsula from Coimbra to Barcelona and crowned his reign of terror in 997 by taking and sacking Santiago de Compostela, the shrine of the Moor-slaying St. James, Spain's patron saint. The smaller bells from that basilica were carried in triumph to Córdoba on the backs of captured Christians; there they were inverted and hung in the

Mezquita to do duty as oil reservoirs. They were sent back to Santiago de Compostela on the backs of Moslem captives as soon as Córdoba fell to Ferdinand III. To appreciate the complicated nature of Iberian politics one should remember that Almansor, the scourge of Christendom, numbered among his wives daughters of the Kings of Navarre and León, freely bestowed. The transaction, for they presumably enjoyed some immunity in consequence, was probably acceptable to all parties; harem life would have been delectable to the girls after the squalid surroundings of their homes and Almansor might have been quite pleased with them, once they had been given a bath.

Almansor's contribution to the Mezquita consisted of a further eight naves on the east side, running parallel with and for the whole length of the previous rows of arches; the patio had, of course, to be enlarged for a similar distance in an easterly direction. The symmetry, with the *mihrab* in the centre of the south wall, was thus destroyed as can easily be verified today. The new portion followed the pattern of the old, with the exception that the upper arches as well as the lower were made in horseshoe style. Simple capitals were used throughout and the arches have their stripes painted on, instead of being produced by alternate voussoirs of brick and stone; the extension, though architecturally sound and congruent, does not impress one as a labour of love, as do the previous additions. Against the north wall, or rather its chapels, the first column as you enter from the oldest part of the mosque shows a rude cross incised in the black marble, and legend has it that it was made by a Christian captive with a nail —some even say a finger nail.

Your next visit should be to the **Cathedral**. Properly speaking, the whole building is the Cathedral as it is consecrated ground, but the word is often applied only to the choir and sanctuary, whose walls and roof rise above those of the Mezquita. Even the naves flanking this building are higher than the rest, though they keep the striped pattern of the arches, but you can see a frieze of Gothic floral decoration in stone on the upper border of each arch and, looking up, the typical ornate rib vaulting used well into the sixteenth century. For this incongruous form of decoration was not used until three centuries after the Reconquest. Until then a narrow nave had been adapted from the beginning of Al-Hakam's addition and the Capilla Villaviciosa served, as stated earlier, as sanctuary and reredos, while the Capilla Real was the sacristy. The people of Córdoba fought hard against the proposed erection of the present choir and sanctuary. In 1523, when the project was launched, the Ayuntamiento or local government issued an order forbidding builders and other artisans to continue working on the Cathedral under pain of death. The document, which was ignored, is still in existence and may be seen in the Castle of Calahorra. The building was begun under the direction of Hernán Ruiz el Viejo, and when he died in 1547 his son Hernán Ruiz el Mozo continued until his death in 1582.

Nevertheless, there is much to admire and enjoy in this addition to the Mezquita, though certainly not the interior as a whole. It is one of those indecisive productions that cannot make up its mind whether to be Gothic or Renaissance, with a ceiling whose ribs divide areas of stucco painted in the Italian style; dropping your eyes in confusion you will recoil from a classical retablo built chiefly in the red marble of Carcabuey. But some of the details are worth studying; the pulpits of mahogany are ostentatious Baroque, with Old Testament scenes carved in relief on medallions, and rest on rather fanciful versions of the Evangelists' symbols, such as a lifesize ox-head in pink jasper resting on a white marble cloud next to a black marble eagle. They are believed to be the work of the French artist Michel Verdiguier, who worked and died in Córdoba towards the end of the eighteenth century. An awesome lamp of gold-encrusted silver, fifteen feet high and nearly six in width, hangs before the altar.

The glory of the **coro** is the wood carving executed by Pedro Duque Cornejo of Seville, a pupil of the famous sculptur Roldán, of the same city. The mahogany has developed the patina of two centuries while losing none of the definition of the sculptor's chisel; the work comprises a large and ornate bishop's throne, a three-seater, part of the central lectern and 106 choir stalls, each with its individual decoration and medallions. The upper row has two of these to each seat, the larger with reliefs of episodes from the life of Jesus on one side and from the Virgin on the other. The smaller medallions also portray biblical scenes, but without any system; the medallions of the lower row of stalls, of inferior workmanship, present various Cordoban martyrs. This, however, is but a beginning: in true Plateresque fashion there is not a square inch without its carving, whether it is the misericords, the columns, arm-rests or cornices that are examined; and there is such a variety of designs, heads, masks, animals, birds and flowers, that one wonders how it could all be the work of one man. The answer is that it wasn't, for Cornejo had a staff of over forty officials and craftsmen under his orders and, like many other sculptors, was responsible only for the design and finish of every part of the work. It took ten years, a short time even in the circumstances, and the surprise is that Cornejo was commissioned to do it when he was seventy years old. When he died at eighty the choir was practically finished and he had already completed ceramic models of the missing portions so that it could be unveiled in the following year, 1758.

The Cathedral contains about thirty chapels, most of them built against the walls, especially those of Almansor's addition. The light in some is poor and an electric torch is useful. The **Capilla de San Pablo** is against the east wall of the Capilla Real and has fine *rejas* on three sides and a retablo as well as an imposing statue of St. Paul; both these as well as the architecture of the retablo were the work of Pablo de Céspedes whose tomb is immediately before the entrance. One is continually reminded, both in Spain and in Italy, of the versatility of the great artists: painting, sculpture and architecture were almost taken for granted and many added another skill such as engineering or, in the case of Pablo de Céspedes, poetry. Almost opposite and adjoining the *mihrab* complex on the south wall, is the **Chapel of Santa Teresa**, a circular structure with decorations of fussy Baroque that are apparently admired. The best thing in it is the statue of the titular by José de Mora, one of the last of the Granada school that was founded by Alonso Cano; she is standing prepared to write in the open book supported by her left hand, her right with its pen poised, the little finger raised in the manner which has now become vulgar, while she looks down at the Holy Spirit, in the form of a dove perched on her right shoulder. Her eyebrows are raised in a questioning manner. St. Teresa was almost made patroness of Spain at one time, just losing to the Virgin Mary; the work for which she was canonised was the reformation of the Carmelites, to which end she founded the *descalzadas* or 'barefoot' branch.

The chapel is used as sacristy and chapter house and was founded by Cardinal Salazar, after whom it is also named, a fact which may be useful when you are asking to be directed there; his sedan chair stands in the centre decorated like other furnishings here, with painted mythological scenes. The treasury opens off this room and contains several notable objects: the visitor is warned here and now that every ivory crucifix in Spain is attributed to Alonso Cano and half the best chalices to Benvenuto Cellini. The gold chalice in this treasury is studded with emeralds and the work is both delicate and beautiful; there is a charming Romanesque *Virgen de la Huerta*, the orchard motif stressed by the fact that she is holding a pear, a very rare attribute which we shall meet only once more in Southern Spain, as the usual one is an apple. The choice of this fruit is symbolic: in Eve's hand it became the cause of our fall from grace, in the Virgin Mary's of our redemption. There is a Mudéjar reliquary which guides will keep on calling Mozarabic, a common solecism for which one should be prepared. The Mozarabs were Christians living under Moslem rule, who later fled to Christian Spain bringing with them an art which fused Visigothic and Oriental elements. True Mozarabic articles are rare but there are two tenth-century manuscripts with typical miniature work, one the *Indiculus luminosus*, the little illuminated index, by Alvaro of Córdoba and the other a parchment codex with beautifully painted capital letters to each chapter.

But the pride and joy of the treasury is the silver and gilt Gothic custodial by Enrique de Arfe (Henri de Harpe), who came from Flanders with Philip the Fair in 1506; it is said that its shape is an echo of a Flemish belfry, like the one at Antwerp. It was first carried in the Corpus Christi procession in 1518; It would be interesting to know at what time of day, for Córdoba is the only city to have a papal bull allowing the procession to take place in the afternoon. I have not been able to discover when or why, but I suspect that the midday heat of June may have something to do with it. The next chapel to the east is that of Santa Inés, important because it joins another called the **Capilla de la Santa Cena** in which hangs the famous *Last Supper* of Pablo de Céspedes, characterised by an unaffected treatment which is not seen again until the sculptured group of Salzillo, nearly two centuries later. Immediately adjacent is the **Altar de la Encarnación**, notable for the fine Annunciation, painted on wood, by Pedro de Córdoba. Although dating from 1475 it preserves the naivety of the Middle Ages; the angel carries a thin scroll, resembling ticker tape, on which one can make out the words, in Gothic lettering, *'Ave Maria gratia plena dominus. . . .'*

There are many other chapels containing works of more or less merit; that of Nuestra Señora del Rosario contains three canvases by Antonio del Castillo, whose work will be considered in greater detail in the Museo de Bellas Artes in the next chapter. Next to it, however, and therefore in the north wall, is the Capilla de las Animas, better known as the Capilla del Inca. The nickname is that of Garcilaso de la Vega, scion of an illustrious family, whose father had been one of the conquistadors of Peru and whose mother was the granddaughter of the last Inca. He was distinguished as a soldier, having served against the Moriscos of the Alpujarras under Don John of Austria, but much more so as a writer and historian. He wrote the history of the conquest of Peru, the source of all our certain knowledge of the Incas, and of the expedition of Hernando de Soto (from whom the automobile got its name) to Florida; his house in Cuzco, Peru, has been made into a museum and the Peruvian parliament has asked that the remains of this much-travelled man make a last journey to his home, where they will presumably lie near the bones of Pizarro.

From the south-west corner of the Mezquita the broad Calle de Amador de los Rios—we shall hear more of this man at Baena—leads to the **Alcázar Real** or New Fortress-Palace, begun in 1328 at the orders of Alfonso XI in the grounds of the old Alcázar. The Catholic sovereigns lived here for long periods during the war that led to the conquest of Granada; Columbus is said to have had his first interview with Isabel during that time and the episode of the *noria* has been recounted. The Inquisition rented it from the end of the fifteenth century until its abolition and from early in the last century it was used as a prison. The towers and octagonal keep, with their curtain walls, rise impressively over the palm grove on the north side, where you will find the entrance. A corridor, furnished with antiques, takes you to the most famous exhibit, a Roman marble sarcophagus of the third century AD that was discovered in the Sierra Morena on the farm of a torero. It is about eight feet long and four feet high and portrays figures in high relief, each holding a scroll; the early Christians adopted this type of beardless figure to represent Christ as Philosopher, just as other Greek Christian communities pictured Him as Orpheus or as the Good Shepherd, the Hermes Criophoros of Hellenistic days. In the centre of the same sculptured side are panels with rams' heads above and lions' below, each of the latter holding a ring in its mouth, like the door knockers that have been in vogue ever since. The focal point of the façade, for this is what it should be called, is a marble door standing ajar, a pleasant conceit to allow the soul of the departed to go in search of paradise. The concept is not unique, for a similar sarcophagus may be seen in the crypt of Palermo Cathedral, its second occupant a bishop of Norman days.

On the other side of the passage there is a small room with a

Roman mosaic portraying a bearded divinity with crab claws protruding from his temples, a common theme and probably related to the belief that maritime creatures can be regarded as emblems of fertility. The main concert hall has larger polychrome mosaics, including one presenting the legend of the Cyclops Polyphemus and Galatea; an interesting detail, demonstrating that this mosaic is Roman, is the fact that the giant is pictured with three eyes, a late innovation replacing the usual Greek practice of portraying him with one central eye. Below there are remains of baths, allegedly Arab, but hardly identifiable as such. Having noted the star-shaped vents, a feature of all eastern baths in Spain, there is little else to tempt one to linger, but a visit to the restful old patio nearby, where the arms of Castile and León survive in fresco, is well worth while.

A walk along the battlements provides not only a view of Córdoba and the Guadalquivir, but a survey of the extensive gardens laid out in Arab style, with rectangular *albercas*, as the ornamental pools are always called, and flowers, bushes and trees conscientiously irrigated, as were the gardens of the original Alcázar by means of the *noria*. All this is floodlit until 1 a.m. and there is nothing pleasanter than to stroll here after the unbearable heat of an August day. At their west end the gardens terminate in another section of well-preserved wall, probably dating from the period of the Almohads in the twelfth and thirteenth centuries, and the **Puerta de Sevilla** with its twin horseshoe arches, believed (though not unanimously) to be a relic of the tenth century. There is, in fact, considerable support for the theory that the arches are Visigothic in origin, based on highly technical deductions drawn from the relation of radius to circumference. Hereabouts was the royal stud farm, where the famous Cordoban barbs were bred. In the eighteenth century there was a strictly enforced law prohibiting the production of mules in Córdoba, as the mares were too valuable to be used for such a base purpose. Riding associations, or *maestranzas*, were formed here and in other horse-breeding centres, each with its own uniform for gala wear, and did much for the improvement of the breed. The barb, by the way, is a distinct North African breed introduced into Spain by the invaders from Morocco and the term 'Arab barb' to designate anything other than a cross is ludicrous. English thoroughbred stock is partly descended from the barb, some say from the pair of 'Barbary horses' that Ferdinand of Aragón sent to his son-in-law, Henry VIII.

CHAPTER THREE

Córdoba – The City

✺

Torre de la Malmuerta—Plazuela de los Dolores—Convent of St.
Elizabeth—Viana Palace—Church of St. Paul Plaza Mayor—
Plaza José Antonio—Synagogue—Zoco—Archaeological Museum
—Calle de Cabezas—Plaza del Potro—Museo de Bellas Artes

The Omayyad line under whose emirs and caliphs Al-Andalus,
as Moslem Spain was called, had been the glory of the west,
ended in a succession of nonentities. Nine of them occupied the
throne at Córdoba in the years 1010 to 1031, some of them twice,
but none exercised any appreciable control over a country torn
by anarchy. Any power that there was lay in the hands of Berber
and Slav mobs, the former a suppressed majority who formed a
large part of the army, the latter mostly slaves from south-eastern
Europe who greatly outnumbered their masters. During twenty
years of civil war Córdoba, with the exception of the great
mosque, became one large ruin and has never since regained
its former eminence. This does not necessarily mean that the
Córdoba of today is less attractive than that of the eleventh
century for, like most eastern towns, it was possibly quite uninspiring until the visitor was invited into the patio which then,
as today, charmed the senses with a fountain and with trees,
shrubs or flowers, according to the owner's means. The inward
look, with family life concentrated round the patio, probably
persisted into the last century, for Théophile Gautier remarked
on the absence of windows and Borrow wrote: 'Little can be said
with respect to the town of Cordova, which is a mean, dark,
gloomy place, full of narrow streets and alleys, without squares
or public buildings worthy of attention, save and except its far-
famed cathedral.'

Today we see a different Córdoba, with clean, cobbled streets
between whitewashed houses, wrought-iron grilles to the ground-
floor windows, balconies before those of the upper storeys. From
these, from over the tops of the walls, even from flower-pots
fixed to the walls themselves, come the cascades of roses and
geraniums that remain in the memory after art treasures have
become a dim recollection. Two magnificent modern avenues
cross near the railway station, their modern buildings and
thronging traffic in strange contrast to the southern part of the
town. But if you stand at the corner for a while the modern
make-believe disappears; in April and May the lines of orange

CÓRDOBA. *Above left*, Plazuela de los Dolores, the Christ of the Street
Lamps; *right*, a gate (restored) in the eastern wall of the Mezquita.
Below, the Roman bridge over the Guadalquivir, with the Mezquita on
the far bank.

The Mezquita at Córdoba. *Above*, the forest of columns and tiered arches. *Below*, the choir of the Cathedral.

1 Conv. of La Merced. 2 Torre de la Malmuerta. 3 Puerta del Rincon. 4 Pl. de los Dolores.
5 Conv. de los Capuchinos. 6 Conv. of St. Elizabeth. 7 Ch. of Sta. Marina. 8 Pal. of Marques
de Viana. 9 Ch. of San Augustin. 10 Ch. of San Lorenzo. 11 Casa de Hernan de Oliva.
12 Casa de los Villalones. 13 Ch. of St. Paul. 14 Ch. of San Miguel. 15 Ch. of San Nicolas.
16 Ch. of San Hipolito. 17 Almodovar Gate. 18 Synagogue. 19 Zoco. 20 Chapel of San
Bartolome. 21 General Hospital. 22 Casa de los Ceas, 23 Conv. de Jesus Crucificado. 24
Minaret of St. John. 25 Pal. del Marques de la Fuensanta del Valle. 26 Archaeological
Museum. 27 Conv. of Sta. Clara. 28 Casa de los Marqueses del Carpio. 29 Portillo. 30
Meson del Potro. 31 Museo de Bellas Artes. 32 Museo de Julio Romero de Torres. 33 Conv.
de San Francisco. 34 Casa de las Campanas. 35 Casa de los Caballeros de Santiago. 36
Ch. of Santiago. 37 Ch. of Carmelitas Calzadas. 38 Arab water mills. 39. Pl. Jose Antonio.
40 Ch. of La Magdalena. 41 Manolete Fountain. 42 La Calahorra.

trees perfume the air with their blossom and charm the eye with
the golden fruit that looks so sweet and tastes so bitter. In the
early morning a donkey cart draws up, the driver reaches behind
him for a tin trumpet and blows the flourish that brings the
housewives running to buy their daily bread, crisp, warm, and
aromatic. Another donkey brings a barrel-organ, all varnished
mahogany and shining brass, and woe betide you if your glance is
encouraging for you will have to stay and look appreciative
while the owner grinds out one of the twelve interminable, jingly
tunes that the instrument is licensed to play. And if you are there
on the hour you will hear not the striking of a clock nor the
pealing of a chime but the amplified notes of a guitar.

C.G.S.S.

D

Walk east along the Avenida del Generalísimo Franco to the spacious Plaza de Colón; half-way along its west side is the old convent of La Merced, one of the alleged sites of the first meeting between Queen Isabel the Catholic and Christopher Columbus, the once dignified patio now made hideous with white paint. Off the north-east corner of the square stands the **Torre de la Malmuerta**, massive and octagonal, with the arch that used to connect it to the city wall still straddling the main road from Madrid. Although it was built in 1404 it is a parvenu in this city of the caliphs, but for all that it is old enough to have collected at least three legends to account for the sinister folk etymology of *mala* (bad) and *muerte* (death): all insist that the tower was built by the Count of Priego, at the orders of Henry III of Castile, in expiation of the murder of his wife. There is a half-hearted version that the count killed his wife because of his unjust suspicions, and another which makes him come home unexpectedly through the underground passage connecting the tower to the family mansion. He not only killed his wife but two of her lovers as well and then, furious that no one had kept him in touch with domestic developments, a manservant, two maidservants and, because the creature could have talked and didn't, the parrot. Though mass murders were frequent enough, this one had that extra dramatic touch which provided Lope de Vega, who usually avoided tragic endings, with material for his play *Los Comendadores de Córdoba*. A flight of stone steps on the south side of the road leads to the entrance of the tower, usually locked and now unused, though it has been an astronomer's tower and a museum. From the gate, however, you may still discern the two friezes of Mudéjar workmanship in the Almohad style that encircle the tower, and from the road the crest bearing the arms of Castile, and what used to be the date of construction and names of the sponsors, now illegible.

If you go south, after returning to the east side of the Plaza de Colón, remains of the great wall that divided the city in half in Moslem days come into view. Other walls, of which no trace now remains, subdivided the complex into five separate townships. The eastern half is entered through the small square called Puerta del Rincón, and by immediately turning right into the Calle de Alfaros, which runs parallel with the wall. From here, or even earlier, it may be better to ask for the **Plazuela de los Dolores**. To see it at its best you should choose a hot summer's night, when the full moon mocks the street-lamps' efforts. In the narrow, cobbled plaza, enclosed by the plain white walls that contrast with the dense, black shadows of the window grilles, stands the *Cristo de la Agonía*, better known as the *Cristo de los Faroles*. By day or night, there is something inexpressibly moving in the lonely marble figure on the crucifix standing in its tiny sanctuary, from whose plinth and railings spring the eight street lamps, like flowers on pliant stalks, that give the group its popular name. Allowed only two glimpses of Córdoba, I should choose the interior of the Great Mosque and the Plazuela de los Dolores.

At one end of the plaza the whitewashed façade of the **Convento de los Capuchinos** makes a perfect background to the crucifix and street-lamps, and the pattern of geometric interlacing on its mudéjar door is worth examining, now that its many coats of paint have been removed. A few steps away, typifying the contrast of Renaissance opulence and the humble, whitewashed house-fronts that used to make up the greater part of Córdoba's streets, stands the **family mansion of the Fernández de Córdoba**, rebuilt in the last century. Its portal is supported by Doric columns; a fine, wrought-iron gate gives access to the *zaguán*, or short entrance-hall, and the large, rather bare patio in whose arches are framed portions of the Roman mosaics that were discovered below the foundations. The simple, wide Baroque staircase enhances the sense of grandeur, though the brown-painted walls and mustard-coloured carpet will not be to everyone's taste. The original owners were the descendants of Spain's most famous soldier, Gonzalo Fernández de Córdoba, the Great Captain, whose life story will unfold during this journey through Andalucía. He had no sons and the persistence of the family name is due to the fact that his surviving daughter and heiress to his fortune and titles (Duchess of Sessa, of Andria, of St. Angelo, Princess of Venosa and Marchioness of Bitonto—all these in southern Italy, commemorating her father's greatest campaigns) married a distant relation, the Count of Cabra, whose family name was also Fernández de Córdoba.

Our next objective is a patio, an example of that coolness and quiet of an interior garden that the Arabs bequeathed to Spain, having themselves adopted the principle from the Romans. To enter them from the grilling heat of a summer's day gives one an understanding of the cool shady paradise that is promised to the pious Moslem: 'It is watered by rivers; its food is perpetual and its shade also; but the reward of the infidels shall be fire.' Returning to the Puerta del Rincón by the Bailío, where one can best see the remains of the central wall of the old city, the **Convent of Saint Elizabeth** (Convento de Santa Isabel) lies a few yards to the east. The entrance projects into the corner where the Puerta del Rincón meets the Calle del Conde de Priego, for like every religious house of olden days, it was founded by a noble family, that of the counts of Priego, many of whom are buried here. In the shade of the old cypresses the plain, irregular courtyard runs up to the simple Renaissance doorway of the church, with its sculptured Visitation in the tympanum and the smaller, Baroque entrance to the sacristy on the right. The interior is pleasing but not remarkable; the cupola, in the shape of a truncated pyramid, is somewhat over-decorated, as might be expected from the exuberance of Spanish art of the mid-sixteenth century. The inscribed medallions inform us that this florid achievement was due to the munificence of one of the Figueroa family—their crest is generously displayed about the convent—who was a knight of the Order of Calatrava. As the convent is *in clausura* the church may only be visited at certain hours.

Behind the convent is the Gothic **Church of Santa Marina**, the oldest in Córdoba, dating from the Reconquest of 1236. The buttressed façade reminds one of a fortress, as the church may well have been in a secondary capacity, but the wheel window relieves the grimness. The north portal is noteworthy for the transitional archivolts springing from worn capitals that portray human and animal masks, a rarity in Southern Spain. Inside there is the customary plan of nave and two aisles with a clerestory of Gothic lights. In the Chapel of the Virgin of the Rosary (*Capilla de la Virgen del Rosario*) are fine paintings by the younger Castillo —those of St. Francis and St. John the Baptist are the best—and competent second-raters such as Fray Juan del Santísimo Sacramento and Gómez de Sandoval have added their quota. The chief attraction is the **Chapel of the Orozco family**, now the sacristy, whose entrance is a fine example of the Mudéjar style, with its intricate arabesques surrounding escutcheons of the cross 'fleury' and rows of stalactites surmounting the whole.

More tourists have seen this than any other church in Córdoba; the reason is that the statue of Manolete, the beloved bullfighter who was killed in 1947, faces the west entrance. Nowhere has the 'cult of Manolatry' reached greater heights than in this, the city of his birth, and nowhere more than in the parish of Santa Marina, cradle of many of Spain's most famous toreros. The house where he spent his childhood is a popular shrine; there is a Manolete fountain with his bronze bust in the Plaza de la Lagunilla, between here and the Tower of Malmuerta, brooding over a paving in which four mosaic bulls are set. In this statue, opposite Santa Marina, the bronze torero stands with cape held low before him, flanked by marble men and horses that recall the *Dioscuri* of the Roman Campidoglio. On the plinth behind him cherubs support a bronze bull's head, perhaps that of Islero who killed him. The complete group unfortunately spoils the simple architecture of an old square.

Going south by the Calle de Morales one soon reaches the **Palace of the Marqués de Viana** behind whose unpretentious Baroque portal lies a stupendous but private museum; it may however be visited when the family is not in residence. The site and possibly the lay-out are those of a palace of the last caliph of Córdoba, who is said to have caught one of his wives exchanging pleasantries through the bars with a certain Spanish Captain Gómez, whom he promptly had killed and buried somewhere on the premises. The palace has 181 rooms and 13 patios, of which eight are interior. Part of the decoration is provided by Roman finds from a Viana farm about twenty miles away. A collection of sporting guns, another of swords, ancient braziers and chests —one of these dated 1030—and a set of Chinese porcelain consisting of 2,000 pieces, brought from China in the sixteenth century, make up some of the gems of this treasure-house. This is but one example from the many sumptuous palaces that maintain their privacy behind a modest front—through a narrow wrought-iron *cancela* in a tiny street one may see three or even four patios, with fountains, palms, lanterns and statuary, and subsequently confirm that this family residence occupies the whole of a block. One such ancestral home, in addition to being a museum of all ages, displays the foundations, floor mosaics and lower walls of a complete Roman house in its basement, though it is unfortunately not on view.

For the energetic there are more churches to be seen in the north-eastern section of the city, as well as a portion of the old walls, flanking the Ronda del Marrubial. There is the baroque **Church of San Agustín**, in the street of that name, whose original Gothic has been heavily overlaid, except in the polygonal central apse. The façade of the **Church of San Lorenzo**, a short walk to the south-east, with its magnificent rose-window (*rosetón*) is certainly the finest in the city. The interior is notable for frescoes of the fifteenth century, rare specimens surviving from a rather sterile era. From here, or from the Viana palace, if the digression was not made, the Calle de San Pablo is easily reached; across the street is a group of interesting buildings that merit more than a glance. First, the **Casa de Hernán de Oliva** with its

Plateresque front. It is named after the famous humanist of Salamanca University and now belongs to a family of superior silversmiths who are proud of the many beautiful pieces they have collected, among them two Murillos and a Juan de Juanés. In a recess a few yards to the west is the best example of secular Renaissance architecture in Córdoba, the **Casa de los Villalones**. Enthusiasm is usually directed to the admittedly fine proportions and decoration of the doorway and the window that surmounts it; little is said of the Italian style loggia with its round arches and delicate columns, that provides a piquant contrast on the upper floor. Next, walking westwards, one sees the **Church of Saint Paul** (*Iglesia de San Pablo*) at the first corner on the left, but first a short lane on the opposite side of the street reveals the Gothic portal of the Church of Santa Marta; the Archaeological Museum of Madrid preserves an interesting Mudéjar ceramic well-top which was found intact in the patio of the attached convent. The interior offers nothing of interest.

San Pablo, on the other hand, has some surprises in store. If you enter from the Calle de San Pablo, though the usual access is from the Calle Calvo Sotelo round the corner, the left wall shows a type of masonry originally used by the Romans, adopted by the Arabs and used afterwards by the Mudéjars, as here. In a brick wall it would be described as alternate 'headers' and 'stretchers', that is laid end-on and sideways respectively. *Soga y tizón*, as it is called in Spanish, is the same system applied to stonework and in the latest caliphal examples there may be as many as three 'headers' to one 'stretcher'. The archivolts of the portal itself are supported by caliphal columns and capitals, of which others are found in the apses. In spite of these features, the church is not a converted mosque but was founded by St. Ferdinand for the Dominicans in 1241. The Oriental atmosphere is due to the employment of subject Moslems and the use of material from the ruined palace town of Medina Azzahra a few miles away. Originally Romanesque, so many styles have been employed and additions made that one loses all feeling of congruity: the side portal is florid Baroque; the Chapel of Doña Leonor López de Córdoba, in which is buried her father, a famous master of the Order of Calatrava, is fifteenth-century Gothic with a coat of limewash, and the ceiling of the nave is a magnificent *artesonado* with geometric Mudéjar decoration. More Mudéjar work is found alongside the sacristy, on the right as you face the altar, where an anteroom is divided by a hand-some, pointed, Oriental arch resting on caliphal capitals; passing through it one sees the interior of a typical Moslem cupola, of the same style as that in front of the *mihrab* in the Great Mosque. The walls are attractively decorated with *azulejos* and arabesque stucco, in which there are mirror-image pairs of Cufic script. Even the most ardent ecclesiophile will by now be threatened with a surfeit, and as some of the churches close as early as 11 o'clock it is as well to devote the rest of the morning to secular sights. Skirting the Church of San Pablo by going down the Calle Calvo Sotelo and then taking the left fork, you soon enter the **Plaza Mayor.** If you have lost your way, or are approaching from a different direction, you may have to ask for the Plaza de la Corredera, or even the Plaza del Mercado, although the ugly market buildings have been removed, for Spanish streets and squares like to fool the visitor by a frequent change of name. The Plaza Mayor is the best example in Andalucía of what has become a typical feature of large cities, such as Madrid and Salamanca. Oblong and built of pale brick, there is a continuous arcade at street level, relieved by the plainest of moulding and the bracket of a street-lamp projecting from alternate spandrels. In the arcade are the shops and the entrances to the upper storeys; there are three of these, with large, severe windows and plain iron balconies where geraniums and rambler roses make a fine show against the brickwork and the ubiquitous dull green sun-blinds.

A few years ago a cobbler showed me two Roman Ionic capitals among the blocks in a wall in his back room, put there perhaps in the 1690s, when the Plaza Mayor was built. Roman finds arouse little comment in Córdoba: I have seen a spiral column revealed about ten feet below street level, when foundations for a new building were being dug, and not so long ago a complete mosaic floor was discovered below the square we are to visit next.

For some centuries one of the chief functions of these squares was to stage bull fights, in which the nobility and gentry pitted their skill against the bulls, under the eyes of their peers in the balconies; deeds of sale of these houses in fact often contained a clause entitling the original owner to retain the use of windows and balconies during bull fights. The formal sequence of today's *corrida* had not yet been devised; the bulls were loosed into the square, one or two or more at a time, and the cavaliers rode against them with spears. Variations were introduced, even to riding the bulls themselves, and may be seen in Goya's sketches in Madrid's Prado Museum.

Leaving the Plaza Mayor at the point where we entered, a left turn takes us into the Calle Claudio Marcelo and so into the **Plaza José Antonio**, alias Plaza de Cánovas, alias Las Tendillas. The buildings are modern, for this is the region of fashionable shops, and in the nearby streets are cafés where the *jeunesse dorée* of Córdoba repairs for Coca-Cola and *perritos calientes*, attractively diminutive hot dogs.

The equestrian statue in the centre of the square, by the Cordoban sculptor Mateo Inurria, is of Gonzalo Fernández de Córdoba, whose descendants' mansion we passed earlier. The features of the statue are quite unlike those of the same Gran Capitán, kneeling in prayer over his tomb in Granada, but they closely resemble the relief on a medal struck in his honour in 1503. Inurria took as his model a popular Cordoban torero nicknamed *El Lagartijo*, The Lizard, and those who have seen the medal, reproduced in a biography by Lojendio, will agree that his choice was inspired.

Gonzalo was a devoted servant of the Catholic Monarchs, Ferdinand and Isabel, and played an important part in the conquest of Granada. Later he fought the Turks in the Ionian Islands, then the French in Italy and finished his active career as first Spanish viceroy of Naples. He reorganised the Spanish army, founding an officers' training college and the infantry formations known as the *tercios*, the pikemen who remained the terror of Europe for nearly one and a half centuries. Gonzalo was one of the last three mirrors of chivalry in an age when kings themselves were unmindful of the proverb: *Honra y provecho no caben en un saco*; 'Honour and profit don't fit in the same bag'. The other two were Gonzalo's enemies and admirers, Gaston de Foix and the Chevalier Bayard.

North of the plaza lies the **Church of San Miguel**, whose exterior provides another of those delightful contrasts that Córdoba offers. The façade is an example of the severe early Gothic; the southern entrance, however, has a horseshoe arch with contrasting voussoirs, with alternate ones bearing arabesque scroll-work, a clear imitation of the portals of the Mosque. Three hundred yards westward along the Calle de Góngora brings you back to the Paseo del Gran Capitán; a glance to the left reveals the handsome belfry of the **Church of San Nicolás**, where Gonzalo was baptised in 1453. The octagonal tower so resembles a minaret that it is surprising to learn of its completion in 1496, nearly three centuries after the Reconquest. Of course the work was largely done by Mudéjars.

The **Church of San Hipolito** is at the end of the first block on the left in the Paseo del Gran Capitán, which ends at the Church of San Nicolás. Alfonso XI of Castile, one of the more efficient and less ostentatious monarchs, ordered its construction but the work came to a standstill when only the Gothic sanctuary and crossing had been built; it was eventually completed in 1736, when the remains of the founder and his father, Fernando IV, were transferred here. Their sarcophagi, of pink marble on black marble pedestals, occupy niches on either side of the nave.

It is possible to see something of the rest of Córdoba in an afternoon, if you realise that business hours extend from 4 or 5 pm to 7 or 8 o'clock, depending on the season, and that many churches are only open during these hours. It is as well for the traveller to conform, to take a siesta during the hottest hours and thus prepare himself for an evening that can be pleasantly occupied in sightseeing or simply strolling, then dinner and a visit to the Alcázar gardens which are floodlit in summer till 1 am. Visitors are often shocked when they see toddlers playing in the parks at 2 am; this only means that the Spaniard has adapted himself to his climate, for the child gets the same amount of sleep as his northern cousin and grows up just as healthy or unhealthy, depending on factors other than the clock.

At the **Almodóvar Gate** on the west side, there is a stretch of the old city wall, with moat and gardens, extending southward. A bronze statue of Seneca stands before the gate and at intervals other, less impressive gates are found; in one of these is the statue of Averröes. Seneca was a Roman philosopher, playwright and tutor of the Emperor Nero. With his father Lucius the rhetorician, his nephew Lucan the poet and his elder brother Lucius Gallio who, as governor of Achaea refused the Jews permission to prosecute St. Paul, he represents at least one great Cordoban family whose fame is likely to endure. Averröes or Abu'l-Walid ibn Rushd was also the scion of a Cordoban family of standing, he himself representing the third generation to hold office as *cadi*. The Almodóvar Gate itself stands between square towers in a section of the wall that still sports its pyramidal Almohad merlons; much of it has been filled with an ugly, squared gateway of later date. In Moslem days it was called *Bab al-Yahud* and even today it is often called Puerta de los Judios, for it gives access to the old Jewish quarter of Judería. Almost immediately a narrow street with strips of squared slabs

winding among the cobbles leads to the right; it carries the name
Judíos, though the Jews were expelled nearly five centuries ago,
and another indicator pointing to the Zoco, the nearest the
Spanish language got to the Arabic *suk*, or market.

Turning into Judíos, whose official name is Calle de Maimonides, you find at No. 18 on the right the old **Synagogue**,
unique in Southern Spain. It was not built in the days of the
Arab emirs and caliphs, for three centuries remarkably tolerant
of Jews and Christians whom they regarded as 'people of the
Book', nor in the time of the Almohads, the last wave of North
African conquerors who were rabid persecutors of Christian and
Jew alike and even of their less fanatical co-religionists, and
destroyed churches and synagogues impartially. It was therefore
built after the Reconquest—the builder's name, Isaac Mejeb,
and the date 1315 are given in one of the Hebrew inscriptions—
and is in Mudéjar style. You descend to a tiny patio, for the level
of the city has risen in six centuries, and one of the family of the
late custodian will show you the stairway leading to the women's
gallery; separation of the sexes has always been a cardinal
requisite of Hebrew worship. Even after the wonders of the
Mosque one can admire the intricate stucco panels, the foliated
arch, the remains of the extensive wall tiling and the frieze of
Hebrew selections from the Psalms. After the expulsion of the
Jews in 1492 the synagogue became a hospital for rabies patients
and in 1588 was acquired by the Shoemakers' Guild, naturally
under the patronage of St. Crispin and St. Crispian. The damage
done by successive occupants has been partly made good since
the building was declared a national monument in 1885. In the
patio is a marble panel commemorating the birth of Maimonides:

> 1135 — 30th March — 1935
> Spain, through its government, expresses its
> homage to the immortal genius of Jewry.
> Córdoba, his birthplace, offers the veneration
> of its remembrance.

Farther down the street we come to the tiny Plaza Tiberiades, in
which a seated statue of the great man shows him in robes and
turban; behind him an old caliphal column is visible on the
street corner. The plinth says simply: 'Córdoba to Maimonides'
in Spanish and Hebrew and gives the dates 1964 and 5724, referring to the Christian and Hebrew calendars respectively.
The Maimonides cult has a firm hold in Córdoba, which regards
him as one of her most illustrious sons, ranking with the Gran

Capitán and only slightly below Manolete. It has no political implications whatever.

Maimonides—Moses ben Maimon—was the son of an outstanding physician-philosopher and a contemporary of Averröes. Both suffered from the intolerance of the Almohads, and in both cases it entailed emigration, for Maimonides to Morocco, where he lived for some years in Fez, concealing his religion. Later he went to Jerusalem and then to Cairo, where he not only became physician to Saladin's family but persuaded that ruler to allow Jews to settle in the Holy City again. Apart from his medical writings, some of which are only now being translated from the original Arabic, his commentaries on Hebrew law made him famous throughout Jewry, and his ever fresh mind brought illumination to a subject already stale. To the Jews his title of Rabbi and his initials provided the affectionate nickname 'Rambam', while Christian scholars made much of 'Rabbi Moyses' and his thesis that Scripture must be accommodated to reason.

From the Plazuela de Maimonides the street changes its name to Calle Tomás Conde and leads to the **House of Góngora**, yet another native in the great series that began with Seneca. The house has long ago been replaced and not even a plaque marks its site, but there is a bronze statue of the seated poet near by. Today Gongorism, as it is called, is regarded as an innovation with the respect that is accorded the Baroque art form. Gerald Brenan says: 'Seen through the perspective of the centuries, he must be called, if not the greatest Spanish poet—the term is ambiguous—at least the greatest and most enchanting artist in the language.' Góngora's statue, or at least the head, is modelled on the portrait by Velázquez, painted when the artist was twenty-three and the poet sixty-one; the original is in the Museum of Fine Arts, Boston, and a copy survives in the Prado Museum where one can see the ageing, aristocratic features such as have been immortalised in El Greco's *Burial of the Count of Orgaz*.

All around are narrow streets with glimpses of patios through the iron grilles that are still so artistically forged by hand. The reader may be confused by the various words used for the grille, the best known being *reja*; those guarding the entrance to the patio are usually referred to as *cancela* and, like window grilles, may also be called *verja*. Hereabouts are many Andalucian restaurants, in which for most of the year the tables are placed in the patio, kept cool by the canvas *toldos* that can be pulled across by an ingenious arrangement of cords and pulleys. Just after a shower is not a good time to eat there for an enthusiastic waiter is almost certain to start drawing the *toldos* back, with the result that they empty some gallons of water on the astonished diner. But the food and wine are good, if not thus diluted.

In the Plaza Maimonides is the Zoco, where local craftsmen display their traditional leather and silver work against a background of greenery and Roman amphorae. Upstairs is another restaurant, where an excellent meal is served before the nightly flamenco show in the patio. This is usually better, and certainly more authentic than the shows to which parties of tourists are taken in the larger towns. The rest of the upper balcony is the **Museum of Tauromaquia**, where you may pass an interesting half-hour among the relics of Córdoba's favourite toreros.

Turning left from the Zoco into the Calle de Averröes, you can see through a railing the patio of the **Chapel of San Bartolomé**, which can, alas, no longer be entered unless the visitor has special permission to use the entrance from the hospital in the Calle de Cardenal Salazar. On the right of the little patio, with its ivy-covered palm tree, are the three pointed arches that rest on two stunted columns and give access to the portico. The builder of this structure, said to be more recent than the chapel itself, but still of respectable antiquity, made use of ancient columns and one Ionic and one handsome Visigothic capital. The central arched portal of the chapel carries a zigzag or chevron pattern, such as may also be seen in the churches of Santa Marina and la Magdalena, a purely Norman decoration which rapidly spread southwards from England.

Round the corner is the General Hospital, and in the little square in front of the portal of 1701 is a bronze statue of the Arab oculist Al-Gafequí, who flourished about 1165. Diseases of the eye being excessively common in the Near East it is only fitting that their study and treatment should have their origin there too. The first systematic text-book on the subject was written in the ninth century and thereafter the practice of ophthalmology was kept alive in Al-Andalus, transmitted to the Christians and developed by them, so that Louis XIV's oculist was a Spaniard and the Barcelona school is today world famous.

In the Calle del Buen Pastor one can see a limewashed Gothic doorway and a plaque to say that St. John of the Cross lived here in 1586; we come across his traces, alive or dead, in many parts of the South. At the end of the street is the Plaza Angel de Torres, often known as the Plaza del Indiano from the celebrated **Casa de los Ceas**, which is also known as the Casa del Indiano, thus keeping up the local weakness for aliases. The rectangular doorway is quite typical of Cordoban architecture and the decoration of lintel and jambs is from the fourteenth or fifteenth century, with a pronounced resemblance to the Puerta del Perdón; both buildings were the work of Mudéjars. Although restored during this century by Inurria the façade, including the lobulated twin window, is authentic. The upper storey, with its Plateresque-Mudéjar decoration round the windows, is an example of the best period, towards the end of the fifteenth century, when large, blank areas were relieved by intensive decoration round doors and windows.

A few yards away the Little Sisters of the Poor occupy the **Convento de Jesús Crucificado**, which has one of the finest *artesonado* ceilings in Spain. In one of the patios is a selection of capitals that includes Roman, Visigothic and Moslem, one of the last being signed (with hammer and chisel) by Ahmed ibn Fateh.

In the Calle Barroso, two blocks away, stands the sadly worn but still handsome **Minaret of St. John** (Alminar de San Juan). The original mosque was given to the knights of the Order of St. John of Jerusalem, who helped in the capture of Córdoba and this accounts for the name of the minaret. Many of the old stones have had to be replaced and the ruined top has been covered with an ugly roof which at least protects the remains from the worst of the weather. Its chief attraction are the charming double, or *ajimez*,[1] windows with twin horseshoe arches separated by slender marble columns; these are among the first Moslem ones known in Córdoba and their capitals have been identified as coming from the workshops of Abderrahman II (822–852). The floor above still shows the remains of tiny columns dividing horseshoe arcades and the interior preserves the spiral staircase by which the muezzin mounted for his call to prayer five times a day.

Behind the next block, in the Calle Angel de Saavedra, is the **Palacio del Marqués de la Fuensanta del Valle**, whose lintel and door-jambs are patterned with *almohadillo*, or quilted, though the impress of a waffle iron would be a more accurate description. No. 29 in the Calle del Heredia has a similar front, which we shall see when we visit the Convent of Santa Clara. The palacio was built about fifty years after the Casa de los Ceas and one can see how in that time local architects and builders had practically

1. The word *ajimez* is not strictly applicable to this type of window but the usage is now established. Like the horseshoe arch it is not a Moslem invention, for examples can be seen in Visigothic buildings.

broken with Moslem tradition, as the full tide of the Italian Renaissance swept through Spain.

Andalucian Baroque is well displayed in the nearby school of the Marist brothers, occupying what was once the House of the Jesuits, opposite the Iglesia de la Compañía, which houses a rather dismal retablo in wood, partly sculptured by Pedro Duque Cornejo whom we know to have been capable of better things. The school contains a fine classical patio and a monumental staircase of marble, veined dark grey, yellow and fawn, the last from the quarries of Cabra, which are still in production; it is not as grotesque as it sounds.

The Palacio de los Páez de Quintano houses the **Archaeological Museum**. The portal is an example of how the classical severity of the Renaissance was circumvented by the compulsion to decorate, the *horror vacui*, call it what you will, of the mid-sixteenth century with its Plateresque additions. The building itself has undergone many alterations since its design by Hernán Ruiz, one of the fashionable architects of the time. But in the second patio there are still some brick and tile windows of the original palace and the low, pointed arch of the Isabelline style in the *alfices*. Round the walls are fine Roman polychrome mosaics, and there is shade, a fountain, and at the far end a pool with a Roman mosaic floor representing fish, and papyrus in the corners of the recess.

The Roman columns, capitals and steles can be examined in comfort, as well as the interesting Mithraic sculpture, showing the usual Mithra with Phrygian cap delivering the death blow to the bull, a dog licking the blood issuing from the neck wound and a scorpion attached to the penis, doubtless—as Morley points out—to demonstrate that the seed never perishes. Note too the Christian sarcophagus with Old Testament scenes in high relief and follow the progress of Christian funerary art through the various halls. There are palaeo-Christian and Visigothic reliefs on tombstones, one dated E 630. The E stands for 'era', inaugurated by Augustus in 38 BC when he began the final pacification of Spain, completed in 19 BC. The era dating was used well into the Renaissance and sporadically even beyond.[1]

In every way the museum has been arranged not only scienti-

---

1. This has been responsible for errors of dating in the past, especially by foreigners, to whom any other system than that reckoned from the Nativity is inconceivable in an ultra-Catholic country. Nearly all have the vague *Vixit annos plus minus . . .* instead of the precise Roman 'He lived six years, nine months, two days and seven hours'.

fically, but artistically. Mounting the broad staircase one sees an apparently endless succession of perfect polychrome mosaics from the city and surroundings, and as the building boom continues, the ever-deepening foundations of the new apartment and office blocks will bring more Roman remains to light. Hall VII has a collection of iron *braseros* with Arabic inscriptions round the rim; this is the last link in a chain whose first is the discovery of clay *braseros* in Hittite settlements of a few thousand years ago, others being the continued use of the same article in modern Turkey, in North Africa, Sicily, Spain and Portugal. A *brasero* is a flat bowl on stumpy legs and its function is to contain glowing charcoal, olive stones, camel dung or any other combustible; it is then placed under the circular table around which the family seats itself on winter evenings, with a long, heavy tablecloth that is draped over the thighs and almost reaches the floor between each pair. In most families, rich or poor—though the former use electric *braseros*—this is the only means of keeping warm in houses designed primarily to keep out the heat. This is why one sees so many women in Spain with mottled, pigmented shins, the inevitable consequence of repeated exposure to radiant heat.

One of the finest pieces is the tenth-century bronze and enamel stag from Medina Azzahra, where it presided over a fountain given by Constantine VII Porphyrogenitus to Abderrahman III. Constantine was one of the great Byzantine rulers, bringing diplomacy and court procedure to their highest level. It is interesting to note how much Byzantium and the Moslem states had in common, even to the wave of iconoclasm which shook Constantinople in the eighth century. Which brings us to the surprise felt by many visitors at seeing this and other representations of animal forms in Islamic art, since so many writers have repeated the statement that they are forbidden in the Koran. No such prohibition is found in the Koran; it comes from the *Hadith*, or *Traditions*, alleged sayings of the Prophet and their interpretation, a verbal collection that was not put into writing until a century and a half later; many Moslems have felt that their divine inspiration is inferior to that of the Koran, which transmits the commands of Allah to Mohamed.

A short street leads to the Calle del Rey Heredia where, turning left, one comes to the **Convent of Santa Clara**, founded for Franciscan nuns by Alfonso X, 'the Learned'. Parts of a pre-existing mosque were utilised as can be seen from the *soga y tizón* arrangement of the worn, fawn-coloured stones. The belfry is the original minaret as high as the level of the battlements and the interior preserves the muezzin's stair lighted by arrow slits; experts believe that it was built by Almansor, during the last phase of the caliphate, certainly before 1010, and this conforms with the use of two or three headers to each stretcher, typical of that era. Going south, the next street on the right is called Badanillas, a name derived from *badana*, a soft leather, a reminder of one of the trades for which Córdoba was renowned. Many of the street names hereabouts show where the various trades had their premises, a practice still seen in eastern bazaars.

Turning left, we enter the street called **Cabezas**, or 'Heads', though this is not to be taken in its nautical sense. Though narrow, it gives access to numerous aristocratic mansions; one of the humbler, No. 18, carries the plaque that explains the street name, and along its side runs an alley, closed by a grating and about three feet wide, typical in fact of many a North African street. It is called Arquillos from the numerous arches which brace the buildings on either side, and the plaque reads:

Two famous Cordoban historians, Aben Hayan and Ambrosio de Morales, and a Castilian ballad singer tell us that in the year 974 Gonzalo Gustioz, Lord of Salas, was captive in this house and that the heads of his sons, the seven Infantes of Lara, killed in the fields of Soria, were exposed on these arches. Truth and venerable legend, of many centuries' repute in the whole of Spain

The complicated tale goes back to the early days of the Reconquest, when García I was second ruler of Castile, after its separation from León. His beautiful cousin Lambra had just married a member of the House of Lara. During the wedding festivities, which lasted several weeks, her cousin Alvar Sánchez boasted of his prowess in the tourney, whereupon the youngest of the Infantes, or sons of the House of Lara, unhorsed him. The ensuing brawl wounded Doña Lambra's Castilian pride; the next day, on her instructions, one of her servants threw a cucumber dipped in blood at the offending Infante, Gonzalvico. Aroused by this remarkable insult, which is stated to be the most serious that could be offered to a Castilian gentlemen, the Infantes pursued the unfortunate servant and ran him through, although he had taken refuge under Lambra's cloak. Doña Lambra easily persuaded her husband to procure her revenge against his own kin. He arranged with Almansor, the dreaded Moslem dictator, for the father to be inveigled to Córdoba and beheaded

SEVILLE. The narrow streets and balconies of the Santa Cruz quarter.

SEVILLE. *Above*, lunette of the Puerta de la Campanilla – the Palm Sunday entrance into Jerusalem. *Below*, the Hall of the Ambassadors in the Alcazár.

and for the sons to be treacherously slain, after being betrayed to the Moslem army. Almansor was too much of a gentleman to kill his guest and kept him in light captivity under the care of his (Almansor's) sister. In a short time the seven heads of his sons arrived and were exposed on the arches. The broken-hearted parent was consoled by his Moslem hostess with such success that she produced a son, whom they called Mudarra. Gonzalo was released shortly after and returned to his wife, and from then on Doña Lambra's servants threw seven stones at their window every morning. Of course Mudarra grew up, came North, avenged the death of his half-brothers and had Doña Lambra burnt alive. In this way the ballad singer was able to finish his story with 'and they lived happily ever after'.

Farther up Cabezas, on the right side, there is a recess in which stands the **Casa de los Marqueses del Carpio**. Although the masonry is like that of the Convent of Santa Clara, the two are not contemporaneous, though some maintain that it was here, and not at No. 18, that the Lord of Salas was kept prisoner. The Mudéjars were conservative and preserved the original Arab methods of building along with many other skills for centuries after they came under the rule of Christian Spain. The interior has a fine patio with some caliphal capitals, including one with a Cufic inscription, dated 353 of the Hegira and taken from the old Alcázar—possibly the only survivor from that vanished building. It is unfortunately often impossible to enter this private residence but, by retracing their steps to the Calle del Cardenal González, the former red light district, visitors can see in the patio of the Taberna de los Palcos two fine columns from Medina Azzahra, dating from the second half of the tenth century. The drill work of the capitals is a form of decoration which had been lost when the Western Roman Empire collapsed and was revived in Al-Andalus at the beginning of the ninth century.

In the Calle de la Feria, at the northern end of Cabezas, is another picturesque corner of Córdoba, the arch called the **Portillo**, doubtless a part of the wall which once divided the city. Here is the essence of old Andalucía, a surviving portion of mediaeval walls, a lamp suspended from the arch, a narrow cobbled street of whitewashed houses, *rejas* and balconies and flowers trailing down. Across the road a short street leads to the **Plaza del Potro**, where a tiled notice on the wall of the Museum proudly announces that this place was mentioned by Cervantes 'in the world's best novel'. An eighteenth-century monument to the Archangel Raphael deserves only a glance, but the fountain is a beautiful creation, its base, where children are usually to be seen splashing with their hands, like an early baptismal font and the centre column topped by the exquisite colt which gives its name to the Plaza.

Opposite the Museum is the **Mesón del Potro**, where Cervantes is alleged to have stayed, but you have to remember that he is credited with as many lodgings as our Queen Elizabeth I. At least the inn is known to have existed in his day, as its venerable appearance suggests. It is the typical Arab *fonduk*, and *fonda* is one of the Spanish words for an inn. It is built round three sides of a narrow courtyard, stables and stores below and bedrooms on the wooden-balconied floor above. A night's lodging may be had for 20 pesetas. Very near, between the Calle Lucano and the Paseo de la Rivera, is another survival, the Posada de la Herradura, or Horseshoe Inn.

You enter the **Museo de Bellas Artes** from the Plaza del Potro. It was originally built in 1443, as a religious foundation and hospital, but the façade is modern. There is a pleasant patio, where a fountain plays and white marble classical sculptures gleam against the dark box hedges. The Museum's collection is largely made up of works of art that became available when the monasteries were suppressed in 1835. The pride of the collection are the paintings of the Cordoban School of the seventeenth century. Local art came to prominence with Augustín del Castillo and his gifted son Antonio and culminated with Valdés Leal. However much the Cordoban masters suffer by comparison with the far greater masters of Seville, their works repay careful study, especially as the visitor is less harassed by guided groups. But in your enthusiasm for painting don't overlook the hall allocated to the sculptures of Inurria, and especially his seated Seneca.

The earliest painting, a head of Christ, is all that is left of a fresco of 1286, by Alonso Martínez; it was discovered in the Villaviciosa Chapel of the Cathedral in 1890 and promptly ruined, though with the best intentions. Upstairs, the school of Pedro de Córdoba, whose Annunciation we saw in the Cathedral, is represented by a St. Nicholas of Bari, resplendent in colourful mitre and robes, with an ornamental wealth characteristic of Gothic painting. From the year 1494, when Renaissance influences became important, you may see a monumental retablo, doubtfully attributed to Juan de Zamora or Alfonso de Aguilar, and a Flagellation by Alejo Fernández, a Cordoban for all that he spent most of his productive life in Seville.

A new trend in realism is shown by Juan Zambrano, pupil of Pablo Céspedes. The latter is commemorated in a plaque over the main entrance and is regarded as one of the transitional painters, whose pupils introduced the earliest and best Baroque painting; his *Wedding at Cana*, partly spoiled, may be seen upstairs, and we saw some of his work in the Cathedral. Another of the transitional figures was Francisco Pacheco, teacher and father-in-law of Velázquez, to whose generation Zambrano therefore belongs; his *David Victorious* reveals the drama and the interest in the human subject that distinguished the artistic revolution of the end of the sixteenth century. The same development in technique and expression can be seen by comparing the *Trinity* of Agustín del Castillo with the *Crucifixion* by his son Antonio, who studied under Zurbarán and whose numerous canvases occupy the further half of the hall at the far end of the entrance corridor, on the left. One of Zurbarán's successors was José Sarabia, justly renowned for his scenes of rustic life, of which *The Adoration of the Shepherds* reflects the dramatic chiaroscuro that Zurbarán used with such effect.

Of the painters from outside Córdoba there are examples upstairs, though many are but attributions—Ribera, Murillo, Zurbarán, Alonso Cano, Ribalta, Giordano (popularly known, from the speed with which he worked, as *Fa presto*) and Anton Mengs. These artists will show up to greater advantage in Seville and Granada, but only in Córdoba will you find two Goya portraits such as those of Carlos IV and his wife María Luisa. The amiable and fat-headed Bourbon king and his ugly but amorous wife had a perfect mania for being painted by Goya, as one may verify in the Prado, and the more plainly he revealed their little souls the more eagerly they came back. Many will know how the beady-eyed Guinevere made a Lancelot of Manuel Godoy, a guards officer fifteen years her junior, and how between them they ruined Spain; studying Goya's portraits of this mother of seven or eight one must reluctantly respect the firmness with which Godoy climbed the beaten path to promotion.

The top floor displays a collection of sketches, most of them pen-and-ink. Among the most interesting are those of Antonio de Castillo; note especially the bold lines and sense of balance in *The Two Male Nudes*. The moderns, among whom are included the successors of Goya, are patchily represented; of particular interest is a painting by Eugenio Lucas Padillo (1824–1870), of 'bull running' in an open square, full of life and excitement. One occasionally meets the inquiring foreigner who wonders why a bull-fight in an enclosed arena should be called *corrida*, or running. This painting gives the answer. It used to be the custom, and still is during the Fiesta of San Fermin in Pamplona, to herd the bulls at a gallop through the town on their way to the *toril*, where they await their turn at the bull-fight next day.

Returning to the patio you will see a double-stored baroque house-front built into one wall. This is the **Museo de Julio Romero de Torres**, in which Córdoba honours one of its favourite sons. It is best to regard him as an interpreter of his own region and he is most successful with two of Andalucía's outstanding products, women and fruit. Some of his portraits of the olive-skinned, sloe-eyed beauties of Córdoba at least received the accolade of being reproduced on the postage stamps and 100-peseta notes of Spain. His group of seven street-walkers, entitled *Vividoras de Amor*, caused a commotion when it appeared and was consistently barred, as immoral, from exhibitions; it hangs here under the title *Nocturno* and no one gives it a second glance.

If you time your visit well you can walk over to the **Convento de San Francisco**, which is open from 7 to 8 pm, badly lighted and noteworthy less for its 'Churrigueresque' decoration than for its collection of artistic treasures. The best known is the San Andrés (St. Andrew) of Valdés Leal (1622–1690), that dynamic Baroque forerunner of the Romantics in whom the seventeenth century revival of art in Córdoba culminated. The St. Andrew hardly shows him at the height of his powers and we may pass on to the statuary, of which the finest is the *San Pedro de Alcántara*, by Alonso Cano's most gifted pupil, Pedro de Mena. In contrast there is an anonymous *La Dolorosa* of the seventeenth century, a sorrowing mother with crystal tears, obviously copied from Gregorio Fernández, whose famous *Mater Dolorosa* may be seen in Valladolid. Fernández, in turn, exploited the realism begun by Juan de Juní, as have a hundred others, so that in this example in Córdoba we have what amounts to a third generation of debased sentiment. No wonder that the Spaniard, always cynical, has for generations referred to the restaurant bill as 'La Dolorosa'.

All this gives you a fair cross-section of Córdoba, artistic, historic and modern. For those who want to see more a last group of buildings remains. Walk down to the embankment of the Guadalquivir and turn left, or upstream. After half a mile turn left again, opposite the weir, along the Calle Ronquillo Briceno; in the second street on your right you will find the **Casa de las Campanas**; one side of its patio retains a rare survival of Moslem civil architecture in the shape of three arches, two of them cusped, resting on antique columns taken from still older buildings. Opposite is the Mudéjar mansion of the Knights of St. James, the **Casa de los Caballeros de Santiago**, later reduced (or possibly exalted) to the function of a bodega and now a school. One patio has no less than twelve lobulated arches, and one can see how these were constructed by allowing every third brick of the arch to project into the opening; subsequent plastering disguised the corners to make rounded, miniature arches; there are also remains of arabesque stucco. Almost next door is the **Church of Santiago**, presumably built immediately after the Reconquest on the site of a mosque, for its bell tower is an almost untouched minaret of the tenth century with the usual spiral stair. The church contains an *artesonado* ceiling, constructed in 1635 by the master-carpenter Alonso Múñoz de los Rios, who was paid 14,000 reals, possibly equivalent to $5,000 today; he was probably able to command high prices because Córdoba was a renowned centre for this work.

The **Church of the Carmelitas Calzadas** near the Puerta Nueva is also in this unspoiled, eastern section of Córdoba. A retablo was recently discovered here, apparently concealed behind an everyday Baroque one; it contains twelve fine paintings by Valdés Leal which merit a visit in the morning, when the light is least bad; it is, however, as well to arrange a time.

CHAPTER FOUR

Excursions from Córdoba and the Road to Seville

❧

La Arruzafa—Las Ermitas—Medina Azzahra—San Jerónimo—Almodóvar—Baena—Cabra—Lucena—Rute—Aguilar de la Frontera—Osuna—Estepa—Écija—Monclova—Carmona

The nearest point of interest is the site of the *Munyat al-Ruzafa* the garden and country house of Abderrahman I. It lies about 2 kilometres north of the city on a road that branches off the Carretera del Brillante, and is approached between files of orange trees. Nothing now remains of the pleasure grounds of the 'Immigrant', as the first Omayyad is sometimes called, except a scraggy palm tree, but it is interesting to recall that the original building was used as a guest-house for important visitors from the days of the founder onward. The present one is The D.G.T. Parador. The story is that Abderrahman I was taking a walk in the country when he saw a palm tree. This was apparently such an event, and his homesickness was so great, that he called it a fellow-immigrant and decided to build a palace there and breed palm trees in his spare time. The story is suspect for two reasons: first, you can't breed from one palm tree alone, and secondly palm trees were well known in Spain from earliest recorded times, some saying they were indigenous and others that the Carthaginians brought them.

The road now leads to an area which was inhabited by hermits from the early days of Christianity, through Visigothic and Moslem times. The Cordoban bishop Osilius seems to have started collecting the solitary anchorites into small communities in the fourth century and traces of their buildings have been found from La Arruzafa into the mountains. During the Mozarab defiance of Islam in the tenth century many Christians suffered martyrdom, but the caves and hermitages went on being inhabited until the present century. To those who have spent any time in a Spanish city the silence of the countryside acts as a magnet and there are few visitors who fail to appreciate the inscription over the entrance to **Las Ermitas**: *Oh bendita soledad* . . ., 'O blessed solitude! You urge to penitence, inspire austerity, contemplation and abstinence. O sole felicity!'

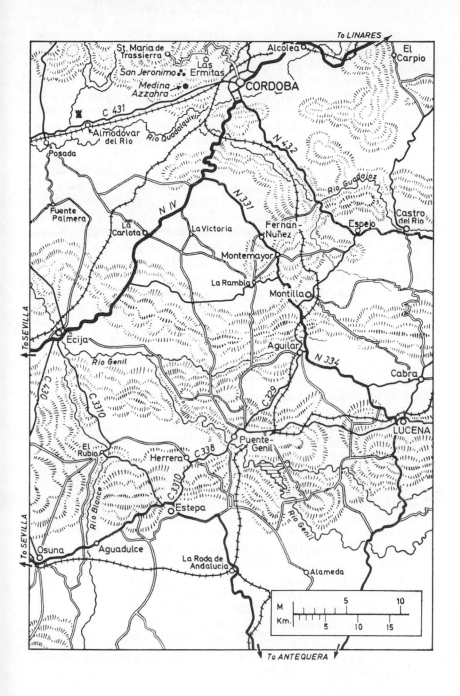

The skull played a large part in the hermit's life and some even used a sawn-off calvarium as a cup. As we enter between the cypresses we come upon a crucifix in whose pedestal there is a barred niche containing a skull and the verse: *Como te ves yo me vi* . . ., a grim warning that the skull once looked like you and that you will one day look like the skull; 'think on it and you'll sin no more'. Meanwhile, there is time to inspect the cells that are on view, with their austere furnishings, and wander along the paths between the shrubs and flowers.

Six kilometres farther, along what is no longer an atrocious road over the mountains, stands the Church of Santa Maria de Trassierra, a converted Almohad mosque of the twelfth century, inside the ruins of a castle.

The ruins of **Medina Azzahra** (Madinat al-zahra—city of the flower) lie 8 kilometres west of Córdoba on a side-turning to the north of C431. To find this you go west along the broad Avenida del Generalísimo and turn left down the far side of the Jardines de la Victoria; the first large turning to the right is signposted to Medina Azzahra.[1] The first view of the ruins is bound to disappoint, especially if you have conscientiously read about the palace-town, and some believe the visit to be a waste of time.

The building was begun in 936 by order of the first western caliph, Abderrahman III. The story of its origin and how it got its name is too good to be true and yet documents discovered in this century have confirmed every detail. One of the caliph's concubines died leaving him her wealth, which was considerable; this fact alone gives an idea of the conduct, customs and advanced civilisation of the western Moslems. The caliph decided to devote the money to the ransoming of prisoners in the Spanish March, that is the territory south of the Pyrenees originally conquered by the Franks under Charlemagne. His envoy, however, brought the information that there were no prisoners to be ransomed. Thereupon his favourite of the moment, named 'The Flower', proposed that the money be used to build a new administrative capital and palace combined and this was begun by the caliph, with his heir Prince Hakam supervising the work. After five years the mosque was inaugurated and four years after that a large reception (a house-warming?) is recorded. The city was named after the Flower and her statue placed in a niche above the main gate, another incredible tale which proved to be

1. The spelling often given is *Medina al-Zahra*; this is orthographically correct, but the 'l' in *al* before 'z' is pronounced as 'z'.

true when chronicles by an anonymous Arab author turned up in the libraries of Madrid and Copenhagen, stating that the Almohad caliph Yakub-al-Mansur ordered the statue over the city gate to be removed in 1120, much to the annoyance of the Moslem inhabitants.

The building programme was on a vast scale and the complete project took over forty years, employing never less than 10,000 workmen. Over 4,000 columns were used, mainly from Tunisia though 200 were sent as a present by the Emperor of Constantinople. All the capitals so far recovered are of various caliphal reigns so that there must have been a large workshop on the premises; some of the capitals are still to be seen in Córdoba, others were carried far afield, particularly to Seville and Granada. The sumptuousness of the palace has been described many times; it is enough to say that it aroused the admiration of all visitors, even those coming from the splendours of Constantinople, and that it included the unheard-of luxuries of an aviary and a menagerie.

After this account of glittering display it is indeed sad to walk round the site and see the painstaking restoration in progress. The city was sacked more than once in the first part of the eleventh century and it seems as though the Berber mercenaries took a fiendish delight in destroying what they could not carry off; the fragments of carved stone that are being unearthed are so small that we can only conclude that systematic destruction was carried out with hammers. Then, when the remains began to be covered with a merciful mantle of soil and herbage, 'Old Córdoba' (Córdoba la Vieja) came to be used as a quarry and provided all the stone for the nearby fifteenth-century convent, among other buildings.

There is nevertheless a melancholy pleasure to be had from walking about Medina Azzahra. The overgrown aqueduct that ran from the sierra, on whose skirt the ruins lie, pierced mountains and leaped gullies; the mosque, of which only the ground-plan remains, is truly orientated to Mecca and not across the Sahara. One hall is being reconstructed and it is quite exciting to watch its progress from year to year; the alternate pink and blue columns, the decorated and particoloured horseshoe arches and the arabesque and *ataurique* that have been restored to panels and door-jambs will one day provide the finest example of Moslem palace architecture in Spain, with four centuries' priority over Seville and the Alhambra. The Cufic inscription on some of the column bases should renew our respect for those who, in deciphering them, have done so much to reveal the history of the palace.

A few hundred yards up the slope of the sierra is the **Monastery of San Jerónimo**, now a residence of the heirs of the Marqués del Mérito. The road is bad and steep and the building is not open to visitors. There is a Gothic cloister and, more important, a fountain from Medina Azzahra in the shape of an animal resembling the stag in Córdoba's Archaeological Museum, standing over an oblong bath. When Gonzalo de Córdoba was about twenty, it is related that he sought admission, possibly because of friction with his elder brother, Alonso de Aguilar; the prior, Antonio de Hinojosa, refused his application, saying farewell and adding, with remarkable foresight, 'for God is keeping you for greater things.' Morales, the historian of Philip II's reign, was a member of this community and, strangely, it is another Morales who relates the above event.

Continuing westward along C431 for 20 kilometres we see the **Castle of Almodóvar** crowning a hill before us. Over-restored it may be, but that great bulk outlined against the western evening sky makes scepticism bad form and turns incredulity into wonder. A good road leads round the hill to the top where the sturdy walls of the Moslem fort still stand; 'the Christians' worry', as Abulfeda called it. Pedro the Cruel was alleged to have kept his treasure here; wherever he kept it, his Italian admiral stole it while Pedro was in Bordeaux enlisting the Black Prince's aid. The view is inspiring, straight down on to the tawny roofs of the whitewashed village, then the long, green and brown fields and at last a knuckle of the Guadalquivir on its majestic way to Seville.

It is as well to arrange in advance for a tour through the castle; the tourist agency at the intersection of the Paseo del Gran Capitán and the Avenida del Generalísimo in Córdoba will help. It is worth the extra trouble, for the views from the top of the towers through the too new pyramidal merlons are still better than from below.

The country south of Córdoba rises gradually to the sierras which guarded the last Moslem kingdom of Granada. The fertility of its low hills can be deduced from the numbers of towns and secondary roads that crowd the map, and their history from the castles and watch towers that crown almost every height. This was the old frontier, the disputed territory between the two religions, after St. Ferdinand had recovered the valley of the Guadalquivir. Its extent can be traced by the towns that still carry the title *de la Frontera*; the country round them is fertile and a formidable barrier of mountains replaces the horizon in the direction of Granada. For two centuries these lands were subject to the destructive *razzias*, the raids that burned crops and carried off cattle and slaves: a school for warriors whose old boys are still famous.

Leaving Córdoba by either bridge across the Guadalquivir, N IV leads off to the right and we take N432 to Granada. After 34 kilometres the massive Castle of Espejo comes into sight on the left, the little village with its fourteenth-century church gathered round it. Eight kilometres farther, again on the left, is the old walled town of Castro del Rio, whose castle and walls look far better from a distance; the best view is obtained from the east, after passing the town. Cervantes was imprisoned here for three months and his room is still shown at the Ayuntamiento. The arrival of Lope de Vega, that prodigy of dramatists, cut short Cervantes' career as playwright and forced him to look for a living as a government official, an occupation which demanded only the primitive instinct of self-preservation. This was the one ingredient lacking in his make-up; he had courage, generosity and genius, qualities unsuitable to his new career and, worst of all, an unbusiness-like confidence in his fellow man. At Castro del Rio, in 1592, he committed the crime of levying a contribution of wheat belonging to a priest, unaware that the clergy were exempt from taxation; this was not his only gaol sentence and it is possible that he employed them all in writing. Certainly, he won a prize of three silver spoons for some verses in 1595 and his literary output may have profited by his enforced leisure. It is thus just possible that Castro del Rio may rival Argamasilla as the birthplace of the incomparable *Don Quixote*.

Baena is 17 kilometres farther, on a hill. You can see the walls of the old, higher town of Almedina to advantage as you approach over a narrow but quite passable road. The hilltop is bare, surrounded by ancient walls and buildings, among which rise the remains of the castle that once belonged to Gonzalo de Córdoba. The square keep is crowned by a possibly unique cupola of a type seen chiefly in the Near East and Sicily, dome and drum in a single piece without a cornice to define them.

Across the open space (it can hardly be called a plaza) is the Convent Church of Madre de Dios, lying north and south, with the high altar at the north end, and the main portal on the east side. This is an example of the felicity with which Spanish styles blend, for it is essentially a late Gothic doorway with an Annunciation in relief above; but the Mudéjar builder placed all this in an *alfiz* and the narthex which shelters it has an old *alfarje* ceiling. The church's pride, for as long as it lasts, is the polychrome stone statue of the *Virgen de la Antigua*, formerly housed in the Church of Santa María la Mayor and presumably destined to return there. She has a peculiarly archaic look, an almost Oriental head-dress and holds a pear instead of an apple. (Baena seems to have trouble with apples; even in the Holy Week pageant representing the Fall the organisers had some difficulty because apples were not to be found in spring. In this predicament an unknown genius proposed an original solution—a lemon—which has been adopted ever since, so that the fruit of that forbidden tree could be duly handed to Adam.) In case anyone thinks of spending Holy Week in Baena, where the processions are picturesque though small, he is warned that drums beat incessantly from Wednesday to Saturday; Baena's most distinguished sons come home at this time from the ends of the earth, simply to join in and make a noise.

Behind the convent church is the shell of Santa María la Mayor, a fine Gothic building burned out during the Civil War. Its fine *reja* and pulpits of wrought iron are still there and will soon be restored along with the rest of the church. Among the rubble in a corner are the fragments of a statue, that of Amador de los Rios (1818–1878) whose fame rests largely on his great *History of Spanish Literature*. His family house is within a few yards of the church and bears the usual commemorative tablet. The statue was there too, until the Civil War, when the digging of an air raid shelter disturbed the plinth and it fell over, killing a child. To avoid disappointment the visitor who expects to see the statue here is directed to the lower town where another statue of the writer, just as good, stands in the Plaza del Generalísimo Franco.

Here you can leave the Granada road and take the one through Doña Mencía to **Cabra**, a distance of 24 kilometres, to find another typical Andalucian town, with that indefinable air that market-towns wear all through the week. The square near the hilltop lies at the side of a school building which incorporates a massive mediaeval tower, all that is left of the great castle in which Gonzalo of Córdoba (how we keep running across him!) was kept prisoner by his cousin because of a family quarrel. Another celebrity connected with Cabra was born there in 1824 and lived till 1905—the novelist Juan Valera, who is ranked among the best nineteenth-century Spanish writers. The third famous figure is that of a blind Arab, Mukkadam of Cabra, who is credited with introducing or adapting the form of poetry known as the *muwassaha,* a fact that will interest the occasional reader of Provençal poetry.

We have kept the best of Cabra to the last. The **Church of St. John the Baptist** (San Juan Bautista) has to be approached by a steep cobbled street which may be difficult to find; many of the inhabitants do not even know the name, for among them it is always called *La Iglesia del Cerro,* 'The Hill Church'. At the top of the street you see the low, whitewashed wall of the church with its three semicircular buttresses. Inside, it is plain and all the more pleasing for that, with a wheel of bells that is used during Mass, a typical feature hereabouts and one that the Spaniards probably imported into Sicily. To support the claim that the church was originally built by the Visigoths is a stele engraved with the record that the 'Baselica' (spelling was never their strong point) was consecrated in E 628 or AD 590. The stoup for holy water, which it used to support, is now fixed to the wall and carries a rather blurred frieze of a running vegetable motif, reminiscent of Byzantine decoration. That is all; distressingly little on which to build pictures of a Visigothic centre, especially when you remember that Cabra (Egabra) was one of the ten bishoprics of Andalucía (Betica) in those days.

Lucena is only 9 kilometres away and distinguished more for its anecdotal than its visible attractions. Like Cabra it provides relief from the universal Andalucian whitewash by incorporating colours and thus presents agreeable if undistinguished sights. A sleepy town that produces the great *tinajas* in which wine is stored in many parts of Spain (though not of course in the sherry lands where oaken casks are necessary), it used also to be renowned for its lamps. The remains of the castle are in the higher part, with one square and one octagonal tower surviving. The latter is the Torre del Moral in which Boabdil, last king of Granada, was imprisoned after his capture by the Count of Cabra.

Behind the towers is the Plaza Nueva, in which you will find the Church of San Mateo, containing a few features of interest: the *artesonado* is handsome, though not outstanding, and the Renaissance retablo, with its sixteen reliefs from the life of Christ is competent. The *sagrario,* not to be confused with the sacristy, is wrongly described as Churrigueresque, 'already granadine', by a Spanish author. There is no Churrigueresque work in Andalucía, the family having practically confined its work to the region between Salamanca and Madrid, and ornate

Baroque is by no means always copied from Churriguera works. The image of Our Lady of Araceli is brought here every year from her sanctuary 4 miles away, where there is another Baroque altar, so that she is hardly better off. On the outside of the church is a plaque relating in detail her elevation to patroness of the countryside.

Lucena has the peculiar distinction of having been a self-governing Jewish town for many years, during which the ruling Moslems occupied their own ghetto. Its peaceful existence was threatened only once, when in the eleventh century a crock of gold was discovered in Granada, under a house formerly occupied by a Jew who had moved to Lucena. As the occupant had been royal treasurer, the king, Abdallah Ibn Boloquín, sent to Lucena asking the deceased treasurer's sons to visit him. Their refusal provoked a quarrel and then open revolt, but diplomacy, possibly combined with a touch of treachery, restored peace and matters were settled in a satisfactory manner—at least according to King Abdallah, who wrote his own memoirs.

From Lucena a digression may be made along C334 to **Rute** (20 kilometres), whose main attraction is a distillery; every kind of liqueur is produced including, very surprisingly, rum made by the addition of an essence, while the bagasse of the nearby coastal sugar plantations goes to waste. No one knows what has happened to the flourishing rum industry that enriched Vélez-Málaga in the eighteenth century.

Five kilometres from Rute, on a bad road that leads to Carca-buey, where they get that rather vulgar red marble, there is a towering hill on the right. At the top can be seen a length of grey curtain wall and two towers, and with field glasses one can see the resemblance between their masonry and that of the Visigothic portion of the fortifications of Carcassonne. Fifteen kilometres farther south is the friendly and far more attractive town of **Iznájar** presiding over the new Genil reservoir that is to be the second largest in Europe. The castle is seen to advantage as you approach. Of its antiquity none of the inhabitants have any doubt, least of all the parish priest who is a keen antiquarian; a local tradition, for instance, sometimes chanted in rhyme, described how the town received Trajan in triumph. This is not entirely absurd, for Trajan was Spanish born and later commanded a unit in Spain. The church has no obvious signs of great age but the parochial records go back to a baptism in 1528. The town's name is derived from the Arabic *Hizn*, a fort, and another name which is believed to be *Chafar*, son of Omar

Ibn Hafsun the rebel. The derivation is suspect on philological grounds and it could just as well be from *achar*, refuge.

Retracing our road along the charming, tree-lined Genil over what will soon be an expanse of water—even now the first inundations of the reservoir are visible—N331 takes us to **Aguilar de la Frontera**. Once again we meet the great Gonzalo, this time through his famous elder brother Alfonso Fernández de Córdoba, named 'The Great', sixth Lord of Aguilar. At the summit stands the old Clock Tower (Torre del Reloj), alone amid the ruins of former buildings; it is Baroque and as pleasing as Baroque can be when it is not trying to please. All that it lacks is a clock. Next to it is a sight which no one should miss although it has nothing of history nor any masterpiece of art. The *Plaza de San José* stands peacefully on the hilltop, surrounded by its octagonal frame of three-storeyed, whitewashed houses, with their balconies and green sunblinds. In the centre is a single tree and a cluster of street lamps; the only entrances are four archways that pierce the surrounding octagon. Here is the Ayuntamiento too, with nothing noteworthy except the newel post at the turn of the staircase, decorated with a Roman female head.

You should also see the Chapel of the *Convento de las Descalzas*, the barefoot Carmelites, farther down in the town. It is hard to disparage an object on which so many centre their devotion, and personal taste should never be the absolute criterion for all climes and times, but this small chapel is covered from floor to ceiling with gilt moulding and twisted columns—if a plane surface does appear it is sure to be covered with a fresco—and nowhere can the eye follow a straight line or be led to the contemplation of a focal point of worship.

The return to Córdoba along N331 presents no difficulty; the town of **Montilla** lies three kilometres to the right of N331 and is famous for being the birth-place of the great Gonzalo. The castle has disappeared without a trace because the ungrateful King Ferdinand the Catholic, jealous of his great lieutenant, had his ancestral home pulled down as a punishment for misbehaviour on the part of Gonzalo's nephew. Montilla and its neighbour Moriles are today remembered for their wine. Devoid of the veneration accorded to the products of the *soleras*, the golden produce of Montilla, confident of its quality, relies on palates instead of posters; the aristocrats of Jerez once used it to enrich their own produce. by which the town is still immortalised in the name *amontillado*.

The **Castle of Montemayor** is on the right as we continue north along N331; one of the residences of the Duke of Frias, it is kept in constant readiness in case of his unannounced arrival. From its terrace one looks out over the broad plain where the battle of Munda was fought between Julius Caesar and the sons of Pompey. The triumph which he subsequently celebrated in Rome was unpopular, for even the Roman crowd was shocked at a public spectacle celebrating the victory of Romans over Romans. Who knows, even this ill-judged triumph may have strengthened the party that opposed and killed him. Four kilometres farther on is the village of Fernán-Núñez, whose roadside is decked out with the cement elements of rural scenes, farm implements, a sower, wine-jars and horses' heads, contributions to a government-sponsored competition for the most attractive village—to tourists of course. We can now rejoin N IV and return to Córdoba.

Osuna is difficult to approach, although it lies on the main road from Seville to Granada. The best plan is to go south from Écija on C430; this is the second road to the left as you leave the town by N IV and leads across bleak but rapidly traversed plains. It is, however, essential to make sure that the road is in good repair, otherwise it is better to take C3310 to Estepa. Écija itself will be described later, as it is on the main road from Córdoba to Seville. The Dukes of Osuna carry the name of Téllez Girón and are said to de descended from the family whose most notorious member was the first Marquis of Villena, Don Juan Pacheco.

The town has little of interest but there are a picturesque market-place and some Renaissance and Baroque house-fronts which promise more than they fulfil. The built-up area stops before the hilltop is reached, leaving you amid bleak surroundings in which a shapeless lump of deliquescent brick marks all that remains of the Roman fort. On the summit of the hill lies the College, founded in 1549, with a fine, plain patio; now a high school, it was originally for students of University rank who were especially bound to defend the thesis of the Immaculate Conception of the Virgin.

The Collegiate Church lies in a commanding position next to the college; during the Napoleonic wars it was converted into a citadel and magazine for the French troops. It is large but unpretentious; its western doorway, with its Plateresque ornamentation, including terracotta reliefs, relieves the severity of the Renaissance design. The entrance to the chapels is on the east side, where a guardian is theoretically available from 10 am to 1.30 pm and from 4.30 to 7 pm (an hour earlier in winter).

The entrance to the Museum, which is the main object of the visit, is on the east side and leads immediately to a delightful, small Renaissance patio, heavily ornamented in the Plateresque style. Thereafter you are conducted through a maze of rooms in which various treasures are displayed, including a Luis Morales portrait of the Saviour. In this painting, as in many others, the artist can be readily identified by the deep shadow he often introduces below the eyebrows. There are also numerous objects of virtu, some less interesting than others, but the pride of the collection are the four canvases of Ribera. Their chief interest lies in the fact that they are among the earliest surviving works of 'Lo Spagnoletto' and pure chance contributed to their acquisition. The Third Duke of Osuna was Viceroy of Naples in 1616, when Ribera achieved sudden, if local, fame through a painting which had been placed on a balcony to dry and had attracted a crowd. The Duke himself was impressed, summoned the young Ribera and gave him several commissions, thus assuring his success. The canvas which was set out to dry is entitled *The Martyrdom of St. Bartholomew* and occupies a place of honour.

There is also a St. Jerome by Pietro Torrigiani, the unfortunate Florentine who sculpted the tomb of Henry VII in Westminster Abbey. He is said to have produced four penitent St. Jeromes, of which the terracotta one in the Museo de Bellas Artes in Seville is held to be the finest, if not the only genuine one. Goya called it the masterpiece of modern sculpture. Torrigiani cared little for the English and his last experience of Spain was anything but happy. Commissioned by the Duke of Arcos to produce a Virgin and Child, he was paid with as much copper coin as two men could carry. When he counted the fee at home he found that it amounted to only thirty ducats, at which he took up a hammer, went back to the Duke's and smashed the masterpiece. This of course drove him straight into the net of the Inquisition, who held that men might make gods but must not break them, and Torrigiani died in the dungeons, voluntarily starving to death.

In other parts of the museum there are tombs to be seen and caskets, desks and cupboards displaying more ingenuity than art. The family chapel of Santo Sepulcro is, however, a little masterpiece with everything in miniature, even to the *coro* of eleven seats placed in the middle of the tiny nave.

Taking N334 to the east we pass through Aguadulce, which once formed a welcome oasis amid brackish pools; when the corn is ripening poppies and marigolds, which are plentiful in most parts, are especially prolific here, forming red and gold carpets whose only rival will be met on the way from Cádiz to Tarifa.

Estepa is about 12 kilometres farther and the ruins of its castle crown the hilltop and stand out black against the sky. Much of the ascent has to be made on foot and is hardly worth the trouble, though the fantastic shapes to which wind and weather have reduced parts of the surrounding wall are remarkable, as is the massive square keep that still survives. This is the ancient Astapa, whose heroic resistance to Scipio Africanus in 207 BC is recounted by Livy; like the immortal defenders of Saguntum and Numantia the inhabitants chose death on a funeral pyre, with their wives and children, rather than surrender. The Church of Santa Victoria has an attractive Baroque tower and the façade of the Palace of the Counts—the Cerverales —is something of a rarity, as it stresses the horizontal rather than the usual vertical trend of Spanish Baroque.

A fair road (C3310) takes us to Herrera, a right turn along C338 to Puente Genil, whence C329 leads to Aguilar de la Frontera and Córdoba.

J'ai vu dans Ecija, vieille ville moresque,
Aux clochers de faïence, aux palais peints à fresque ...
                                        THÉOPHILE GAUTIER

N IV leaves Córdoba as it entered, wide, smooth and uninteresting. Low hills with olive groves, fertile fields or fallow greet our eyes as we bear away from the Guadalquivir. Occasionally a cluster of houses stands beside the road and at 30 kilometres we pass through another of Olavides' settlements, La Carlota; here you can best see the standard type of house which was planned for the northern settlers, a window on each side of the front door and a broad, shuttered aperture above, hayloft and guest-room in one, while a modest outhouse clings to one flank. They are not nearly as elaborate as the farmhouses built for the settlers in the reclaimed Pontine marshes south of Rome, but the fact that they are still standing speaks well for their builders.

At 55 kilometres we descend to the valley of the Genil, a river which is born in the melting snow of Mulhacén, highest peak of the Sierra Nevada, winds past Granada and here flows past **Écija**, the hottest town in Spain, the frying pan of Andalucía.

The average traveller is so keyed up at the prospect of seeing Seville that he rarely stops at this, one of the most charming towns in the South, with its tall church steeples, of which there are about a dozen, reaching up like shining projectiles. They seem to have shed every trace of Baroque heaviness, and instead have assumed an air of fantasy—with their mellow brick and brightly coloured tiles they remind us of fairy tales rather than the Counter-Reformation. The reason is not far to seek, for almost every tower was built in the eighteenth century and can be confidently placed after the disastrous earthquake of 1755, which flattened Lisbon and capriciously picked out other Iberian towns for punishment. Écija was one of them. So here is a Baroque without ulterior motive, that neither threatens hell-fire nor promises salvation, but sets out to please.

We cross the Genil on what is still called the Roman bridge, a claim that will not stand up to careful examination for the caliphal forces not only destroyed it completely in 913, when Écija was a strong point of Ibn Hafsun's rebellion, but also demolished the greater part of the city's defensive walls. Nevertheless, you can still make out the remains of the Arab flour mills in the River Genil and the names of the old city gates are preserved in plazas where no gate has been seen for ten centuries.

At the first cross-street the Palacio Vilaseca stands in a recess on the right, its heraldic crest supported by 'wild men' or woodwoses, and across the road is the extraordinary façade of the **Palace of the Marqués de Peñaflor**. The entrance is in two storeys of heavy Baroque that dominate the narrow street, classical below and fancy Salomonic above. We shall be seeing a lot of these 'barley sugar' columns, an integral feature of Sevillian more than any other style of Baroque. From the portal the main building stretches away in a majestic curve that follows the winding street, with simple arched windows to the ground floor and french-windows above, giving on to the longest balcony in Spain that dwindles into the distance along with the frescoed wall from which it juts. Entering the palace through a small patio you find a sensible interior arrangement, for the stables face you and you have only to turn to the right to reach the living-quarters and the upper storey; over each manger is a plaque, some still bearing the name of the equine tenant. The main patio is severe but attractive, the staircase monumental, with a ridged dome, the *media naranja* or 'half-orange', over the first landing where there is also a retablo of the *Virgin of the Rosary*.

The second turning to the right from Emilio Castelar, leads

to the Plaza de España, more commonly called the Plaza Mayor, and the Church of Santa Barbara, whose chief attractions are the large Roman columns which have been used as door-jambs. The Plaza Mayor is one of the most beautiful in Spain. There are arcades with balconies above that drip flowers; where they have forgotten to put up the arcades the balconies project anyway. At the far end stands the Ayuntamiento with its embryonic museum. Its most precious possession is the Roman polychrome mosaic showing the punishment of Queen Dirce, who was tied to the horns of a bull by Amphion and Zethus. For those who may later find the Church of Santa Cruz closed, there is a good copy here of the so-called sarcophagus of San Fulgencio.

A hundred yards from the south end of the once fashionable Calle de Sor Angela de la Cruz is the **Church of Santiago**, a fine building of the early sixteenth century. The door carries the scallop shells of Santiago or St. James the Greater, Spain's patron saint, and the exterior brickwork and *alfiz* over a window are typical of the Gothic–Mudéjar style. The interior is roomy and uncluttered; it has a good, simple *artesonado* and the retablo mayor, behind the high altar, is a rich example of the late Gothic–Isabelline style of the early 1500s, carved and gilt, with dark canvases from the brush of some forgotten artist. The north-east chapel contains two crucifixes, a shiny one by Roldán and a curiously dark one called the Cristo del Gonfalón, from the banner, the *gonfalón de la Victoria*, with which it was associated.

The **Parish Church of Santa Cruz**, in the Plaza de Nuestra Señora de Valle, though built only in the eighteenth century, marks the site of an older church built over the ruins of a mosque, which itself was presumably erected over a Visigothic church. This was therefore the episcopal seat of St. Fulgentius, one of a family of four who created a record by being canonised without exception. St. Leander was Bishop of Seville; St. Isidore, 'the egregious doctor', followed him and their sister, St. Florentina, is patroness of a nearby convent. A stone sarcophagus, with Byzantine-style carving of the sixth century, is said to contain the saint's relics, and can be seen as an altar frontal on the right of the high altar. But most of the interest of this recently rebuilt church lies outside. In the orange patio is a pointed horseshoe arch, its surface covered with arabesques except where heraldic shields are carved, precisely as we saw on the Puerta del Perdón in Córdoba; it is therefore a Mudéjar work. One at least of the very weathered columns on which the arch rests suggests a Visigothic origin.

The front of the bell tower, which stands apart from the main building, gives us our most intimate glimpse of court life under the Caliphs. Here are two stone plaques with Arabic inscriptions, of which one, dated 977, commemorates the setting up of a public fountain at the bidding of *al-sayida al-kubra*, the great princess. She was the Basque concubine of Hakam II—a man of forty-six and childless when he came to the throne—and she alone of all the harem produced two male infants. As the only fruitful partner she naturally took the title *umm-walad*, 'Mother of a Son', and the infatuated caliph followed an old Baghdad custom by giving her a male name, *Chafar*, which was prefixed to her own Basque name of Dawn, or *Subh* as she was called in Arabic. It is still undecided whether her new name had anything to do with her habit of wearing male costume. Through her influence and infatuation, young Abi Amir rapidly became her adviser, as well as treasurer and guardian of the surviving royal offspring, who later came to the throne as Hisham II. On the death of Hakam Abi Amir soon took over the role of Caliph, both in and out of bed, and Hisham was relegated to obscurity while his mother ensured her lover's career, of which we have had a glimpse under his later name of Almansor. It was inevitable that she should lose her power once Almansor was *de facto* ruler of Al-Andalus, and all that was left was hatred for her former lover and two fine ivory caskets, now in Madrid and Fitero (Castejón).

Back on N IV a drive of a quarter of an hour takes us to another settlement, La Luisiana, and shortly thereafter a signpost in a copse on the left points to **Monclova**. The castle was restored in 1910, using the ruins of the Convento de la Merced in Lorca and Roman columns from Córdoba. Today it is as handsome a country house as you could wish to see, and even if you cannot enter you can see, through the wrought-iron *cancela*, the white marble Renaissance patio with its two rows of arcades, in whose spandrels are the crests that constitute the sixteen quarterings of the arms of the Duke of Infantado, the present owner. The floor of the patio is laid out as a formal garden round the marble well-head in the centre, and flower-pots decorate the upper arcade with green and red and white. The chapel is built on to the outside of the palace and is still used in the old feudal manner by lords and labourers; the complete Infantado crest is displayed on the wall near by.

Carmona can be made out on the right of the highway for

some time before you arrive; the steeper side of the hill, with the
ruins of a fortress, faces you across the wide plain and in a short
time you can look down and realise your insignificance. The
town is ancient of course; anything beginning with *Car* is attributed to the Iberians, except when the prefix *Cart,* meaning city,
takes us back to the Phoenicians of Carthage. Cars may be parked
in the shadow of the great tower of San Pedro (1704), for this
town, with its remains of all ages, is best seen on foot.

The **Puerta de Sevilla** is still largely Roman, a double portal
with a guardhouse between, in the shape of a passage about
40 feet long, with barrel vaulting. It forms part of the *alcázar
de abajo*, the lower fortress (*alcázar* or *kasr* is said to be derived
from the Latin *castra*) and has undergone many changes at the
hands of various owners. The Roman masonry, which is also
seen at the base of the two miles of circuit walls, is unmistakable
with its massive blocks; it is interesting to try to pick out the
areas where Visigothic builders added to or repaired the structure with smaller stones, and then the *soga y tizón* of the Moslems.
The highest part of all is often an unimpressive and mediaeval
rubble, and the horseshoe arches were, of course, added in the
days of the Moslems.

Standing at the bottom of the steep Calle Domínguez de Asa,
the tawny bell tower of San Bartolomé, an exact match for the
ancient walls, is visible over the roofs, its tiles mellowed to a
soft green with lichen. The rest of the church has been rigorously
limewashed, inside and out, even to the flowered capitals of the
Gothic south portal that continue as a string course. The sacristy
contains the charter of a *cofradía*, one of the guilds about which
we shall hear more in Seville, dated to the fourteenth century.

A short way up on the right a doorway leads into the market
place. Until the last century this was the Convent of Santa
Catalina and presumably became municipal property at the
dissolution of the monasteries in 1836. Perhaps the change is for
the better; certainly nothing could please the eye more than the
mounds of tomatoes, green peppers, cauliflowers, aubergines
and oranges; the walls are brilliant with whitewash, picked out
with faded maroon and the inevitable touch of blue that wards
off the 'evil eye'.

In the Plaza Mayor, close by, one of the houses is resplendent
with bright blue *azulejos* of varying shades that cover the walls
of the second and third storeys. They look modern and vulgar,
but are actually an early seventeenth-century production. At one
corner a spirally carved Roman column attracts antiquarians

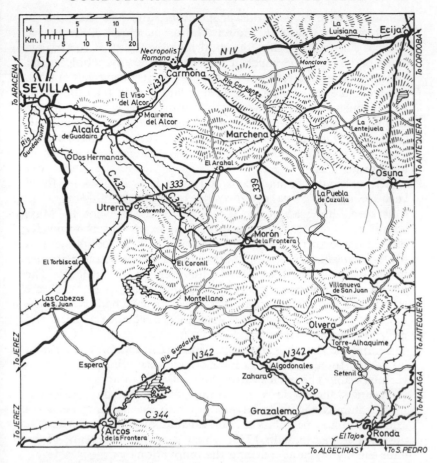

and dogs; next to it is the Ayuntamiento. In the council chamber are portions of Roman floor mosaics, framed and hung, and in the patio there is a complete one, about 20 feet square, that was found only three feet below the road surface during repairs. It is worth studying, both for its completeness and the intricacy of its designs. The continuous border of ivy recalls the mosaics of Piazza Armerina in Sicily, which helped to identify the owner of the villa as the Emperor Maximianus Herculius. The geometric patterns in the panels are in many cases the forerunners of Christian symbols, though the central Medusa head, of course, identifies this mosaic as pagan.

Along the street the Church of El Salvador is a rather ordinary

Baroque edifice of generous proportions, and near it is the fifteenth-century **Church of Santa María**, or Nuestra Señora de
Gracia. The patio of this church, originally a part of the orange
court of the mosque which it replaced, makes the whole ascent
worth while, even on the hottest day; six horseshoe arches of brick
survive and even now more are being laid bare in the other walls
of the courtyard. As if a Moslem ablution court was not enough,
we find that the builders made use, as usual, of whatever materials
came their way and among them is a priceless column dating
back to Visigothic times with an engraved *calendario*, or list of
local saints' days.

Before leaving Santa María it is worth while looking for a
very special brick on the south side. It commemorates the occasion seven hundred years ago when a count went to Mass
attended, as usual, by a servant. The priest absent-mindedly
offered the Host to the servant first, at which the count slapped
his face thus demonstrating that whatever might be the priorities
in the life to come, they were rigidly defined in Carmona. The
matter could not of course rest there and various penances were
inflicted on the count, one of which was that he had to press the
offending hand into wet clay that was baked into a brick and
built into the church wall.

Behind the church is the large *Plaza del Marqués de las Torres*
in which three antique columns have been incorporated in
various walls. The palace of the Marquis has an impressive front
of Rennaissance style with Baroque overtones; the Doric and
Ionic columns and the triglyphs point to the building being an
example of the neo-classical revival and one of the earliest at
that, for it was built in 1755, which is within five years of the
date usually taken as marking the innovation.

From here a maze of cobbled streets between single-storey
houses leads to the **Puerta de Córdoba**, which marks the eastern
end of what was the Roman *cardo*, or main cross-street, beginning
at the Puerta de Sevilla where we entered the town. It occupies a
narrow valley between hills, and consists of a restored Renaissance gateway between two octagonal towers on Roman bases,
flanked in turn by curtain walls. The restoration has emphasised
the massive proportions of the gate and hence indirectly the
importance of Carmona. All through the history of Moslem
Spain we find rivalry smouldering between Córdoba and Seville
and more than one rebel found Carmona a safe retreat. The contrast between the grand gate and the humble earth road that
passes through it is quite laughable until you remember that this

was the Roman highway to Córdoba. About a mile away is the Roman bridge of five arches that took the highway over the Rio Corbones (or one of its tributaries); it is still worth a visit, if the walk does not deter you. The paving of the bridge has almost disappeared but even this is not a total loss as you will be able to study the various layers that went to make a Roman road.

On the highest part of Carmona's hill stand the remains of the upper castle, the **Alcázar de arriba**, from where one can enjoy the finest view of the fertile plain. It was of course built by the Arabs but so extensively altered by Pedro the Cruel that it rivalled the Alcázar of Seville. He also used it as a royal prison for Leonor de Guzmán, his father's mistress, and later it became a favourite residence of the Catholic Sovereigns. Severely damaged in the earthquake of 1504, it was allowed to degenerate into its present state of neglect. The climb up to it is between very humble dwellings, but none so lowly that the women are not busy with a stick, a rag and a bucket of lime; when the walls are pulled down or repaired, the masonry is usually found to be Arabic.

The ruins cover a huge area and parts have become quite shapeless from centuries of wind and rain; the result is that one can distinguish two building methods introduced by the Moslems, the *tapia* and the *hormigón*. The former is known to us as *pisé à terre*, earth rammed between the boards of a framework; the latter is made by pouring mortar and small stones into a similar mould. Both methods produce a wall which is almost as hard and resistant as stone and which can be readily recognised with a little practice. The east gate survives and consists of three arches behind the usual horseshoe; recent work has uncovered frescoes which may be early Gothic on the ceilings between the arches.

On your way back to the Puerta de Sevilla, which you cannot miss if you always go downhill, you should try to bear right as often as possible in order to see something of the daily life of a small town. You will see brick steeples hooded with moss or weeds, and an occasional Baroque house-front; far more interesting are the sealed houses, *casas saladas* in the local version of what should be *casas cerradas*. These were at one time closed because of some religious transgression and some have remained so ever since; the older inhabitants are reluctant to discuss the matter and profess to know nothing of this old custom, reminiscent of primitive taboos that forbid the occupation of a house in which a death has occurred. Nothing special distinguishes these houses except the fact that they remain unoccupied year after year.

Leaving again by the Puerta de Sevilla, one can visit the **Church of San Pedro**. Apart from the extraordinarily rich interior and the number of polychrome wooden statues, of which Southern Spain contains literally thousands, there is a ceramic baptismal font with the maker's name on it in relief. It constitutes one of the rarer forms of religious furniture, for the making of earthenware baptismal fonts was forbidden in Spain at the end of the sixteenth century, though others consisting of lead or the shells of giant molluscs were evidently permitted. No transgression need have been committed here, for the church was built in the second half of the fifteenth century and the font could well have been installed long before the prohibition. But extensive renovation was undertaken in the eighteenth century and the Chapel of the Sagrario of 1760 is our first introduction to Sevillian Baroque.

The founder of the school was Leonardo de Figueroa, who was helped and succeeded by two sons and a nephew. It is inevitable that their work will continue to be labelled 'Churrigueresque' although, as previously pointed out, that family confined its efforts to north-western Spain; furthermore, Leonardo was slightly older than José de Churriguera. It takes time to get used to either of these Baroque schools and only when the underlying architectural simplicity, and even majesty are appreciated, does one begin to accept the wealth of ornament, the display of gilt and the shining bits of glass. Stripped of all this frippery, the lines and proportions of the Sevillian Baroque are usually classical, and it was in revolt against this severity that the Figueroas and their successors adopted two expedients: first, to avoid straight lines at all costs, and secondly to produce a composite impression of light, mass and movement. To the latter can be attributed the bits of glass, the exaggerated chiaroscuro and the gesticulating saints. The Chapel of the Sagrario was the work of Ambrosio, the second son, and features all the good points, as well as all the bad, of the Figueroa system. In his book, Lees Milne shrewdly emphasises the latter in describing the wavy entablature as like pleated muslin, and the marbled dado as like *carne de membrillo*, Spain's delicious quince jelly.

While here, it might interest the visitor to see the inside of what is nowadays called a *pensión*, formerly a *fonda*. There is an excellent example near by in the Casa Gamero, in which the rooms are small and scrupulously clean, with running cold water, and where a satisfying typically Spanish meal can be had for less than five shillings. The most expensive accommodation costs about 40 pesetas and no one need be afraid of spending a night at this or any of the equivalent inns in Carmona.

Carmona is perhaps best known for its **Roman Necropolis**, which will be found along a signposted turning to the right before leaving the town on the road to Seville. Some of the tombs are only humble trenches, others *columbaria* in which the ashes were kept in niches in the walls, resembling a dovecot, an arrangement copied in many modern Spanish cemeteries. A description in detail serves little purpose and the visitor will be shown the traces of fresco that have miraculously survived on the damp walls; one, showing a female harpist, is in the large patio known as the Tomb of Servilia; and the circular, domed mausoleum so like an Etruscan tomb should also be examined. The clumps of prickly pear seem to add an Oriental touch to the Roman background; it is all the more surprising to learn that this ubiquitous plant comes from America and that no Arab or Moor in the history of Al-Andalus ever set eyes on it. The contents of these tombs and of the prehistoric ones situated near by are to be found partly in the recently enlarged museum built at the site and partly in other collections.

From Carmona N IV continues as it began, wide, smooth and uninteresting, to reach Seville after 30 kilometres.

CHAPTER FIVE

Seville – The Cathedral

✤

*Hercules built me, Julius Caesar encompassed
me with walls and towers, the Saintly King
took me.*

So reads an inscription over one of the gates of Seville, giving only
a small selection of the famous men who have lived here or
passed through. Hercules was frequently credited with the foundation of pre-classical Spanish towns, having allegedly passed by
on his way to or from the theft of the cattle of Geryon or of the
apples of the Hesperides. Caesar certainly took an interest in it
and gave it the name of Colonia Julia Romula, but many other
adventures befell it before St. Ferdinand took it from the Moors.

Under the Visigoths it achieved importance by its opposition
to the Arian creed, pioneered by the viceroy Hermengild; he was
killed by his father, King Leovgild, and had to wait a thousand
years for canonisation. St. Leander and St. Isidore, who were
mentioned in the last chapter, were archbishops here and achieved
quicker results; the former was actually responsible for weaning
Hermengild from the Arians. Then came the Moslems, and
Seville led a fairly quiet life until the Vikings sailed 70 miles up-
river to destroy the town and kill the male inhabitants. By then
the Roman walls had apparently disappeared, so new ones were
built. When the caliphate collapsed Seville became the centre of
one of the splinter-states, or *taifas*, until the threat of Christian
reconquest brought help from Morocco, two waves of reformers,
Almoravids and Almohads, who made life fairly unpleasant for
the easy-going Andalucians. It was the revolutionaries who drove
out the Almohads and lost the town to King Ferdinand III, the
Saint, in 1248; the remains of the town walls that survive date
from the twelfth and thirteenth centuries, and are at least the
third set.

St. Ferdinand appears on the banner that is displayed in the
Ayuntamiento. His son Alfonso the Learned gave the city another
crest and motto in gratitude for its loyalty during the rebellion of
his son Sancho. The rebus looks like an '8' between the syllables

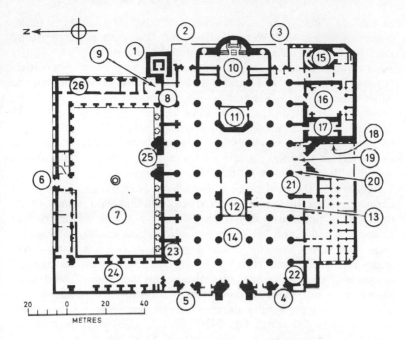

PLAN OF SEVILLE CATHEDRAL

Numbers follow the route taken in the text.

1. The Giralda
2. Puerta de los Palos
3. Puerta de la Campanilla
4. Puerta de San Miguel
5. Puerta del Baptisterio
6. Puerta del Perdón
7. Patio de los Naranjos
8. Puerta del Lagarto
9. Chapel of Nuestra Señora de la Granada
10. Capilla Real
11. Capilla Mayor
12. Coro
13. Chapel of the Concepción Chica
14. Grave of Hernando Colón
15. Sala Capitular
16. Sacristía Mayor
17. Sacristía de los Cálices
18. Fresco of St. Christopher
19. Tomb of Christopher Columbus
20. "La Gamba"
21. Chapel of La Antigua
22. Chapel of San Laureano
23. Baptistry Chapel
24. Church of the Sagrario
25. Puerta de la Concepción
26. Biblioteca Capitular Colombina

no and *do*. The '8' represents a skein of wool or *madeja*; to make it more difficult *nodo* means 'knot'; but the rebus is meant to be read *no m'ha dejado*, 'it has not abandoned me'. Above it sits Alfonso the Learned, often rendered as 'The Wise' with little reason, flanked by St. Leander and St. Isidore. A similar tribute was paid by Charles V, after Seville had remained faithful during the Comunero rising of 1520, when he gave it a new motto: *Ab Hercule et Caesar nobilitas, a se ipsa fidelitas*. Pedro the Cruel lived in the Alcázar, which today is much as he restored it, and during all his troubles the city also remained loyal to him, but was let off without another motto.

Seville was the birthplace of Hadrian, Trajan and possibly the Emperor Theodosius; of Velázquez, Murillo and many other painters; of poets and playwrights such as Fernando Herrera and Lope de Rueda; and least substantial but best known, of Figaro, Don Juan and Carmen. It is a large and busy town and as you enter it for the first time you may wonder about its alleged properties, the ebullience, the colour; unlike other Andalucian towns it is not even whitewashed. Undoubtedly much of the aura imputed to Seville dates back to the days when it was Spain's chief link with the New World, the river harbour to which the argosies were legally bound to come. The people of such towns—you have only to think of Alexandria, Naples or Venice—were always known to live at a faster pace, to be more restless and more artful. And so, for long after Seville lost her monopoly to Cádiz, she still retained her reputation and the old fourteenth-century saying lingered on: *si a Sevilla pidiese leche de pájaro, se encontraría*, best rendered as 'if you ask for pigeon's milk in Seville, you'll get it'. The wonders of Seville dawn on you slowly, for few of them engage your attention in the streets themselves.

One exception is the **Cathedral**, whose bell tower, better known as the Giralda, is a landmark for many miles. The site has had an interesting history, for a Visigothic cathedral of great richness stood here and seems to have been sanctioned for Christian worship after the Moslem conquest, as frequently happened under the emirs and caliphs. The fanatical Almohads demolished it in 1172 in order to build a mosque which was to be the second greatest in the whole of Islam.

It was this mosque which Ferdinand handed over for Christian worship immediately after taking the city on 23 November, 1248. It was built of brick and internal alterations had to be made. By 1401 the Church of Santa Maria de la Sede, as it was now called, was in such a sorry state that the Dean and Chapter recorded: 'That inasmuch as the Church of Seville threatens to fall into ruin because of the earthquakes ... that there should be built another church such and so good that no other may be its equal ....' So enthusiastic and, indeed, devoted were the clergy that they decided to take for their own use only as much of their salary as was essential for their bare needs; and in their religious exaltation they resolved: 'Let us build a church so great that those who see it completed may take us for madmen.' Hence an old saying quotes the Cathedral of Seville for its size, that of Toledo for its wealth and that of León for its beauty.

No single architect can be credited with the plan of this, the largest Gothic cathedral in the world and one of the three largest Christian temples. We know the names of several who worked on it, including two Normans, in the 104 years it took to build. Four years after its completion the great cupola with its lantern fell in, 'with a noise that startled the whole city', and Juan Gil de Hontañón was chosen to carry out repairs and is responsible for the present roof. After the second accident, the collapse of a pillar and part of the roof in 1888, it was repaired without any alteration in design. The Cathedral stands today without equal not only in size and proportion, but as the greatest achievement of fifteenth-century Spanish architecture; remarkable, as Gudiol says, for the synthesis of its different stylistic elements. It is also one of Spain's greatest museums and treasure-houses, thanks to the prudent removal of its portable contents to safety in Cádiz before the arrival of the French.

A good plan is to view the outside by starting at the ticket office at the east end, situated outside the main building and close to the Giralda. The nearest door is called the Puerta de los Palos, from a wooden fence that used to connect it with what was the Courtyard of the Elms (Corral de los Olmos) where the Dean and Chapter met, on the site of the present Archbishop's palace. The tympanum has a fine relief of the Adoration of the Magi, by the Frenchman Michel Perrin, who may have taken his inspiration from the same subject in the Cathedral of Como, by Bernardino Luini. Note that the third king, Balthasar, is portrayed as a Negro, a convention which, like the kissing of the Infant's foot by the senior magus, was adopted very tardily in France, though common in Germany and Italy.

To the south you pass what should be the main apse of the Cathedral, but is actually the east wall of the Royal Chapel, and then come to the Puerta de la Campanilla, named after a temporary bell tower that signalled the start and finish of working hours during the building's construction. Here the relief of the lunette is also by Perrin and represents the Palm Sunday entry into Jerusalem; note the figure of the child who has climbed the palm tree immediately above the Saviour. It would be interesting to trace the origin of the palm in this scene, for the gospels mention only 'branches of trees' and palm trees are not a feature of the Judaean highlands; yet this scene commemorates the origin of Palm Sunday.

Before leaving the east side of the Cathedral one may pause for a moment to appreciate the proportions and dignity of the Plaza de los Reyes, assuming that it is not yet filled with motor coaches. At the far side the Archbishop's palace presents an early example of Sevillian Baroque in its portal by Lorenzo Fernández de Iglesias (1704), an obvious follower of Figueroa. It demonstrates how much Spanish Baroque owes to the sculptors of retablos, for nothing could resemble a retablo stuck on to the outside of a building more than this doorway does. As so often in urban scenes, the contribution of the central clustered street-lamps must be given its proper due.

Turning the south-east corner the old Lonja, or mercantile exchange, lies at an angle on the left, its rose and grey elevation making a pleasant contrast to the great sombre mass on the right. The southern aspect of the Cathedral is immense and impressive, but relieved by buttresses, towers, pinnacles and crockets. There is a fine modern imitation of a fifteenth-century Gothic portal, built in the last century at the expense of Don Francisco Jiménez Bocanegra. The great arch still looks incomplete with its niches waiting for their saintly occupants.

The western or principal façade is on Seville's busy Avenida de Queipo de Llano, and the centre of the three main entrances is reserved for the archbishop or, when there is one, the king. It is also an example of recent building—the ornamentation is nineteenth-century work, with a fine Assumption and 39 saints by the celebrated sculptor Bellver. There are still 53 unoccupied niches and one wonders whether they ran out of saints or money.

Artistically finer is the Puerta de San Miguel, sometimes called Nacimiento from the terracotta Nativity in the Lunette, the work of Lorenzo Mercadante, a Breton of the mid-fifteenth century. His school is represented by Millán, who made some of the inferior, smaller figures of the prophets. Mercadante's work is outstanding, even though the original polychrome has almost vanished; the terracotta is, however, weathering to a pleasant, dull russet. Apart from the other delightful features of the Nativity, this sculpture shows a group of shepherds dancing, with smiles of joy on their rustic faces. The other flanking door, to the north of the main entrance, is for obvious reasons called *del Baptisterio*, and is distinguished by the fine sculpture of a whole array of Sevillian saints, whose sensitive portrayal again reveals the master hand of Mercadante.

The last, or north side of the Cathedral rises from a stepped pavement, already mentioned by Cervantes, and some of the marble columns that hold the chains are from the old mosque. *Las gradas*, as the steps are called, were used as a gallery where artists exhibited their work and where crowds gathered to criticise or admire. Many an artist, Murillo among them, owed his success to this free exhibition. There are many modern equivalents, such as the Via Margutta in Rome.

The main feature of the wall is the **Puerta del Perdón**. In essentials this is very similar to the gate of the same name in Córdoba, which was copied from this one. The workmanship here is, however, somewhat finer and it stands as an unrivalled Mudéjar masterpiece grafted on an Almohad doorway. Even the bronze doors are similar, with their panels of Cufic maxims from the Koran interspersed with *ataurique* ornament, and their magnificent knockers. It also gives us an opportunity to examine larch wood at close quarters, for this forms the main leaves of the door. Larch (*alerce*) was used almost exclusively by the Moslem carpenters who made the intricate *alfarje* ceilings and the inlaid geometric patterns of doors and window-shutters, for it possesses considerable resistance to the ravages of time and to wood-borers.

As at Córdoba there was previously a Moslem gate here, and this one too leads into the Patio de Naranjos, the Orange Court, which is one of the few relics of the Almohad mosque. The gate's present appearance may be criticised for the multitude of styles which form an uneasy partnership. The doors are of 1478; the stucco work of the *alfiz*, in Plateresque style, is of 1522 and was made by one Bartolomé López; the saints alongside, with the high relief above, were made later by Miguel Florentín, sometimes confused with Perrin. The relief is another fine Renaissance work and shows Christ driving the money changers out of the Temple.

The patio itself gives an impression of size that is partly due to the wide spacing between its trees, and there is an atmosphere of tidiness. Morgado, who saw it before the reconstruction of

1618, was captivated by perfume and shade, flowering orange
and lemon trees, cypresses and palms. In the centre was a kiosk,
presumably for ritual ablution, with a Visigothic, octagonal
marble fountain. This at least survives, though two sides of the
arcaded and crenellated patio have been put to other uses; but
seven of the original horseshoe arches remain on the east side
and twelve on the north.

Here too, built against one of the pillars of the arcade and
perched on a marble column, is a historic pulpit, entered by
worn steps at the side through a door originally belonging to the
mosque, and covered with a little marble roof. The names of
some famous occupants are inscribed; some of them will be unknown to the average visitor, but others have attained almost
universal fame or notoriety. St. Francis of Borgia (Francisco de
Borja), great-nephew of Pope Alexander VI, who gave up the
material advantages of being the Emperor's confidant and Duke
of Gandía to become General of the Jesuits, was a man whom by
any standards we would judge to be *simpático*. St. Vincent Ferrer
preceded him by nearly two centuries and was unequalled as a
rabble rouser in the days before there was money in revivalism;
it is questionable whether he burned more souls in this life than
he saved from the flames of the next. There has been much
argument as to whether his father was English or Spanish;
strangely enough, each nation claims him for her own.

The arcade behind the pulpit leads to one of the entrances to
the Cathedral, the **Puerta del Lagarto**, a relic of the mosque with
Gothic carving rather incongruously within the pointed horseshoe arch. Too few sightseers stop to look up at the Mudéjar
artesonado and the strange objects that are suspended from it.
the most striking is a crocodile (*lagarto*), which gave its name both
to the 'nave' of the arcade on the east side of the patio and to the
Cathedral door.

The chronicle of Alfonso X, the Learned, tells of an embassy
sent by the Sultan of Egypt, requesting the hand of Alfonso's
daughter Berenguela. In somewhat unflattering exchange the
Moslem sent a giraffe, an elephant and a crocodile. Whether
Alfonso found his daughter more attractive or whether, as the
chronicle states, she declined to marry an infidel, is not known for
certain. Alfonso seems to have kept both his daughter and the
crocodile. Stuffed and hung outside the door of what was still the
converted mosque, the crocodile's body was popularly believed
to bring good luck or avert the Evil Eye; the elephant's tusk
next to it had the same significance. Both these objects either

fell down or disintegrated and are now represented by competent copies in wood.

The other suspended objects are a lance and a horse's bit, said without any justification to have been that of El Cid's charger Babieca. There are various explanations for this bizarre collection. Some have said that the bit belonged to the giraffe; many are satisfied with the trite interpretation of Prudence for the crocodile, Strength for the tusk, Justice for the lance and Temperance for the bit.

The **Chapel of Nuestra Señora de la Granada** is immediately on the left before passing through the Puerta del Lagarto. It is rarely opened but enough may be seen through the glass door; it is small and dark and the altar piece has little artistic merit, but the light picks out a rare and beautiful arrangement of six Visigothic capitals, in perfect preservation. It is thus quite possible that this little chapel is a part of the Almohad mosque, for the Moslems made use of any previous ornamental work that they came across. Two of the capitals are on columns that form the door-jambs and the other four are arranged as though supporting a ciborium; not the least of their attractions is that although all are different in design they make a homogeneous group.

Through the Puerta del Lagarto you arrive in the same bay as is reached by entering through the more orthodox Puerta de los Palos, next to the ticket office. It is as well to try and fix some landmarks before examining the hundreds of details that will be encountered. The aisles cross your line of vision at right-angles, seven of them if you include the outside ones that are filled with chapels. The vast space before you is broken up by three interruptions. Before you and to the left is the complex of the Capilla Real (Royal Chapel), occupying the eastern end of the nave and adjacent aisles. Next, the nave contains the high altar, then there is another interruption and the *coro* fills the two bays immediately west of the crossing. By having the three structures in a line down the nave, the huge interior is conveniently landmarked; this amply repays the broken perspectives thus produced.

The placing of a *coro* in the centre of the nave always raises protests from art lovers and in some churches it has even been removed; Seville Cathedral, however, is big enough to contain the above three structures and still look empty. Before examining the museum pieces, one should admire the stately, sober arrangement of clustered columns that divide the nave and aisles, many of those in the centre covered with hangings of crimson velvet trimmed with gold, an offering from the shipping magnates in 1694. There is nothing to add to the stock accounts of the soaring, aspiring arches of the Gothic interior, so often described; but there is one feature of this noble building which is rarely mentioned. The Gothic style of church architecture was based on the striving for more light, achieved by buttressing the walls and weakening the intervening parts by building larger windows— Seville has employed the means without trying to achieve the result. Light was needed in the north, in the lands of cloud and mist; in Spain it can be a positive embarrassment and churches— León Cathedral is a notable exception—tend to be cool and restful through the deliberate exclusion of glare.

The adoption of the Gothic style was a matter of fashion, or of making use of the only method with which some of the foreign architects were familiar, and so we have in this cathedral the basic plan which was meant to bring God's light into His house, along with an arrangement that allows the minimum of illumination to penetrate the ninety odd windows. Many of them are masterpieces and the names of outstanding mediaeval glass painters are recorded as having worked here. Reconstructions and replacements have been necessary, so that some strange scenes and subjects can be found, preferably with field glasses as the windows are for the most part extremely high up. In one of them the dance of the *seises* is reproduced; another, entitled *The Nativity*, reproduces the Adoration of the Shepherds, a copy of the retablo by Luis Vargas in the first chapel on the right as you enter the Cathedral through the Puerta del Nacimiento—a fact which also explains why that door is so named and adorned with a Nativity in the tympanum.

The **Capilla Real** makes a good starting point for a detailed tour of the Cathedral. As previously stated, it occupies the extreme east end of the nave and adjacent two aisles, and also therefore the apse which bulges out between the doors of Los Palos and La Campanilla. The chapel is principally dedicated to the 'Saintly King' who captured Seville, Ferdinand III of Castile who, like his cousin St. Louis IX of France, was a great-grandson of our Henry II and a descendant of the Cid in the fifth generation. (His daughter was that Eleanor of Castile who married our Edward I; it was she who sucked the poison from her husband's wound in the Holy Land, and crosses were erected by her sorrowing widower to mark the stages of her journey to the tomb.)

Both cousins displayed a humility rare in the royalty of that age and Ferdinand was kindness itself to the Moslem king of

Granada, who came to him abjectly seeking to be his vassal. From this act stem various happenings, and the story of the final conquest of Granada should always be viewed as the dispute between liege lords and their disobedient vassals. But that is all in the future; what interests our assessment of Ferdinand's achievements is the fact that his capture of Seville was aided, and perhaps even made possible, by the military aid of the Moslem king of Granada, who was frankly ashamed of the part he had to play.

The magnificent *reja* of the Chapel was erected in 1771 and portrays St. Ferdinand receiving the keys of Seville. Once inside your eyes are immediately held by the broad steps that lead to the altar, and the special feature of the enclosure in their centre; here rests the uncorrupted body of the saint, in a silver-gilt casket of 1729, so brightly and profusely decorated that there is little chance of the visitor overlooking it. The casket stands on a pedestal which comes from the original resting-place of St. Ferdinand, with inscriptions ordered by his son, Alfonso the Learned, in Hebrew, Arabic, Latin and Spanish.

The central feature of the retablo is the famous *Virgen de los Reyes*, a Romanesque statue of the Patroness and Child, said to have been given to his cousin by St. Louis of France. The head is of wood, the rest of other material, and the statue is so articulated as to look comparatively natural, at least for a carving of the thirteenth century. Both the Virgin and Infant were canonically crowned in 1904, which rather detracts from their charm; but we can picture this precious image as it was taken by St. Ferdinand on his campaigns in a magnificent carriage. She would not in those days have been so overdressed as she is today, nor wear round her neck a silver ribbon with the Spanish national colours but, like most Romanesque statues, she still radiates the simple sincerity of her maker.

To the left of the altar is a small gate through which one descends to the Royal crypt in which lie, like deed boxes in a lawyer's office, the plain brass-bound caskets of some of Castile's royalty. Perhaps the most interesting historically are those of Pedro the Cruel and his mistress Maria de Padilla, here designated as the wife of Pedro, a claim to which he swore during his lifetime. Its importance has long ago dissolved, but if it were true then John of Gaunt was rightful heir to the throne of Castile through his marriage to one of the daughters of this union.

The pride of this crypt is the *Virgen de las Batallas*, an ivory statue about 17 inches high of the Virgin and Child, which St.

Ferdinand also took into battle, seated before him on his saddle bow. These images were quite well known in mediaeval days and originated with the Greek emperors of Byzantium, where they were called *socia belli*, war companions. They were seated figures with a small door opening underneath the throne, and thus served as reliquaries. Many warriors, especially Spanish, carried such images fitted upon a pin (*perno*) that protruded from the left side of the saddle bow. In this way the talisman, for that is what the image amounted to, would sit in the shelter of the warrior's shield, securely held by the *perno* that fitted into the square hole placed where it would be least noticeable.

Among other treasures of the Capilla Real are the authentic sword of St. Ferdinand, which used to be taken out on important expeditions, his spurs, the buckles of his belt and a silver reliquary containing one of his fingers. The paintings include a good Dolorosa and a fair St. Ferdinand by Murillo and small works by Pacheco and Alonso Cano. There are sacred vessels used in the first mass said in Mexico, attended by Hernán Cortés, in 1519, and show-cases of the Virgin's jewelry, among which two gold watches—not even wristwatches—look out of place. Lastly there is an ivory crucifix of beautiful design, possibly Romanesque, which came from the private oratory of Hernán Cortés.

In the wall on the left of the Capilla Real is the tomb of Beatrice of Swabia, first wife of the Saintly King, and in a symmetrical recess opposite is that of their son Alfonso the Learned. Both are fine examples of Renaissance tomb carving, the kneeling figures especially admirable, and it is therefore surprising to learn that they are contemporary sculpture, with one of the artists a woman.

As we leave the Royal Chapel we face the back of the **Capilla Mayor**, or Chapel of the High Altar, which is quaintly built to resemble a house-front of the early sixteenth century in Plateresque style, with Gothic niches for upper windows in which are rows of terracotta bishops. Few visitors spare it a glance, which is a pity, for it provides a little light relief among the masterpieces that envelop you. To the right is the Capilla de San Pedro, whose retablo contains paintings of the life of St. Peter by Zurbarán. Their especial interest lies in their being the first of many series painted by this great artist, the Caravaggio of Spain, as he has been called. Philip IV called him 'painter of the King and king of the painters', a compliment indeed during the lifetime of Velázquez.

The first impression of the Capilla Mayor is undoubtedly one of richness, the striking result of its beautiful gilt *rejas* on three sides. Whatever opinions may be held of the merit of Spanish painting, sculpture or architecture during the flowering of Renaissance and Baroque art, none can deny that wrought iron here achieved perfection; and of all Spanish *rejas* these may well claim to be the most exquisite. They are best appreciated during Mass, from the benches which stand before the *coro*, when their dull gold tracery and the crimson velvet hangings that frame them glow against the sombre background. They are the visual complement of the organ's pealing anthem or the Requiem Mass of Tomás Luis de Victoria.

The great Maestro Bartolomé, whose *reja* of the Capilla Real in Granada is also considered the finest in Spain—among a dozen examples, whichever you happen to be looking at is supreme—worked under Sancho Múñoz on the side portions, and also on the *coro*, which we shall see later. The western, or front panel, with its embossed *Entombment*, was by Francisco de Salamanca, a Carthusian friar, whose name deserves to be venerated outside Spain along with better known artists. In 1518 Archbishop Diego de Deza donated 100,000 golden doubloons for this work and the gilding of the retablo, which is why his arms figure so prominently in the lower sequence of the latter. On either side is a wrought-iron pulpit with bas-reliefs, another work of Fray Francisco, which would engage our whole attention in surroundings less sumptuous. The one on the right is especially interesting.

The retablo is beyond description. In size it outranks any other in the world and the statistics which follow cannot prepare you for what is intrinsically a superb example of Gothic art and contains many important features of historical interest. In cold figures, it stands nearly 70 feet high, towering over the Chapel of the High Altar, and is 60 feet broad. In this immense space are forty-five niches, framed in flamboyant Gothic style, in which scenes from the lives of the Saviour and the Virgin are portrayed in high relief. As the higher tiers recede their figures are made imperceptibly larger, so that the effect of perspective and distance should be diminished. All this intricate carving, as well as the thousand-odd figures, is variously stated to be made from walnut, larch or chestnut and each scene would be regarded as a masterpiece if it was displayed separately. Dancart the Fleming worked on it for the first ten years, and after 1492, when it was decided to add the wings, a whole team was employed. The gilding, an operation requiring considerable skill and experience, was done by two outstanding artists of the day, Alejo Fernández and Andrés de Covarrubias, and completed in 1526.

In the lowest tier are some very interesting compartments. One, representing St. Leander and St. Isidore, includes a model of the Cathedral as it was before the construction of the Royal Chapel, and of the Giralda; the other portrays the patronesses of Seville, St. Justa and St. Rufina, with a model of the city as it was about the year 1510. This may be compared for antiquarian interest with the relief of the old minaret of the Córdoba Mezquita over the Gate of Santa Catalina which, by the way, also figures on old seals of that city. An intelligent restoration of the retablo was made in the present century and the cost defrayed by a distinguished and pious member of the Osborne family, whose great sherry bodega is at Puerto Santa María.

At the foot of the retablo and behind the altar is the late thirteenth-century statue of the *Virgen de la Sede*—after whom this cathedral has been named since its foundation—made of cypress wood, partly silver plated, partly painted. It is said to be the identical image mentioned by Alfonso X in *Cántiga No. 256*, which refers to an illness of his mother, Beatrice of Swabia.

The Capilla Mayor should be seen at different times of day in order to appreciate its beauties, which are largely Teutonic, in various lights. The best illumination is in the early afternoon. But before leaving you might like to pass through one of the small doors, carved in the same style as the retablo, that lead to the Sacristía Alta, behind the altar, not of course to be confused with the other sacristies that we shall see later. There is a Mudéjar door, believed to be of the fourteenth century, which is said to come from the old Sagrario, with typical geometric inlay. The ceiling is a fine artesonado of the Plateresque epoch and there are three well-known paintings by Alejo Fernández, portraying the Conception, Nativity and Purification of the Blessed Virgin.

The third building in the nave is the **coro**, whose beautiful *reja*, also by Fray Francisco de Salamanca, faces the great entrance of the Capilla Mayor. The space between them is directly below the fine vault of the crossing 132 feet above. The *sillería*, or choir stalls, are the main feature of interest and in the direct line of wood carving that was introduced into Spain by Philip Vigarny or Felipe de Borgoña (though there is no evidence that he was in fact a Burgundian). He communicated his secrets to Gil de Siloé, Berruguete and other famous artists whose influence can be traced uninterruptedly from teacher to pupil. The *sillería* here is held to be the best in Southern Spain and is in mixed Gothic, Mudéjar and Plateresque style. It consists of 117 seats of oak and fir, inlaid with other woods, and as usual is divided into the upper *sellia*, for the canons, and the *subsellia* for those in receipt of benefices, which might include artists, enabling them to lead a secure and sheltered life.

Each seat has carvings different from the rest, and the Giralda, which forms the crest of the Cathedral, can be distinguished among the reliefs and inlays. There are also 216 statues carved in wood, and on the second stall of the *sellia* on the left, in Gothic script, is the statement that 'Nufio Sánchez, whom God preserve, the woodcarver made this *coro*, finished in 1478'. This seat, by its royal arms, was reserved for the King of León and Castile. Nufio Sánchez was assisted in this work by the same Pieter Dancart who carved most of the great retablo. We saw the *sillería* of Córdoba Cathedral by Duque Cornejo; we can compare his style with that of the older masters, for he was responsible for the organ cases here.

The outside of the *coro* must not be overlooked. The *trascoro*, or western face, is a pseudo-classical accumulation of coloured marbles that bears no relation to the *coro*, the Cathedral or refinement. But the lateral chapels, also known as the Capillas de los Alabastros, must be seen. The late Gothic and early Plateresque style of the carved alabaster and the fine *rejas* are too often overlooked. Furthermore, the chapel of the Concepción chica contains one of the finest works of the Andalucían sculptor Montañés; we are to see his birthplace and many of his works, but none finer than this. The Immaculate Conception, of polychrome wood, 'is so beautiful', wrote a Spanish critic, 'that with the modesty, gravity, devotion and loveliness of her face it refreshes the souls of those who see her.' The sculptor himself, scorning false modesty, described it as one of the best things there were in Spain and the best which he had made, and it was the favourite model of his brilliant pupil Alonso Cano. The Sevillians call her *La Cieguecita*, 'the little blind one', from her downcast eyes; the neck has a delicacy of moulding outstanding even in this perfect work, and a peculiarity not often commented on is that she is serious when seen from the left but smiling from the right.

In the marble pavement to the west of the *coro* can be seen the grave of Hernando Colón, younger son of Christopher Columbus, or Cristóbal Colón; the caravels and part of the inscription incised on the tombstone can still be made out. The inscription, *A Castilla y a León, Nuebo Mundo dió Colón*, was responsible for many a writer of the last two centuries thinking that this was the grave of Cristóbal, who had indeed given a new world to Castile and León; meanwhile the bones of the father were resting in Havana, whence they were brought here in 1899.

To complete your visit to the Cathedral you can begin at the south-east corner and make a circuit of the chapels built into the outside aisles, in a clockwise direction. The services of a guide are useful, for not only are they knowledgeable about the treasures, but most important of all they know where the electric light switches of the various chapels are placed. The Sala de Ornamentos has a rich and varied collection of sacred vestments, which interest few visitors, and a Persian rug of the fourteenth or fifteenth century, called the *terliz de la montería*, as some of the animals are hunting. It is of silk with gilt thread and one of the oldest existing specimens. Here too is the banner used by St. Ferdinand at the capture of Seville, purple, white and gold nearest the staff, fading to pink and yellow farther away.

The oval Sala Capitular or chapter-house of the Cathedral has admirable proportions but is best known for the Immaculate Conception by Murillo and the eight portraits of local saints in medallions, by the same painter; there is also a St. Ferdinand by Francisco Pacheco, founder of the Seville school of painters, teacher and father-in-law of Velázquez. In this painting on copper can be seen the only originality he ever showed, the moustache and 'Imperial', which were quite contrary to tradition.

The **Sacristía Mayor**, a spacious Plateresque hall whose beauty caused Philip II to tell the canons 'you have a better sacristy than I a royal chapel', contains many noteworthy treasures. The entrance-doors are delightfully carved by Guillén, a master woodcarver whose work nevertheless seems insignificant compared with the proportions and decoration of those great artists Riana, Siloé and Gil de Hontañón. But few have leisure to admire this fine hall which 'shines next to the Cathedral like a brilliant planet on a night of full moon', as one Spanish writer expressed it. As you enter, you see on the right the bronze candelabrum, the *tenebrario*, a work of Bartolomé Morel. It is placed under the crossing during Holy Week and twelve of its candles are extinguished one by one during the *Miserere*, to suggest the desertion of the apostles, while the thirteenth, representing the Virgin, remains alight. The maker of this 26-foot masterpiece also carved the great *facistol*, or lectern of the *coro*. Balancing the *tenebrario* is another giant on the left, the silver custodial of Juan de Arfe which is carried in procession on Corpus Christi and used to be placed in the great wooden *monumento*, erected over the grave of Hernando Colón, during Holy Week; the component parts of the *monumento* were so old that it has not been put up during recent years.

A Descent from the Cross, by the Flemish Pedro de Campana, is regarded as the finest painting in the sacristy and is truly a work of great realism and tenderness. This is the very painting that Murillo admired so much and before which his body was placed, at his own wish, in the Church of Santa Cruz. There is an Immaculate by Pacheco, in which a wonderful effect is achieved by the burst of light from behind the figure of the Virgin; it is a pleasant change from the stereotyped Murillos, of which there are many examples. We know, of course, that Murillo depended for his livelihood on religious paintings and his Immaculates were always in great demand; nevertheless one gets the feeling sometimes that they became a habit that he could not shake off. The portraits of St. Leander and St. Isidore by Murillo show far more warmth, that of the latter especially, as the sitter was an old friend. But we must be grateful for all Murillos that are left in Spain, as they were highly prized by Marshal Soult.

Just as it is impossible to do justice to every painting, so the jewels and other solid works must be mentioned very briefly. The Alfonsine Tables are famous and were bequeathed to the Cathedral by the learned king. There are two historic keys which were said to have been handed to St. Ferdinand by the Moslems and the Jews when he entered Seville. Fortunately, it is now believed that the whole story of the surrender of these ornamental keys is a fabrication, and that they resemble keys of honour or of dedication, which were often specially made and offered to kings as symbols of power.

Proceeding westward you enter the Sacristía de los Cálices through the Capilla de los Dolores. Here is another of the best of the works of the 'Sevillian Phidias', Juan Martínez Montañés, a startlingly lifelike, or rather deathlike, Crucifixion. There are some forty pictures by famous artists, including a wonderful Holy Family by Murillo, who is represented also by four other works. To the art student it is enough to say that there are examples of the work of Valdés Leal, Morales the Divine, Zurbarán, de Vargas, Roelas, Pacheco, Titian and Alejo Fernández. Owing to the rarity of his works in Southern Spain, visitors spend most time before one of Goya's few religious paintings, *SS. Justa and Rufina*. These young women are the patronesses of Seville, being female potters from Triana who were martyred under the Romans for being rude to a heathen image. They are equipped with their standard properties, pottery, a broken idol, palm branches and the Giralda in the background, for their only miracle was to support the tower when the powers of evil had whipped up the wind to knock it over. Not one of Goya's best.

A finer subject, even if the painting is not regarded as among the best in this art exhibition, is the monk Fernando de Contreras by Luis de Vargas; the date 1541 given with the artist's signature is believed to be wrong, as de Vargas was in Italy at the time. Contreras, who belonged to the Order of Mercy, dedicated himself to the ransoming of Christian captives in North Africa; so fine was his character that the infidels accepted his staff as security for the payment of ransoms. Small wonder that he earned the title 'Apostle of Seville' and that, on his death in 1548, he was laid in his shroud by noble ladies.

Next comes the south transept and its door, called the Puerta de San Cristóbal. It is the rule for Spanish churches to have an immense figure of St. Christopher near one of their entrances, for it is well known that whoever has looked upon the saint will not come to a violent end that day. This huge fresco was the work of an Italian, so it is said, named Mateo Pérez de Alisio of Lecce; it would not be unusual for an Apulian to have a Spanish name and the well-known anecdote about him, which is related below, requires an Italian speaker. Here also is the tomb of Christopher Columbus, an original work of 1891. The sarcophagus is supported by four more-than-life-sized heralds representing the four kingdoms that make up Spain: Castile, León, Navarre, Aragón. A strangely effective result is produced by the stone pall-bearers, the late Gothic portal and the giant St. Christopher.

The first altar after crossing the transept is the famous **Altar de la Concepción**, better known as de la Gamba. The name originated from the story that Luis de Vargas was painting the fine retablo that shows the Virgin and Infant appearing to a selection of Old Testament characters; the composition, drawing and colouring are excellent and, although the influence of Raphael and Vasari is often cited, the features of the subjects are unmistakably Spanish. Adam appears in the foreground, and the story is that Pérez de Alisio took a few minutes off from his St. Christopher to look at Vargas' work, was enchanted with Adam's foreshortened leg and exclaimed, *piu vale la tua gamba che tutto il mio San Cristoforo.* Most critics agree with him that

Adam's leg is worth more than the whole St. Christopher, but the story loses its point unless the artist is an Italian, for *gamba* in Spanish means prawn. It loses still more when you discover that Pérez de Alisio painted his St. Christopher in 1584, sixteen years after the death of Vargas.

The next is the largest and most sumptuous of all the lateral chapels and is called **Capilla de la Antigua**. The Virgin after whom it is named is not quite as old as is usually claimed, being neither Byzantine, Visigothic nor Mozarabic; it is a fourteenth-century fresco, probably modelled on a Byzantine icon, as the most cursory glance shows. From the chapel a small door on the right leads to a sacristy in which are kept about thirty paintings by well-known artists, including Ribera, Valdes Leal and Alonso Cano; Zurbarán's St. John the Baptist deserves special mention for the sitter's natural pose. Behind this and the neighbouring chapels are extensive apartments devoted to the business of the Cathedral, including its archives, and in these are enough paintings by famous artists to equip an art gallery; visitors are unfortunately not allowed inside. The next chapel, of San Hermenegildo, has a fine *reja* and contains a masterpiece of flamboyant Gothic sculpture. This is the alabaster tomb of Cardinal Cervantes, by Lorenzo Mercadante the Breton (1458), whose work is also found on the western portals. The portrait of the dead archbishop is renowned, not only for its realism, but for the expression of peace into which the worn lines have fallen. Note the deer at his feet and the others on his crest, a canting emblem *cierva*—Cervantes.

At the south-west corner is the last chapel of this series, that of **San Laureano**. This local martyr is believed to have walked and talked after being decapitated and the miracle may be seen portrayed here. The chapel is more noteworthy for the fact that it covers the site of the first stone laid in the construction of the present Cathedral and was used for divine service during the period of building.

On the west side and immediately inside the Puerta del Nacimiento is the Altar del Nacimiento with a Nativity by Luis de Vargas, showing the Adoration of the Shepherds. Before reaching the main entrance there is a fine Murillo of the Guardian Angel, over the Altar del Angel de la Guarda. Hereabouts stands the enormous silver custodial, at least forty feet high, which has taken the place of the old *monumento* for the Holy Week services; it makes up in bulk and intrinsic value what it lacks in taste. At the next corner is an entrance to the Church of the Sagrario,

which is better approached from the street but is not of prime
importance, and there we turn to the right inside the Puerta del
Baptisterio and enter the straight.

On the left is the **Baptistery Chapel**, with the world-famous
Vision of Saint Anthony of Padua by Murillo. Two-thirds of the
canvas are occupied by Murillian cherubs doing their acrobatics
on a cloud of glory. In 1875 an unknown thief displayed astonish-
ingly good taste by leaving the cherubs and cutting out the figure
of St. Anthony; it was sold in New York, whence it was promptly
restored to Seville. The line of repair can still be seen. The
Cathedral Chapter then resolved to employ watchdogs at night
to prevent a recurrence of the theft, but in the ninety-odd years
that have elapsed the matter has not progressed beyond the
planning stage. Though the light in the Baptistery is not good,
one may see that this is in Murillo's last style, the *Vaporoso*, in
which outlines are lost in the light and shade, some say because
he could thus work more quickly. The vase of lilies, attribute of
St. Anthony, is painted with great verisimilitude. There are other
paintings in the same chapel, difficult to see in the poor light, but
a small *Virgin and Child* in the Murillo style faces the main
canvas and is said to be the work of his servant, Sebastián
Gómez the Mulatto.

The neighbouring chapel has various names, of which the
Capilla de Scala is thought to be the most correct, for it contains
the ornate tomb intended for the bishop of that see. The chapel's
chief attraction is a glazed terracotta relief by Della Robbia,
though some say it is by Luca, the founder of the family workshop, and others that it is the work of his nephew Andrea. The
next chapel, that of Santiago, contains another Della Robbia, *The
Virgin of the Cushion*, and a battle scene, *Santiago at the Battle
of Clavijo*, by Juan de las Roelas. This artist was a leader in the
revolt against mannerism in Spain and therefore an early expo-
nent of the Baroque which, in his hands, became a vehicle for
the naturalistic style. The subject deals with the miraculous
appearance of St. James the Elder at the battle of Clavijo, when
he descended from Heaven on his white charger and slew
thousands of Moslems. Hence, in this guise he is known as the
'Moor Slayer', *Santiago Matamoros*. It is now known that the
story really refers to the capture of the small fortress of Albelda,
converted into a major battle by a twelfth-century forger;
fortunately the deception was only discovered recently so that
Santiago was not precluded from appearing in Mexico to help
the Spaniards against the Aztecs.

In the transept, to the left of the Puerta de la Concepción, which leads from the Patio de los Naranjos, is the Altar de Nuestra Señora de Belén, which houses one of Alonso Cano's most typical portraitures. His paintings have been said to show feminine grace mixed with realism, a resigned piety rather than a deep mysticism—note the tenderness of Our Lady of Bethlehem and the famous, downcast 'Moorish' eyes. There is one more chapel which merits a moment's pause for reasons other than artistic, the Capilla de las Doncellas, though a glance at the *reja* and the polychrome Cuenca tiles will not be wasted. The chapel's name derives from a *cofradia*, or society, whose purpose was the collection of dowries for poor maidens (*doncellas*); we shall be hearing more of these societies and there is some confusion about them. They are not trade guilds; they are not wholly composed of parishioners; they are not even always made up of men, for the girls of the tobacco factory, from which Prosper Merimée drew his inspiration for Carmen, had their own *cofradia*. They can best be defined as a voluntary society banded together for a religious, often charitable, object.

In the north-east corner of the orange patio is the **Biblioteca Capitular Colombina**. The staircase which brings us to the library has Roman and Visigothic inscribed plaques. The collection is really a fusion of two distinct libraries, the chapter-house collection and the bequest of Hernando Colón, acquired after litigation with the Dominicans of San Pablo. To penetrate the aura of romance that surrounds the great explorer and to see a book of excerpts in his own handwriting is to bring him back to human proportions, grandiose but mundane. Obviously well-read, Christopher, along with his brothers Bartolomé and Diego, made annotations in the margins of Cardinal Pierre d'Ailly's *Imago Mundi*, the work of a great theologian and philosopher who had been dead for more than half a century. He had read and annotated Seneca, Eneas Piccolomini who was to become Pope Pius II, Pliny, Marco Polo and Abraham Zacuth, whose perpetual calendar is dated 1496. His marginal notes were sometimes in Spanish, at others in Italian or Portuguese. In an edition of Seneca, published in Venice in 1510, is a note by his son Hernando, 'This prophecy was noted by my father.' Map maker, navigator and scholar, his discovery should be viewed less in the light of the importance that the new continent subsequently acquired, than as a triumph of the human intellect.

The **Giralda** represents the minaret of the great mosque of the Almohads and was begun in 1184, shortly before the death of the

Sultan Abu Yakub Yusuf; work was temporarily interrupted and it is said that its resumption under his successor Yakub Al-Mansur is marked by the change from stone to brick courses. The names of various architects are mentioned but it is generally conceded that the minaret of Seville at least was designed and begun by a Spanish Moslem, Ahmed Ibn Baso, and completed by Ali de Gomara.

The original minaret was 250 feet high, its slender upper section crowned with a cupola of *azulejos* and topped with the four gilded brass balls or 'apples' of diminishing size. It remained unaltered until the balls and cupola were dislodged in an earthquake on 24 August, 1356. Thereupon a small brick bell tower was built in their place. This can be verified in the Chapel of the Evangelists, next to that of the Doncellas; St. Justa and St. Rufina are shown with the Giralda as it was in 1555, when the artist Ferdinand Sturm painted the retablo. In 1558 Hernán Ruiz was commissioned to add a more imposing bell tower and this gave an extra 60 feet to the minaret—Baroque and Moorish harmonising surprisingly well. The name Giralda is derived from the colossal statue of Faith, containing over a ton of bronze. It was cast by Morel, who also made the beautiful *Tenebrario*, which acts as a weathercock or *giraldillo*, a marvel of engineering as well as art, and turns at the slightest breeze. She is said to be holding the labarum, or Constantine's *chi-rho* banner, but most see only a Roman standard in one hand and a palm branch in the other.

The stones of the lower courses are Roman and came from an earlier alcazar than the one we shall see; careful search even discloses the remains of Latin inscriptions on some of them. The brick is of the usual, flat type that the Romans introduced, and is laid with the most admirable precision. Inside, the pattern has been plastered over and the size of the bricks disguised, and over the plaster a hundred thousand visitors have scribbled their names. From outside, each face of the tower is divided into three vertical panels, of which the central one is filled by a succession of *ajimez* lobulated windows with balconies. The central pillar of each is of white marble and the capitals are caliphate, brought from Medina Azzahra, some of them still displaying a trace of gilding. The side panels bear a typical Moorish pattern made by the intersection of diagonal, wavy lines that thus produce a series of lozenges, known in Moslem architecture as *sebkas*, and in English as reticulated tracery. For all the detail of raised brick and the blind arcades, the façades give no impression of fussiness but rather one of dignity; they are the authentic prints of true Moorish, as distinct from Islamic, art, just as the Spanish custom of giving a visitor anything he incautiously admires stems from the Moroccan Marinids.

The bells are reached by a ramp instead of stairs, winding between an inner core and the outer wall. Eventually it reaches a promenade round a wall that is decorated with lobulated blind arches and more caliphal capitals. There are twenty-five bells, each with its own name, such as San Pedro, or Santa María which is the largest; three more storeys with diminishing girth succeed each other, the second known as that of the clock as it contains the bell which strikes the hours. The mechanism was set up in the eighteenth century, but there is one bell that is a relic of the first mechanical clock in Spain, erected on the 17th June, 1400, as Latour was told. He said that in 1848 he could still hear the movement that was originally blessed by Archbishop Gonzalo de Mena.

The view is, of course, impressive and, more to the point, useful for later exploration of the city: there is the Guadalquivir, running north and south, the main city on the left bank, Triana on the right. Here and there you see one of the twelve Arab or Almohad minarets that still, though in an altered form, rise from the crowded roofs. Perhaps still more attractive are the extensive parks to the south, the gardens of the Alcázar and the feathery tops of the palm trees that rise singly from some of Seville's smaller squares.

CHAPTER SIX

Devotions and Diversions in Seville

❧

Holy Week—The Dance of the Seises—Flamenco—The Feria—
The Bulls

Seville is not the only town in Spain to celebrate **Holy Week** with
processions, but it is without doubt the one where this old ritual
can best be seen. The visitor must know in advance, however,
that the unforgettable spectacle is subject to several drawbacks.
First, hotels may refuse bookings for less than the whole week,
as they also do a little later for the week of the Feria; secondly,
the processions take priority over all traffic and make it quite
impossible to enter or cross some of the most important thoroughfares during the whole of the day and part of the night. Thirdly,
only the connoisseur of Christs and Virgins will want to see
more than a certain number of floats proceeding hour after hour
through the streets, and in any case the effigies can be seen far
more comfortably at any other time in the churches where they
are housed. Fourthly, the renowned *saetas* can be heard only
outside the Cathedral, where many hours of standing are
necessary unless you wish to hire a chair for the whole week, or
at the home church of the image. If all this does not dismay you,
programmes of the various processions can be bought and are,
in fact, essential for the addict.

Each one of the series of processions is provided by a *cofradía*.
Each *cofradía* has its own colours for cape and cowl, and its
own holy images that are escorted from their home churches to
the Cathedral for blessing, and back again, a trip of ten to twelve
hours. Each *cofradía*, furthermore, takes its images out once only
during the week. It is easy enough to compare the processions,
the *cofradías*, the statues and their rich clothing with pagan
examples; Ford did so and thought he had proved something
that would please Protestant English readers. We are, or should
be, more broad-minded today. To enjoy the experience of Holy
Week, or for that matter much else that is Spanish, you must
ignore the sneers that foreigners so often direct at the 'waxwork'
holy images. They and their Baroque churches were not made

and decorated for the benefit of twentieth-century art critics, but for the devout illiterate, to whom a perpetual verisimilitude had to be presented in days when there was no cinema, no television, not even a comic strip. It is therefore senseless to complain that the images are too lifelike: they are meant to be, for they have a message to impart.

The processions—their number varies from forty to fifty— begin at the parish church of their *cofradia* and make their way to the Cathedral. They all finish this journey by passing south along the Calle de las Sierpes to the Plaza de la Falange, where the mayor and city council sit in rows on the stand in front of the city hall, the Ayuntamiento. Tens of thousands watch the processions from the street, or fill the windows that overlook it. The biggest crowd of all congregates at the entrance to the Cathedral in which the Cardinal Archbishop blesses the images.

A procession is usually headed by a band, which may belong to the police, the *guardia civil* or the army. The dress of the brothers, for members of the *cofradia* are not necessarily penitents, is well known and customarily compared to that of the Ku Klux Klan, to avoid tedious description. Gown and cowl are of various colours, usually different, so that a number of distinguishing combinations is possible. The brotherhood is merely the escort of the *pasos* or floats; the first, sometimes preceded by a file of Roman soldiers, represents a scene from the Passion, the second is one of the numerous Virgins that are housed in the churches of Seville. The *pasos* are encased in repoussé silver work and brocade hangs from the sides to hide the sweating bearers. These are hired porters whom one can see from time to time, when the *paso* is lowered for the rests that are needed every few yards. They look happy whenever you see them, for they are well paid for this labour of love and can earn up to 5,000 pesetas in the Week. After the *pasos* come more members of the brotherhood, some of them with chains round their ankles and carrying heavy crosses; it is not really correct to call them penitents either, for they are expressing their gratitude for divine intercession in answer to prayer.

The Virgin is greeted with passionate enthusiasm in the neighbourhood of her own church and her superiority over all the other Virgins of Seville loudly upheld. The Virgins have lovely faces, preferably adorned with tears of glass or even pearl, and gold-encrusted velvets and brocades that sweep down and out in a great train. Their crowns frame their faces, their jewels almost hide throat and fingers, and they are surrounded by white carnations and candles. Two Virgins are outstanding in popular veneration, *la Virgen de la Esperanza* of San Jacinto in Triana, and the Virgin of the same name, also called *La Macarena*. The passion scenes, in contrast to the attempted idealisation of the Virgins, are realistic and even gruesome. Two again deserve special mention. The *Jesús del Gran Poder*, from the Church of San Lorenzo, is one of the finest of Juan de Mesa's works; the other comes from Triana, from the Capilla del Patrocinio. It is the far-famed *Santo Cristo de la Expiración*, made in 1682 by the little-known sculptor Francisco Antonio Gijón. In the same chapel are two Dolorosas, but the one that accompanies this Crucifixion in the procession is the older one, the work of Cristobal de Ramos. The *Cristo de la Expiración* is regarded as the last great work of the Sevillian school; the people of Seville affectionately call it *el Cachorro*, the Puppy, because that was the nickname of the dying pauper whom Gijón used as a model.

The **Saeta** was originally a spontaneous tribute to Son or Mother given as the porters rested for a spell. Over the murmur of voices and the shuffling of spectators' feet would come a long, clear note that demanded silence; then come the grace notes, and the words lengthen unbearably, or else half a dozen will suddenly be crowded together. The music is without rhythm, harmony or counterpoint, melody is of the simplest and the *saeta* is distinguished by its arabesque of quarter notes that wander away from the main line and return in time for the singer to take breath. Occasionally an animal cry breaks in, expressing an insupportable anguish. The words are simple enough and few, but may be repeated several times. *Y yo no sé, María, como te vas tu sosteniendo*, says one, 'I don't know, Mary, how you go on bearing it'; another is addressed to her Son, *Encorvao y sin fuerzas ya*, 'Bent down and bereft of strength'. For three or four minutes the waving chain of notes echoes from the buildings while the silence holds; then the *saeta* ceases and the applause begins while the floats get under way again.

The *saeta* is, of course, largely Oriental, with its microtonic Arabic scale and profusion of *fioriture*; like most Southern Spanish music and poetry there is no unanimity about the proportionate influence of Hebrew, Arabic, Moorish and primitive Spanish elements. *Saetas* can today be bought in recordings, accompanied by guitars or bands, sung by Spaniards or gypsies, men or women; they have one thing in common that is unique— nowhere else in the world can you hear their like.

Religious dancing is as old as the history of religion and has always had a great hold in Spain, from the days of Bishop Priscillian, burnt for heresy in 385, who introduced dancing into the service of the Church. It had obviously become popular by 589, when the Third Council of Toledo condemned it, and all through the Middle Ages until well into the eighteenth century travellers report dancers heading religious processions. The **Dance of the Seises**, so called because there were originally six dancing boys, is performed only during the octave of Corpus Christi and the Feast of the Immaculate Conception on 8th December, but its origin is not precisely known. It is recorded in the Cathedral archives as early as 1508 and has been tentatively ascribed to the time of the foundation of Corpus Christi.

There are ten dancers among the boys and a further sixteen who sing. Originally the boys were dressed as angels, later as pilgrims and as shepherds; now their clothes are of the seventeenth century and would not be out of place on a page boy in a Velázquez painting. The dance takes place before the high altar of the Cathedral, inside the *reja* and to the accompaniment of an orchestra, the performers using castanets. If the visitor misses the feasts on which the Seises dance he may at least inspect their costumes in the school where they are trained, nearly opposite the Cathedral.

There is much confusion on the question of **Flamenco** singing and dancing, a subject so complicated that even experts disagree. To most visitors the term is taken to mean 'gypsy dancing', with recollections of an evening in the caves of Sacromonte in Granada. It is impossible to reduce the subject to reasonable proportions. The dances of Andalucía may be divided into the 'pure', which are danced without castanets, and those in which *palillos* are used. I purposely introduce the Spanish word for castanets here— used far more frequently than *castañuelas*—because in some parts it is used to denote finger-snapping (*pito*) to mark the rhythm.

Flamenco songs and dances are of comparatively recent origin and are derived from the *cante jondo*, 'deep song' expressing some profound emotion, rarely seen today. They are less sombre and physically more demanding, but preserve, or should preserve, the element of 'possession'. The word, meaning 'Flemish' or 'flamingo', is of doubtful origin in this connotation. It may refer to the additional auditory and visual colour that the gypsies have contributed for Flamenco, though basically Spanish, has been modified by the gypsies, whose influence is particularly strong in the *pito*, the *palmada*, or hand-clapping and the *taconeo*, a highly energetic form of tap-dancing. Castanets are never used, except in the fandanguillo, a comparatively recent addition to the bulerías, tangos, fandangos, jaleos and the virile farruca, to name only a few. Audience participation is an integral part of the flamenco dance, and encouraging cries from the guitarist and other members of the troupe stimulate the dancer.

The female figure that is thought appropriate for the true, 'pure' Andalucian dance does not have buttocks like apples and breasts like melons; rather has the Spaniard inherited the tastes of the poet Hazim al-Quartachanni, who wrote: 'If you describe her from above down, she is a moon over a branch over a heap of sand'; and according to García Gómez, the contrast between the massive thigh and the willowy body represented for the Andalucians the acme of feminine beauty, as it did for the characters in the *Arabian Nights*. Great stress was also laid on a rosy complexion, teeth as white as daisy petals and, by most aesthetes, blonde hair.

The dances which are classified as those using *palillos* are said to descend from rural ones and some would trace them back to the Bacchic orgies. These dances are more mobile than the *jondo*, the whole body moves, often with leaps, and, of course, dancers' castanets supplement the rhythm of the guitars. The gypsy performances that come the tourist's way belong more to this type than the *jondo*, but it is rare indeed to get more than a disorganised jumble of various dances and improvisations, often based on the zambra. The best flamenco dancing, apart from the spontaneous Sevillana at the Feria, is to be seen in some of the half-dozen flamenco cabarets of Madrid, but even these can present only the technique and not the spirit of a vanishing art.

Seville is always a lively place and has an air of spontaneous mirth, but after the emotional tension of the *Semana Santa* is over and the **Feria** begins an additional ebullience appears. The city is full, every bed in every hotel, pension and private apartment booked months before, every bar bursting with jostling, chattering throngs, and still they arrive, from town and country, in cars and lorries, in farm carts and on horseback.

The plazas everywhere are redolent of orange blossom, even above the petrol fumes. Behind the Fábrica de Tabacos and the Plaza de España, in the Prado de San Sebastián, a whole town springs up. Square tents, striped in red or green with paper roses strung across the ceilings, garish paintings on the gable ends and wooden floors for the dancing that is to come, fill the blocks. The plan lists over 450 of them; some are private and the owner invites his friends there; others are free, which means that entrance is free, but the owner will be amply recompensed, for this is one time when the Andalucian lets himself go, and the consumption of wine per head becomes startling in this sober land. The streets between have nine rows of Chinese lanterns, red and white, over each pavement, separated by less than 2 feet, so that the whole fairground is brighter at night than during even the most brilliant spring day. The only thing missing is the cattle sale, the original function that gave rise to this week of celebration. But that too can be found, if seriously sought.

At about noon, while the *casetas* are making sure that they have enough supplies for thirsty throats at night, small groups of riders appear in every part of the city and converge slowly on the fairground. Both men and women wear the broad-brimmed, low-crowned Cordobes hat, white shirt buttoned at the throat without cravat or tie, grey or black Eton jacket and half-boots with spurs. Their knees are covered with brown, embroidered leather *zajones*, the chaparrejos of the West, and their feet rest in box stirrups that have not changed since Seville was captured from the Moors. A few of the women ride side-saddle with incomparable grace. Old farmers, young bloods with the pallor of the city, tots of five or six, dressed like their parents, riding their spirited ponies with the absence of concentration that marks the confident rider.

At night the whole Prado is ablaze. The huge arch at the entrance, built to resemble (though only slightly) the Triana Bridge, has more than 20,000 lights which electricians have for days been installing. The Chinese lanterns along the streets outside the *casetas* now look so close together that you feel you are walking under red and white snakes. Troops of youngsters roam the streets, many of the girls in Andalucian dress, in bright colours, flowers in their hair, barbaric earrings twinkling. Hand-clapping echoes, a ring forms and above the heads can be seen the twining hands of the dancer. Time loses all meaning, gallons of manzanilla course down thousands of dry throats, and as the half-light before the dawn appears, the youngsters troop off, still chattering and still clapping their rhythms.

In spite of the rising popularity of football, **the Bulls** still attract large audiences on Sundays and feast days, and high-lights from recent *corridas* are shown on television once or twice a week during the season. The *corrida*, as mentioned earlier, no longer means a 'running' but the meeting. A torero is any one of the bull-fighters; the matador or espada is the principal, who has his own assistants, the *cuadrilla*. The season begins on Easter Sunday and daily corridas are put on during the Feria. At one of these, for a mere 50 pesetas, you may buy what is called a 'programme'; the date and the names of the matadors are printed on the cover and inside in three languages, is an introduction to the noble art. The writer, it is true, is unfamiliar with punctuation and uncertain about spelling, but he is confident in his vocabulary, for if an English word escapes him he uses a Spanish one.

Having mastered the principles you can now enter the bull-ring, one of the most famous in Spain and formerly one of the most beautiful, but now largely defaced by advertisements. Seville is one of the cities that takes its bullfighting seriously, and is irritated by Ronda's seniority but consoled by the fact that Ferdinand VII chose it for the foundation of his School of Tauromachy. The President's box faces the *toril*, or enclosure, from which the bulls enter the ring. Foreigners do not realise the mass of regulations that exist in this sport: they cover everything from the number of artery forceps in the sick-bay to the maximum weight of the quilts that prevent the picadors' horses from being wounded. The President is charged with the maintenance of these rules, but it seems to be impossible to prevent infringements. It is well known, for example, that some breeders use cattle feed that artificially 'brings on' their bulls, so that although they may pass as five-year-olds in weight and dentition, they are in fact much younger and far too weak to be dangerous.

The signal for each animal to be released is given from the President's box by laying a white handkerchief on the front ledge; those who have seen Roman consular diptychs will recognise the *mappa* which the consul used for signalling the start of the games. There are two other handkerchiefs in reserve: a red one to signal that black banderillas are to be used, a sign that the bull is below standard and a disgrace to the breeder—a rare but salutary lesson. The green handkerchief is even rarer, and is displayed when a bull has shown such courage that its life is ordered to be spared; this is so unusual that its first re-corded use in Barcelona, where bullfighting has been staged for many generations, was in 1968. The bull's wounds were treated with several hundred million units of penicillin and appropriate amounts of other antibiotics.

Protocol rules every stage of the spectacle. Even the entry of the three matadors and their cuadrillas, in parallel files, is arranged so that the junior is on the left and the senior in the centre. Today's audiences at Feria time are no longer as picturesque as they were but the colour in the ring has not changed. The capes are still mauve, with yellow backing, the matador's stockings pink, his coat of many colours and the *muleta*, or square cloth attached to a batten, bright red. This is very nice for the spectators but makes little difference to the bull, who is colour blind. His vision is in any case poor and he charges only moving objects, so that the statuesque pose of the classical matador, who would throw down his hat and stand on it throughout his *faena*, or solo performance, was not so dangerous as it looked. From the spectators' viewpoint a series of passes with the bull led round the stationary torero is far more thrilling than the dancing and evasive action that has become the rule today; but as all the old men say, and always will, bullfighting is not what it used to be.

The novice spectator may see little purpose in much that goes on. Why, for instance, should the bull be encouraged to attack horses and perform the incredible feat of lifting horse and rider on his horns? Why does the picador attempt to keep him off with a guarded lance that he thrusts precisely to the side of the hump? And finally, why does the matador, after practically taming the beast with a series of passes, get him nicely lined up for the kill and then walk away and start again? The answer lies in the obligatory method of delivering the sword thrust. On either side of the spine and on the inner side of the shoulder blades there is a small opening through which a sword thrust will reach the heart or great vessels. In order to allow this opening to attain its maximum size, and even that is ridiculously small, the forefeet must be together and the head held low. By weakening the neck muscles the second object is achieved; spectators will also observe that the matador holds the *muleta* low with his left hand and allows the bull to follow it down with his head. When the matador, sighting along his sword, suddenly turns away, it means that the bull has made a movement that has separated the forefeet.

A bull is in the ring for twenty minutes and if, at the end of that time he is killed with a single accurate thrust you may say that he has had a better life and death than the victim of our Sunday joint. But even the most skilful matador may only wound and may fail to kill at the second and third attempt too. This is where the *lidia* degenerates into butchery and the bull may be despatched with the special sword called the *verduguillo*, 'the little executioner'. This form of slaughter, or *descabello*, also calls for special skill as the weapon has to be inserted between the vertebrae of the spinal column in the neck, while the matador stands in a particularly vulnerable position should the bull summon up a reserve of strength and aggressiveness. The *verduguillo* has a guard exactly 100 millimetres from the tip according to the regulations, and 78 millimetres in length. The reason for the guard is a strange one and goes back a comparatively short time. An unguarded sword occasionally had an unexpected career and on one occasion, in Corunna, Juan Belmonte killed a spectator when the bull tossed the unguarded sword out of its neck and into the audience. Those who prefer front row seats may now rest assured that they will sustain no more than 100 millimetres of steel if the performance is repeated.

One member of the audience deserves a brief mention, the *espontáneo*. Many an enthusiastic amateur, balked for too long in his efforts to belong to the élite of the bull ring, leaps over the barrier and begins to play the bull with his jacket until the attendants lead him out. The Rules legislate for him too, the fine is specified, his enforced absence from corridas set at two years. And yet they go on doing it, for this is one way to catch the eye of the talent scout; they may interrupt the set course of the fight, they may even put the official toreros in danger by breaking the spell which they have begun to weave over the bull, but dozens of leading bullfighters have begun their career in this way; Ortega and El Cordobés are only two who have broken into the game by an unexpected leap into the ring.

Not all foreigners realise the importance of the corrida in Spanish life. It has been the subject of legislation, litigation and almost assassination. It has inspired novelists, painters and poets. Among the latter Rubén Dario has perhaps most aptly summarised the Spaniard's subconscious justification of the bullfight; here is a dialogue:

BULL: Yesterday the air, the sun; today the executioner. What more horrible than this martyrdom?

OX: Impotence!

BULL: And what darker than death?

OX: The yoke.

CHAPTER SEVEN

Seville – The Northern City

✣

Palacio de la Condesa de Lebrija—Santa Catalina—Palace of the Duke of Alba—Convent of Santa Paula—La Macarena— Torre de Don Fadrique—Calle de la Feria—Museo de Bellas Artes

If you spent a fortnight in Seville, planned your visits intelligently, found all the churches open at the right moment and didn't linger to look at things, you could probably get round all the sights that are usually listed in guide books. I shall pay most attention to the visits that embody something different, rare or amusing; however much we respect the masters, we must remember that Montañés and Murillo turned out hundreds of works of art in their lifetimes. We shall see many of them; to try to see all seems to me to be mere record hunting.

To see the northern half of the city begin at the Campana, a busy intersection hard by the public garden of the Duque de la Victoria, which used to be the private garden of the Duke of Medina Sidonia. The name *campana*, or bell, commemorates the fire brigade that used to be quartered in this strategic position at the geographical centre of the city. To the south is the narrow and unremarkable Calle de las Sierpes, intended for pedestrians, and given over to cafés, clubs and commerce. The name *sierpes*, meaning snakes, is probably taken from an old inn sign that used to hang here.

As you walk east from La Campana the next turning on the right is the Calle de Cuna, or Cradle Street, where the Foundling Home used to stand; Ford castigated it for the neglect of the unfortunate inmates whom he saw, apparently ignorant of the fact that mortality in similar institutions in England, France and the United States of America at that time varied from 75 to 90 per cent. Not far down on the right is the **Palacio de la Condesa de Lebrija**. A short *zaguán* leads to a beautiful wrought-iron *cancela*, through which arrangements can usually be made for a subsequent visit; groups are made especially welcome. While you are there, examine the Roman pavement below the screen, a fine

1 Campana
2 Palacio de la Condesa de Lebrija
3 Old University
4 Church of San Pedro
5 Ch. of Santa Catalina
6 Palace of Duke of Alba
7 Ch. of San Juan de la Palma
8 Ch. of San Marcos
9 Convent of Santa Paula
10 Ch. of Santa Marina
11 Almohad fortifications
12 Hospital de la Sangre
13 Ch. of San Gil
14 Ch. Omnium Sanctorum
15 Conv. Santa Clara
16 Torre de Don
    Fadrique
17 Market
18 Museo de
Bellas Artes

example of *opus sectile*, and the eighteenth-century tiles which
form the magnificently coloured dado. Inside, there are examples
of Roman mosaic flooring in the large patio and in every living-
room of the ground floor; all this, as well as the busts and statues
which adorn the corners, comes from the former city of Itálica.
There are many smaller antiquities in show cases, and over the
grand staircase are the *artesonado* and Mudéjar stucco panels
from the former castle of the Dukes of Osuna at Marchena.

Returning to the main east-west street, the last house on the
right (No. 3) is that of the Motilla family, said to be descended
from the Scottish knight, Laurence Poore, who was the first to
climb the Giralda after the reconquest of Seville. Round the
corner you find that the Old University building is continuous
with this mansion, its entrance being in the Calle Laraña. It

occupies the old Jesuit House and has done so since 1771, but recently most of the faculties have moved to the former Tobacco Factory of operatic fame. The Old University is chiefly notable for its church, which contains many fine works of art by Roelas, Alonso Cano, Montañés, Juan de Mesa and others. The church is *en obras*, alleged repairs that are equivalent to a life sentence, without hard labour. One suspects that the excuse is put forward when works of art have reached an advanced state of dilapidation; certainly the rest of the old building, with tiles falling from the walls, cries out for restoration.

To the east is the Church of San Pedro on the left, notable not so much for the fine *Liberation of St. Peter* by Roelas, as for the fact that Velázquez was baptised here in 1599. Farther on, (the street is now named after Juan de Mesa) is the Church of Santa Catalina. The brickwork of the Mudéjar apses, with their lobulated blind arcades, is noteworthy, as are the crenellated Mudéjar tower rising from what was probably an Almohad minaret and the square chapel with cupola nestling against it. For those who can stand sudden changes the overloaded Baroque interior is worth a cautious glance.

Behind Santa Catalina the Calle de Gerona leads to the Calle de las Dueñas by a cross-street, María Coronel; this lady was alleged by some to have been the mistress of Pedro the Cruel, by others to have deliberately burned her face in a pan of frying doughnuts in order that her disfigurement might save her from the fate that was worse than death. Turning right you reach the **Palace of the Duke of Alba**, part of which can be seen when the family is not in residence. It has been rescued from the ruin which threatened it at the beginning of the last century and is now a fine example of an Andalucian upper-class residence. The palace should not be visited as a museum, but as an example of the happy blend of all fashions and styles from the Mudéjar onward.

About two hundred yards to the west is the little Church of San Juan de la Palma whose treasures are of slight interest; the best known is the statue of the *Virgen de la Amargura* (Virgin of the Bitterness), one of the favourites of the Holy Week processions, carved by La Roldana, the gifted daughter of Pedro Roldán, a leading sculptor of the seventeenth century. The church is remarkable, however, for being built on the site of a mosque from which an interesting inscription, now in the Archaeological Museum, has been recovered. It records, in raised Cufic characters, that Itimad Al-Rumaikiya, wife of Al-

Mutamid, king of the *taifa* of Seville, ordered the building of the minaret. In the usual fashion the names are a genealogical table in themselves, but among all the inscriptions reading 'whom Allah preserve', and 'may Allah look on him (her) with favour', one finds that she was the mother of a son and that the dedication was made towards the end of 1085.

Rumaikiya was the favourite wife of the last Abbad king of Seville, whom one might call Mutamid the Unpredictable, poet and murderer. Their mutual affection, which lasted until he died a prisoner of the Almoravids, began in the following way. Mutamid and his best friend Ibn Ammar the vizier, whom he later killed, were walking along the riverside promenade, near where the present bull ring is situated; the poet-king made up a couplet which his companion was supposed to expand into a quatrain. While Ibn Ammar was thinking a girl in the passing crowd answered with an appropriate second couplet. The impulsive king ordered a eunuch to conduct the girl to the palace. where he found that her name was Itimad, that she was a slave, usually called Rumaikiya after her master Rumaik, and worked as a mule driver. On hearing, too, that she was unmarried, he announced that he would buy, and then marry her.

Behind the Duke's palace is the Church of San Marcos, or rather the façade and tower, all that remain after a disastrous fire. The former is of a simple Gothic style, with dog-tooth ornament, in an *alfiz* ornamented above with the *sebka* pattern found on the Giralda. There are stone statues projecting from the wall, just as are so often seen on Romanesque church fronts, only these have the characteristic Gothic canopies. The result of this strange mixture is one of the most attractive church portals imaginable.

The **Convent of Santa Paula** is at the end of the street of that name, a hundred yards farther on. Its church portal, approached through a quiet garden, is another example of the happy union of various styles; this time the Mudéjar element is enhanced by being built of brick, while Renaissance additions consist of medallions and heraldry in glorious ceramic, most of it the work of the celebrated Niculoso of Pisa. It was he who added Renaissance concepts to the ancient art of Sevillian pottery and not only gave his name to the Pisano tile but introduced two new colours, rose and violet. This doorway is regarded as one of his masterpieces, though part of the credit must go to Pedro Millán. The interior is notable for three things: the *artesonado* ceiling, the

Gothic apse and the three ceramic tombs. The ceiling is one of the works of a Christian-Spanish carpenter, Diego López de Arenas, who deserves immortality for writing the first and only authoritative work on the Moorish or Moslem type of woodwork. The *Carpinteria de lo Blanco* has run through several editions and gives information obtainable nowhere else, even though we cannot guess the meaning of many of the numerous Arabic words and phrases that he employs.

The tombs, which are built into the walls at the other end of the single nave, are of rare beauty. Their fronts consist of *azulejos* in groups, heraldic crests and inscriptions in Gothic characters, all of ceramic. They house the bodies of the founder and benefactress, Doña Isabel Enríquez, a Portuguese lady descended from kings of Castile and Portugal, and wife of the Constable of Portugal, who lies here too. Their tombs are on the left; on the right lies her brother, Don León Enríquez, whose tomb preserves the only original inscription, as the others are recent replacements. It is difficult to describe the charm of these tombs; the *azulejos* are divided into panels which look very much like hanging Oriental rugs. Their colours are restrained, one using only blue, green, brown and white, even for the blazon which quarters the arms of Enríquez and Portugal.

Five hundred yards along the Calle de San Luis, from San Marcos, is the façade of the burnt-out Church of Santa Marina, which also has stone saints with canopies on the wall. Both churches have converted Mudéjar towers with lacy brick patterns and blind arcades. Farther along the street is the *Puerta de la Macarena*, in the Almohad fortifications which extend to the right in a well preserved state for about half a mile. Beyond that the great road that circles the town follows the line of the old Almohad walls, of which traces can be seen here and there. Here at the gate they show the typical Almohad *antemuro*, a lower outer wall castellated in the same way as the main one, and at various distances seven square towers and one octagonal. The name Macarena is that of a long-forgotten Arab damsel, daughter of one of the local rulers; the whole district, for long a poor and unsavoury one, is called after her; so too is the most famous Virgin of them all.

Outside the city, opposite the Puerta de la Macarena, is the **Hospital de la Sangre** or Cinco Llagas: whether called 'Blood' or 'Five Wounds' it sounds ominous to those not steeped in Catholic tradition. It is a fine building of the sixteenth century, a combination of Renaissance and Baroque styles, and its church contains the usual ration of painting and sculpture; its pleasantest feature, however, is the steeple on the left, with its covering of *azulejos*. The fact that it lies outside the walls suggests that it may originally have been intended for infectious cases; occasionally one reads of a Seville hospital for *las bubas*, the syphilis epidemic that raged through Europe in the sixteenth century, and we know that the poet Juan de Salinas was rewarded with the lucrative post of superintendent. It seems just possible that the Cinco Llagas was at one time set aside for this disease, like the hospital at Úbeda.

Inside the gate is the **Church of San Gil**, one of the earliest Christian foundations and probably built on the site of a mosque. The name is taken from the Church of San Gil in Segovia, whence the founder, Bishop Raymond, received the first baptismal water for his font. Only the apse remains of the first church, but this is worth a visit, for its interior has geometric mosaic tile designs of the late thirteenth century and represents a landmark in the long history of Sevillian pottery. In the left aisle a small passage leads to the modern basilica built to house the celebrated *Virgen de la Macarena*, or more properly *de la Esperanza*. She is a Dolorosa of the seventeenth century, attributed to Pedro Roldán or one of his school; some say that only a woman's sympathy could have produced a work of such deep feeling and Pedro's daughter Luisa, la Roldana, is usually credited with the work.

As in other representations, the Virgin is far too young to be the mother of a man of thirty or more and her display of jewellery accords ill with her mood. Nevertheless, the Duchess of Alba lends her own jewellery each Holy Week to increase the aura of divinity produced by the golden crown, the gold-encrusted velvet cloak, the silver candlesticks and the banks of white carnations. La Macarena is the protector of the poor, who are particularly numerous in her parish, and of bullfighters. Even Manolete, Cordoban born and bred, presented her treasury with his 'suit of lights' when he returned unharmed from a tour of Mexico.

Returning through the narrow, winding streets of this populous quarter you should take a look at the Church of Omnium Sanctorum for its Gothic-Mudéjar façade and the Mudéjar tower with its *sebka* decoration. Across the historic Calle de la Feria is the **Alameda de Hercules**. This promenade, built to replace an offensive swamp in the reign of Philip II, has two great columns at each end. Those at the south are genuinely Roman, presumably from a temple, and were brought here with an effort comparable to the labours of Hercules, as an inscription on one of them states. Quite fittingly, they are crowned with statues of Hercules and Julius Caesar, sixteenth-century works by Diego de Pesquera.

About two hundred yards to the west is the Convent of Santa Clara; its entrance patio, or *compás* in the Andalucian dialect, is one of Seville's most beautiful squares, quiet, cobbled and studded with orange trees. In the grounds stands the **Torre de Don Fadrique**, a landmark that can be seen from the Giralda; its architecture is transitional Romanesque-Gothic, agreeing with the date 1252 mentioned in the verse engraved over the door. Fadrique was a younger son of St. Ferdinand III, who died in the year that the tower was built, and therefore brother of Alfonso the Learned. He was killed at the orders of the third brother, Sancho the Wild, who thus inherited the throne by a method too often used by the monarchs of Castile. The tower stands in the rather unkempt garden and consists of three storeys; the ceiling of the top one has ribs which spring from corbels carved to resemble human heads, certainly the first examples of mediaeval sculpture in Seville.

You should now return to the **Calle de la Feria** where a weekly open-air market has been held for centuries. If you have arranged the visit for a Thursday you will encounter the same thronged and noisy atmosphere in which the young Murillo sketched every week. His best-known child studies, *Los Niños de la Concha* and *El buen Pastor*, both in the Prado, embody the angelic-looking little rogues one still sees in the Calle de la Feria.

Follow the street southward and you face what was once an Arab palace given to the Duke of Feria at the time of the Reconquest. The Calle de la Feria is said to take its name from the fair that we have just seen; but it could have been called after the first Christian owner of the palace. During the last century it belonged to the Count of Benamejí, whose daughter eloped with a bandolero. The entrance is in the Calle Viriato and the Renaissance gateway leads into a narrow lane that runs between cottages and has its own street-lamps. All this is inside the old palace and the lane was presumably one of the main corridors, for the old *almenado* tile frieze runs along both walls.

At the end, a turn to the right brings you to a picturesque if neglected patio, whose walls still sport the tile frieze. A horseshoe arch, possibly a relic of the Arab palace and unfortunately white-washed, leads to a larger patio surrounded by cottages. In this

I

there is a charming centre-piece of two palms, a cluster of orange trees and a street-lamp. A narrow passage at the far end preserves most of its ceramic dado and leads through a more modern building that was once a government school of art, to the Calle Gerónimo Hernández. Immediately facing you is the back entrance to the central market. Picking your way between heaps of oranges, and piles of prawns and hake you emerge opposite the Old University, a few yards from La Campana again.

To find the **Museo de Bellas Artes** is simple, for you start again at La Campana and go westward along the Calle de Alfonso XII. It is best to plan the visit for a morning, as the art gallery is open for only an hour in the afternoon. After five minutes' walk you come to a small formal garden on the left of the street, in which stands a bronze statue of Murillo. Behind it is the massive museum building that was originally the Convento de Nuestra Señora de la Gracia, or de la Merced, one of whose inmates in the early seventeenth century was Tirso de Molina, creator of Don Juan; his portrait in Madrid shows the face of a satyr over the habit of a monk. The Museum of Art was founded in 1838, two years after the suppression of the monasteries, and its nucleus was formed by art treasures salvaged from the abandoned convents.

The entrance corridor and most of the passages and patios are lined with dadoes of sixteenth and seventeenth-century tiles, brought here through the efforts of Dean Manuel López Cepero. The lay-out is continually changing and the threat of *obras* hangs over any old building in which walls may dampen or roofs leak.

The first patio is called *del Aljibe*, from the central well, and on the wall there is a picture in ceramic, signed by Cristóbal de Augusta in 1577, representing the Virgin sheltering monks and nuns under her outstretched cloak, a theme to which we shall return later. The first room on the left contains works of Valdés Leal (1630–91), a contemporary of Murillo who adopted the latter's *vaporoso* style, blended it with Venetian tricks such as the use of a red ground smeared with lighter colours, and produced some unfortunate results. Most of the examples shown here are of his later mannerist style in which restlessness predominates; among the exceptions are scenes from the life of St. Ignatius Loyola.

In the large *Camino del Calvario*, showing St. John leading the Virgin and the three holy women to the site of crucifixion, the facial expressions and the diagonal leaning forward of the figures produce the desired effect of urgency. Less successful is the *Temptation of St. Jerome* by four of the least appetising females ever put on canvas, even by fashionable portrait painters. The most sympathetic work here is the *Head of John the Baptist*, in which the absence of limbs and the inappropriateness of facial expression force the painter to rely on drawing and chiaroscuro.

On the way to the large patio look for the green ceramic baptismal font of the fifteenth century, with its floral decoration in relief, a product of the Triana potteries. Off the passage along the glassed-in patio, or cloister, is a seated Madonna in terracotta by Torrigiano, perhaps the very one that made the Duke of Arcos eager to possess a similar work, with such unfortunate results for the artist. Farther on is the only El Greco in the Museum, the portrait of an artist with brush and palette. Since it has been shown that the features are identical with those of the worshipper in El Greco's *Virgen de la Caridad* at Illescas who has been established as the artist's son, we can be certain that we have here a portrait of Jorge Emanuel Theotocopulo.

In what was the convent church you will find the cream of this collection, which itself ranks second in importance in Spain. First come three statues, two of them by Montañés, representing St. Bruno in Carthusian habit and St. Domingo de Guzmán penitent. The latter is customarily shown holding a cross in his left hand and a knotted rope for flagellation in his right. The third statue is a St. Jerome by Torrigiano which is said to have had a great influence on subsequent Spanish sculptors.

To the right are the sanctuary and crossing of the old convent church, now wholly devoted to the works of Murillo. There are more than twenty of his works here and though a few may be cloying, none is objectionable. Among them can be distinguished his three styles. The first, the *frío*, or cold, is based on the hard outline that he learned from Zurbarán and the dull blacks and dark browns that he acquired from his master, Juan del Castillo. The *negro de hueso* was, as the name implies, made from the beef bones of the stew-pot, and was a favourite pigment of Sevillian artists until well into the present century. The second, or *cálido* style infused some warmth by paying more attention to colour and chiaroscuro, while retaining the hard outline of his earlier work. An anonymous critic is credited with the original remark that Murillo's faces now appeared to be compounded of milk and blood. The phrase *el rostro bañado de leche y sangre*, 'the face bathed in milk and blood', was in fact used by Tirso de

Molina, who trod this very floor several times each day, in his play about Don Juan, written before Murillo was eight years old. The last style is called the *vaporoso*: by softening the tones and outlines a more ethereal effect was produced.

Murillo's *Immaculate Conception* paintings were discussed earlier; the demand for them was endless and he cannot be blamed for trying to satisfy it. Among the four examples in this museum is the largest and most famous, in which four cherubs support the Virgin as she stands with raised, joined hands and blue cloak floating behind.

Among the other Murillos here are a Dolorosa and the *Virgen de la Servilleta*. The story of this small but charming Mother and Child is that Murillo painted it without a previous commission: he had been working at the Capuchin convent and when his task was done the lay brother who had cooked and served his meals asked for a painting from the artist's own brush as a mark of friendship. Unfortunately, the story goes, Murillo had used up all his canvas, so the cook produced a table napkin on which the artist painted this memorable picture. The serene mother, proud and patient, and the lively Child, seemingly attempting to push Himself out of the picture, have never been surpassed for tenderness and realism.

Most authorities agree with the artist that his best painting— he used to call it simply *mi lienzo*, 'my picture'—is *The Charity of St. Thomas Villanueva*. The subject, an Archbishop of Valencia, was a favourite of Murillo and you could say that Murillo practically illustrated his career, from the time when, as a boy, he distributed his clothes among poor children. The saint's figure dominates the large canvas and each figure in the foreground repays study. There is the lame, half-naked beggar receiving alms, the urchin delighted with the coppers that have been his portion, and another with ringworm, characters that obviously date back to the artist's days in the Calle de la Feria. Ringworm seems to have been quite a favourite with Murillo and his famous St. Elizabeth of Hungary, which we shall see in the Caridad, gives an accurate clinical picture of a child's head with *tiña* (from the Latin *tinea*, a gnawing worm). There is nothing morbid about this preoccupation; the disease must have been extremely common at that time for special hospitals to have been set aside for its treatment.

It was probably the combination of wealth and decadence that allowed philosophy and the arts to flourish; perhaps that is why such a galaxy of outstanding painters were born in the last quarter of Spain's Golden Century or the first quarter of the succeeding seventeenth. Herrera the Elder, who once taught Velázquez; Pacheco, who also taught him and became his father-in-law; Velázquez himself, Ribera, Zurbarán, Alonso Cano and Murillo: all were working in the year 1650. Most of them may be seen in this converted church or the adjoining halls.

Herrera the Elder, *el Viejo*, so called to distinguish him from his artist son *el Mozo*, was a peculiar person. Impetuous and gifted, his fiery genius not only produced works of the highest quality but alienated his family and his pupils, Velázquez among them. So deserted was he at one time that he had his maidservant apply the paints with a coarse brush, then moulded and modified them to their final form. If this is true it would fit well with his use of impasto, anticipating in some ways the use of the palette knife. He was also a skilled engraver on copper, and used this ability to make counterfeit money, which got him into trouble. He fled to the Jesuits' College for sanctuary, and there painted an altar piece portraying the Apotheosis of St. Hermengild. The ground floor is occupied by those two standbys of Seville, St. Leander and St. Isidore, and by the son of Hermengild, crowned and kneeling. After Philip IV, patron of artists, visited Seville in 1624 and asked who had painted the masterpiece he was admiring, Herrera was released from sanctuary to return home, and again become unbearable.

The tremendous influence on art of Fràncisco Pacheco through his patronage of Velázquez need not be stressed again, but we must not forget his great contribution, *The Treatise on Painting* (*Arte de la Pintura*) for which he is most famous, and which was published when he was seventy-eight years old. In the neighbouring gallery he is represented by his portrait of San Pedro Nolasco embarking on one of his voyages to ransom Christian captives in Barbary. Little is known about the saint's life, or that of the co-founder of the Mercedarian Order, St. Raymund Nonnatus, except that the latter owed his cognomen ('not born') to his alleged delivery by Caesarian section. When Philip II died in 1598, Pacheco was selected to paint the grandiose catafalque for the official mourning in the Cathedral.

Juan de las Roelas, Zurbarán's master, is known chiefly for his altar piece in the Church of St. Isidore, described in the next chapter. Here in the Museum he is represented by another crowded canvas, the Martyrdom of St. Andrew, where the elevated body of the apostle just manages to bridge that awkward horizontal line, so characteristic of Spanish Baroque Art. There is a story that Roelas asked the College of St. Thomas, for whom the picture was painted, for a fee of 2000 ducats; the College offered 1000. No compromise could be reached and the picture was sent to Flanders to be valued. To the surprise of the College the picture was valued at 3000 ducats, which Roelas insisted on receiving.

Zurbarán has been left as the climax, for no one will dispute his pre-eminence among the artists in the nave. Stirling-Maxwell called him 'the peculiar painter of monks, as Raphael is of Madonnas and Ribera of martyrdoms.' Zurbarán is said to have learned the chiaroscuro, not from his master Roelas, but from Ribera and thus at second-hand from Caravaggio. In his portraiture he may even exceed the Italian master: for instance that of Luis Beltrán, mistaken for Enrique Suzón, in monk's robes and cowl, and the various subjects in the great *Apotheosis of St. Thomas Aquinas*. In this great canvas we see not only the customary two horizontal levels, but a third, upper one in which can be distinguished the Trinity, the Virgin, St. Paul and St. Dominic. St. Thomas Aquinas' features are said to be those of Don Augustín Abreu Núñez de Escóbar, prebendary of Seville. In the lower part is another portrait, easily recognised as that of Charles V, the first kneeling figure on the right; immediately behind him is a face reminiscent of Velázquez's self-portrait, which is said to be that of Zurbarán himself.

The St. Thomas may be labelled Zurbarán's greatest picture; most visitors will find others here far more to their taste. There is the procession of holy women in their gorgeous dresses, originally painted for the Hospital de la Sangre. We may guess that the models for these lovely saints were chosen from the aristocracy, for there are still traces of the rouge which all the ladies of the court used in 1665. There is the somewhat posed interview of St. Bruno and Pope Urban II, in which the carpet in the foreground is sadly out of perspective, and St. Bruno's champion and helper. St. Hugh of Grenoble, catching the Carthusian monks in the act of eating forbidden meat.

All these paintings, with their emphasis on light and shade, their restrained, rich colours and their three-dimensional impact, bring Zurbarán into the front rank of painters of any nationality. Though he was painter to the king, little remains of the work he was called on to do and we remember him chiefly for his religious studies.

A strange history attaches to the *Virgen de las Cuevas*, in apricot gown and with cherubs holding her blue cloak over kneeling Carthusian monks. The same theme was seen in tile in the first patio and it is repeated in the Alcázar. The protection of the Virgin's mantle goes back to fifteenth-century France, where it is frequently pictured in painting and bas-relief. Here in Spain she is the Virgin of the Caves, allegedly because her cloak acts as a shelter; it is far more likely that she is so called because this picture is one of those that Zurbarán painted for the Carthusian monastery of Santa Maria de las Cuevas in Seville. Strangest of all, this Carthusian group owes its origin to the Cistercians. Early in the thirteenth century a Cistercian monk is recorded as having recounted a dream to his abbot: he had been in Heaven and seen the Church triumphant. The prophets were there and the apostles and the innumerable crowd of monks; all were there—except the Cistercians. Boldly he asked the Virgin Mother why there were no Cistercians in Heaven. At which, opening her arms, she showed him the monks of Cîteaux hidden under the folds of her great mantle; she wanted them there because she loved them more than all the others. We cannot tell whether Zurbarán knew of this pretty story; it seems to be quite forgotten in the Spain of today.

Upstairs are the moderns, but before seeing them you may pause in a small room, the Sala Gestoso, devoted to ceramics and armour. On the wall hangs a lustre barber's bowl, a rare enough piece. All barbers' bowls have a curved section taken out of the rim, which can then be fitted below the chin for shaving or against the arm for blood-letting. A bowl of this kind, made of brass, used to hang outside every barber's shop until quite recently; it is the same bowl that Don Quixote mistook for Mambrino's helmet.

Several halls are devoted to the romantics and moderns; there is a Bacaresas entitled *Sevilla en Fiesta*, an explosion of light amid clashing colours, and Múñoz Degrain, Picasso's teacher, is represented by a seated huntsman. Various townscapes are on view in the Sala de García Ramos, an artist who lived near by at No. 14 Calle Fernán Caballero, the very house that had been occupied by Fernán Caballero herself. Ferdinand was a woman novelist, Cecilia Böhl von Faber, with a German father and a mother of mixed Irish and Spanish descent. Though no one reads her novels today, she deserves to be remembered for her collection of folk poetry, Andalucian *coplas* that she helped to save from oblivion.

CHAPTER EIGHT

Seville – The Southern City

~

La Magdalena—The Ayuntamiento—El Salvador—San Isidoro
—Casa de Pilatos—Barrio de Santa Cruz—The Alcázar—Archivo
de Indias—Fábrica de Tabacos—Hospital de la Caridad—Triana
—Parque de María Luisa—Archaeological Museum

The Plaza Nueva is a good beginning for a tour of the sights of
the southern half of Seville. It is also called the Plaza San Fernando, because the centre of its palm garden has a modern
statue of the conqueror of Seville. Of more interest was the stone
statue of the Commander of Calatrava, which used to stand in the
cloister of the Franciscan convent here. In the original play
about Don Juan, written by Tirso de Molina, the Commander
was Gonzalo de Ulloa. He was killed by Juan while trying to
avenge the honour of his daughter Doña Ana, and his statue
features in the second half of the play's title, *El Burlador de
Sevilla y el Convidado de Piedra*. Juan is of course the Joker of
Seville; the Stone Guest is Gonzalo's statue which accepts Juan's
mocking invitation to supper, after having its stone beard pulled
insultingly, and finishes the party by squeezing its host to death.

Two hundred yards north-west from the Plaza Nueva is the
Church of la Magdalena, which has to be seen in a digression from
our route. The building itself is typically Sevillian Baroque, by
Leonardo de Figueroa, and occupies the site of the former
Church of San Pablo; for this reason it preserves the Gothic plan
of three aisles with transepts and a wide crossing. Inside, it is
chiefly notable for the profusion of frescoes, the work of Lucas
Valdés, son of Valdés Leal. The Chapel of la Quinta Angustia
has a Mudéjar cupola with the typical sunburst pattern of interlacing wooden strips, or *lazo* work. The design is usually described
as *lazo de diez, de doce*, etc., according to the number of rays;
this one has sixteen. In the Capilla Sacramental, on the right, are
two Zurbaráns that demonstrate his usual mastery of lighting,
colour and drapery. That showing the miraculous cure of the
Blessed Reginald of Orleans is attractive for the dull violet and red
robes and for the charming still life on the invalid's bedside table.

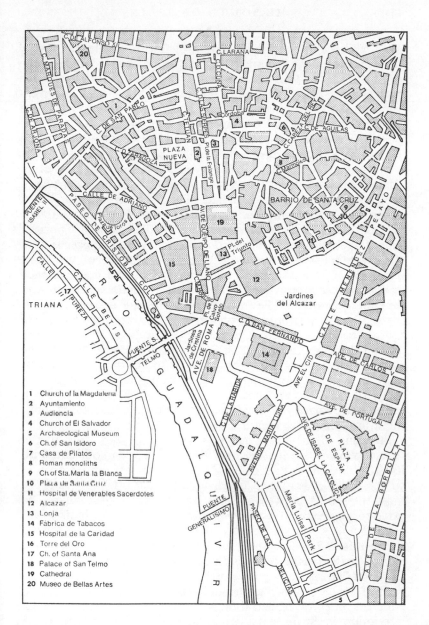

1 Church of la Magdalena
2 Ayuntamiento
3 Audiencia
4 Church of El Salvador
5 Archaeological Museum
6 Ch. of San Isidoro
7 Casa de Pilatos
8 Roman monoliths
9 Ch. of Sta. María la Blanca
10 Plaza de Santa Cruz
11 Hospital de Venerables Sacerdotes
12 Alcazar
13 Lonja
14 Fábrica de Tabacos
15 Hospital de la Caridad
16 Torre del Oro
17 Ch. of Santa Ana
18 Palace of San Telmo
19 Cathedral
20 Museo de Bellas Artes

La Magdalena saw the baptism of Murillo on the 1st January, 1618, and the investiture as bishop of Bartolomé de Las Casas, the Apostle of the Indians. Born in Seville and ordained in the West Indies, he fought against the ill-treatment to which the natives were being subjected. Though doubtless given to exaggeration, his intentions were good and he was able to rouse the conscience of Cardinal Cisneros. It has been said that the supposedly beneficial introduction of Negro slaves into the Western Hemisphere was the result of Las Casas' pleading.

Returning to the Plaza Nueva you see before you the severe Renaissance façade of the **Ayuntamiento**, or *Casas Capitulares*, built mainly during the first half of the sixteenth century. The other side, the east façade, looks on to the Plaza de la Falange Española and straight across to the Audiencia, the Court of Appeal, rebuilt after a disastrous fire in 1918. The east side of the Ayuntamiento is universally regarded as one of the finest examples of Plateresque architecture, its classical lines softened and embellished by the multitude of animal, vegetable and fanciful decorations. The entrance is on this side and the interior, especially the vestibule, is typical of the transition from late Gothic to Renaissance. The municipal archives upstairs rank among the most important in Spain, preserving as they do the rarest of documents from the reign of the Catholic sovereigns. Here in a glass case is the famous city banner, with its seated figure of St. Ferdinand, made in the second half of the fifteenth century to replace the previous one which was becoming worn out after a mere two centuries.

Standing in the Plaza de la Falange with your back to the Ayuntamiento, the Sierpes opens immediately on your left, with its attractive shops and cafés. At the north-east corner a short curved street leads to the **Church of El Salvador**. This is one of the most interesting as well as least known sights of Seville. The exterior may remind you of a railway station, with its exaggerated finials and volutes, but the interior and the patio make up for this. You can enter it either from the Plaza del Salvador, alongside the façade with its three doors, or from the Calle de Córdoba that runs along the north boundary. This was the courtyard of Seville's principal mosque, that of Omar Ibn Adabbas, built by order of Abderrahman II in 829. The oldest Arabic inscription in Spain, carved in Cufic characters, tells us these facts and may be seen in the Archaeological Museum. The mosque itself survived the Vikings' attempt to burn it down in 844, was thereafter regarded as having been preserved by a miracle and became an object of great veneration. Periodic floods, from which Seville suffered until the construction of proper embankments at the end of last century, deposited alluvial mud and raised the ground level; 'improvements' swept away the orange trees and central ablution fountain in 1671. But the walls of the patio remain.

The tops of the columns project only a foot or two above the ground and their bases are said to be about 6 feet deeper. The capitals are Roman and Visigothic—in fact some believe that a Visigothic church once stood here—and they support the brick arches between which modern houses have been built. The minaret, now the bell tower, was situated in the north wall of the patio, next to the entrance, exactly like the one at Córdoba. The lower courses are still those of the caliphate, with Almohad additions, all of yellow sandstone with the tell-tale *soga y tizón*. Most of it fell down in the earthquake of 1079 and Mutamid (he who married the slave girl), built it up again in a month, as inscribed on the marble tablet over the holy water stoup at the entrance to the church. Above this part is a section of Gothic tower, and at the very top it is Baroque; adjoining it is the house of the bell ringer who reaches his front door by the internal spiral stair that the muezzin climbed a thousand years ago.

As you enter the church from the patio, passing the tablet of Mutamid on your left, you see another stoup and over it a fine relief of the Adoration of the Shepherds by Juan de Oviedo, salvaged from the old *retablo mayor*. The present huge retablo, which Ford would undoubtedly have called 'a fricassée in gilt', may please some; probably more interesting is the giant St. Christopher on the left, the earliest known work of Martínez Montañés and one of his most admirable.

On the right, in an ornate niche, is the *Virgen de las Aguas*. Her title is derived from a quaint tale: St. Ferdinand had ordered several images from which to choose and could not make up his mind which to take. He was therefore in a dilemma, *entre dos aguas*, 'between two waters', as the Spanish phrase expresses it, and his predicament was transferred to the Virgin of his eventual choice. On the right of the entrance to the sacristy is a pleasing group, St. Anne instructing the Virgin, by Montes de Oca who carved so many subjects, including this one, in La Magdalena. The Passion figures by Montañés and his favourite pupil Juan de Mesa are famous; the latter made the well-known *Cristo del Amor* with an exaggerated crown of thorns. The name is derived from the story that an incredulous or agnostic artisan dreamed that one of those long thorns pierced his breast and woke up converted, with his heart full of love.

From El Salvador to the **Church of San Isidoro** is another hundred yards to the east. The south entrance is through a Gothic portal, with zigzag ornament on the archivolt, and under a bell tower crowned with *azulejos*. Among the works of art inside one should see the *Tránsito de San Isidoro* by Juan de las Roelas. Though the word *tránsito* denotes the death of the saint, it happened that his body *was* transferred from Seville to León about four hundred years after he died. King Ferdinand I of León and Castile, who had reduced the *taifa* king of Seville, Abbad Ibn Mohamed, Al-Mutadid, to a sufficiently respectful dependent, sent an embassy to ask for the body of the virgin St. Justa. I have emphasised before the importance of holy relics in the Middle Ages, so there is no need to stress the consternation when Al-Mutadid confessed that no one knew the whereabouts of the saint. But Bishop Alvito, head of the embassy, had a dream, three times repeated in which a venerable ecclesiastic appeared to him saying, 'As the divine will does not consent to the city being deprived of this virgin, God in his mercy, not wishing you to go away empty-handed, has granted you my body instead.' With justifiable caution Alvito asked the apparition whom he had the honour of addressing, and received the reply, 'I am Isidore, the doctor of the Spains and bishop of this city.' This was good fortune indeed, for Isidore ranks fairly high among the saints; the usual phenomena, such as the divine odour of the remains and assorted miracles, confirmed it and the body was conveyed to León, performing more miracles as it went.

Behind S. Isidoro is the Calle Cabeza del Rey Don Pedro. The story of why Pedro the Cruel's head should be reproduced in stone on one of the walls, is too long to be told in detail. Briefly, during his nocturnal wanderings he had murdered an inoffensive citizen and disappeared without being seen. His police were unable to find the culprit, to the king's pretended annoyance, until an old woman, living at the corner of the Calle del Candilejo, came forward and said she had heard the murderer walking away, his knees clicking in the way peculiar to Pedro himself. Known as *el Monarca Justiciero*, Pedro had to find a solution to this predicament; he therefore ordered an effigy of himself and handed it over to the authorities for summary execution, stipulating that its head should subsequently be displayed at the scene of the crime.

The Calle de Águilas brings us to the **Casa de Pilatos** which ranks nearly as high as the Cathedral and the Alcázar as a 'must' for the visitor. The entrance gate of marble is the work of Genoese sculptors, Apprile and Bisono, of 1533, and carries three examples of the Jerusalem cross; this consists of an ordinary cross with a small one in each of the four compartments. The building was begun towards the end of the fifteenth century by Pedro Enríquez and his wife Catalina de Ribera; their son, Fadrique de Ribera (note the use of the mother's name) completed it and enriched it with marbles brought from Italy. Fadrique was a great traveller and did the Jerusalem pilgrimage in 1519—which was responsible for the unfounded belief that the palace was modelled on the praetorium of Pontius Pilate; a belief which also prompted some of the *cofradías*, whose Holy Week processions were at one time symbolic of the Via Crucis, to begin at the Casa de Pilatos, visit various sites marked out as Stations of the Cross and finish at the Cruz del Campo outside the city walls. The starting point of the Via Crucis is marked on the wall to the left of the entrance by a recessed cross in jasper, and near it is a plaque commemorating the canonisation in 1960 of Juan de Ribera, a relation of the founder.

Inside is the usual plan of an outer court and an inner patio which, in this case, is the principal one. Here again is an example of that happy mingling of Mudéjar and Plateresque. The general lay-out with two storeys, is typically Renaissance, as is the low balustrade above. The slender marble columns, the dentate arches, the ornate stucco, the geminate windows with their *alfices* and, above all, the tiles, all take us back to Moslem traditions. The series of *azulejo* panels, up to twelve feet high, that decorate every wall with patterns reminiscent of Oriental rugs, is perhaps the chief glory of this palace. The colours are mainly those favoured by the Almohads, caramel and honey, green and dark purple, the last produced by burnt manganese; the majority are the so-called Cuenca type, in which the pattern is produced in bas-relief by a stamp.

There are also examples of the *cuerda seca* technique, where patterns were originally outlined by string impregnated with manganese before baking, so that the cord separates the various colours and the finished product shows a dark line of demarcation. In each corner of the patio is a Roman statue, two of them representing Minerva; it has been proved convincingly that these were copies of the celebrated *Lemnian Athena* of Phidias, of which other Roman copies exist in Bologna and Dresden. In the centre stands an elegant fountain with dolphin supports and a bearded head of Janus to top it, while the greenery round the base relieves the coldness of stone and marble.

To the right is the *Salón del Pretorio*—every part of the building is named after some place or event in the story of the Passion—which is notable for its beautiful Plateresque *rejas*, through one of which another *reja* can be seen in the garden, a favourite subject for artists. The wooden shutters are original and possibly represent the most artistic and best preserved of all Mudéjar carpentry. The ceiling is a marvel of patient labour and emphasises once more the wedding of Renaissance and Islamic themes; it is coffered in the style of the former and several of the compartments show armorial bearings, but the others have exquisite *alfarje* with polygonal inlay of ivory. This is a good opportunity for studying the *racimos*, or 'clusters' which hang from many of these panels. These ornamented wooden cones are carved in various patterns, some resembling fir cones or pine-apples, others with the stalactite or *mocárabe* design that imitates a honeycomb. Outside the hall is a smaller patio, with old *olambrillas* or tiny ornamental tiles set among the bricks of the paving, and capitals from Medina Azzahra.

The antechamber to the chapel is called the *Sala de Descanso de los Jueces*, the judges' retiring room, and contains opposing kneeling statues of two females, one probably Catalina de Ribera. Each stands on a plinth beautifully decorated with *azulejos*. The chapel itself has a florid Gothic ceiling with gilded, ornamented ribs on a Mudéjar stucco background. The *cuerda seca* tiles here are among Spain's best examples. In the centre stands a broken column, said to be a copy of the pillar of scourging preserved in the Church of Santa Prassede in Rome and presented by Pope Pius V; the size and shape are certainly similar but whereas the Roman, allegedly original, column is of black and white jasper, this one is fawn and brown. From the antechamber a small door leads into the *Salón de la Fuente*, so called because of the small ceramic basin in the centre; this gives another opportunity to examine a fine Mudéjar ceiling with *lazo*, *mocárabes* and heavily gilded *racimos*.

The next room is used as a small museum of Roman statues and busts and beyond it there is another patio, the *jardín grande*. In a small room is an ugly sixteenth-century table of *opus sectile*, trustingly shown by some as the one over which Judas was paid his thirty pieces of silver. Here and there above the dadoes lime-wash has been removed to reveal traces of old fresco; as in other Mediterranean countries, an outbreak of plague led to the

extensive application of lime, thus impairing art without disturb-
ing the flea that carries the infection. The last showpiece is the
dome over the turn of the monumental stair, a *media naranja*
or half-orange, with the ribs of the segments well marked, the
whole composed of the most ingenious and artistic lacework of
wood and various inlays. The upper storey, whose rooms are
usually locked, contains the archives of many Andalucian towns,
a fact not generally known but useful to the historian.

The picturesque **Barrio de Santa Cruz**, the former Jewish
quarter, retains most atmosphere of old Andalucía. Here are the
narrow, winding streets of houses washed white or yellow, tiny
patios, street-lamps on wall brackets, pavements of brick in
herring-bone pattern, and oriels that project only a foot from the
wall and are furnished with lattice screens, the direct descendants
of the *mushrabiyyah*, which enabled the inmates of the harem to
watch the street without being seen. Here you can find comparative relief from the usual city noises, and the perfume of
orange blossom, stocks and jasmine.

It is quite impossible, and indeed undesirable, to follow a given
route through this maze. The Calle de Mármoles is the nearest
point of interest; there is a gap here in the line of houses and
from an excavation fifteen feet below rise three huge Roman
monolithic columns of marble, as the street name implies. They
have no capitals and the bases are invisible, for water has collected round them and is covered with a brilliant green carpet of
duckweed. There is the Church of Santa María la Blanca which,
like its counterpart in Toledo, is a converted synagogue; it contains a painting by Vargas and a Last Supper attributed, against
considerable opposition, to Murillo. There are a dozen bewitch-
ing plazas, of which that of Santa Cruz is best known, with its
beautiful wrought-iron cross among the oranges and magnolias.
The other, Plaza de las Cruces, is triangular and has three similar
crosses mounted on columns of which one at least is Roman.
There is the Calle de la Pimienta, Pepper Street, commemorating
the days when spice merchants had their own bazaar and pepper
was worth more than its weight in gold; when Catherine of
Braganza married our Charles II she brought as dowry not only
Bombay and Tangier, but over half a million pounds' worth of
pepper, obviously for use as currency rather than for the royal
table.

In the centre of the Barrio was an old playhouse named Doña
Elvira. Though not mentioned in the original play about Don
Juan by Tirso de Molina, somewhere in the long line between

him and Da Ponte, who wrote Mozart's libretto for *Don Giovanni*, an Elvira does appear and the name is surely more than a coincidence. On the playhouse site was built the Hospital de Venerables Sacerdotes, a home for aged priests, in 1675. The sunken patio of red brick, with its orange trees, myrtles and pot plants and its tile steps leading down to the central fountain, is particularly charming with its suggestion of cloistral seclusion. The church is gay with frescoes and illustrated with subjects that are outside the usual range, such as Frederick Barbarossa doing homage to the Pope in Rome and an episode from the life of Attila. There is a Last Supper by Roelas as part of the *retablo mayor*, with the peculiar feature of hovering angels. This is where the *cofradías* exhibit their treasures, except during Holy Week, and in fact the Hospital may be found by following the signposts to *Tesoro de las Cofradías*.

Opposite the Hospital is the picturesque Hostería del Laurel, which appears in Zorrilla's version of the Don Juan story, and was the home of another new character, Inés. It is a cool and fragrant spot, redolent of wine maturing in the cask; from the ceiling hangs a multitude of hams and on the counter can be seen an endless variety of *tapas*, the snacks that seem to constitute the Sevillian's main nourishment. The Laurel is famous for its variety of *tapas*—there are prawns, whelks, squid, sardines, snails, chicken livers and lobster claws, apart from the usual ham, hot dog, sausage and *morcilla* (which is how Lancashire black pudding turns up in Spain). There is a grill on which kebab, called *pinchitos* here, can be prepared in a moment, with a cunning sprinkling of spice.

One should leave the Barrio by the delightful Plaza de la Alianza and the Calle de la Alcazaba; on the south-east side is a stretch of Almohad wall with five square towers, and beyond are the famous gardens of Murillo. Keeping the wall on your left you will turn a corner and soon come to the main entrance of the **Alcázar**, the last of Seville's famous triad. The castle-palace is said to have been founded originally by Julius Caesar and then adapted to their use by each subsequent ruling nation. Like most Spanish alcázars it is continuous with the city walls, but unlike most it has been used as an occasional residence by every head of state or province for over two thousand years. In spite of occasional finds of Roman masonry and the repairs of recent years, the bulk of the defensive work is twelfth-century Almohad.

One enters beneath a ceramic crowned lion bearing a cross and a motto, possibly *ad utrimque*. In front is the arch in the wall that leads on the left to the only Almohad survival other than military, the *Patio del Yeso*. This is not generally shown to visitors but a custodian will usually unlock the entrance door if special interest is shown. The patio is rectangular, with a shallow ornamental pool of the same shape in the centre. Many travellers will have seen the Court of the Myrtles in the Alhambra of Granada and will recognise the standard lay-out in this one too; one minor difference here is that clipped pomegranate trees about two feet high take the place of the myrtles. The walls and the horseshoe arcades are well preserved, with their typical Almohad ornamentation, mainly because a private house was built over the area.

Leading off this patio is the *Sala de Justicia* built by Alfonso XI in the fourteenth century; his son, Pedro the Cruel, was responsible for building most of the present palace, which is a hundred yards away from this section and of a quite different style. The walls show two levels of stucco frieze, with the lozenge pattern that is so prominent on the Giralda, and *arcos de colgadura*, arched recesses in which the curtains of the pierced stone windows could be hung. The ceiling is an octagonal pyramid, if the term is permissible, with the usual wooden lacework (*enlacería*) and inlay—one of the first examples as it was constructed in the early days of Mudéjar labour. In the centre of the hall is a fountain with a shallow drain down to the Patio del Yeso, and round the walls are brick and tile benches. One foreign touch is given by the chicken wire that hangs down to block the entrance, for birds love to nest in the ceiling and spoil the precious *alfarje* by sharpening their bills on it.

The large courtyard that lies before you as you pass through the Almohad wall is called the *patio de los leones*, allegedly because it was once used as a menagerie. The one on the left is the *patio de la montería*, the court of the huntsmen (*monteros*) of Espinosa; these were for centuries the bodyguard of the kings and originally recruited exclusively from the small town that lies on the high plateau of Castile, south of Santander. Before you is the façade of Pedro's palace, to be examined later; on the right is the Chamber of Commerce, the *Casa de Contratación*, founded by Isabel for the regulating of trade with the newly discovered Indies. The additional qualification *de las Américas* was not used in her day as Amerigo Vespucci's name was not generally attached to the new continent until after her death. A tablet at the entrance refers to 'the Indies' and states that the first circumnavigation of the globe was organised in these offices.

Passing through the entrance-hall, hung with Flemish tapestries of mythological subjects, you enter the audience hall with its fine *artesonado* and continue to the Chapel. On the end wall is the celebrated painting of the *Virgen de los Navegantes* showing the Virgin, as protectress of seafarers, spreading her cloak over assorted characters believed to range from the Emperor Charles V to American Indians. Alejo Fernández painted this popular work after 1530, so many of the so-called portraits must be imaginary. There is the additional interest that the lower part reproduces every type of craft in use at the time.

As you leave the Chamber of Commerce a staircase on the right leads to the royal apartments. It is easily dated by the tiles which ornament the wall to a height of five feet. The top row consists alternately of the arms of Castile and León, the triple tower and the lion, and the personal crest of Charles V; this has two pillars as supporters, inscribed with the words *Plus Ultra*. The classical phrase associated with the pillars of Hercules, or Straits of Gibraltar, was *nec plus ultra*, 'thus far and no further', and Charles was now the first ruler of an empire on which the sun never set. Here we can not only calculate the reign in which the staircase was decorated, but the age of the tiles, which are of the best sixteenth-century Sevillian manufacture.

The first room at the top of the staircase is called the *saleta* and served as a waiting-room. The ceiling is a complicated *artesonado* among which the yoke and arrow badges of the Catholic Sovereigns can be distinguished with difficulty. It was typical of their day that married couples would each select an emblem that began with the initial of the partner. Thus Ysabel (as she was spelled) chose the arrows, or *flechas*, and Ferdinand the yoke, or *yugo*. The walls are hung with Flemish tapestries and the view through the windows, across the entrance courtyards and battlements to the Cathedral and Giralda, is superb. The next room is small but rich, barbaric in fact. It has an octagonal *alfarje* ceiling, whose central part is supported by twelve marble columns with gilded caliphal capitals.

The Oratory of Isabel the Catholic is a small room with a ceiling in the Gothic style, famous for its ceramic altar by Niculoso of Pisa, some of whose work is also in the Convent of Santa Paula. It is possible that he learned his craft in Faenza; at all events he introduced the first method of producing multicoloured tiles that did not have the ridges and grooves of the *cuerda seca* or Cuenca types. The altar is entirely covered with these tiles, on which various subjects are painted, principally in blue, white and yellow. In the centre of the retablo is a five-foot tall picture of the Visitation. The frame of the picture is provided by the Tree of Jesse, from whose breast sprout the branches that provide the genealogy of the Saviour. Jesse himself reclines below, propping himself up on one elbow. The decoration of the rest of the altar is typically Plateresque, and includes the yoke and arrows, mythical creatures and floral designs.

The remainder of the apartments upstairs contain nothing as fine or interesting as those below. Pedro's bedroom is not as bad as the rest and has a fine *artesonado* and some decorative inscriptions on the walls. Over the door is a very poor painting of five skulls, said to represent those of five unjust judges whom he had executed. There is a silver group of Isabel II and her family, showing her features little changed from those painted by Vicente López when she was a child; her body, however, is lymphatic. Among other portraits are two of Isabel II's sister, Maria Luisa, later Duchess of Montpensier, after whom the park on the south border of the city is named. In the music room is a piano of 1850, and some portraits by Anton Rafael Mengs, the Bohemian Teuton of partly Danish descent who discovered Velázquez, whose work was threatened with oblivion in the latter half of the eighteenth century.

We now come to that part of the Alcázar which is often cited as being the finest surviving example of Mudéjar art. Descending to the Patio of the Lions you find on the right a rectangular doorway flanked by its blind arches and *sebka* work. The centre combines the best features of Mudéjar with themes reminiscent of Granada, and especially the Alhambra. This is not surprising, as Pedro had helped to restore Mohamed V to the throne of Granada in 1362. (Mohamed had lost it to a usurper, Ismail Ibn Yussuf, who was assassinated by Abu Said, a vicious character better known as Mohamed VI, el Bermejo, the Red. Eventually the people of Granada asked Mohamed V to return, which he did, helped by Pedro.) In return for this help, Mohamed V loaned Pedro his craftsmen, which explains why so much of the Alcázar reminds one of the Alhambra.

The upper storey presents double and triple windows and is flanked by open balconies. Below the windows runs a blind arcade topped with the *sebka* work with which we are now so familiar. A similar frieze, the work of builders from Toledo, runs below the magnificent overhanging canopy of the roof, supported by carved and gilded beams and lateral corbels. Below it is a curious panel on whose rim runs the inscription in Lombard lettering: 'The very high and very noble and very powerful and very conquering don Pedro by the grace of God king of Castile and of León ordered the making of these alcázars and these palaces and these doors which was done in Era one thousand four hundred and two', that is in 1364. The larger central portion has a blue and white tile design that looks purely geometric but is actually rectangular Cufic, and repeats the sentence 'There is no conqueror but Allah' eight times. It may seem strange over the door of a Christian king's palace; we shall find it in an even stranger place.

The interior follows a lay-out that is a regular feature in the homes of kings, presidents and general practitioners. There is one area devoted to official and business duties, and another for private life. The official area is situated round the *Patio de las Doncellas*, the private round the *Patio de las Muñecas*. The former is a great galleried courtyard, with dentate arches supported on pairs of slender marble columns and much *sebka* decoration. It was used by the ladies-in-waiting, *doncella* being a damsel of high degree, just as *doncel* is a royal page. Extensively restored under the Catholic Sovereigns it now has Renaissance–Plateresque details; the oldest, and possibly handsomest part is the fourteenth-century dado of *azulejos*. This patio gives on to three rooms, of which the first and most splendid is the **Salón de Embajadores**.

The main entrance to this Hall of Ambassadors is guarded by fine double doors dated 1366 and decorated with *enlacería* of the usual geometric kind. There is an Arabic inscription on the outside, stating that it was made by Toledan workmen, and Gothic writing on the inside, containing excerpts from the Gospel of St. John and Psalm 53. The latter was obviously chosen in a mood of depression—easily understood perhaps, for it was in that year that Pedro's bastard half-brother Henry of Trastamara took the title of King of Castile and invaded Spain. The contest was to last three years, involving English and French expeditionary forces and finally terminated by Henry's dagger. So Pedro had little time left to enjoy his splendid palace.

Inside, the Hall of Ambassadors is a blaze of mosaic tiles and painted stucco and gilt. It rises two storeys and is crowned by an intricate cupola, larger and richer than that of the Casa de Pilatos. The geometric pattern of larch-wood strips encloses pieces of painted stucco and the octagon and squinches on which the dome rests are a mass of honeycomb stalactites. Downstairs, triple

Above, Roman arch in the patio of the Church of El Salvador, Seville. *Below left*, the Puerta de Agua, Niebla; *right*, the Puerta de Losal, an early Mudéjar work, Ubeda.

Above left, triple-arched Visigothic plaque in the wall of Santa Maria de la Granada, Niebla; *right*, a caliphate column capital with Cufic inscription in the Bar de los Palcos, Córdoba. The Corinthian parentage is clear. *Below*, the patio of the Casa de Pilatos, Seville, with Mudéjar arcading and Renaissance balcony and fountain.

entrances in each wall open under horseshoe arches supported by caliphal capitals. Above them there is a fantastic display of painted stucco, in panels, arches, on bosses and in Arabic script, all alive with pink, yellow and blue, while the balconies have gilt bosses on their iron rails and are supported by dragons with gilt wings. There is a frieze of royal portraits, installed under Philip II, which encircles the hall above the level of the balconies and is best seen from them. Above is a continuous line of Cufic Arabic; then come the Gothic niches, each with its portrait of a king. Neither Isabel the Catholic nor her mad daughter Juana are represented. Below are the names, the personal crest, dates and duration of reign, and below that another frieze of Arabic script, this time Naskhi. It was in this hall that Don Fadrique was murdered by his half-brother Pedro, and the wedding of Charles V and Isabel of Portugal took place.

One room that must be mentioned is the *Salón del Techo de Felipe II*, which is named after its plain, coffered ceiling. The walls, on the other hand, are covered with stucco of a very different pattern from that which we have seen so far, and includes outlines of animals. One of its doors is called the Puerta de los Pavones, from the peacocks that wander among the endless vine pattern. This panel is confidently regarded by some as Toledan; others maintain that Persian artists were responsible. From here you enter the *Patio de las Muñecas*, named after the tiny, doll-like faces that adorn the spandrels of the arcade; as it is the centre of the private part of the palace the decoration, though exquisite, is on a smaller scale. The capitals are largely brought from Córdoba, presumably Medina Azzahra, and are all different, so that a close study of them, preferably in company with an expert who can date each type quite accurately, will be interesting. For the rest I would suggest that little attention be paid to the names of the apartments, but that the visitor wander through them for his own pleasure.

The courtyard of María de Padilla is a rather sombre patio with cypresses and myrtles. María was Pedro's mistress or wife. She seems to have been a good woman as well as a beautiful one and Pedro remained devoted to her, apart from an occasional bout of backsliding, until her early death. In María's day the patio was completely covered, and a part of it still shows the tops of windows that illuminated the cisterns below, known for centuries as the Baths of María de Padilla. The story that the gallants of Pedro's court used to drink her bath water in order to curry royal favour was probably invented to provide the build-up for a joke; for one courtier, it is said, declined the drink on the grounds that, having tasted the sauce, he might covet the partridge.

Charles V's Palace is beyond this patio and is a Gothic building of earlier date than Pedro's. The tapestries are world famous and were commissioned by Charles to illustrate his conquest of Tunis, to which he took an artist from Brussels to observe the combined operations. The artist's name was Jan Vermayen, called impartially Longbeard or The Dashing, and he was fond of including a self-portrait in the cartoons he produced for the tapestry makers. The weaving, too, was done by a Fleming, William Pannemaker; the silk and wool thread was sent to him from Granada and the gold from Milan. Before the twelve tapestries were finally sent to Spain they were ordered to be exhibited in London, on the occasion of Philip II's wedding to Mary Tudor, first cousin of his father. A pleasing feature of the series is the running commentary in Spanish and Latin woven into each piece. All in all, as good a documentary of those days as one is likely to see.

The gardens of the Alcázar are also justly famous, and are representative of Arab, Renaissance and modern tastes. There is a large pool with a wall of Baroque rustic masonry, there are tiled seats and there is the famous pavilion of Charles V, with Cuenca *azulejos* of strange and varied patterns reaching up ten feet from the ground and surmounted by Arabic writing and stucco arabesque. Inside there is a coffered dome, typical of the mid-sixteenth century. It is delightful to wander along the paths among fountains and trees, splashing water and scented breeze; under palms and between orange trees planted by Pedro the Cruel; past jasmine and bamboo, alongside box and myrtle hedges and through a giant chessboard of roses. Andrea Navagiero, Venetian ambassador to the court of Charles V, called this garden the most peaceful spot in Spain.

Leaving the Alcázar by the Plaza del Triunfo, the old buildings of the Lonja, now housing the **Archivo General de Indias**, is on the left. It was designed by Juan de Herrera, the architect of Spain's greatest century, who expressed something of his country's grandeur in the massive Escorial. Other works have been modelled on his severity, but none are so satisfying in their classical proportions. The Lonja was designed under Philip II to accommodate the merchants who used to disturb divine service in the Cathedral by their vociferous business dealings in the Patio de los Naranjos. How appropriately Perrin's *Money Changers* sits over the Puerta del Perdón!; and quite coincidental, for it was put there half a century before the merchants made a nuisance of themselves. The *Casa Lonja*, or Long House, was established in 1598, and nearly two centuries later Charles III, the best of the Bourbons, founded the Archives in the same building. The classified records embrace every aspect of life in Spain's colonies, from religious to commercial. Today they are under the direction of the erudite and gracious Señorita Rosario Parra Cala, one of the many women who today, as in the past, foster the traditions of Spanish art and culture.

This building also saw the opening of an Academy of Art on 1 January, 1660, with Murillo as President and Valdés Leal and the younger Herrera as co-founders. On admission each pupil had to say *Alabado sea . . .*, 'Praised be the most Holy Sacrament and the Immaculate Conception of Our Lady'. And who more suitable as President than the man who had painted so many of them?

There is a permanent exhibition, in which one may see original letters from Columbus, Cortés, Balboa and other famous explorers and conquistadors; there is one from Alvaro de Bazán announcing the victory of Lepanto. Also here is the will of Elcano. The name is almost unknown outside Ibero-America, yet he was the first to circumnavigate the earth, for he was Magellan's lieutenant and Magellan himself died during the voyage, in the Philippine Islands. Elcano's letters patent and coat-of-arms can be seen, the latter with the motto, in Latin, 'I was the first to encircle the globe'. Charles V's letter of thanks and endowment pays no attention to the profound scientific and philosophic import of Del Cano's feat (this is how Elcano himself spells his name in his will), but mentions five times the Spice Islands and cargo of spices that he brought home. Ginger was more valuable than geography, and turmeric than trigonometry.

Also displayed are painted designs of clothes to be used at a reception aboard a Spanish frigate in the Philippines in 1776. The guest of honour was a special emissary from 'the Nabab, Hyder Ali Bahader'. This illiterate adventurer, the greatest threat the East India Company had ever known, came near to overthrowing it, and became a partisan of the French in the struggle for India. The Spanish had no love for Britain in those days, who was depriving them of colonies at an alarming rate; it follows that the paintings of Oriental musicians, dancers and acrobats on the programme of the reception can be regarded as secret weapons in a cold war. In the collection, an etching of

Seville of 1878 shows the extensive changes the capital of Andalucía has undergone in less than a century. The great promenade along the Guadalquivir was then a stretch of untidy foreshore; the towers of gold and silver were still united by a length of the Almohad city wall and in the background can be seen a long stretch of the aqueduct, whose meagre remains now accompany the road outside the Puerta de Carmona.

Going south along the busy Avenida de Queipo de Llano, a few minutes' walk brings you to the attractive Plaza de Calvo Sotelo. This is the part most visitors know best, for at two of its corners are the excellent *de luxe* hotels of Alfonso XIII, with the typical white and fawn façade, and the Cristina, where reasonably good flamenco dancing is usually staged in the basement.

East of the Hotel Alfonso XIII is the great square building of the **Fábrica de Tabacos**, now the University, where thousands of women used to work. One of them was a creation of Prosper Mérimée and her name became famous in the world of opera— Carmen. The building itself was planned and built mainly by military architects, and it has been said that the moat on three sides and the built-in sentry boxes were absent-mindedly included by those who had designed nothing but fortresses for years. Others said that the defensive system was to prevent the cigars from being smuggled out rather than men from getting in. So lucrative was this evasion of excise duty among the *cigarreras* that, according to Ford, 'these ladies undergo an ingeniously minute search on leaving their work, for they sometimes carry off the filthy weed in a manner her most Catholic Majesty never dreamt of.' The floor space is second only to that of the Escorial and the elevation, though much admired, is simply one of many Sevillian examples of a severe Renaissance exterior adorned with pineapples and pinnacles.

What most people miss in the big plaza is the charming **Chapel of Maese Rodrigo**, the only surviving building of the first University of Seville, occupying a sharp corner on the north side. There is a Gothic-Mudéjar portal and a Gothic window in the side wall. The chapel has a single nave with a really fine *artesonado* and the retablo, by Alejo Fernández, is as good an example as you could wish of primitive Sevillian painting of the Byzantine type in a Gothic setting. By now you will probably be familiar with the appealing, if formalised style of the sixteen canvases that make up the retablo, for the Antigua of the Cathedral and the Virgin of the Sailors in the Alcázar were by the same artist. The Cuenca tiles in the presbytery enhance the attraction of the east end of the chapel. There is one interesting feature, a tile let into the wall on the right of the altar, which marks the height to which the flood of 1892 rose. This catastrophe caused so much damage to the town that it was at last decided to build the embankment which now protects it.

To visit the **Hospital de la Caridad** you can cut through the Calle Maese Rodrigo opposite. A slightly longer route, however, takes you along the broad Calle de Queipo de Llano towards the Cathedral. On the right is a white-washed horseshoe arch, inside which a Gothic one has been built; a plaque says that this is the *Postigo*, a postern gate of the Alcázar, mentioned by Cervantes. The Hospital is pleasantly situated opposite a small garden in which is a bronze statue of Don Miguel de Mañara carrying in his arms a dying beggar from whose belt hangs the *olla* and a spoon, counterpart of the begging bowls of Oriental mendicants. In this garden, too, one can buy the freshest flowers in Seville, at a market gardener's hut. The façade is a simple Baroque one, adorned with five pictures of blue and white ceramic, alleged to have been designed by Murillo. They portray Faith, Hope and Charity and St. Roch and St. George, five subjects that are repeated over the high altar within.

The legend that has gathered round the founder is that Miguel de Mañara, after a profligate life, turned to good works. The immediate cause of the change is attributed to two adventures: returning home from a carouse he met a funeral procession and, on enquiring whose body was being taken for burial, was shown his own likeness; in the second he pursued a veiled woman and on overtaking her and lifting her veil found himself confronted with a skull. These are merely legends and there is almost no support for the belief that Mañara was the prototype of Don Juan Tenorio of Tirso de Molina's play. However hotly the contrary may be maintained it must be emphasised that Tirso de Molina probably wrote the play before 1625, and certainly before 1638, when his last play was produced. The profligate Mañara, born in 1626, was thus between minus one and twelve years old when Tirso allegedly took him as the prototype.

What we do know about Mañara is that he was a Knight of Calatrava and that he was excessively preoccupied with death. He was widowed at thirty-four and there is every reason to believe that it was the loss of his wife that turned his thoughts to practical Christianity, though not of a very cheerful kind. His *Discourse on Truth* begins with the old Latin tag, 'For dust thou art and to dust thou shalt return', and reads on: '... go to an ossuary and distinguish between the bones of rich and poor, wise and foolish, small and great . . .'; 'What is as horrible as a dead man?'; 'Oh instant, which changes all! Oh instant, from being to not being!', and more in the same vein. Where Mañara differed from the general run of Jeremiahs is in his practical philanthropy; he did find a dying beggar and carry him to hospital in his arms. He did rescue the tumbledown Hospital of St. George and make it into a working institution under the Hermandad de la Santa Caridad . . ., the Brotherhood of the Sacred Charity of our Lord Jesus Christ, of which he was an Elder. It still shelters the sick and the aged. At the entrance is the site he chose for his tomb, with the epitaph on which he wanted everyone to tread, 'Here lie the bones and ashes of the worst man there has ever been. Pray to God for him.' Fortunately the Brotherhood had its own views and moved his body to a place below the high altar seven months after his burial.

The *Patio de Acceso*, immediately at the entrance, has fine proportions, and is a rectangle divided by an arcaded passage that goes well with the cloistral lay-out; in each half is a marble fountain in the Italian style. On the walls is a series of blue and white Dutch tile pictures by one De Wet, studiously ignored in most descriptions of the Hospital. The title is *Der tien Geboden*, the Ten Commandments, but the subjects do not include anything relevant to that theme. There is Jonah and the whale, Abraham preparing to sacrifice Isaac, and other Old Testament episodes which have been used to foreshadow the New.

In the Church there is a painting by Valdés Leal, the spine chiller, portraying a skeleton striding over the world's vanities, with the motto *In ictu oculi*. Facing it is the well-known *Finis gloriae mundi*, a faithful representation of a dead bishop and an even more obviously dead knight of Calatrava, about which Murillo made the celebrated remark that it made him hold his nose each time he looked at it. The knight, whose shroud carries the cross of the Order, is believed to be a portrait of Mañara himself. It is quite probable that it was painted to illustrate the sentence from Mañara's discourse, 'What is as horrible as a dead man?'

In striking contrast is the delirious gilt retablo of the altar of Pedro Roldán, which uses every device of High Baroque, splendour, movement and wavy line. The larger than life tableau of the Entombment is highly appropriate, for one of the activities of the Brotherhood was the Christian burial of executed criminals. Among other celebrated works of art are several Murillos that were missed by that great art collector Soult. *Moses striking the Rock*, in the upper gallery, is in the *vaporoso* style and both it and the companion *Multiplication of loaves and fishes* have the unusual feature, for Murillo, of a fairly detailed background. Note the horns of Moses' halo; the Vulgate states that his face was *cornutus*, horned, when he came down from Mt. Sinai and some believe that the Hebrew *Keren*, shining or radiant, was mistaken for *Karan*, or horned, a pardonable mistake in documents where only the consonants are written.

St. Elizabeth and the boy with ringworm has already been mentioned; in its portraiture, depth and restrained chiaroscuro it should rank among the artist's very best works. The small crucifix painted by Murillo is said to have hung at the head of Mañara's bed and to have been in his hands when he died. Other items of interest are the delicate wrought-iron pulpit and the *Cristo Implorante* of Francisco Antonio Gijón, sculptor of the *Cachorro* to be seen in Holy Week. A painting of St. John of God by Murillo perpetuates the features of Mañara himself; one of the latter's unsuspected gifts was that of painting and he too is represented by an Immaculate Conception.

Behind the hospital can be seen the narrow stair that Mañara used so frequently on his visits to the chapel, and an old street sign *Calle del Ataud*, Coffin Street, where a plot to kill Mañara was hatched, but thwarted by God's intercession so that he might be spared for his good work. The brick Gothic arches are important for they represent all that is left, apart from others incorporated in the main building, of the *atarazana* or shipyard of Alfonso el Sabio, said to have been founded by Alfonso X in 1252, though possibly dating back to an Arabic *Dar Assina'a*, house of work, which occupied precisely the same spot three hundred years earlier—as shown in a surviving plan of the city reproduced by Lévi-Provençal.

Leaving the Hospital, the Artillery School is on the right, with the date of its foundation given as 1587. Before the front entrance is a strange wrought-iron cross with lamps. To the left the street gives a view of the *Torre de la Plata* which with the *Torre del Oro* was part of an Almohad fortification running from the Alcázar to the river-bank. There was also a subterranean tunnel to a wharf, a normal precaution for those times. The Silver Tower is whitewashed and inhabited and can be recognised by its battlements, above which rises a primitive penthouse.

The Tower of the Gold is far more impressive, a twelve-sided structure from which a chain could formerly be extended to the opposite bank. Its name derives from the gilt tiles which used to flash in the sunlight and have been reproduced in the present century. There are of course fables connected with it, for the word 'gold' has always excited human interest. The tale that the treasure of Pedro the Cruel was stored here is false, as is that which connects the tower with the gold that Columbus brought from the New World. The truth is that Columbus brought back very little gold from any of his voyages, in spite of which numerous treasuries in Spain and Italy exhibit objects said to have been manufactured from the first gold brought back from the Indies. About as much truth attaches to the legend that St. Ferdinand ordered a usurer to be imprisoned there, with the task of counting an uncountable hoard of captured gold coins under the supervision of a demon-captain. On windy nights, they say, when children put their ears to the ancient stones, they hear the chink of coins, the groans of the miser and the stern voice of the demon saying, 'Count! Count!'

Today the Tower is used as a naval museum, of interest to specialists. There is a good view from the wide walk that crowns the lower part and one can see where the River Guadalquivir has been dammed on the north side, upstream, and led westward round the far side of the Triana suburb. The second storey, of brick, is decorated with blind arches, some lobulated, some of simple, pointed horse-shoe pattern, interrupted by panels of *sebka*. The most interesting feature is the type of *alfiz*, almost unique in the chequered green and white tile ornamentation, an untouched survival of the thirteenth century.

From the Torre del Oro the riverside promenade, Paseo de Cristóbal Colón, runs north to the Puente Isabel II, which one may cross to visit the suburb of **Triana**. On the right is the Plaza de Toros and on the left one looks over the stagnant arm of the blocked river and the railway line that runs beside it. Triana itself is no longer the romantic haunt of gypsies and potters. The castle that once guarded the ancient bridge, which stood where that of Isabel II stands today, is no more. Apartment blocks rise on every side; the suburb's name, a corruption of the Emperor Trajan's, is the oldest thing hereabouts, and the sightseeing attractions are limited. There is the Capilla del Patrocinio, for those who want to see the *Cachorro* at close quarters, and the Church of Santa Ana.

This is believed to be the oldest of Seville's many churches and the longitudinal ridge-rib is quoted as evidence that builders

Above, the Cathedral at Cádiz. *Below*, fishermen near Málaga.

JEREZ DE LA FRONTERA. *Above*, sherry casks in a bodega. *Below*, large casks in a Gonzalez-Byass bodega.

from Burgos, whose Cathedral was built before 1250, took part in the construction. There are traces of Mudéjar workmanship from the following century and so many Baroque additions as to produce confusion in place of unity. Its treasures are many and of varying merit: Alejo Fernández has a Virgin of the Rose and Niculoso of Pisa a ceramic tomb. Taking into account the capricious hours of opening it is doubtful whether the visit is worth the trouble, again except for the specialist. Application at No. 90, Calle de Pureza, on the east side, may secure admission, which should be suitably rewarded.

From now on the rest of Seville may be seen most enjoyably from an open victoria. From the Hotel Cristina or the Alfonso XIII the Avenida de Roma passes on the left the Palace of San Telmo and on the right the delightful triangular Jardines de Cristina. The palace was originally built as a college for naval officers and pilots and emphasises the part played by Seville in communications with the Americas. It is a fairly plain two-storey building in the prevailing brick and stone colours, and the doorway, much abused by puritan critics, is simply another retablo stuck on the front by the Figueroas, and is one of Ford's fricassées of marble. María Luisa Fernanda, sister of Isabel II and Duchess of Montpensier, bought the building and its extensive grounds and on her death-bed willed the former to be a religious seminary. The beautiful gardens that extend southward along the river are still called after her.

A drive through the **Parque de Maria Luisa** and the adjoining and aptly named Jardines de las Delicias, with its palms and citrus and a hundred other trees, makes a pleasing contrast with the noisy bustle of Seville. The houses that were put up by the former American Colonies for the 1929 Exhibition are each typical of the country of its origin. Then there are reproductions of Spanish styles, especially towards the south end, where you can see Spanish Gothic, Mudéjar and Plateresque palaces. They do this reproduction very well in Spain, as anyone will agree who has seen the Pueblo Español at Barcelona.

The **Archaeological Museum** is housed in the Plateresque Palacio de Bellas Artes, at the far end, in the Plaza de América. The usual collection of prehistoric and Iberian exhibits is presented, showing evidence of Phoenician and Greek influence. The Roman Halls contain numerous finds, especially from Itálica, among which the Greek Hermes, recognisable by his winged sandal and here called Mercurio, and the bust of Trajan are regarded as outstanding. Perhaps the most agreeable arrangement is of four Roman columns and a fountain, with a relatively complete Diana, who has only lost her hands, reflected in the basin. But the pride of the Museum, and its latest acquisition, is the **Tartessian Treasure** from El Carambolo, a few miles away. Beautifully lighted and displayed behind glass are over twenty pieces of solid gold, weighing goodness knows how many kilos, in all their barbaric splendour. Sixteen of them are plaques measuring six inches by two or three, and two are enormous armlets; each one is in repoussé with gold plates welded to the under-surface. The remainder are the pieces of an elaborate necklace ending in a pendant of seven plum-sized, decorated drops. This magnificent exhibit came to light with no clue as to its origin. From internal evidence it is thought to be of native origin, a survival of the Tartessians with whom the Phoenicians traded, from the land whence Solomon's navy brought 'gold, and silver, ivory, and apes, and peacocks'.

On the east side of the park is the great, semicircular building that houses the Capitanía General and other government offices. The work of Aníbal González and the main building of the 1929 Exhibition, it is built entirely of brick and tile. It can best be described as Renaissance–Baroque with Mudéjar touches; the architect's genius is evidenced by the fact that it copies no other building in Spain and yet is wholly Spanish. Inside the semicircle and across the diameter runs a Venetian type of canal and access is gained over a bridge whose upper works are completely encased in *azulejos*.

Opposite, in the María Luisa Park, are several quiet retreats which are dedicated to Spain's intellectuals, while the avenues themselves commemorate her explorers and conquerors. Two of the retreats deserve special mention: a monument to Gustavo Adolfo Bécquer and a fountain named for the brothers Álvarez Quintero. The former was a tuberculotic poet of the romantic age and a Sevillian by birth. Technically his poetry is unpolished but he presents the sentiment of his period, much of it modelled on Heine, with a melancholy verging on morbidity and an imagination that often becomes mere fantasy. The Álvarez Quintero brothers were playwrights, born in Utrera in the early 'seventies of the last century, who spent their constructive lives in Seville. Their plays were numerous, light, witty and a little sentimental.

Both Bécquer and the Álvarez Quinteros are honoured in a novel and gracious manner; at the shady tree of the one, and the ornamental fountain of the others, brick and tile bookshelves are filled with the complete works of the writers every morning and until the late afternoon. Here, surrounded by mellow brick, *azulejos* and books, you may sit undisturbed by anything louder than bird calls or splashing water, and drowse away the afternoon. Imagine sitting in cool shade or warm sunshine, reading Yeats or Barrie or Shaw, in perfect quiet and in an ambience of orange blossom, flowering myrtle, or whatever else the season offers.

CHAPTER NINE

Excursions from Seville

❧

*San Isidoro del Campo—Itálica—Alcalá la Guadaira—Utrera—
Morón de la Frontera—Marchena—Castilleja de la Cuesta—
Castilleja de Guzmán—Sanlúcar la Mayor—Nuestra Señora del
Rocío—Villalba del Alcor—Niebla—Huelva—La Rábida—Palos
—Moguer—Rio Tinto—Aracena.*

The shortest tour, to the north-west, goes through Triana and
across the new course of the Guadalquivir. In less than 2 kilometres, at La Pañoleta, a right fork diverges along N630 to the
village of Santiponce. Here is the **Monastery of San Isidoro del
Campo**, originally founded for the Cistercians in 1298 by Guzmán
el Bueno, hero of Tarifa. In 1431 it was handed to the Order of
St. Jerome and remained in its care until the dissolution of the
monasteries in 1836. When H. V. Morton visited the deserted
buildings in 1954 he found a voluntary caretaker looking after
them by day and night. Since then the Hieronymites have returned and José María Geniz Bazán is happily installed in an
official capacity, still faithful to his trust. His dearest possession
is a copy of Mr. Morton's book, well thumbed, you may be sure,
on page 196 where the Monastery is described.

The massive outline of the buildings is made sterner still by
the fortified apses of the twin churches and their heavy buttresses.
The old fifteenth-century entrance is no longer in use and today
one enters through a simple door into the sacristy. The monastery
is now *in clausura*, so that all its beauties may not be visible, but
in the not too distant future the twin churches should be opened.
The older one was pure Gothic until the seventeenth century,
when 'restorations' obliterated much of its simple beauty but,
though limewash and Baroque have done their worst, the proportions and the vault ribbing of the apse still witness their
Cistercian past. The carved retablo is regarded as the culmination
of Spanish polychrome sculpture and includes the finest work of
Martínez Montañés. The central figure, of the Penitent St.
Jerome, is detachable and is carried in processions; on the right
is the Epiphany, with the figures grouped in two files, the Magi

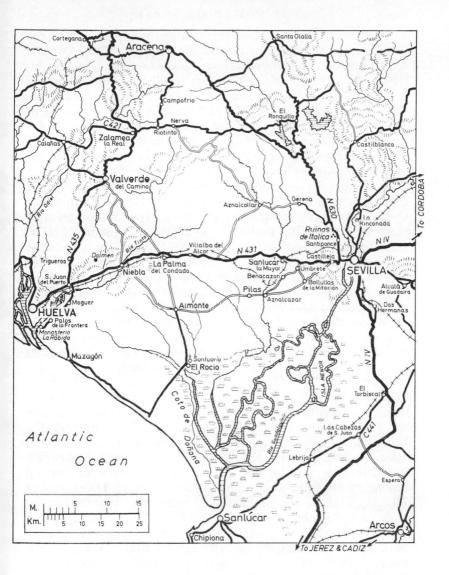

in one, St. Joseph, the Virgin and Infant in the other. The attitudes and expressions of tenderness are full of charm and in the figure of the Saviour Montañés portrayed the Infant Jesus type which, according to Gudiol, he himself created and which is so much admired in Andalucía. On either side of the sanctuary are the kneeling effigies of Guzmán el Bueno and his wife, also the imaginative work of Montañés.

C.G.S.S.

L

An archway leads to the second church, built parallel with the first by Juan Alonso Pérez de Guzmán, son of el Bueno, in the fourteenth century. Here is the tomb of the founder, it is thought, typical of the late fourteenth-century Sevillian sculpture. Facing it, and therefore on the right side of the presbytery, is the famous tomb of Urraca Ossorio, wife of Juan Alonso, who was burnt alive by order of Pedro the Cruel. The reason for this atrocity is not clear. Pietri states that it was because her son, Alonso de Guzmán, refused to accompany the king in his exile. The inscription on the tomb reads '. . . in order to take her treasures and riches', and elsewhere one is told that it was because she rejected the king's advances. As she was well over sixty at the time this showed considerable strength of mind. The inscription also recounts how Urraca's maid or companion, Leonor Dávalos, shielded the body of her mistress with her own, as the flames exposed it, and shared her fate; it is only reasonable that her ashes should rest in the same casket as those of her mistress.

There are two patios to which access is now almost impossible; the first, *de los Muertos*, is a two-storeyed cloister, of which the upper one has arches resting on typical octagonal brick pillars of Mudéjar type; the other, or *Patio de los Evangelistas*, is also Mudéjar, as evidenced by the *alfices* over the Gothic arches, and has fifteenth-century frescoes in poor preservation.

A very short distance up the road and on the left are the ruins of **Itálica**, the first Roman foundation in Andalucía (or Baetica as it then was) built by Scipio Africanus Major for veterans of the second Punic War. This great leader also conducted the brilliant, lightning capture of Cartagena, defeated Hasdrubal Barca at Bailén, Hannibal at Zama and introduced the Spanish sword into the Roman army. Itálica became important, having among its other claims to fame the birthplace of Trajan and of Hadrian's father, and declined only when the Visigoths located their capital in the nearby riverain village of Hispalis (Seville). Though experts point out streets, water supplies and cisterns, baths and a gymnasium, the only exhibit likely to interest the casual visitor is the great amphitheatre, largely in ruins. And for the only human touch he must go to Madrid, where the Archaeological Museum displays a copper plaque from Itálica, on which is engraved an ordinance of the Emperor Marcus Aurelius ordering a reduction in the pay of gladiators.

The second expedition, a much longer one, takes you through the historic and fertile district south-east of Seville. Leaving by the Puerta de Carmona, you immediately see on the right a few arches of a tiered aqueduct. Traces of this remain in various places and in the seventeenth century this particular portion was long and impressive, judging by an etching in Latour's journal. It is doubtful whether the aqueduct was ever Roman, as Hispalis was a relatively insignificant town; certainly it was used by the Moslems, and the first village you pass commemorates the *Caños de Carmona* in its name, Torreblanca de los Caños. About a kilometre from the Puerta de Carmona a domed brick building with open sides houses the *Cruz del Campo*, an ancient Calvary that was probably put up at the same time as the Riberas built the Casa de Pilatos. As mentioned previously, it was once a part of the Holy Week processions.

The country is rich but uninteresting until, after about 10 kilometres, the road forks; the right branch takes you, after 3 kilometres, to **Alcalá la Guadaira**. It is worth while stopping as the road descends to cross the Guadaira, for the outline of the old castle is a fine sight. The walls of *tapia*, or *pisé à terre*, and the stone towers rising at intervals, give one the impression that this was once a whole walled town; on the hilltop in the centre is the Church of San Miguel, so called because the town was captured by St. Ferdinand on that saint's day. From here the sainted King gazed at Seville for several days before venturing to receive its surrender. Pictures, incidentally, which show him receiving the key as he is about to enter on horseback are dramatic but erroneous; he was given them only after the affairs of the inhabitants had been settled to everyone's satisfaction, about a month later.

A century later Alfonso XI gave the castle to his mistress, Leonor de Guzmán, mother of the bastard brothers who eventually killed Pedro the Cruel and founded the Trastamara dynasty. Pedro himself made use of the place as a prison for Trastamara supporters, notably Diego de Padilla, a relative of his own mistress. Among the legends of those stirring, if bloody times, is that of how Diego wrote appeals for help with his own blood; tying these to the tails of rats he used the creatures as postmen.

The road takes us over the river, then up into the castle and to the church. Parts of the old mosque can still be recognised from outside and the bell tower is, as you might expect, a converted minaret. Inside, it is easy to pick out the Gothic stone apse, with its ribbed vault, from the older building. The most impressive feature here is a simple piece of wrought iron, the great candelabrum that hangs like a horizontal wheel over the centre of the nave.

In the retablo of the high altar is one of those overdressed Virgins with an undersized Infant that you see so often. She is known locally as the *Virgen del Águila*, because she was discovered by an eagle, instead of the usual shepherd, after the departure of the Moslems. The lecterns are for this reason supported on double-headed eagles.

The Hapsburg eagle came into the Spanish escutcheon through Philip the Fair, husband of Joan the Mad and father of Charles V. The Hapsburgs got it because they, as Holy Roman Emperors, claimed to be the successors of the Byzantine 'Roman' emperors. They in turn took it from the Moslems, who had it from the Persians, and via Assyrians and Hittites, from the Babylonians. The Turks also adopted the emblem, and great must have been their surprise at Lepanto when they saw their own eagle on the banner of Don John of Austria, son of Charles V.

The castle is of vast extent, obviously a refuge for man and beast when the frequent raids, or *razzias*, devastated the no-man's land between Christian and Moslem. The famous grain-storage cisterns are no longer visible, but the fame of their flour persists in Seville, where the town is still called Alcalá de los Panaderos, 'Bakers' Castle'. Weeds and wild flowers grow in the crevices of the walls and towers, even between the steps of the towers' spiral stairs. Wide panoramas and shady corners, the scent of flowers and the hum of bees make this the pleasantest, if not the most important of the places you may visit.

Twenty-one kilometres along C432 is **Utrera**, another prosperous town in the midst of fertile fields. Your first sight of it is Santiago Matamoros, as a weather-cock mounted over his fifteenth-century church. The west portal, with its flamboyant, late Gothic decoration, ogee and *alfiz*, is reminiscent of the beautiful entrance to San Jacinto in Córdoba. Inside the narrow and lofty Gothic church there are only a few items of interest: the crypts, a dark brown and very ancient Crucifixion, and twin stoups of a rare pattern, as each of them is half of a giant mollusc, more than a yard across, sent from the Philippines. The other church is that of Santa María de la Asunción, better known as Santa María de la Mesa. If you ask why she should be called St. Mary of the Table you will be told that the word is a contraction of *Meseta*, the plateau, but no one really knows why she should have been given this name either. She is connected with Utrera's famous image, whose sanctuary has to be visited. The *reja* of the Plateresque *coro* is a handsome one and there is a good kneeling statue of Diego, one of the less important members of the family of Ponce de León. The general effect of the painted and gilded Gothic interior is unpleasant.

In the town the house of the brothers Alvarez Quintero is distinguished by a commemorative bas-relief, but not otherwise noteworthy. The Sanctuary of *Nuestra Señora de la Consolación* is on N333 at the outskirts of the town, approached by a pleasant, tree-lined avenue. She is regarded as Utrera's greatest claim to fame, a miracle-working Virgin whose *ex votos* hang in her sanctuary by the thousand; she is venerated all over Spain and in many parts of Spanish America. The miracles began in 1560, when a lamp before her shrine filled with oil and lit itself. Thereafter in unbroken succession she has aided those who invoke her aid. In the inundation of December 1962 she saved the town which, in gratitude, made her perpetual Lady Mayor; the rough work is, however, still done by an elected *alcalde*.

The Sanctuary has a plain Baroque front and the building itself dates back to 1619; its chief attraction, despite the claims of the chapels, the jewels and the altars, is the great Mudéjar *artesonado* over the single nave. An attempt has been made to add an Oriental flavour, perhaps to go with the ceiling, by introducing scalloped arches and Arabic writing, both in gilded stucco and in painted fresco. It is as well that the standard of Arabic is poor among the devout townspeople, who attended the ceremonious coronation of the Virgin with tears of pride and joy, for otherwise they would read in her sanctuary, over and over again, 'There is no Conqueror but Allah'.

Nine kilometres along N333 you can turn right on C342 for **Morón de la Frontera**. To the right is the Sierra de Morón, outpost of that great jumble of mountains that forms the core of Andalucía. It is easy to picture the massive, ruined castle as it was in the old frontier days, when the men rode out to intercept the fierce Berber raiders from the sierra, and the women and livestock took shelter within the sturdy walls. Or even earlier, when the Moslems who built the castle fought the fierce Christian raiders from the north.

As with most towns, Morón is best seen on foot, after leaving the car near the Ayuntamiento. Making for the Church of San Miguel one walks east between the white-washed walls of the low houses; there are some interesting side-streets on the left, especially that named after Fernando Villalón, a local poet. The street consists of a row of steps and down the centre a series of miniature gardens in tiled boxes displays some of the roses which grow so well in these parts. Extracts from Villalón's works interrupt the pattern of the lowest tiles; one of them is addressed to the *sereno*, or night-watchman, a typical Spanish official about whom every traveller writes. *La noche serena*, of course, gave them their popular name. The Church of San Miguel lies in the saddle between Morón's two hills. Before the high altar is a magnificent *reja* with something new in design, geometric patterns that suggest *enlacería* worked into the upper and outer sections.

If you turn north on leaving San Miguel the perfume of roses may entice you up a flight of about forty steps; at the top you find a small rose garden with a wonderful view. Behind is the ruined castle and before you the rich plain; a few stone benches support the oldest inhabitants, who day after day gaze at the monument in the centre of the garden. Probably none of them, or the park keeper who trims the rambler rose that climbs the plinth, knows what the bronze cock without feathers signifies. It in fact commemorates the revolt of the citizens against a tax collector who was considered grasping, even for one of his profession. They set upon him, beat him and pulled the clothes off his back, laughing with pleasure when he fled with loud lamentation. The expression *sin pluma y carcareando* (plucked and squawking) was so suitable that the town chose this method of reminding its citizens of the episode. When you descend the steps take the first turning to the right, into a street containing some good Baroque house-fronts; one of them, on the right, houses the local branch of the Ministry of Agriculture. In the entrance-hall is the usual dado of *azulejos* and here again we find a frieze of tiles declaring that there is no conqueror but Allah; they have unfortunately been put in upside down.

From Morón to **Marchena** is twenty-five kilometres due north on C339. The line of houses beside you is built into, on to and from the wall of the old Moslem town, and an occasional tower can still be made out. Opposite a branch-street to the left is the horseshoe arch of the entrance, set at an angle to the line of the wall in the usual way, so that attackers must present their unprotected right side to the garrison. It is very quiet inside and there are picturesque corners, with street-lamps on the house fronts, *rejas* and tiled roofs, a palm tree here and there and the blinding white of the walls that reflect and magnify both light and heat.

There are two churches in the old town, Santa María and San Juan. The former has some *azulejo* patterns on the bell tower, like many another Andalucian church, and two Gothic portals, one whitewashed and the other built up. San Juan is Gothic–Mudéjar and too large to be anything but forbidding, as it stands in the silent square; two of the façades, with *alfices* over the portals, are partly restored. The interior, with its five naves, is grandiose but there is little to see beyond the cedar-wood carved stalls of the *coro* and its fine *reja*. The retablo contains Flemish paintings of the sixteenth century but few except specialists will be drawn to them; if the church happens to be open (and 'happens' is the operative word) during the heat of the day, its coolness will be worth more than its contents. The tower is another storeyed one, with a pyramidal *azulejo* cap. Don't waste time looking for the Palace of the Dukes of Arcos, of the Ponce de León family. In its place the hilltop is covered with streets of humble cottages, whose inhabitants, if asked where they live, will reply, 'Why! In the Palacio.' Adjoining is a convent *in clausura* but you can always manage a look into the patio where a fine old horseshoe arch fills the right-hand corner.

An attractive way back to Seville is by continuing on C339 to Carmona. On leaving Carmona the road forks, the right branch being N IV with a signpost to the Roman Necropolis. In the centre of the fork is a large grain silo and our road, C432, goes to the left. Many are surprised to learn that it is the old main road to Seville, and travellers of the eighteenth century invariably described the route through the Alcors and Alcalá de Guadaira. After Viso del Alcor and Mairena del Alcor a narrow but restful road, that has not even graduated to being numbered, leads between banks of wild flowers to Torreblanca and Seville.

The third possible excursion is due west and touches the Atlantic coast-line. To complete the trip will require a stop of one, and preferably two nights, so that those who cannot afford the time are advised to return to Seville from Niebla. Leave Triana as though for Itálica but continue straight on at La Pañoleta on N431. In less than a kilometre you find yourself climbing the main street of **Castilleja de la Cuesta** and on the left is the large Instituto de la Bienaventurada Virgen María. If this is too much of a mouthful just ask for the Irish Convent (*Convento de las Irlandesas*). The majority of the nuns are Irish, but the Lady Abbess is Spanish and speaks excellent English. Cortés died here, forgotten in the feverish march of events of Spain's Golden Century. Everyone knows how he conquered Mexico with 400

Spaniards and a few horses; fewer know that he discovered and explored the coast of California and sandwiched the conquest of an empire between fighting in Italy under the Great Captain and taking part in Charles V's disastrous expedition against Algiers. Even after a gracious welcome from his king, he preferred retirement and oblivion; it is not surprising to read that he was a fine orator and a stylish writer. His horse Estrella was buried here in the Convent, though the grave is unmarked. Cortés, less fortunate, was transferred to Mexico after his death.

But this does not exhaust Castilleja's roll of honour. This is a town of pastrycooks, and their products, tarts and *magdalenas*, confections of flour and egg-yolk in the shape of a shuttle, are avidly consumed in Seville. And though the average citizen may not know that Cortés died here, he will almost certainly tell you that a leading confectioner of this town was the grandfather of Rita Hayworth.

Opposite the Convent a narrow road leads to Castilleja de Guzmán, where a castle of the great family of the Dukes of Medina Sidonia passed through various aristocratic hands before becoming the Government Colegio de Santa María de Buen Aire, for girls at the University of Seville. The entrance arch still carries the Guzmán crest; the buildings are white, with light brown borders to the eaves and openings. The chapel is new and the retablo is of tiles, the upper half reproducing the *Virgen de los Navegantes* in the Alcázar and the lower the oratory of Isabel the Catholic in the same palace.

From here you can, if you wish, retrace your route to the main road, or you may choose to work through a maze of picturesque lanes that lead through Valencina de la Concepción, Salteras and Olivares to **Sanlucar la Mayor**. The signposting in this district is poor and the inhabitants' local knowledge poorer. It is a sleepy town with two sights particularly worth a visit. The Church of Santa María is a converted Almohad mosque, but most of the present structure is Mudéjar. The façade is especially exuberant and has obviously been restored with the intention of giving the beholder a bit of everything. There is a brick Gothic portal with three archivolts, its *alfiz* surmounted by a row of zigzag merlons. Then comes the plain, whitewashed front, relieved by brick windows, Gothic and *ajimez*, in plain brick *alfices*, the central one having a second frame in the shape of a horseshoe, too good to be true. To complete the dazzling picture, the trees in front have their trunks whitewashed too. The interior preserves the three naves of the mosque, with their pointed horseshoe arches, and a thirteenth-century sanctuary in which Roman columns and capitals have been used as supports. The bell tower is of course the old minaret, with a ramp instead of a winding stair, as in the Giralda.

At the far end of the town is the Church of San Pedro; it is doubtful whether it was, as stated, within a castle. It is curiously situated at the end of a lane that runs between iron railings, outcrops of rock and prickly pear; it is certainly built as though to withstand a siege, with pyramidal merlons and lancet windows as narrow as arrow-slits, but placed inside a blind horseshoe arch and then finished off with an *alfiz*. The interior is notable for the monumental stair leading up to the high altar. This typically Spanish feature is here embellished by the old tiles in the rises of the steps, partly replaced with new ones through the centuries, so that the enthusiast can date each patched-up section. Another unique feature is the presence of three altars at the east end, the two side ones being situated half way up the stairs.

Returning on N431 you will have a straight run through to Huelva. If time is not important, however, you should turn east as though for Seville. After four kilometres a signposted right turn takes you south to Umbrete, Benacazón and Aznalcázar. The great brick church of Umbrete has a fine *azulejo* dome, and Aznalcázar has more battlements on its church and a Roman bridge just beyond the town on the road to Pilas.

Four kilometres take you to Pilas, another village without intrinsic interest.

As you leave Pilas, four kilometres farther on, on the road to Almonte, almost the last wall on the left conceals a typical Andalucian *cortijo*, with living-quarters on one side and all the other appurtenances of a mediaeval manor grouped around. Though it now belongs to a Marquis it has had a more distinguished tenant, Murillo. His wife, Doña Beatriz de Cabrera y Sotomayor, was born here and continued to live here with the family after his death. An easy road takes you to Almonte and even earlier the signposts read **Rocío**.

There are three great festivals a year in these parts, and if you miss Holy Week and Corpus Christi you may still be here to see the **Romería de Nuestra Señora del Rocío**, the Pilgrimage of Our Lady of the Dew. Her sanctuary lies at the northern border of the great *marismas*, the swamps that accompany the Guadalquivir in its last stretch, near the River Rocina. The effigy is known affectionately as *La Blanca Paloma* and this is but one detail that reminds us of the worship of Astarte, that has assumed so many modern forms in the south of Europe. At Whitsun, or Pentecost, the *cofradías* converge, traditionally in trains of tented, ox-drawn wagons on two wheels, while the men ride alongside, dressed as they were for the Feria. At night camp-fires are lighted and there is a continuous sound of the clapping of hands, the thrum of guitars and the trilling roll of castanets.

The town itself is a large and straggling collection of cabins round a huge, bare centre that bakes in the sun, except beneath a single clump of trees. The population is 300, rising to 20,000 at Whitsun, and each *cofradía* has its inn, marked with the name of the parent town. The celebrations last at least two days and three nights and for the whole of this time sleep is out of the question. The Virgin's tour is the climax of the pilgrimage and the rivalry between *cofradías* for the honour of carrying her a few yards gives the impression that bloodshed is imminent; but somehow she makes her circuit, contusions are shrugged off and the walking wounded remain in the mob. People under a vow or hoping for a miraculous cure are still enabled to touch her *paso*, and she then returns for another year's rest.

The surrounding country is partly being reclaimed from marshland and huge plantations of eucalyptus, a thirsty tree, stand sentinel over the new fields. Nature lovers who wish to visit the bird sanctuary and study the wildlife of the marshes may continue from El Rocío to Coto Doñana, after seeing the D.G.T. representative in Seville, who will arrange an introduction to the **Estación Biológica de Doñana**. From here on vines will be seen with ever greater frequency, for the sherry barons draw their raw material from a widening area.

By returning to Almonte and then continuing due north you reach the main road, N431, at Palma del Condado. If you now turn to the right, in the direction of Seville, five kilometres bring you to **Villalba del Alcor**, The White Town of the Hill. This detour is unnecessary unless you propose to continue to Huelva and stay there for a night or two, returning via the Rio Tinto mines. As you descend the steep part of the narrow main road, the church, now a national monument, is on your left and somewhat back from the road. The façade is a curious mixture of a Baroque portal, a Gothic one and a walled-up, pointed horseshoe window, a reminder of the Almohad mosque. Another survivor is the tower at the end on your left, whose lower courses are in *soga y tizón*. The caretaker's house is immediately opposite. Inside you find the curious feature of a Gothic church built on to the old mosque at a right-angle. Thus the nave has seven

Gothic arches, all of brick like the rest of the interior and the cupola over the altar has compound squinches, an Oriental touch. The arches of the nave, on the other hand, help to support the roof by embryonic pendentives, a more sophisticated method, best seen on the left side, where the solitary aisle runs. At right-angles to the sanctuary, on the left, is a chapel which is the remaining part of the mosque, with horseshoe arches and a groined roof. The tower, originally the minaret, is entered from inside the church and preserves part of its winding stair.

Turning westward again and continuing along N431 you will come to what is undoubtedly the noblest ruin that ever excited the senses of a romantic. After only sixteen kilometres you see the misty outline of a town on the crest of a hill; the mistiness is fortuitous for, though **Niebla** means mist, its name is actually derived through *Ilipula* (Roman), *Elepla* (Visigothic) and *Lebla* (Arabic). The first Count of Niebla was the Guzmán who married Beatriz, daughter of Henry of Trastamara, but this by no means inaugurated the city's greatness. Scipio defeated the Lusitanians here; the Visigoths made it the head of an episcopal see, and after the downfall of the Caliphate of Córdoba, Niebla became the capital of a small but independent *taifa*.

As you approach the town you encounter the Rio Tinto, familiar to every stockbroker, for the first time. The rocky bed of the river, whose waters are not so highly coloured here as its name suggests, is a bright gold from the metallic oxides that have been deposited through the ages. The road crosses the river by a Roman bridge in good repair and in a few minutes the *tapia* walls with their forty-six towers and stone reinforcements are on your left hand. A narrow entrance leads through a hole in the wall next to the original town gate; the gap is not prominent enough to modify García Gómez's statement that Niebla has the only complete Moorish town wall in Spain. The old Puerta de Socorro has a round horseshoe arch, whose proportions are Visigothic, and leads through a guard-room and a right-angled turn, a common safety device, into the town. In the plaza that faces you there is an isolated stretch of wall with a horseshoe arch; your car may be conveniently parked in its shade. On your left a piece of Roman masonry now serves as the front steps of a house.

Straight ahead, which is due south, is a fascinating bell tower, with *ajimez* windows on all four sides, much restored and partly bricked up but still proclaiming their Visigothic origin. Above is a modern clock face and above that again a round arched window through which you can see the great bell; the smaller ones are housed on the floor below. The roof has a tiny garden of wild flowers that seems to cap the ancient relic suitably. Behind is the Church of Santa María de la Granada, restored since its near-destruction in the Civil War. Note the alternate courses of brick and stone, and the little entrance patio which was once the Court of the Oranges of the mosque. There are remains of two rows of arches, also of horseshoe design, but it is impossible to say whether they are from before, during or after the Moslem occupation. Lying about are fragments of Roman columns and capitals and a stone catapult ball. The church's north wall has a foliated arch and near it a precious Visigothic survival is set flush in the white-washed wall, a triple window with primitive decoration, the whole carved from a single piece of stone. The interior is disappointing but there is one double window of Moslem days that uses a white marble Visigothic column in its centre, carved with a typical design in bas-relief.

The east gate, the Puerta de Sevilla, is Roman and lies down-hill, past the humble single-storey cottages that are reproduced everywhere, so that hardly a roof shows above the wall. The south gate, or Puerta de Agua, is also approached down a steep lane, and overlooks the river. They say that the women used to pass through here to fetch water, hence its name, but this is hardly likely as Rio Tinto water is undrinkable and not even used for washing clothes. There was a quay here, however, in the long past days when iron-ore shipments were sent down-river to Huelva. The last gate is on the west side—the town in fact keeps to the rudiments of what may once have been the square Roman plan—and is called the Ox Gate, Puerta del Buey. It is another Oriental one, with horseshoe arch, *alfiz* and a blind arcade of brick above it. From here there is a wonderful view of the river and countryside, vivid green in spring, relieved by the shimmering grey of the restless olive leaves.

This is almost all; there is a ruined Church of St. Martín, which hardly repays a visit, and opposite the bell tower is the old hospital of Nuestra Señora de los Ángeles; most of it is now a shop, but some of the old patio still survives. Those who cannot spare the time for two nights at Huelva could now return to Seville along N431, a distance of about sixty kilometres.

The road continues to **Huelva**, twenty-eight kilometres farther, situated at the confluence of the Rivers Odiel and Tinto. It is sheltered from the Atlantic by the Island of Saltes, at one time intermittently occupied by metal workers and Vikings, the former vacating the area whenever the latter were sighted. Huelva, the home of the fandango, the centre of Spain's longest stretch of sandy shore, the Costa de la Luz, home of culinary specialities. . . . The fact remains that Huelva is a convenient headquarters for sight-seeing and nothing more. It is a pleasant town without particularly notable monuments, and when communications are better, will undoubtedly be the centre for the finest bathing beaches in Spain, at least as regards extent.

There is one visit, however, which should be paid; a drive of about three kilometres along the Paseo del Conquero reveals a marvellous panorama of the two rivers and their lagoons, and finishes at the Sanctuary of Nuestra Señora de la Cinta. When Columbus was returning from his first voyage in the half-decked caravel Niña, his own flagship having been wrecked, he encountered a succession of storms so violent that they immobilised the seaborne traffic of the whole of Western Europe. Driving under bare poles, every piece of canvas shredded, Niña was hit by a fresh storm on the 3rd March, 1493. In his diary Columbus wrote, 'He [the Admiral] cast lots to send a pilgrim to the shrine of Santa María de la Cinta in Huelva, who should go in his shirt, and the lot fell on the Admiral.'

The Virgin of the Belt was a shrine for seafarers long before the visit of Columbus made it famous. The legend first appears in Christian writings as the story that St. Thomas, arriving after the Resurrection and Assumption of the Blessed Virgin, refused to believe the facts suggested by the empty grave, at which Mary, in order to convince this resolute sceptic, threw her girdle down from heaven. We can trace the story's origin to the Near East, to Ashtaroth and her Greek equivalent Aphrodite, the Roman Venus. Aphrodite's magic girdle was famous throughout the classical world. Aphrodite of Eryx, and Ashtaroth before her, protected seafarers and these took her cult to every part of the Mediterranean and beyond. But the orthodox legend (for pagan goddesses had long been assimilated into the one, supreme Mother of God) runs differently, as may be read in the blue and white tile pictures inside the sanctuary. This is how the story goes:

There was once a poor shoemaker called Juan Antonio. Having no children of their own he and his wife Lucia gave shoes to poor ones every Christmas. One day in the country he was overcome with pains in the belly, against which he invoked the aid of the Virgin Mary. Putting on a belt, which he found conveniently to hand, he was miraculously cured. He therefore built a small sanctuary and asked a painter friend to portray the Virgin holding a pomegranate in her left hand and supporting the

Infant Jesus on her knee with her right. He stipulated that the Infant was to wear shoes and hold a belt. This was duly done and the picture gained great fame, being hidden during the Moslem occupation of five centuries and miraculously discovered by a shepherd in the year 1400.

To visit the other sites so intimately connected with the Columbus saga you follow the Avenida de los Pinzones along the bank of the Odiel estuary for a distance of five kilometres. This brings you to the Punta del Sebo whence the ferry crosses a few hundred yards of Rio Tinto to the **Monastery of la Rábida**. On the nearby promontory is the colossal statue of Columbus made of granite blocks by the sculptress Gertrude V. Whitney for the Columbus Memorial Fund and erected here in 1929. Across the river the Monastery gleams white above the palms, mimosa and umbrella pines that flourish in the sandy soil. A path through a pleasant garden, in which an unfinished monument commemorates the fourth centenary of the voyage, leads to the porch of the Franciscan convent with its engaged octagonal brick columns that are repeated in the second patio, evidence of Mudéjar builders.

Most will know the story of how the white-haired stranger arrived at the monastery with his little son, how he interested the good fathers in his project to sail westwards to the Far East, and how they cared for his son and furthered his quest. It is quite understandable that the Monastery should today be an important museum of Columbiana and that annual classes should be held in a so-called University of Santa María de la Rábida. Many obscure details of the great adventure are only now being brought to light. There is of course far more to see than can be described: the alabaster Virgin of the thirteenth century, Nuestra Señora de la Rábida, is said to have been brought from Palos and therefore to be the identical one before which Columbus knelt in prayer before sailing. In the chapel there are also a fourteenth-century Crucifixion and processional cross, and opposite is a horseshoe arch leading to the patio that is evidence of the antiquity of the building; many believe that it is built on the site of an Arab watch tower, as the name *rábida* would imply.

Among the exhibits are the study in which Columbus and the friars held their conferences, the Mudéjar patio above which he slept during a six months' stay, models of the expedition's three ships, portraits, largely imaginary, of the main actors in the drama and various objects from the New World, such as a box made of jacaranda wood. There is mention, too, of a little-known benefactor, Mariano Alonso Castillo, Governor of Huelva, who in 1851 saved the Monastery from threatened demolition. A recent discovery in the shape of a document is claimed to prove that Columbus was a Spaniard, a patriotic belief quite at variance with the accepted one that he was born in Genoa.

Salvador de Madariaga put forward the hypothesis that Christopher was the son of a Spanish *converso*, a Jew who had embraced Christianity and gone to live in Genoa. In a sense this would make him a Spaniard, but it may be relevant that the suggestion was made from the security of Oxford, often the home of lost causes. The only authentic portrait of Columbus is his profile on a bronze medal made in 1505, that is during his lifetime, by the Italian Guido Mazzoni; the original is in Germany but a plaster cast here does nothing to combat the *converso* theory.

The little towns of **Palos de la Frontera** and **Moguer** lie along the new road that takes us back to Huelva overland. Both are seedy and seem to exist only as reminders of past importance. In Palos is the Church of San Jorge (St. George), where the royal authority for Columbus's expedition was proclaimed; the iron pulpit from which it was read, or supposed to have been read, is pointed out. Outside the Gothic-Mudéjar portal, the Puerta del Novio, is the little square where the inhabitants were summoned and ordered to make up crews for the two caravels that were requisitioned from the seaport of Palos. The other showplace is the old Arab fountain, sadly neglected now, where the crews of the expedition are said to have filled their water-casks.

Moguer is another neglected town, of interest as the birthplace of the Nobel prize-winner Juan Ramón Jiménez. His house with a small museum is on view. In contrast to most of his enormous output of verse, one prose poem stands out, *Platero and I*. Platero is a donkey, Juan Ramón is his own shy, sensitive, retiring self and the work is the freshest and most mature, the lightest and deepest account of life in an Andalucian town, an elegy that reflects something of every facet of small-town life.

A road of five kilometres takes you to San Juan del Puerto. About 8 kilometres from here, along the road to Seville (N431), you see a *venta* on your right and a few yards farther is a private earth road to La Lobita. This is a ranch where *toros bravos* roam and where you can study them at close quarters; be certain that you replace the barbed wire gates—there are six of them—each time you pass through, and have no fear that the bulls will attack you; they are perfectly tame as long as there are no cows about. You eventually come to a country house which is closed up except for a week every year, when the owner comes to select the breeding stock for the current year. No one believes that all bulls are the same, the breeder least of all, and it is widely held that the virtues of courage and aggressiveness are inherited from the female parent, so that the breeder selects those cows that show these qualities in good measure. There is a miniature bull-ring here, with three rows of seats, a *toril* and *burladeros*, those wooden screens that allow the man, but not the bull, to squeeze out of the ring. In this *tentadero*, as the trial ring is called, the promising cows are tested with capes every year; those that show the necessary qualities are kept for breeding; the rest are eaten. So deeply rooted is the matriarchal principle in the mind of the breeder that a strange custom is still observed—the killing of a cow that produced the bull that kills a torero.

Returning to San Juan del Puerto you now take N435 for Valverde. The country becomes sparsely populated as you ascend the foothills of the Sierra Morena and vast areas are covered with *Cistus*, a wild shrub with a white flower four inches across, con-sisting of five petals with ruby-red markings setting off the yellow stamens. The flower has no perfume but if you break the stem an intensely sticky, white substance exudes which has a pleasant odour. The peasants call it *lábdano*, a gum-resin, a word that goes back to the Persian, via Latin and Greek; a well-known variant of it is laudanum. This sticky exudate, however, goes to the scent factory instead of the apothecaries. The soil now becomes thinner and cultivated fields give way to plantations of cork and ever-green oak. The former has a bark of pure cork, up to an inch thick, stripped once every nine years to the height that a man can reach. The latter, which you will see during the greater part of this trip, covers hundreds of square miles and is used solely for the acorns on which pigs are fattened, and have been fattened for centuries. The Labours of the Months, a theme repeatedly painted or carved in Romanesque churches, always shows the flogging of oak trees in October and the pigs rooting hopefully below.

Zalamea la Real has the customary steep streets of these parts and the brick church tower with *azulejo* steeple. If you want to see a mining town, *Rio Tinto* is close by, but it is a dull town where the only light relief is provided by the semi-detached villas that used to belong to the British employees of the Rio Tinto Company. The whole hillside has been nibbled away here, since the days of the Phoenicians, and in the giant steps that surround the great hole the black mouths of the adits show where the veins of metal have been followed. The mine dumps are dark red to chocolate in colour; the older ones are beginning to sport a cover of vegetation and even pine trees are growing on the oldest. Up here the Rio Tinto is a narrow stream, but brightly coloured even above the mine workings.

A good but tiresome, winding road goes on to **Aracena**, a favourite resort for Sunday excursionists from Huelva, Seville and Southern Portugal, coming to see the cave, the Gruta de las Maravillas. Huge stalactites and stalagmites greet you at every turn in these magic caves, deep pools of crystal water reflect the lamplight on to the fretted roof in arabesque intricacy, and the colours change according to the prevailing mineral, so that one cave may be festooned with ruby stalactites and the next with emerald.

Crowning the hill that is honeycombed by the grotto are the ruins of an Almohad castle, and a Templar's church, that of Santa María de los Dolores, stands on the site of the old mosque. It is Gothic, with nave and two aisles separated by square piers with engaged columns, and the foliate capitals of these continue as a frieze round the whole pier. Over the west entrance a shallow central arch supports a raised choir, the *coro en alto*, possibly a later addition, for it cannot be of the same epoch as the Romanesque transitional western façade. It is a feature that was brought to perfection at the end of the fifteenth century, one of the best examples being in the Church of San Juan de los Reyes in Toledo. On the left side of the sanctuary, behind a beautiful *reja* portraying kneeling figures, is the tomb of Prior Pedro Vázquez, of about 1500, in glazed terracotta which at first sight appears to be alabaster. It is a work of great charm and sensibility. One is sometimes told that it is the work of Miguel Florentino, by which Michel Perrin is probably meant; this is unlikely if the date is correct, for he was not born for another nineteen years.

In a small chapel on the left, now used as a store, there is a primitive fresco of the Virgin, of the same school as the Vargas Antigua in Seville Cathedral. All else has vanished, for the miners of Rio Tinto in 1936 imitated the rabid Berbers of 1010 and destroyed everything that had a claim to beauty.

The two best parts have been left to the end. First there is the bell tower of the Templar Church, with its Almohad foundations and lobulated arches, all in warm red brick, then the usual *sebka* and above it a Templars' cross. The second attraction is the excellence of the restaurants and bars that cater for the hungry excursionist. All the inns are recommended, the Casas Restaurant from personal experience.

An hour's drive through oak forests and heather takes you back to Seville along the high road from Portugal; hawkers will tempt you with flowers and bunches of mountain asparagus, and in the distance the Giralda beckons.

CHAPTER TEN

From Seville to Jerez

❧

Las Cabezas de San Juan—Lebrija—Sanlúcar de Barrameda—
Chipiona—Rota—El Puerto de Santa María—Jerez de la Frontera

Leaving Seville for the last time, you follow the broad road that
runs south along the left bank of the Guadalquivir, the Paseo de
las Delicias. By following N IV for the whole of an uninteresting
drive one can do the journey of under 100 kilometres in just
over an hour. It is far more interesting, however, to skirt the
southern border of the Marismas, the swamp-land that flanks the
lower course of the Guadalquivir, and you should therefore
branch off at the village of El Torbiscal, nearly forty kilometres
from Seville, along C441 to the right. Before reaching this branch,
you will probably have by-passed the uninteresting town of Dos
Hermanas, a name that goes back to at least the twelfth century,
but famous only for the fact that Don Juan's seduction of
Aminta took place there, on his way to Lebrija.

The first town on C441, **Las Cabezas de San Juan**, shows up as
the usual splash of white, this time on the flank of a solitary hill.
It was a fortified station on the Roman road from Seville to
Cádiz and from that time on achieves only an occasional mention
in the chronicles. As the centre of a fertile district it is only to be
expected that its contributions to the war effort against Granada
are the chief entries. The inhabitants derive a vicarious satisfaction from the punning motto, *El Rey no puede hacer nada en su*
Consejo sin Las Cabezas, 'The King can do nothing in Council
without Heads'. The St. John in the town's name is the Baptist,
for he is the patron of the *parroquia*, but the 'heads' is because
the old name of the town was San Juan del Cabezo, or St. John
of the Hill; the change of a single letter to *cabeza*, or head, and
subsequent reversal can easily be understood.

The Ayuntamiento stands at one end of a small and unimpressive square, the opposite side of which is formed by the steep
main street. The balcony of an otherwise undistinguished house
that looks across the square is pointed out as that from which
Colonel Riego read his *pronunciamento* in 1820. This was the
beginning of one of Spain's numerous struggles between per-

jured politicians and crooked kings. Ferdinand VII, who had relieved the tedium of his captivity in France by congratulating Napoleon on his victories, was restored to the throne by his suffering countrymen and swore to uphold the liberal constitution of 1812, promulgated by the government of the Resistance in Cádiz. The King broke his word, troops ready to sail to the South American colonies to restore order there refused to embark, Riego became the tool of the Freemasons, opponents of Church and King. The revolutionaries retired to Cádiz taking King Ferdinand with them, and France sent the hundred thousand Sons of St. Louis, whom we met at Andújar, to restore the *status quo*. Enough of politics; the plaque that marked this house of destiny was removed in 1936.

Farther up the hill is the comparatively recent Church of San Juan Bautista, which houses some interesting objects. The well-worn theme of St. Anne teaching the Virgin how to read is rendered by an anonymous sculptor, in a style similar to that of Juan Montes de Oca, but with more sensitive features and expressions. Also here are a Crucifixion by Juan de Mesa and the charming *Pesebre* by La Roldana, the gifted daughter of the sculptor Pedro Roldán. Compositions in miniature of Nativity scenes were popular at one time and survive above all in the former Spanish possessions in Sicily and Southern Italy. As examples of eighteenth-century *genre* they give us much information regarding the customs and costumes of the time. The best example in Spain is to be found in Murcia.

Lebrija is the next stop on this road and is richer in interest than one would imagine. The parish church is called *Nuestra Señora de la Oliva* and clearly exhibits its origin as an Almohad mosque. The bell tower shows its minaret parentage, at least in the lower courses, and the interior of the church has three horseshoe arches on each side, separating the nave from the two aisles. The aisles each have four cupolas with a different pattern of rib vaulting; seen from the hilltop, they are reminiscent of the roofs of mosques with their attached *madrassehs*, or religious schools.

The retablo has an interesting history. Miguel Cano was commissioned to produce a new high altar, at an estimated cost of 3,000 ducats, but died in 1630 before the work was well under way. His son Alonso completed it in 1636 so successfully that he was paid a bonus of 250 ducats, astonishing generosity from clergy who too often went back on their bargains. Alonso Cano ranks as one of Spain's greatest artists and the Lebrija retablo as his first triumph. It portrays four notable pieces of sculpture, a Crucifixion above, statues of St. Peter and St. Paul in the second level and an image of the Virgin in the Camarín behind the altar. This beautiful statue, said to be carved from a single olive tree, deserves all the praise that has been lavished on it, combining as it does Spanish strength with Italian, Raphaelesque tenderness. Somewhat boldly for a young beginner, he incorporated console scrolls in the frieze of the entablature; this kind of innovation had not been attempted for nearly a century, since Pedro Machuca in fact.

The headless Roman statue that was at one time worshipped locally as the Virgin and called the *Marequita del Marmolejo*, more correctly *Marmoleña*, was removed to Cádiz Archaeological Museum in 1902.

All that remains of the castle are a few shapeless lumps that once were walls on the hilltop. The castle chapel, which they call Mozarab here, is actually Mudéjar and so well whitewashed inside that no masonry can be seen. The nave and aisles are separated by pointed horseshoe arches, themselves sufficient to discount the Mozarab story. The inhabitants make much of a wooden Christ with articulated arms; the figure lies in a glass coffin for most of the year but on special occasions can be attached to a cross by nails through the holes in the hands and feet. Its attribution to the fifth or sixth century is quite incredible.

From Lebrija a rough road leads north into the Marismas, gradually being reclaimed, where rice is planted and where fighting bulls are bred; here the bird-watcher may study egret and heron, eagles and owls and a hundred other species, while every now and then a wild camel may be seen in the distance. They have been here since the eighteenth century, when they were used in public works, probably in the vast Arenas Gordas nearer the mouth of the river. They are not the first camels to be imported into Spain; during the barbarian invasions in the sixth century there were complaints about the stabling of camels and other animals in the churches, and under Moslem rule they were used as beasts of burden in the building of Medina Azzahra.

The Guadalquivir has a variable course and canalisation by man is also changing old landmarks. The Isla Menor, northwards towards Seville, was once a river-girt stronghold of the Vikings who made their headquarters there in 844, while they sacked the surrounding country at their leisure. Their reign of terror ended when the troops of Abderrahman II, well disciplined and well led, disposed of all but one detachment; these were surrounded and offered their lives if they became Moslems. They settled down in the Marismas hereabouts and became successful dairymen, producing cheeses famous as far as Córdoba.

C441 now continues to **Sanlúcar de Barrameda**, an old town that lies on the south bank of the estuary of the Guadalquivir. It saw the departure of Magellan and Elcano on the first circumnavigation of the globe, and that of Columbus on his third voyage. Today it still has a few treasures for the visitor. The large, rectangular block of a seminary, the Colegio de San Francisco, was once a hospital for English sailors founded by Henry VIII, an indication of the amount of trade then existing between England and the Spanish wine ports, fostered perhaps by Henry's marriage to Catherine of Aragón. The concept of a hospital reserved for sailors is by no means far-fetched, for there was another hospital, that of San Pedro, maintained exclusively for field workers. The façade of San Francisco must have been added later, for it is pure Baroque, relieved in summer by storks' and swallows' nests, but there is a spacious Renaissance cupola which may be part of the original structure. Miss Epton, in her book *Andalusia*, gives a more detailed and credible account of the building of an English Church of St. George, whose brotherhood founded a hospital for English and Irish refugees in 1591. It is a hundred years since the hospital was last heard of and an authoritative account of its history and the preservation of its surviving portions, if any, should certainly be undertaken, as Miss Epton suggests.

The Parish Church of *Nuestra Señora de la O* is well worth a visit and will be found adjacent to, and communicating with, the Palace of the Dukes of Medina Sidonia. Few Spaniards are puzzled by the Virgin's title, but none seem to know its derivation; even the priests seem to have accepted the curious title without a second thought and Spanish books of reference are singularly reticent, confining themselves to the statement that she is equivalent to our Lady of Expectation. The most likely explanation seems to be the substitution of an 'O' for an egg; we know that a female holding an egg was an old fertility symbol which can be found, for instance, in Etruscan tomb paintings. The Virgin, furthermore, is sometimes portrayed in the same way, as in Murillo's *Sagrada Familia del Pajarito* in the Prado.

The church has an impressive front which includes a restored Gothic portal inside an astonishing *alfiz*, of which the top strip consists of stone corbels, much weathered, with faces carved on them. Then comes a zone of *sebka* work rising from a line of closely set columns, and below this, in turn, two crests with lion supporters and various ornamental designs, mostly geometrical. Inside, the nave and both aisles have attractive *artesonados*, and a private pew some twenty feet up, near the chancel, is guarded by an intricate lattice screen which is continued along the entrance from the adjacent palace. Here we have, in fact, the exact counterpart of the *pasadizo* that the emirs and caliphs of Córdoba used for their visits to the mosque.

Above the church there is an old castle; below, the weathered Gothic façade of a palace that once belonged to the Duke of Montpensier, brother-in-law of Isabel II.

Godoy had an estate near Sanlúcar and, surprisingly in those days, as he was of gentle, if not of noble, birth, proved himself an excellent landlord and a born farmer. It is customary to decry his title of Prince of the Peace, and foreigners even hint that he arrogated a dignity that belongs to the Saviour. This is nonsense; the title was bestowed on him in 1795 on the conclusion of the peace treaty with revolutionary France, just as it was bestowed on a Count of Haro for a similar reason a century earlier. But our connection with Sanlúcar goes back to long before Godoy, or even Henry VIII.

Pedro the Cruel was watching the tunny-fishing here in 1356 when the Catalan fleet of Aragón passed by on its way to attack England; this was the precipitating cause of war and indirectly of Pedro's defeat and death. Tunny-fishing is still an annual event along the whole Atlantic cost, but the local delicacy is the so-called *langostino*, the Dublin Bay prawn. Sanlúcar lies on the south bank of the estuary of the Guadalquivir and there is a long, sandy beach called the Bajo de Guía, behind which are bars that specialise in this delicacy. To some nostrils this beach is excessively fishy and discriminating visitors go a mile or two to the west, where clean sand and Atlantic breezes improve the bathing. The *langostinos* are tasty but it needs a zoologist to distinguish them from the familiar *gambas*, the prawns which are eaten by the million as *tapas* in every corner of Spain; or an economist, for the unwary can be charged as much as 10 pesetas for one of these puny celebrities. The traditional apéritif here is Manzanilla, a dry type of sherry that is by many preferred to the more orthodox. It can be ordered anywhere in Spain (with due care that the camomile tea of the same name is not produced) and costs from five to ten pesetas a glass. Here, on its native soil, the price is twelve pesetas.

Across the estuary is the region of sand-dunes called Arenas Gordas and another, but more arduous approach to the Coto

Doñana Nature Reserve. Our road leads westwards to the mouth of the estuary and the growing resort town of **Chipiona** where one sees a form of symbiosis that will be met again and again round the coasts of Southern Spain. There is a first-class hotel, with a fine bathing beach, down at the end of a straggling and not very attractive village whose sole contribution to the night life of the locality is a cinema in which one may see such offerings as *Dinamita Jim*, with Spanish sub-titles. It is only fair to add that, according to residents, the weather is unreliable except from July to September; the hotel staff contradict this statement.

Rota is due south along the coast and, being a Hispano-North American treaty base, is surrounded by California-type houses and served by excellent roads. There is a good hotel, where Spanish food is still served, and an excellent bathing beach, whose fine, clean sand contrasts with most Mediterranean resorts, being the result of Atlantic tides. Rota is traditionally the port from which sacramental wine is shipped to England; the name 'tent' wine is nothing but a corruption of *tinto*, *tintilla*, or red.

A new road now leads across the estuary of one of Spain's numerous Salado rivers to **El Puerto de Santa María**, at the mouth of the historic River Guadalete. Situated in the outer bay of Cádiz harbour, this delightful town looks across at the gleaming provincial capital on its peninsula. Santa María is notable as a holiday resort, a wine town, a fishing harbour and for a historical museum. Many prefer it to Jerez and it is certainly more attractive to the holiday maker, with its ready access to fine beaches and its daily boat trip to Cádiz.

Its history takes us back to the Port of Menestheus, of which there remain scanty relics in the castle of San Marcos, originally a Roman temple. Under the Moslems this became a strong fortress and its siege by Alfonso the Learned in 1264 gives the clue to almost every item of interest. It stands near the centre of the town, next to the mansion of the Dukes of Medinaceli, who ruled this area with almost absolute power. (Through a female member of the family the castle passed to the De la Cerda branch and their crest is still to be seen on the palace's façade, above the blank space where that of the Medinacelis used to show.) During the siege, Alfonso dreamed one night that the Virgin appeared to him and promised him a successful outcome, and the corner tower on which she appeared is still pointed out. Such a miracle deserved commemoration and the Parish Church is therefore named after *Nuestra Señora de los Milagros*, to whom Alfonso also dedicated several of his *cantigas*. It has an impressive

Plateresque south portal above which may be distinguished the effigy of the Virgin standing on a tower.

The fishing harbour is best visited during the morning, when the boats discharge their cargo, all neatly sorted and arranged on trays during the journey back from the fishing grounds. Here you find the *rape*, a large and flabby, pale-coloured fish with no taste, but which some hôteliers seem to consider just the thing for the international menu. For those who like to taste what they are eating there are conger eel, red mullet, hake and a dozen varieties of smaller game, all waiting on crushed ice for the day's lunch. On one of the sheds is a curious and heart-warming inscription on a plaque, thanking the fishermen of Alicante and of Portugal for helping the local fishing industry find its feet after its near extinction.

The **Fortress of San Marcos** is without doubt the most important building in Santa María. On one of the walls of reddish stone is a plaque commemorating it as the residence of Columbus and Juan de la Costa, pilot of the former's flagship *Santa María* and first map-maker of the New World. Other famous explorers lived here too, in the days when Santa María was larger than Cádiz, and the old houses that one sees everywhere might have sheltered Pedro de Villa or Amerigo Vespucci, who was to give his name to the yet unnamed continent. Unfortunately San Marcos is private property, belonging to the Caballero family, who took it over from the Medinaceli. But the Caballeros own one of the three bodegas in the town and Don Luis, who directs the firm, may be kind enough to send a servant with the keys, if he feels that visitors are sufficiently interested. Previous owners have perhaps been too zealous in restoring the old castle but once inside it is not difficult to let the imagination take you back to the Middle Ages. The tallest tower is said to have been the minaret of the castle mosque and is crowned with a small belfry on which storks have nested. The mosque, now a chapel of course, is the true glory of San Marcos and has its own little *patio de naranjos*.

The entrance is Gothic and leads straight into the sacristy, which has a Cufic inscription on one of its walls. The chapel itself is an almost intact mosque, with three naves and seven bays, comprising a total of thirty-three pointed horseshoe arches, resting on piers of varying structure, in which a selection of Roman columns can be identified. The Baroque altar stands before the untouched *mihrab*, an octagonal chamber in the style of Córdoba, with fresco decoration instead of mosaic; inside, the tiny vault has crossed ribs. On either side of the altar there is a small shelf resting on *mocárabes*, or stalactite supports, and behind, to each side of the *mihrab*, is an ornament that is possibly unequalled in Europe. At first sight you may take it for a remarkably vivid and well-preserved tapestry but on closer examination you realise that it is a repoussé leather panel, painted and gilded. The skin is camel, for bovine hides were little used in Spain in the Middle Ages, as they had the reputation of perishing too fast. The work is an Arab speciality called *guadamacilería*, an art whose practitioners occupied a whole street in Córdoba, the Calle Placentines. Perhaps our oldest record of its use in Christian Spain is in the *Poema de mio Cid*, written in the first half of the twelfth century, relating the well-known episode of the pledging of the empty coffers to the Jews in return for a loan, where they are described as *cubiertas de guadalmecí*.

On the north side is the Chapel of the Sagrario, closed by a superb gilt *reja* portraying the Crucifixion. Inside is a Romanesque statue of the Virgen de la Granada, sometimes called La Virgen de España, here, with a pomegranate in the right hand and the Infant on the left arm. Two stained glass windows at the west end have scenes from the *cantigas* and portraits of the Virgin and Alfonso X. An Arab type door, with wooden *enlacería* inside and a bronze sheath without leads to the little patio, which still has its orange trees and a central stepped basin surrounding a fountain that has long been dry.

Possibly without noticing the change, you passed between vineyards of white, sandy soil on your way here and will pass between many more on the road to Jerez. It is on this poor ground that the white grapes grow best and though 'sherry' should strictly mean the produce of that town, it may be extended to include the manzanilla of Sanlúcar and the wines of Puerto de Santa María. There are three bodegas of great repute here and many visitors find it pleasanter to be shown round these than to be taken on the more organised tours of the great houses of Jerez. Apart from the Caballero firm, Santa María is the home of the Terry and Osborne bodegas; English and Irish names need cause no surprise, for much of the wine industry was originated by refugees from various foreign countries and there are particularly strong ties with England and Ireland.

The production and consumption of sherry have been the subjects of innumerable commercial pamphlets with which the earnest visitor is loaded at the least display of interest. He is told not only how the grapes are grown, how the ground is cared for, the grapes picked, the juice expressed, and fermentation and maturation regulated; he is even instructed in the correct method of drinking sherry. You are told at what temperature the wine must be served, exactly how it should be poured and into what glasses, at what time of day and even with what kind of conversation in which company and, of course, how the glass should be held.

There are, of course, noble wines that demand a discriminating palate and a certain ritual, but they are few and difficult to find. The vast majority are pleasantly aromatic, dry enough to prepare the palate for a good meal, or sweet enough to drink with dessert, but endowed with no more subtlety than that which distinguishes one common brand of Scotch whisky from another.

Every step in the preparation of the wine has a purpose and the aim is to produce wines that will not vary from year to year; every step in the process is a scientific measure necessary for this single object.

Of the different varieties of grape the Palomino is the commonest and the Pedro Ximénez the sweetest. When wine is made from the latter the grapes are allowed to dry out for weeks in order to increase the sugar content, as is done with the Rhenish *spätlese*. The name is said to derive from a Spanish soldier of the time of Charles V, who brought back a cutting from the Rhine valley, itself the descendant of a vine from the Canary Islands. In the eighteenth century Pedro Ximénez sherry was so popular as a dessert wine that it was exported to France in quantity and known as Pérochimelle.

At the wine harvest the grapes are no longer trodden with special cleated boots; modern machinery can do everything that the old method achieved, as well as getting rid of solid matter by centrifuging. When the barrels of must arrive at the bodega it may be assumed that each contains the juice of half a ton of grapes. After the must has quietened the contents are moved from the *mosto* shed to the main bodega, rather than to cellars where there would be insufficient circulation of air. The *Solera* system, which is the essence of continuity, entails the 'education' of new wine by putting it through a succession of nursery barrels called *criaderas*. The operative mechanism is a fungus of the yeast family, which forms colonies on the wine called *flor*, or flower, and a good bloom round the bung-hole indicates a successful growth. The *flor* is extremely sensitive and requires an exact concentration of between 14 and 15% of alcohol to survive.

The barrels are arranged in three superimposed rows, the lowest, or *soleras* (from *suelo*—floor) containing the mature wine. Never more than half of its contents are removed for bottling, and the deficiency is immediately made good by *criadera* No. 1, which is directly above, and this in turn is replenished from No. 2. These operations are performed by siphonage and the necessary preliminary sucking is termed 'calling the wine', *llamar al vino*. The same system of siphonage is used for the pure alcohol that may be required to make up the correct alcoholic content, or bring up the strength of the finished product to enable it to travel.

Brandy is a sideline product, distilled from wine that is not behaving well; the result is called *Holandas*, presumably from some reference to the distillation of gin, and is allowed to rest until harmful alcohols have disappeared. It derives its colour, as does Scotch whisky, from being kept in barrels which are made from oak; the North American variety being considered most suitable. Barrels that are to be used again in the maturing of wine are carefully treated with superheated steam, ammonia and burning sulphur sticks, then primed with the lees of a drained cask. This is but a brief outline of an industry in which the wine takes eight years to be educated and the vintner a lifetime.

Jerez de la Frontera means many things to different people. Those with social aspirations turn away after a time from the closed society, with its English overtones, that forms one of the last European outposts of a sporting aristocracy. To most people Jerez is simply the sherry town *par excellence*; to a few it is a treasure-house of monuments, mainly ecclesiastical; to others it is one of the remaining centres for the breeding of an equine nobility, rightly earning the 'Golden Horse' trophy offered by the Ministry of Information and Tourism. The glorious Carthusian breed of greys, said by some to be ancestor to the Lippizaner breed of the Spanish Riding School in Vienna, still shows its paces in the ring, and the Hispano-Anglo-Arab, in which a thoroughbred strain has been judiciously bred back into the mixture of Barb and Arab, is one of the most adaptable breeds.

The *rejoneo*, or bullfighting on horseback, is the sole remaining form of the old-style *corrida* and is still largely the province of the aristocrat. Local horse and rider give a good account of themselves, and the well-schooled horse of Jerez, answering to leg and balance, nimbly evades the bull's charge while the rider, with a *banderilla* in each hand, plants them deftly and accurately. Jerez may be summed up by saying that a street and a square are named after Domecq; that the Domecq bodegas advertise throughout the town and signpost their roads of access; and that Álvaro Domecq ranked as one of the greatest *rejoneadors* of all time and then retired from the ring to become mayor of the city. Jerez was taken by St. Ferdinand in 1251 and lost again under the reign of his son, Alfonso the Learned. The last defenders were Garcí Gómez Carrillo and his ensign Fortún de Torres; such was their bravery that the besiegers tried to avoid killing them and in the end had to drag down the indomitable Garcí Gómez with grappling irons, tend his wounds and restore him to the Christian camp. The Alcázar, where this took place, is a prominent landmark and forms the south-east corner of the primitive town, whose walls are still visible here and there. The Alcázar itself is much restored; the octagonal tower may be Almohad and other parts are known to have been constructed in the fifteenth century. There are items of interest within, but the building, though a national monument, is private property; a hotel is being built against one end and the privilege of viewing the interior is no longer given.

From here to the **Church of San Miguel** is only a short distance. Its name commemorates a battle, one of the forgotten victories of the long drawn-out war in which the Christians were given victory by the appearance on their side of St. James, that is to say their patron Santiago, and the Archangel Michael. When Jerez was eventually captured a small hermitage outside the walls was dedicated to the Archangel in recognition of his assistance. The west front is an impressive late Gothic display, with the usual stylised ogival arch in a highly ornamented *alfiz* and more than a suggestion of Mudéjar workmanship. The interior repays an unhurried examination. The piers vary in style from plain to late Gothic, and a variety of patterns, no two alike, have been traced by the stone webs of the vaults. Six bays are so covered, as well as the apse and four chapels, and in each there is an attractive design, often geometrical and reminiscent of Oriental motifs. In the Chapel of Nuestra Señora del Socorro there is an additional feature, pairs of grotesque figures in bas-relief between the ribs and a recently deciphered plaque giving the name of an unknown sculptor and the date 1547.

The huge retablo has been the subject of much controversy and many names have been mentioned as part-authors of the work. It has now been shown that most of the famous names, including that of Alonso Cano, were introduced in the planning stage and, as so often happens, remained there. Martínez Montañés was the principal craftsman selected and eventually, when he was over sixty, produced the final plan, deputing the lateral panels to a capable but less known sculptor, José de

Arce, and to his wife María. It takes the eye of an expert to distinguish the work of the contributors, so well finished are their carved reliefs. The central reliefs—the Battle of the Angels, the Transfiguration and the Ascension—as well as the free-standing figures of St. Peter and St. Paul, are by Montañés. This really exhausts the artistic treasures of San Miguel, though there is a horrifyingly realistic Crucifixion in the last chapel on the left and on the right, in the *Capilla de Pavón* (a family name, not a peacock), a painting of Veronica's kerchief, attributed to Zurbarán.

From San Miguel it is only a hundred yards to the large **Plaza de los Reyes Católicos**. As General Miguel Primo de Rivera was born in Jerez it is only fair that his equestrian statue should occupy a post of honour among the palm trees. Bas-reliefs of some of his triumphs in the Moroccan war adorn the plinth and there are allegorical figures, perhaps alluding to the years 1923–30, when he directed the nation's destinies. The ensemble shows more enthusiasm than artistry and parts of it demand the services of a guide.

A short distance along the Calle de Calvo Sotelo is the Plaza Escribanos, also called Plaza de la Asunción. Although Jerez is larger than its provincial capital, Cádiz, it is remarkable how little charm the centre of the city holds and it is therefore wise to linger here a while. The south side of the square is formed by the Italianate Renaissance front of the **Civic Library and Archaeological Museum**. The former contains over 25,000 books, some of them rare, but few visitors have the time or knowledge to browse among them. The Archaeological Museum, on the other hand, though small, contains certain items of general interest, including a Greek helmet of the seventh century B C, found in the bank of the River Guadalete. If the Greeks were indeed here—and some have even supposed there was a Greek colony called Xera—this is the only trace of their presence, though extensive excavations have been made at the site of Asta Regia nearby, a Roman colony possibly built over the ruins of the semi-mythical Tartessus. Another item of interest is the marble inscription in Cufic characters which surmounted one of the now-vanished gates of the fortified city. The traces of walls that are left, with the exception of the Alcázar, are hardly worth a special search. Perhaps the most curious exhibit, at least as regards its modern associations, is the Roman head of a girl with her hair done in the style then prevalent in Southern Spain; the most noticeable feature is the pair of kiss curls pointing inwards, in the centre of the forehead, a fashion that is still found among the gypsies in these parts and nowhere else—or so the experts say—and called *nene*. Tracing fashions has its own fascination and even the grave St. Isidore, in his *Etymologies*, follows the modifications made in Roman earrings, collars and brooches during the Visigothic era.

The east side of the square is occupied by the **Church of San Dionisio,** named as usual after the saint on whose feast day the town was recovered from the Moslems. Not only is the exterior a curious and interesting combination of styles, chiefly Gothic and Mudéjar, but on the south side the pavement forms the third side of a tiny patio. Orange and lemon trees perfume the backwater and continue down the pavement in front of the church. The interior follows the usual plan of a nave with two aisles and leads to a huge Rococo retablo, about sixty feet high, which came from the Convent of Santa Ana at the time of the expulsion of the Jesuits. A feature that is usually overlooked but will interest many is the decoration of the piers; there are pairs of slender columns that cross and recross every few feet, a pattern not unknown in Italian Romanesque, but these, instead of finishing in sculptured capitals, merge into a double row of Arab stalactite work. Next to the church is a Mudéjar tower called the *Torre de la Atalaya* or its Spanish equivalent *de la Vela*, from its function as a sentinel's post whence smoke or fire signals could be made out in the chain of fortresses and towers that at one time followed the frontier. Each side has its own decoration and a delightful blend of *ajimez* windows, foliated arches and *alfices* over Isabelline Gothic arches.

The Collegiate Church is built on the site of what was once the chief mosque and it is surprising to learn that this, adapted to Christian worship and eventually in a ruinous state, survived until the seventeenth century. The church possesses religious, if not artistic, priority over all the others of Jerez and owes its immediately impressive effect largely to the monumental stairway that leads up to its west front. The free-standing bell tower is another feature that is popular in Spain where, as previously remarked, the conjunction of mosque and minaret seems to have taken firm root in the southern mind. There the church squats, golden or grey according to the weather, a mass of stone crowned with a cupola and adorned with rather superfluous flying buttresses. A look at the interior gives you a foretaste of the New Cathedral of Cádiz, built by the architect who completed this church, Torcuato Cayón de la Vega. Although building was begun in 1562, less than half had been completed by 1755, when the great Lisbon earthquake caused such damage that Cayón de la Vega was summoned to take over what had already passed through the hands of several architects; perhaps it was the fear of a repetition of the earthquake that prompted the flying buttresses, a Gothic feature that looks so out of place on a Baroque building.

Of all the works of art that are proudly shown, the Sleeping Virgin by Zurbarán is probably the most famous, no doubt owing much to the lack of serious competition; the posture—asleep on her knees while propped against a chair with one elbow—is unreal as well as uncomfortable, but the bowl of flowers in the background has the authentic master's touch. There is also a Black Virgin, of which there are many in these parts, a strange cult object that probably had its origin in Byzantium and can be found as far afield as Russia. There are some paintings on copper too, and for some reason, certainly not their artistic merit, sacristans everywhere attach special importance to these. The historian will be enthralled with an exhibit in the church library, the letters of Cardinal Cisneros to a canon of Toledo, written in cipher and with the key provided. Dated 1516, they throw much light on the troubled times that were bequeathed to the cardinal-regent at the death of Ferdinand the Catholic.

The imposing stairs that lead one to the Mudéjar bell tower and the Collegiate Church are the scene of the September harvest festival, the *Vendimia*. The vintners' patron saint, Ginés de la Jara, is brought here. Even though the whole ceremony, the costumes, the flower games and the *bulerías*, or local variety of flamenco, are organised with one eye on the folklore enthusiast, there is still enough natural exuberance to make the festival a worth-while spectacle for the September visitor.

There is talk of a Shakespeare statue to be erected somewhere in Jerez, in grateful recompense for Falstaff's advertisement in his speech on 'good sherris-sack' and for making Stephano describe his arrival from the wreck to Prospero's island: 'I escaped upon a butt [*bota*] of sack [*seco*], which the sailors heaved overboard...'

Five kilometres from Jerez, on the Medina Sidonia road (C440), is the celebrated Carthusian monastery, **La Cartuja de Nuestra Señora de la Defensión**. The monastery owned not only works of art but much of more negotiable value until, that is, the arrival of the French. In the year 1835, at the time of the dissolution of the monasteries, the abbot was still complaining of the depredations of Napoleon's troops. Fortunately the pictures were taken safely to Cádiz, where one may now see them. The famous stud of Carthusian greys was also scattered, a tragedy which made Ford write, 'the loss of the horses will long be felt, when that of the friars is forgotten.' In 1949 the friars returned, but not the horses. At present the monastery is *in clausura*, but the entrance is well worth seeing and there is always hope that visitors will one day be permitted to see the interior.

If you continue along the road for a little less than a kilometre you come to a humped bridge over the Guadalete, built in 1581, from which you can view the fertile, bushy banks of the river that saw the end of Visigothic rule. The *Guada* is, of course, the Arabic *wadi*, or river, and the rest of its name is much older— there is a story that when Decius Brutus was taking part in the conquest of Spain, his Roman soldiers refused to cross the River 'Lethe', believing that it must be that one of the underworld, whose waters brought oblivion. There is a small hill here which some still call *el real de Don Rodrigo*, and which is supposed to mark Roderick's last encampment at the time of the fatal battle, during which he disappeared. The mystery of his death has intrigued the Spaniards ever since; the legend grew that Roderick's overthrow was the result of his seduction of Florinda, daughter of Count Julian, who had sent her to the royal palace as to finishing school, the custom of those days. Thus was the treachery of the Visigoths rationalised, their despicable bargain with the Moslem forgotten, and the legendary Florinda given such substance that Walter Scott, eleven centuries later, could write:

And if Florinda's shrieks alarmed the air,
If she invoked her absent sire in vain,
And on her knees implored that I would spare . . .

To return to the disaster of the Guadalete and its aftermath. Roderick's war-horse Orelia was found by the banks of the river, but the rider's absence was considered mysterious enough to loose a swarm of legends, comparable with those that surround the ultimate fate of many an unfortunate leader, from Barbarossa to Marshal Ney. You probably passed near his fictitious tomb at Calaña, between Huelva and Aracena. Another, better-known story is that told by the serving-woman in Don Quixote. According to this popular tale, Walter Scott's 'foul ravisher' was last heard of in an underground dungeon which he shared with snakes and toads, and from which arose the dismal plaint:

Ya me comen, ya me comen,
Por do más pecado había.

'Now they eat me, now they eat me, in the place where most I sinned'.

CHAPTER ELEVEN

Jerez to Cádiz

꿎

Arcos de la Frontera—Medina Sidonia—Cádiz

The low hills over and between which N342 from Jerez winds its way are a welcome change from the flat lands that we have traversed since we left Seville. After 10 kilometres an old tower rises on a steep, low hill to the right and a short drive up the earth road takes you to the remains of the *Castillo de Melgarejo*. There is a short section of crenellated wall with a pointed archway, and next to it a grey stone tower, square at the base and octagonal in the little that remains of the upper part, with its machicolations. In its north wall one can just make out the ghost of an *ajimez*, walled up some years ago. On either side this short stretch of ruin continues as the whitewashed wall of a *cortijo*, whose yard is the old parade ground, the *plaza de armas*. The castle was probably one of a chain of watch towers and refuges in the old frontier days, when news of a Moslem raid would set the signal fires blazing and the sentry on the Torre de la Atalaya in Jerez would get the news from this tower.

Arcos de la Frontera is 21 kilometres farther, the old part of the town crowning a steep bluff on the north bank of the Guadalete. Take the left fork on entering the town, and follow the steep, ever-narrowing streets that are signposted to the Parador of the D.G.T. Passing under an archway, the street opens into the Plaza de España, with the modern and entirely admirable parador on your left and a balcony before you. From this you can enjoy a view which will not be equalled until we reach Ronda. Below, the placid river winds past its islands and sandbanks, joined on your right by an irrigation canal that passes under the hill on which the town is built. Straight ahead, southward, are low hills, wheatfields and olive groves; vines are rare, for the winters here are severe.

In the south-west corner of the Plaza is the tiny Ayuntamiento, soon to take in all the buildings along the west side; there are two good *artesonados* for those who are interested. Immediately next to it an archway leads along a cobbled street to the Castle

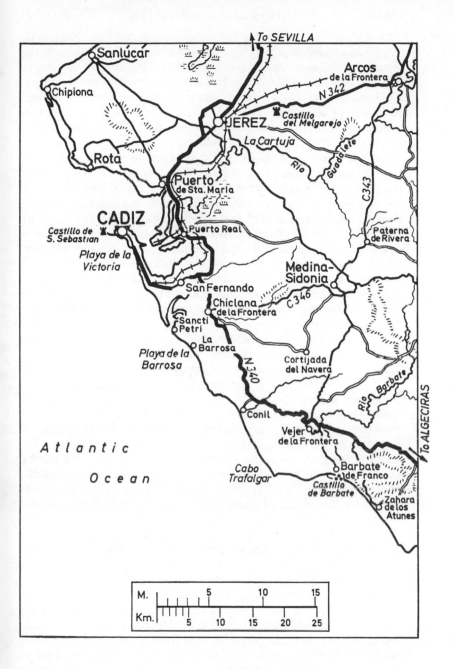

entrance; unfortunately for the sightseer it is the Marchioness de Tamarón's residence and only friends are invited through the Gothic portal with its *alfiz* and the two crests. Another view of this old Moorish castle can be had from the plain on the west side; the long, low crenellated walls with their square towers occupy the crest of a broken hill, on whose slope the tawny rock is visible through a covering of bush and wild flowers. Palm trees stand silhouetted against the walls.

On the north side of the Plaza de España stands one of the two parish churches; each of the twin peaks of Arcos had its patron and the rivalry between them is still alive. The Church of Santa María de la Asunción was originally a Visigothic foundation, but nothing is left of any structure older than the sixteenth century, except on the outside of the apse, where evidence of Mudéjar work remains in the interlaced blind arcade of brick. There is a Baroque façade below the clock tower, with its *azulejo* pattern on the campanile that crowns it; the west entrance is reached by descending steps at the north-west corner, and is a florid Gothic-Isabelline work, so placed that one cannot stand back to admire it.

Inside, the same period shows itself in the overdone ornamental ribs and bosses of the ceiling. The piers terminate above as spreading ribs, the earliest example of this in Spain being in the Church of San Baudel de Berlanga in Soria Province, where eight horseshoe arches radiate from a central pillar and produce the 'palm tree' effect. The best known are those of the *Lonjas*, the exchange buildings, of Valencia and Palma de Mallorca, of about the same date as the interior of this church in Arcos. The effigy of the patroness, the Virgen de las Nieves, is in the second chapel on the right and is called Our Lady of the Snow allegedly because she wears a white frock. It is far more likely that she was originally the Virgin of Santa Maria Maggiore in Rome, whose basilica was built at the command of Pope Liberius in the fourth century, because of a miraculous fall of snow on the Esquiline hill. In the very next chapel is the Virgen del Rosario, who was patroness up to 1936, the year of the Civil War, after which she was demoted, though no one professes to know why.

The font, like so many others in Catholic countries, contains salt water, for it is customary to place a little salt on the infant's lips during baptism as a symbol of protection against evil, in the same way that salt protects food from corruption. Oil, being the symbol of the Grace of God, is frequently found floating on the baptismal water and needs no explanation. There is a poor painting of the *Virgen de la Leche*; some long-forgotten priest had the bare breast of the suckling Mother painted over with the colour of her dress, so that the unfortunate Infant is being offered nourishment through a linen filter.

Though there may be nothing architectural left over from the Middle Ages, the removal of a retablo from the wall of the left aisle uncovered a Byzantine type of painting in tempera, of the Coronation of the Virgin, from the thirteenth century. In the sacristy is an ivory crucifix reputed to be by Montañés. There is also a hole in the wall whose history goes back to the Peninsular War; when the arrival of the French was realised to be inevitable, the hole was made and the church valuables hidden in the cavity behind it. The authorities chose an Immaculate Conception of the school of Murillo to hang over the hole, and whether by accident or design selected one by a student who must have been bottom of the class. At all events, not even the French made a move to steal it, or they would have discovered the hiding place of the gold and silver plate.

Round the Parish Church of San Pedro is everything you expect to see in Andalucía. The brilliant whitewash has been applied so often that it has softened the outlines and rounded the corners of the buildings, and the narrow, oval cobblestones are laid with such art that the streets serve as drains while the stones themselves make surrealist patterns. Antique columns buttress street corners, tiny arches span the narrow lanes, flowers pour down the walls, bricked-up Gothic and Plateresque doorways mark the entrance to the palaces of long ago. The old Puerta de Metrera, with its ceramic plaque of the Virgin as María Auxiliadora, spans one of the steepest streets, where the glaring white is relieved by grass between the cobbles, and moss on the tiles and on the twin merlons that crown the little that remains of the city walls.

You may possibly be invited into a patio, probably shared by a number of families, and itself the walled-off fraction, a quarter or an eighth, of what was once a Renaissance courtyard. All that is left from the days of its glory are two or three arches with their slender marble columns, supporting a crumbling wooden balcony. The brick floor slopes gently to the well-head in the centre, and all around are flower-pots or miniature gardens in their little brick cubicles, or even an orange tree; swallows wheel and swoop to their clay nests under the eaves with alarming speed, while singing canaries and decoy partridges watch wistfully from their cages. It is not surprising that Arcos has had its share of poets and painters. A bird painter's wife bought the castle from the bankrupt estate of the Duke of Osuna, leaving it to her niece, the present Marchioness of Tamarón.

The masonry of the Church of San Pedro indicates that it was once part of the Moorish fortifications. Over the entrance to the northern transept hang two Moorish banners, captured at the Battle of the Salado in which Alfonso XI soundly defeated the Marinids, successors of the Almohads and the last Moroccan dynasty to make Spain the scene of a holy war. There is a Gothic retablo of about the same date, 1347, behind the high altar but its paintings need cleaning. Two Pachecos and some Zurbaráns are hung high on the north and west walls. There are two mummified saints, Vitus and Fructuosus, but it seems unlikely that their bodies are authentic in view of the numerous claims from Westphalia and from various parts of the Iberian peninsula to own their relics.

In the open, bare Plaza de la Caridad is the Hostel of the same name, *para los viejos desamparados*. Old people in Spain are usually well looked after by their descendants, but now and then an old, abandoned creature is found, and for these the Little Sisters of the Poor do their noble work, unseen and unheard except when they gently ask for alms. Those of the old folk who are not paralysed have some little task; an old woman can still milk the cow, and old men plait straw for water-jars, or weed in the tiny garden. Funds are in short supply; but there is an excellent, modern kitchen whose food is appetising and accompanied by a glass of wine twice a week. There is a small Rococo chapel and a pharmacy with a store of modern drugs.

Thirty-seven kilometres along C343 take us across the River Salado and between olive groves to the hill on which the ancient town of **Medina Sidonia** stands. The old Phoenician town of Sidon is commemorated here, with the comparatively modern *madinah* of the Arabs, which is only twelve hundred years old. As you enter, a cobbled space on the left houses the town's sole petrol pump. At the far end, up a stepped, grass-grown street, the cobbles continue to the *Arco de la Pastora*, the double horseshoe town gate that survives from Moslem days. An empty niche inside shows where the Shepherdess stood, the Virgin in her role as protectress of the flocks.

The town is best known to us through the title of the commander of the Invincible Armada, Alonso Pérez de Guzmán el Bueno, Duke of Medina Sidonia. Unable to get out of the awful responsibility of command, and burdened by the mistakes of the intended admiral, the brave but dilatory Marquis of Santa Cruz, the Duke obeyed his sovereign's orders like a Spanish gentleman and put his trust in God. Unfortunately the ships and the stores were rotten and the project ill planned, and when he finally brought home the fleet, he was put ashore at Santander so weak that he had to be carried.

At the top of the town, approached by a very steep cobbled street is the Parroquia de Santa María Coronada. Next to it is the single remaining tower of the old castle, in which took place the murder of Blanche of Bourbon, at the orders of her husband, Pedro the Cruel. In the same castle Leonor de Guzmán, mistress of Alfonso XI and mother of the bastard half-brothers of Pedro the Cruel, took shelter from inevitable murder that finally found her out in 1351. Blanche's murder, at the hands of the archer Pérez de Rebolledo, is commemorated in a plaque on the wall.

The roomy church interior is of a beautiful cream-coloured stone, as clean as on the day it was built, during the transition from Gothic to Renaissance. The great retablo—no two authorities agree as to who was its sculptor—portrays scenes from the life of Christ, the upper row, or Calvary, being especially impressive. At the end of the right aisle there is a Franciscan monk, allegedly by Montañés, and the portrait of an old man by Ribera. Caution is advised concerning these rustic attributions. The choir is uncommonly far back, a pleasant change from the usual arrangement, and in front of it stands part of an old bench which was used by the Inquisition on state occasions. One seat has the crest of cross, sword and palm branch, though not the motto, 'Arise, Lord, and vindicate thy cause!', and the next has the simple cross of the Dominicans. These must have been the seats of the mighty, for the Dominicans, or *domini canes*, 'the hounds of the Lord', as they were jestingly called, were the chief instrument of the Holy Office. Over the entrance to the Baptistery a devil's mask is carved in stone illustrating his proverbial dislike of holy water.

From Medina Sidonia C346 takes us to Chiclana de la Frontera, pretty but unremarkable, and from there N340 goes north to San Fernando, a modern town that houses the Spanish naval headquarters. Soon the road passes uninterruptedly over the string of islands that make the peninsula of Cádiz. On the right is the vast inner harbour and on the left we soon come to the Playa de la Reina Victoria, two miles of golden sand that can hardly be bettered in Europe and an ideal spot for the bather who likes Atlantic breakers. Behind the beach there are only the causeway and the railway line. The **City of Cádiz** occupies the

far end of the promontory and is reached after a journey of only
46 kilometres from Medina Sidonia.

Cádiz has a charm whose source is difficult to define. Poets and
advertisement writers shower it with epithets: *aireario*, said
Juan Ramón Jiménez, whom we met at Moguer; *salada claridad*,
wrote Manuel Machado, brother of a still more famous poet,
cleverly fusing the ideas of clean and salty air. Byron called it
'Siren of the Ocean'; its people, with better taste, 'Little Silver
Cup'; and José Maria Pemán, the city's most famous living
citizen, addressed his birthplace as *Señorita del Mar, Novia del
Aire*. 'Sweetheart of the Air' is not a bad compliment to the
whitest, cleanest seaport in Spain.

So tightly does the city fit into its sea-girt bounds that there is
little chance of antiquities remaining above ground. But even the
name, like that of Medina Sidonia, takes us back three thousand
years to the Phoenicians who founded Gaddir as a rival for the
trade of Tartessus. This was the farthest settlement of the known
world, placed so as to receive tin and amber from the cloudy,
unknown North. So far was it from the haunts of civilisation
that an ancient tomb found here bore the inscription: 'Heliodorus,
a Carthaginian madman, ordered in his will that he should be
put into this sarcophagus, at the farthest extremity of the globe,
that he might see whether any one more mad than himself would
come so far as this place to see him.' The labours of Hercules
brought him here, to take the cattle of Geryon that were pastured
on the Isla de León, and the hero's temple used to stand at the
tip of the promontory.

In Roman days Gades was still of great importance; it produced Lucius Cornelius Balbus, first foreign-born consul of
Rome, and his nephew of the same name who also attained
consular rank and almost rebuilt his home town, equipping it
with docks and a theatre. Much of the wealth of Iberia was
shipped from here to Rome, silver, copper, wine, wool, salt fish
—Gades had a monopoly of this trade—and dancing girls. These
puellae Gaditanae were a famous attraction at dinner parties of
the first century. As Cádiz claims to be the home of flamenco,
it is interesting to read in Juvenal of the *testarum crepitus*; this
can be translated either as clicking of castanets or clapping of
hands, both fundamental elements of Spanish dancing.

The town as we see it today dates almost entirely from the
seventeenth and eighteenth centuries, for the destruction produced by the Earl of Essex in 1596 necessitated much rebuilding.
A road surrounds the whole town and where the streets open on

to it at an acute angle, as they usually do, the sharp edge of the corner house reminds one of a liner's prow. The houses themselves are flat-roofed and most of them sport a small tower, on which the owner would stand in the old days to watch for the homecoming of his fleet.

From these roofs the people of Cádiz listened to the thunder of the guns at Trafalgar, among them the Böhl von Faber family whose daughter Cecilia was eight at the time. It was soon after this catastrophe that Cádiz faced her greatest crisis: as the naval and mercantile station on the life-line that connected Spain with her American colonies, she had to face the prospect of losing her golden monopoly. Her daughters were suddenly her sisters and she was no longer the capital of Latin America.

Cádiz should be visited on foot or in a victoria and without urgency. The Hotel Atlántico with its lovely garden, is a good place to start. If you walk south on the circular drive that once ran inside an unbroken line of fortifications you will see on your right, as you take the first bend, the Castle of Santa Catalina, and far out, facing it, that of San Sebastián, connected to the city by a causeway. The bay between them is called La Caleta, which is only the Spanish diminutive of an Arabic word for harbour. Cabins, a dining-room and balconies have been built and the bathing here should be pleasant from July to September, a proviso that applies to the whole Atlantic coast. One of the local dishes is named after this old fishing harbour, *sopa caletera*, containing rice and ham as well as the ingredients of the usual fish soup.

After La Caleta the road turns east and on the left is the large psychiatric hospital which now incorporates the Chapel of Santa Catalina or *de los Capuchinos*. Like most buildings in Cádiz it has fixed hours for visitors, a refreshing change after the small towns. The chapel's chief interest lies in the fact that it punctuates Murillo's artistic life-span. On the left is his first *Inmaculada*, painted when he was eighteen. In the Sagrario on the right is his *St. Francis Receiving the Stigmata*, showing the progress of the artist's maturity, particularly the masterly foreshortening of the right hand.

The huge retablo is crowned by the *Marriage of St. Catherine*, during the completion of which Murillo fell on to the altar, sustaining internal injuries from which he died a short time later in Seville. This and the other canvases were completed by Murillo's pupil, Meneses Osorio. For sheer virtuosity I recommend the first chapel on the right in which a whole Calvary, dominated by a *Mater Dolorosa*, is carved out of a single block of wood. The artist is Salzillo, whose major works we shall see at Murcia; this one is nevertheless one of his finest, a documentary in the round.

Continuing eastward we see the squat mass of the **Cathedral** before us, with its shallow dome; in its grey, solid pose it seems to symbolise an island that has withstood the storms and seas of so many thousand years. It was designed by Vicente Acero in 1720 but took over a century to build. The façade, seen from near by, is actually of a brown stone rather than grey, spoiled by the later addition of a Neo-Classical upper storey in white. There is something vaguely familiar about the side elevation, and we understand the reason for it when we go inside, for here is the same interior as we saw in the Collegiate Church in Jerez, built by the same architect, Torcuato Cayón. It is, curiously, the only wholly Baroque church in Spain and, though the materials are not all of the best, the general impression is one of restrained magnificence.

The polygonal ambulatory that supports the huge dome of the sanctuary at times persuades one that the building is a rotunda with a nave added as an afterthought; the plan owes much to Diego de Siloé and has more than a superficial resemblance to the Cathedral of Granada. The massive piers, with their engaged, fluted, Corinthian columns, support round arches with the dome of the crossing resting on four of them by means of pendentives. A flood of light pours on to the free-standing altar and emphasises the contrast of light and shade on which this type of architecture depends for its effect. The crypt is a masterpiece, its dark grey stone blocks so accurately hewn that no mortar was needed in the original construction. It uses the principle of the arch, adapted to the lowest of low domes, with a central aperture, like the Pantheon in Rome. It is plain and induces a mood of solemnity —soon to be dispelled in the Treasury—and has extraordinary acoustic properties, for an echo can be repeated fifteen times. Here, under a slab of Granada granite, rest the bones of Manuel de Falla, one of Spain's greatest composers, brought home to rest from the Argentine. Best known for his ballet compositions, *The Three-Cornered Hat* and *El Amor Brujo* (*Magician's Love*), and for his *Nights in the Gardens of Spain*, he may yet earn posterity's greatest thanks for his interest in, and preservation of, Spanish folk music. One wall of the crypt separates it from the sea, whose crashing waves can be clearly heard on stormy days. This is most appropriate, for he died before finishing his great cantata *L'Atlántida*, and Gaditans are proud of Pliny's claim that Cádiz represented the sole surviving part of the lost continent. What Falla did request, and what was faithfully carved, was the simple epitaph, *Sólo a Dios el honor y la gloria*, 'Only to God the honour and the glory'.

The Treasury is unbelievably rich and of great educational value, for it explains why rioters in Spain have always opened proceedings by looting the nearest church. In this case the loss would be considerable in a financial, but only in a financial, sense. There is a custodial of solid silver that is brought out for the Corpus Christi procession; it stands eighteen feet high and weighs thirteen hundredweight, but fortunately it moves on wheels. Inside this is placed the gold custodial of Enrique de Arfe, a fine example of flamboyant Flemish work of the Gothic period; it is known popularly as *el cogollo*, for it sits in the silver giant like the heart in a lettuce. Enrique's son Juan is represented by a gold processional cross and there is a gold chalice by Benvenuto Cellini. There is a modern gold custodial, said to be made in imitation of the façade of Barcelona Cathedral and quite impressive, if you don't know Barcelona Cathedral. To show that the minor arts still flourish in Spain, there is also a silver and gold monument of fine workmanship by Cabella Baeza. Your guide hurries you past the thorn from the Crown of Thorns in its gold and glass reliquary, and the processional cross which is said to incorporate the gold sword hilt of Alfonso X. The main showpiece is the *custodia del millón*, so called because it appears to be studded with at least a million jewels. This outrageous monstrance was presented in 1721 by Miguel Calderón de la Barca, Viceroy of Mexico; history is reticent about who really paid for it.

Among the works of art, as distinct from craftsmanship and ostentation, is an ivory Crucifixion by Alonso Cano, with a head far too small for the body, and a painting of the same subject by the same artist, who thus demonstrates two of his three skills. The *Ecce Homo* by Zurbarán is not up to his usual standard, but a Holy Family by Morales, another Extremeñan, explains why he was called *el Divino*, and a scene from the Passion by Alejo Fernández is also noteworthy. But the finest exhibit is the Mary Magdalene of Murillo.

As you leave the Cathedral and descend the broad steps into the Plaza Pio XII, a plaque on the wall at the corner of Calle Prim opposite marks the house where Admiral Gravina died of the wound he received at Trafalgar, five months after the battle. Though he was commander of the Spanish squadron, he does not receive the same veneration as his second in command, Admiral Churruca, who was killed during the action. And yet, if Gravina's advice had been followed, France might have been spared her greatest defeat until Moscow. Villeneuve, in command of the combined fleets, had stringent orders to sail, admitting of no excuse, from Napoleon himself. While Churruca and Alcalá Galiano, another Spanish admiral, all thought the move to sea would be disastrous, it had to be Gravina who allowed himself to be persuaded against his better judgement. The story runs that Villeneuve deliberately played on the well-known sensitivity of southern pride, and when Gravina gave as one reason for staying in harbour that the glass was falling, Villeneuve replied, 'No, it is your spirit.' Gravina replied by reproaching Villeneuve with his cowardly conduct at Finisterre and high words ensued, the argument ending in Gravina's angry order to put to sea the next day. It is of course, possible that one reason why Churruca is the more popular hero is that Gravina was a Sicilian. His death earns him our respect for, when the end was finally approaching, he told Dr. Fellows, his English physician, that he was going to join Nelson, 'the greatest man the world has ever produced'.

The Old Cathedral, now the Parish Church of La Santa Cruz, is a hundred yards away. It was once a fine building, but was almost completely gutted by Essex. When Drake singed the King of Spain's beard in 1587 he captured or destroyed thirty-seven vessels, but never set foot on shore. The only civilian casualties on that occasion were twenty-five women and children crushed to death in the rush for shelter in the castle. Essex was far more thorough, for the English stayed for two weeks; and one of Cervantes' *Novelas ejemplares*, *La española inglesa*, deals with the capture of a little Spanish girl and her upbringing in London in a crypto-Catholic family.

The Calle Prim leads to the pretty Plaza de Emilio Castelar, a republican leader of the time of Isabel II. Palms and cypresses rise from the bushes and flower-beds and the bronze statesman himself, with an enormous bronze moustache, stands on a plinth in the pose of a frock-coated conjuror. The Plaza de San Juan de Dios, with its tall palm trees, faces directly on to the quay and is the gayest corner of the city. There is always a slight shock on seeing liners berthed in the harbour so soon after turning one's back on the Atlantic at the Cathedral, but it is a reminder of the slenderness of the promontory. Just off the south-east corner is the Hospital de San Juan de Dios, with two delightful patios, whose walls still sport the *azulejos* of three centuries ago. Ford detested the unmusical clang of Spanish church bells, but the carillon of this hospital chapel makes a notable exception. The neo-classical Ayuntamiento, with the city's titles *muy noble* ... on the façade, fills the back of the Plaza.

Past the Hospital de San Juan de Dios is the Santa María quarter, where you can sample the celebrated sea-food at a *freiduría*, best described as a fish-bar and peculiar to Cádiz. The whole Atlantic coast, from Portugal to Tarifa, is justly renowned for its sea-food, whether it be *raya en pimentón* (rayfish in pimiento sauce), *almejas a la marinera* (an appetising stew of winkles), *atún con tomate* (tunny fish) and, a great favourite throughout the South, *sopa al cuarto de hora*. Be careful about this last one, for it denotes a broth whose virtue derives from the fact that the fish ingredients should be given no more than a quarter of an hour to impart their flavour to the brew. It is as well to look at your watch when ordering it, for an equally strong but less refined soup can be made by soaking half the ingredients for twice the time. Most of the sea fish eaten here have only zoological names in English, but the earnest gastronome should not overlook the *choco*, whose cousin the *calamar* or squid is, of course, everyday fare throughout the Mediterranean.

Walking towards the quay the last street on your left is the Calle del Duque de la Victoria. Under the street sign is a ceramic plaque of a victoria, a relic of the days when Cádiz had one-way streets long before they were adopted in larger cities. In a short distance the street name changes to San Francisco and in the fifth block on the left from the Plaza is the Church of San Agustín, which you enter from the parallel street on the left. Here the main show-piece is a Cristo de la Buena Muerte by Montañés, in the right transept. There is also a Neo-Classic retablo with the Virgen de la Correa in her *camarín*, the round chamber behind many Spanish altar pieces, which has the unintended advantage of allowing visitors to examine the statue of the occupant unseen, even while mass is being said. No satisfactory explanation is forthcoming for the Virgin of the Strap and one presumes that she is the Virgen de la Cinta whom we saw at Huelva.

Back on the Calle de San Francisco we continue north-west. One can get into the Oratory of La Santa Cueva through No. 11 of the Calle de San Francisco, although the main entrance is in the parallel street. The Oratory is circular and has five lunette paintings of religious subjects, three of them by Goya; his religious works were few and these are among the best. An interesting point is found in his Last Supper, said to be based on a drawing by Poussin. The participants are portrayed recumbent, as they would be if they were celebrating the Jewish Passover; there is considerable doubt as to whether indeed they were doing so, and if they were it is strange that fish and not lamb was eaten, and that the bread, instead of being unleavened, was of the same shape as the loaf still baked in Andalucía.

At the end of the street is the entrance to the patio of San Francisco, remarkable for the Mudéjar ceilings in its cloister and its varied flora. From among the moon flowers spring loquats, apricots and magnolias, and a palm tree clothed in ivy towers over them. Behind this block is another pretty square, the Plaza del Generalísimo Franco, in one of whose houses Manuel de Falla was born.

The Archaeological Museum is here and will even be open one day; at present the building is in such bad repair that it would be criminal to expose valuable exhibits to the risk of flooding. Nevertheless the efficient and courteous Directress, Señora Blanco de Torresillas, goes on with the work of classification, so that any of the shrouded items and their provenance can be located in a minute. Here you will find the headless Mariquita from Lebrija, known also as María Piña when she stood in the corner of a house in the last century, though no one remembers why she should have been called a pine cone. There are three Roman male heads that resemble recognised portraits of Augustus, Tiberius and Claudius, though the latter could possibly be Germanicus. The expression on the face of Tiberius duplicates that of other portrait busts and some of the coins issued during his reign. All three wear sidewhiskers, the *patillas* that have never ceased being fashionable in Spain, except during the pointed beard era of the sixteenth century. A Phoenician column capital, of the seventh century BC, has the 'ram's horn' volutes that came into classical art through the Ionian colonies in Asia Minor, and are therefore an Oriental motif; it is the Museum's proudest possession.

Next door, the Academia de Bellas Artes houses the **Museo de Pinturas**, containing a varied selection of paintings. In the first hall (I) are the primitives and others, with Morales included among them; his triptych, the *Ecce Homo* (No. 332), is wonderfully expressive and as always one is impressed with the even standard of excellence that he achieved. Murillo's *Ecce Homo* is also here and cannot stand the comparison. The Flemings are well represented, two of their best being the *Deposition* of Campana (No. 100) and that of Roger van der Weyden, as a triptych (No. 103). Room IV has a small but famous Holy Family by Rubens, measuring about 12 by 8 inches only, and the Virgin in this is one of the artist's few females who are not blowzy. Hall V contains modern works, some of them most attractive, especially the work of the romantics. Hall VI has much of interest; there are portraits of Carlos IV and Maria Luisa by Antonio Carnero, a pupil of Goya and rather more tactful than the master. Even he could not instill much intelligence into the face of the cuckold King, or make the Queen anything but revolting. No. 404 is of Mendizábal standing, writing the decree to dissolve the monasteries, the *Proyecto de desamortización*. He was tall, dark and handsome and his features are consistent with his alleged Jewish ancestry. Of course, this allegation may simply be the result of his financial policy, which enriched the state temporarily by confiscating much church property and forcing thousands of drones to work for a living.

It is strange how Cádiz keeps cropping up in the story of Spain's attempts at liberty, liberalism or libertinism. Mendizábal was born in Cádiz; the Cortes that framed the first liberal constitution did so in Cádiz during the Peninsular War, and Colonel Riego, the balcony of whose *pronunciamento* we saw at San Juan de las Cabezas, kept the standard of liberty flying in Cádiz until Angoulême and his French troops liberated Ferdinand VII.

In the same room is a large canvas by Rodriguez Barcaza, entitled *The Inauguration of the Cortes of Cádiz* and it is surprising to learn that it was awarded first prize in the Paris exhibition of 1867; it is impossible to accept the claim that it won the prize on its merits. Before leaving this room, look at the self-portrait of the gifted Victoria Martín de Campo (No. 181), teacher of painting at the local art school.

In Room VII they make much of Zurbarán's *Vision of St. Francis*, symbolising the rebuilding of the Porziuncola at Assisi; all who have seen this humble chapel in its monstrous new shell will agree that the subject is best left alone. In any case, Zurbarán is at his best with small groups or single figures, as we saw in the procession of female saints in Seville, and as can be seen again in the twenty more that are on view in Room VIII. Nine of them, including three of St. Bruno, were acquired from the Cartuja of Jerez when it was emptied by Mendizábal's decree; one hopes they will never go back, to be shut away from the light of day and the admiration of the spectator. Among the imaginary portraits of celebrated Carthusians is that of St. Hugh of Lincoln, carrying the swan that is his symbol; perhaps this is the origin of the saying that all his geese are swans.

From the Plaza del Generalísimo Franco the Calle San José leads south through the geographical centre of the town. The fifth cross-street is Santa Inés, and here we come across another landmark in the history of the nineteenth century. The Oratory of St. Philip Neri is a Baroque construction which was selected as the seat of the Cortes, a Chamber of Deputies, during the siege of Cádiz in 1811–12. The walls carry numerous reminders of the occasion and the adjoining stair, leading up to what is now a school, was the scene of the promulgation of the new constitution in 1812.

The siege is often imagined as isolating the city at the level of the causeway. In fact, although the French did at first occupy the whole coast-line on the far side of the bay, and even bombarded the city from the Trocadero promontory, they were soon forced to retire and their line of investment for the next two years ran from Rota to Chiclana de la Frontera without occupying Puerto de Santa María, Puerto Real or the Trocadero peninsula. This was as well, for Cádiz had no water of its own and relied largely on supplies from Puerto de Santa María.

The liberal constitution, that was to become an ideal for much of Europe in the next fifty years, was excellent in concept but doomed to failure. The trouble with Spanish democracy has always been the lack of capitalists who can use it to their mutual advantage. So while the Cortes of Cádiz was planning the future of Spain, history was preparing the reaction and its supreme joke—their overthrow by the king for whom they were fighting, by the masses whose emancipation they were planning, and by the French allies of their king, who at that moment was a prisoner in France.

The Trocadero Peninsula, with its fishing village and fort, played a decisive part in the final liquidation of the liberals' brain-child. We have seen how in 1823 Ferdinand VII appealed to the French and how the Hundred Thousand Sons of St. Louis marched to his rescue, welcomed everywhere by a proletariat who did not fancy life without fetters. The only difficulty was encountered at the Fort of Trocadero, where a courageous resistance was offered; once this was overcome, the captive King was handed to his rescuers as a matter of course, along with

Colonel Riego as an example of Punic faith in this once Phoenician stronghold. The brilliant feat of arms was commemorated in
France, where a small hill in the Paris suburb of Passy was re-
christened, the name Trocadero being used in turn for a palace,
a *place*, a *Métro* and an aquarium. The fort, whose poor ruins
do not repay the approach over an impossible road, was finally
immortalised in a London restaurant.

To return to the Oratory. It is a small, pleasant but not impressive building and its contents are limited to a Murillo—
needless to say an *Immaculate Conception*—and a terracotta
Head of St. John believed to be by Pedro Roldán. St. Joseph
would have been apter, for it was on his day that the Constitution
was promulgated; and from this fact it got the name *La Pepa*, as
Pepe is the diminutive for Joseph. It thus came about that consti-
tutionalists came to use the slogan *Viva la Pepa*!

The building next door houses the Historic Museum, mainly a
collection relating to the years we have discussed. There is an
accurate model of the city as it was in the eighteenth century,
and you can see that every house had its patio and every patio its
well, in which the water collected from the roof was stored. There
are some serious paintings, of no artistic importance, one portraying the promulgation of the Constitution, with the Royal
Standard of Great Britain and Ireland standing alongside the
arms of Spain. There are four portraits of Ferdinand VII, his
expressions varying between self-indulgence and cold intolerance;
none of them capture the shiftiness which Goya brought out so
well. A crude daub of the dying Admiral Churruca, waving a
sword, is by a painter who wisely remains anonymous. Strangely,
there is no portrait of Gravina in the whole of Cádiz, though
there is a mirror from his house.

Joseph Bonaparte, *el rey intruso*, is well caricatured, special
attention being given to his alleged love of wine. With wine cups
painted on his coat and goblets on his pantaloons, he holds a tray
with decanter and glasses, while sitting on a cucumber. The last is
a pun on his nickname Pepe, whose diminutive is *pepino*, also
cucumber. The verse, for satire was heavy in those days, begins,

> *Botellas, copas, pepino*
> *Son los títulos, José*

'Bottles, glasses and cucumber are your titles, Joseph.'

Whether or not he was a drunkard, he certainly appreciated the
wines of Jerez and there is even a story, no doubt unfounded,

that the well-known Tio Pepe, or 'Uncle Joe', was named after Pepe Botellas, or 'Bottle Joe'.

On leaving, you should go east along Calle Santa Inés to the end of the block, then turn right along General Queipo de Llano, a main, though narrow, artery across the peninsula. The second turning to the left, Calle Obispo Calvo y Valero, brings you immediately to the *Hospital de Mujeres*, or de Nuestra Señora del Carmen (not to be confused with the church of the same name). This old hospital is now part of the bishop's residence, but the patio is worth visiting for the adaptation of *olambrilla* work on the walls, dating from the eighteenth century. In the courtyard each palmetto grows out of a tiled earth box, and a fine double staircase of marble leads to the upper floor. In the Rococo chapel is one of Andalucía's few El Grecos (we saw the other two in Andújar and Seville), an Ecstasy of St. Francis, which is inevitably compared with the same subject by Murillo that we saw earlier in the Chapel of Santa Catalina. The colouring here is so sombre that a black-and-white drawing would have given almost the same effect, and it is easy to see that the grave Castilian, which El Greco became by adoption, could not identify himself with St. Francis' frequently light-hearted devotion. It is striking to realise that you have not seen in Cádiz a single trace of the five centuries of Moslem rule. Whether it is because Cádiz has always looked westward, or whether the limited space of the sea-girt city does not allow preservation of ancient relics the fact is there.

The *Parque Genovés* runs parallel with the sea front. The palms reach up above the topiary work, children play along the broad paths while soldiers and nursemaids repeat the age old theme. An open-air theatre promises enchanted evenings in the summer, an old fort still houses a garrison, and Cádiz honours her sons with statuary. Here you will find Celestino Mutis, the botanist, suitably placed among the rarer plants. Among these is a fine example of *Dracoena draco*, the dragon Tree; of many plants which have the name 'dragon', *dracontium* or *dracunculus* attached to them, this is the only one that exudes the red resin, the genuine 'dragon's blood'. Here, too, is José María Pemán, the poet and essayist whose features lend themselves to the Roman style of portraiture adopted by the sculptor.

A pleasant walk may be taken in the direction opposite to that which goes to Santa Catalina and the Cathedral. First you pass the Genovés gardens, then meet the sea at the Candelaría Battery, whose guns were never a threat to the many raiders that terrorised Cádiz. Behind the old fortification is the Church of Nuestra Señora del Carmen, a Baroque building that is nevertheless different from all the others we have seen. To appreciate what makes it so different you should really go to Central and South America, where the same adaptation of Baroque can be seen from Mexico to Valparaiso. Just as the Mudéjars modified Gothic buildings by incorporating their own style of decoration, with the support of the conquering Christian, so did the Indian craftsmen add their exotic touch to the Baroque. Then, just as old customs and language tend to perpetuate themselves in the colonies and eventually return, long out of date, to the land of their birth, so did the sixteenth-century architecture of Spain, two centuries later. Only by the time it came back it had absorbed much from the Indians, for the natives of Mexico and Peru were skilled in the arts of stone cutting and carving long before the arrival of the Spaniards. That is why the Church of the Carmen contains something exotic in its façade, the powerful influence of a submerged civilisation, the hint of an Aztec temple.

From the northern promenade, or Alameda de Apodaca, you may watch the liners coming and going between Spain and her grown-up daughters, still perhaps carrying the fighting cocks that were ordered by the fancy in Caracas. The cargo ships still bring mahogany, though every desk, wainscotting, chair and cupboard in Cádiz seems to be made of it—mahogany with brass handles is one of the most vivid memories you will take away with you. A small détour brings you to the Plaza de España, where the grandiose monument to the siege and the Cortes dominates the lawns and the ornamental trees. On the way there you will cross the Calle Isabel la Católica, where a plaque on No. 12 announces that José Maria Pemán, whose statue we saw in the Parque Genovés, was born within.

CHAPTER TWELVE

Cádiz to Ronda

✦

Sancti Petri—Barrosa—El Conil—Véjer de la Frontera—Zahara
de los Atunes—Laguna de la Janda—Bolonia—Tarifa—Castellar
de la Frontera—Gaucín

There is only one land route in or out of Cádiz, and you therefore have to return along the narrow promontory to San Fernando, after which N340 branches southward. On both sides
there are salt-pans, an ancient method of obtaining this chemical
so essential to metabolism and Oriental hospitality. The shallow
pans are a guarantee of fine summer weather, for the salt,
obtained by the evaporation of sea-water in them, is stacked in
glistening pyramids—they are not even covered with loose tiles,
as in Sicily, and a good rainstorm would quickly wash away the
result of a month's work.

You cross the canal or inlet of Sancti Petri on leaving San
Fernando, and when you reach Chiclana de la Frontera (through
which you passed on your way from Medina Sidonia), a turning
to the right leads to the **Castle of Sancti Petri**, eight kilometres
away. It is now a lighthouse, but this rises from the ruins of the
castle which, in turn, was built over the remains of the far-famed
Temple of Hercules. The Roman construction is said to be the
successor of the Phoenician temple; this would be dedicated to
Melkart, equated with the Greek Heracles. There can be little
doubt about the Roman temple, for fishermen still occasionally
find statues fouling their nets, and Roman coins of Gades are
also commonly unearthed. Arab authors describe the impressive
lighthouse and temple, with the colossal statue of Hercules on
the summit holding an iron key in its left hand.

The Arabs were steeped in superstition to at least the same
extent as their Christian neighbours, and the legend that the
building was filled with gold dust and that a treasure was buried
under the foundations was not even questioned. When, therefore,
the Admiral Ibn Maimun revolted against his Almoravid masters
in 1145, his first undertaking was a treasure hunt. He had the
foundations excavated, at the same time supporting the super-

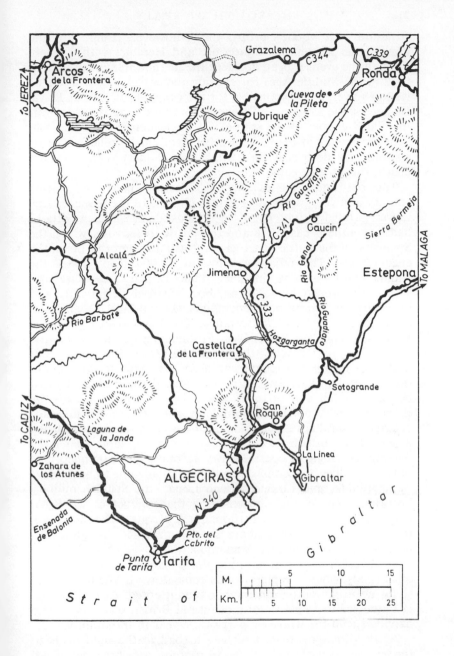

structure with wooden props; these, however, caught fire and down came the temple, lighthouse and Hercules with a crash. Though the event was an accident the method was precisely that used in the Middle Ages for causing the collapse of a defended wall or tower, and responsible for the original title of our Royal Engineers, the Sappers and Miners. All that the ruins yielded was the gilded copper of the statue and the leaden cramps that had kept the stones in place. The other firmly-held belief was that anyone who destroyed the temple would meet with a violent death; this at least came true.

The road now passes through pleasant but uninteresting country and very rarely affords us a glimpse of the sea, although we run parallel with it. The French blockade of Cádiz in 1810–12 had its southern base here and the **Battle of Barrosa**, which the Spanish call the Battle of Chiclana, was an attempt to break the encirclement. The relieving army of 17,000 men, under the command of La Peña, included 4,000 British under Graham. These, abandoned by La Peña, bore themselves gallantly and saved the day, capturing French guns, generals and a regimental eagle, in that order of importance. The bayonet charge of the 87th Foot, later the Royal Irish Fusiliers, earned them the title of the 'Faugh-a-Ballaghs', the 'Clear the Ways'; in the course of it their Sergeant Masterson captured the first French eagle in the Peninsular War. The battle epitomised the mutual distrust between British and Spanish allies, for La Peña, with all the effective cavalry under his command, forbore even to take advantage of Graham's victory and, in Napier's words, 'no stroke in aid of the British was struck by a Spanish sabre that day.' Among the tangle of contradictory accounts given by historians of the two allies, this contest is almost the only one to be marked by unanimity, and Colonel Priego López, the Spanish military historian, joins Napier in censuring the conduct of La Peña. Quite recently, during excavations for a private swimming pool, the skeletons of several casualties were unearthed though identification, even of their race, was impossible.

The coast at this point has nine glorious miles of uninterrupted quiet sands, where the pine woods come down to the beach, and so far no urbanisation scheme has been mooted. At El Pinar de la Francesca there is a colony of retired British servicemen who happily spend the whole or part of the year in tranquillity.

At 19 kilometres from Chiclana a road to the right leads to the seaside town of El Conil de la Frontera, self-christened 'Pearl of the Atlantic.' It is certainly a pleasant region and about forty

British families live here, in houses supplied with electricity and running water. The beach is excellent, and the climate cooler in summer than that of the Costa del Sol. The local bodega now centres round the square keep of the castle, the rest of which has almost disappeared.

Véjer de la Frontera is 11 kilometres farther along N340. This ancient town, which St. Ferdinand declared free of tilth and pasture during the short time that the Christians remained in occupation, has had an eventful life. It was finally recovered by Sancho IV, *El Bravo*, and formed part of the estates of the Guzmán family, of whom we are to hear more. The later generations, Dukes of Medina Sidonia who instituted and owned the hundreds of beehives for which Véjer was famous, as well as the tunny fisheries off the coast, attempted to deprive the citizens of their privileges; the reaction was so strong that they were restored under the name of *hazas de suerte*, a face-saving formula. The blindingly white town, perched on a hilltop from which Trafalgar, Morocco and the Sierra de Ronda can be seen, is there for the traveller's pleasure but is not a must for the sightseer.

From the modern town at the foot an entrance arch surmounted by a balconied window leads steeply upward and gives passage to a representative slice of Andalucian life. Mules and donkeys step daintily on the stone sets, each carrying its straw panniers or containers for milk, wine or water. These last, the *cántaros*, still conform to the specifications of the Water Sellers' Ordinance of 1516, which specified a minimum load of six vessels and that the *cántaros* themselves 'shall be of round shape, and not the Moorish ones, as those have long spouts; each *cántaro* has to be closed with a cork.' Although the women differ in no way from those of other small towns, the story is zealously kept alive that 'only the other day' they were still wearing the *cobijada*, a kind of hood or veil with eye-holes. They would have you believe that it was a picturesque survival of Moslem days, as at Mojácar; in both towns it is probably no more than another device for protecting the female complexion from the sun and wind.

You should ask for the *Convento de las Monjas*, long abandoned by the nuns, whose weathered arch and pilasters support the claim that it was a Roman temple. Along its side runs an alley spanned by four arches leading to a belvedere from which the next green hill can be seen, crowned by a windmill. The castle has largely been rebuilt, but an original tower remains, as well as another lower down in the town, to be entered through the patio of a once aristocratic house. From these viewpoints one may see the River Barbate running past the foot of the hill and the site, five miles to the south, of the Battle of Guadavicea, between Vandals and Visigoths. One of the world's forgotten battles, it may still have its place in the web of history. If the Vandals had not been forced to emigrate to Tunisia, Justinian might not have sent Belisarius to conquer North Africa; and there might never have been a Byzantine exarch, Count Julian, in Ceuta, whose daughter's dishonour provoked the Moslem invasion of Spain.

Before going on to the site of the first battle of that conquest, a visit to the Sanctuary of Nuestra Señora de la Oliva takes only a short time. There is no trace of the original Visigothic chapel nor of the primitive image. Over the entrance are the words *Quasi oliva speciosa in campis*, a quotation from the Apocryphal book of Ecclesiasticus, which probably gives us the clue to Our Lady of the Olive, wherever she is encountered. The actual passage, indeed the whole chapter, is a glorification of Wisdom and as wisdom is feminine in any language, her attributes can easily be adapted to the Virgin.

The annual *romería* on 7th May is like many others in Spain and more typical than the highly organised one of El Rocío. Perspiring police try to keep a passage open through the milling crowds so that cars, motor-cycles, bicycles and loaded buses can discharge their passengers and find parking. Gypsies sell the wares that they always sell in Spain, copper and tin, their ancient craft, but nowadays mass-produced for them in the big towns. Ice-cream merchants do a roaring trade. Everyone is happy, for the noise is indescribable and incessant; a loud-speaker is attached to the roof of the Sanctuary and relays flamenco with the maximum of volume and the minimum of tuning. Every soul for miles around must be here and it is nothing for a woman, with a baby in her arms and three or four children between the ages of three and seven, to be resolutely walking the four miles from Véjer, quite prepared to do the return journey uphill during the night. For that is when the fun of the fair begins; bonfires, flamenco dancing, noise and still more noise, *pinchitos*, the local kebab, snapped up as soon as they come off the vendor's charcoal brazier, wine-skins passed from hand to hand, the thin jet deftly directed into the mouth without the waste of a drop; couples imperceptibly melting into the night from the fringes of the crowd. The devotional side of the outing arouses little enthusiasm and there are about twenty worshippers in the Sanctuary for two thousand holiday makers outside. The crowd shows the usual mixture of races; blonds, redheads, swarthy Moors and even Negroid features reflect the history of the South.

The main road continues to a cross-road, where an inn, *Venta El Cruce*, is well patronised by lorry drivers and therefore to be recommended. The road to the right takes us to **Zahara de los Atunes**, a sleepy fishing village that wakes up only in the tunny season. All along this coast the ancient method of trapping the fish in a maze of nets and then clubbing and stabbing them to death is still practised, as in the Mediterranean. Drowsy though the hamlet may be, it too has had a past, for Cervantes ranked this *finis terrae* of the rogues and their victims alongside the Zocodover of Toledo, and other thieves' kitchens that he knew and described so well. You may find it called the 'Academy of the Tunny Fishers' in his short story entitled *The Illustrious Kitchen Maid*. Near by was fought another important battle, when in 1340 Alfonso XI defeated the combined armies of Granada and Fez, the latter led by Abu'l Hasan, the 'Black Sultan' of the Marinids. The Moslems were supposed to have used cannon, and it is claimed that this was the first time they were used in Europe, though it is recorded that England's Edward III used 'crakys of war' against the Scots in 1327.

Back on the main road we soon see the **Laguna de la Janda** on our left; in spite of drainage it is still largely under water in winter, but in summer it provides an immense grazing ground for cattle, including the *toros bravos* of the Medina Sidonia estate. In spring the wild flowers stretch away into the distance, each species keeping to itself, so that the gently rising ground to the east is chequered with great patches of violet, crimson, yellow and white. The coastal strip between the Laguna and the sea is narrow here, accounting for the number of battles I have mentioned. It is the natural route for an invading army that has landed from Africa and it is believed to be here that the first encounter took place between the small Berber force of Tarik and the great army of the Visigoths under Roderick, whom the Witiza faction called the usurper and other names less polite. It must have been here that the wings of the Visigothic army, foolishly entrusted to Witiza's sons, went over to the enemy.

Much is made of the part played by cavalry in this battle, and the old belief that the Visigoths were superior to the Berbers in this branch is now questioned. All the evidence points to the facts that the Visigoths had few mounted men, while the Moslems relied on clouds of horsemen. Furthermore, the tactics of the Orient always included the use of lightly armed, mobile horsemen against the slower, mail-clad Christians. Such at least were the methods employed at Dorylaeum and Manzikert. The style of riding adopted by the opponents was also antithetic. The Christians, then and thereafter, used the saddle with high cantle and long stirrup, riding *a la brida*, as it is called, while the Arabs introduced a lighter saddle and shorter stirrup, the style known as *a la jineta*, approximating to the modern forward seat. Later, the Spaniards preserved both styles and a good horseman was one who could be at home in both saddles.

The road now winds between low hills in moorland country and after 68 kilometres we turn right at the abandoned Chapel of San Juan del Valle, where a military post of conscripts is established. The new road passes behind the mountain of Silla del Papa—no one knows why the Pope should sit there —and descends after eight kilometres to a fishing village, **Bolonia**, still named after its Roman predecessor, whose ruins are now called Baelo. It lies in a beautiful, unspoiled bay of golden sand, with the whole stretch of the Moroccan coast on the horizon. Even those who have no interest in archaeology will find the trip worth while for the scenery, the view and the bathing.

The Roman remains are at first sight disappointing, and it is easy to pass them without realising what they are. However, the enthusiasm of Don Isidoro Otero Rodríguez, who keeps a bar in the village, brings the town back to life, and he is justifiably proud of his probably unpaid post, having inscribed on his visiting cards 'Guardian of the Ruins of Baelo'. Even if you don't know Spanish he will point out the *templos*, the *teatro* and other easily understood remains. There is a barely distinguishable forum and then, on the rise behind, three small temples side by side, each on its own foundations. The cellae measure only twenty feet square, and are identical; they are known to have been dedicated to Juno, Jupiter and Minerva. The theatre retains vestiges of grandeur, perhaps because of its overgrown condition, and forthcoming restoration may detract from its charm. Down on the foreshore, street corners protrude from the sand and one can still see the troughs in which fish were salted—their function was proved conclusively by the discovery of thousands of fish bones, most of them recognisable as those of the tunny. This find, made in 1966, is of course entirely in keeping with the monopoly of salt fish known to have been enjoyed by Cádiz in Roman days. The objects recovered from the excavations have been removed and, as most of the team were French archaeologists, they are chiefly found in Paris, though one or two mutilated statues are in Madrid.

Tarifa, which is on the Punta Marroquí about 18 kilometres beyond the turning where we left the main road, is the most southerly town in Spain and the point nearest to Africa, for here the Straits of Gibraltar are only eight miles across. This is also the end of the Costa de la Luz, a stretch of almost uninterrupted beach that we have now followed from Huelva, near its northern end. From now on we exchange the tides, the rolling waves and the pounding surf for the languid shores of the Mediterranean.

Tarifa, like so much that we have seen, is first heard of in connection with the Moslem invasion. It is named after a Berber, Tarif Ibn Malluk, who is often confused with Tarik Ibn Ziyad, victor of Guadalete or wherever it was that he defeated Roderick. With the help of Arabic chronicles that were unknown thirty years ago, the legends relating to the fateful years 709–11 have been found to contain more than a grain of truth. There *was* a Count Julian, governor of Ceuta and vassal of the Arab rulers of North Africa, but we still do not know whether he was the Byzantine exarch, a Visigoth or a Christian Berber.

The story of his daughter's seduction appears in every account —in Spain she is still called 'La Cava', from an Arabic word for a prostitute, which seems unfair. After it, Julian went to his overlord Musa Ibn Nusayr who lived in Kairouan, religious capital of Tunis, proposing an invasion of Spain. Cautiously, Musa ordered Julian to make a reconnaissance, which he did in 709, returning from the Bay of Algeciras a few days later with booty and captives. Musa now requested permission from his supreme commander, the Omayyad caliph at Damascus, to undertake an invasion, but was advised to make further raids, gain more local knowledge and, above all, not to expose Moslems to the dangers of an angry sea.

So the second raid was made by Tarif, a Berber officer, who took 400 men, of whom 100 were horsemen, in four ships supplied by Julian. In July 710 they landed at the island which lies off the town of Tarifa (and which was called after him, Gezirat Tarifa). In various forays they captured much booty and many captives of startling beauty, and it was when Musa received his share of these that orders were given for the invasion proper. This, to complete the story, was directed by Tarik Ibn Ziyad, a freedman of Musa and, it is thought, a Persian. In the spring of 711 he crossed the straits and fixed his headquarters on Mount Calpe, thereafter to be called Jebel Tarik, and the Mount of Tarik has now become Gibraltar. When his army had been ferried across he fixed on a small island to the west as a base of operations, calling it the Green Island, *al-Gezira al-khadra*, that gave its name to the town of Algeciras; the island off-shore is still called Isla Verde.

If it is summer you would be well advised to stay in one of the hotels that have been built on the highway within a few miles of Tarifa. The one on the east side, on the road to Málaga, is high in the Sierra del Cabrito among ferns and cork trees; seen at night, these look white and ghostly where the bark has not been removed. From here, on a normal clear day when the *levante* is not blowing, you can see the whole coast of Morocco from Ceuta to Tangier, a line of jagged mountains with Jebel Musa on the east, so that both the Pillars of Hercules are now named after the Moslem conquerors. Far away to the south rise the peaks of the Atlas Mountains, snow-covered for the greater part of the year.

There is really only one way into the town of Tarifa, and that is through the pointed horseshoe arch where the main road takes a sharp turn to the east. The Puerta de Jerez, as it is called, opens invitingly between flower-beds and palm trees through a section of the town wall completely covered with ivy; just enough is cut away to reveal the plaque announcing 'The very noble, very loyal and heroic city of Tarifa, taken from the Moors in the reign of Sancho IV, El Bravo (the Wild), on the 21st September, 1292.' There is not a great deal to see, but as you wander through the clean, white streets something more than the map tells you that you are only a few miles from Morocco. All roads lead downhill, but any that bear left will bring you to the late Gothic Church of San Mateo, built over the site of the chief mosque. St. Matthew was chosen as patron, of course, because his feast day falls on the 21st September. The bell tower might well be built on the foundations of the minaret; note the elaborately pierced stone windows on the north side and the contrast of the grey stone Baroque façade with the brick walls. There is little of interest inside; the usual overdone rib pattern adorns the roof and the whole is of an ugly dun colour caused by an unfortunate choice of limewash. The church is famous for a Visigothic tablet dated 674, discovered by the parish priest in the hills five miles away and now hanging outside the Sagrario, which is the last chapel on the right.

The **Castle** was originally built by Abderrahman III and

completed in April 960; it and the Castle at Marbella were designed to discourage the Fatimids of Egypt who were threatening the western Mediterranean. A Cufic inscription over one of the original town gates gives the date and, on close examination of the worn part at the end, the name of the vizier, Ibn Badr, who was in charge of the work. It is an imposing building, at present occupied by the military, but permission is readily given to inspect every part under the guidance of one of the garrison. Cameras must be left at the entrance. From the extensive walk round the battlements you have a fine view of the town, and can easily trace the circuit of its walls. On the seaward side are the harbours, the end of the mole furnished with an outsize statue of Christ. Beyond is the original island of Tarifa, now called Isla de las Palomas, connected with the mainland by a causeway and closed to the public. Between the harbour and the causeway is a small beach which is sheltered and well frequented; it may be here that Alfonso VI in 1082, with prophetic vision, rode his horse into the sea and exclaimed, 'I have reached the limits of the land of Andalucía!'

A double wall, with a narrow walk running along its top, connects the castle with an outlying, octagonal tower, the Torre de Guzmán. This is said, though without much certainty, to be the one from which Alonso Pérez de Guzmán gained eternal honour. Two years after the capture of Tarifa, Southern Andalucía was again invaded by Moors and the castle closely besieged. The seneschal, Alonso Pérez de Guzmán, had spent three years as a mercenary in the service of the King of Morocco, which was no matter for adverse comment as he undertook not to fight against his own king. But one of King Sancho's brothers was fighting on the Moors' side—which gives one an idea of what loyalty meant—and he had one of Guzmán's sons in his power, possibly assigned to him as a page. It thus happened that Guzmán was summoned to the walls and faced with the alternative of surrendering the castle or having his son killed; his answer was to throw his dagger down and walk away. Various heroic and some trite statements have been attached to this typically Spanish gesture, and were repeated during the siege of the Alcázar of Toledo in 1936. The only unanimity refers to his return to the battlements when the shocking deed had been done, and his theatrical explanation, 'I thought from the outcry that the enemy had penetrated into the castle.'

Rewards were showered on all who were concerned with the gallant defence of Tarifa. Months later Guzmán received a letter from King Sancho, comparing him to Abraham, and decreeing that henceforward he and his descendants should enjoy the additional name of *El Bueno*. The King, being no etymologist, could not know that Guzmán itself had the same meaning, being a Visigothic name, 'good man'. Among the Teutonic tribes, 'good men' were used for certain legal purposes, whence come our 'good men and true' of the jury, and the Spanish *hombres buenos* who to this day have a special function in civil law. Three years later, his father Sancho having died, Ferdinand IV conferred on Guzmán the castle, town and demesne of Sanlúcar de Barrameda. The family much later became dukes of Medina Sidonia, and that is why in 1588 another Alonso Pérez de Guzmán el Bueno, 'Goodman the Good', Duke of Medina Sidonia, was plucked away from his comfortable palace in Sanlúcar to lead the Invincible Armada.

The Ayuntamiento also commands a wide view and there is an especially good bit of the city wall visible at the north-east corner, which is now called Boquete de la Cilla (originally *silo*, as it was one of the food stores). At the Ayuntamiento can be seen the city arms, three keys representing the three gates of the old city; we entered through that of Jerez, the Puerta del Retiro was at the site of the breach made in 1811 and has now disappeared, and the Puerta del Mar is part of the castle and carries the Cufic inscription referred to earlier. Here too is a wonderful collection of original documents granting and confirming the privileges of the town. The east wall is practically untouched, even to the breach made by the French during the siege of 1811–12. Laval, the French commander, sent an envoy demanding the surrender of the town and was answered by Oliver Copons, the Spanish commander, that he would meet him at the head of his troops in the breach in order to discuss matters. The heroic defence, coupled with a cloudburst, resulted in the withdrawal of the French after considerable losses, bearing up the reputation expressed in one of Spain's thirty thousand proverbs, *A Tarifa la guerrera, no se toma ahí como quiera*, 'You can't take warlike Tarifa just as you please'.

From the tangle of conflicting accounts one retains nothing but admiration for the heroic Copons, but the part played by the British is ignored by some Spanish authors. Admittedly, they were under the command of an incompetent leader, but some of the subordinates made up for his deficiencies. The small garrison, assisted by the weather, amply sustained the town's reputation and themselves brought about the retreat of the French; their success was quite contrary to the forecast made by Wellington and on this occasion it is evident that Spanish tenacity in defence, with the assistance of some of the British officers, played a vital part in the outcome of the Peninsular War. Even the Tower of Guzmán featured in the narrative, for an eighteen-pounder was mounted on the roof and would no doubt have caused much damage to the French, had not one of its shells exploded prematurely, wounding a Tarifan, at which the British commander impulsively ordered it to be spiked.

West of the castle is a rather depressing *alameda*, with palms instead of poplars, and a statue of Guzmán el Bueno in white marble, getting ready to throw his dagger. Beyond is the narrow causeway that leads to the island, with the sheltered beach on its east side and on its west the Playa de los Lances. This is a strip of sand facing the Atlantic, about two miles long, with good bathing at the far end. The beach's name signifies the casting of a fishing net and may thus date back to before the days of a local fishing fleet, now the town's main industry. The last, but little-known attraction in this delightful and secluded town is a French restaurant, one of the very few in Spain. It is run by a family in the traditional way and the food is mainly Spanish, but with a certain *je ne sais quoi*, and the décor, with its chequered table cloths, is that of the veritable bistro; it should not be missed.

From Tarifa we follow N340, now signposted 'To Málaga' but destined to reach Alicante and thence to accompany the east coast as far as Barcelona. It crosses the Sierra del Cabrito after about 8 kilometres, and the cork trees, that look so ghostly at night, can be examined by daylight, with their naked, black trunks extending as high as a man can reach with the grey and wrinkled branches above. The view of the Straits of Gibraltar and the northern part of Morocco is stupendous; we saw it earlier and we shall catch glimpses of it as we look back from the mountains on our way inland, but we shall never see the like of this panorama. Ceuta is on the left, and then comes the great mass of Jebel Musa and the whole wrinkled shore line to Tangier and Cape Espartel.

The descent takes us, after another 10 kilometres, to Algeciras. 'There is only one thing to be done in Algeciras,' says J. B. Trend, 'and that is to take tickets for Cádiz.' This is perhaps appropriate if you are looking for its historical associations or the Andalucian atmosphere. There is a fine view of the Rock, there are modern hotels, of which the María Cristina is the best known and has for generations been frequented by week-end visitors from Gibraltar. It has recently been bought by a British company. It is a fine town for the holiday-maker or the honey-mooner, and a delightful stop-over on the way to Morocco. But of its glorious past not a vestige remains. The Green Island from which the town took its name is now built over and connected with the mainland by an ugly pier. There is no trace of the massive walls that were stormed by the army of Alfonso XI in 1344, and only a faint echo of the famous siege in *The Canterbury Tales*, whose Knight numbered it among his campaigns. It is impossible to imagine the grim walls before which the twelve champions of Úbeda gained such honour that the crest of that city perpetuates their memory in its twelve lions. We cannot even meditate on the scars left by the first iron cannon balls used in European war-fare; they are as intangible as the far more important Black Death that was about to change the course of Europe's history while it wiped out a quarter of her inhabitants, among them the same Alfonso during his siege of Gibraltar in 1350.

The road now skirts the Bay of Algeciras, heading for San Roque, a comparatively modern town, built to house the refugees from Gibraltar when it fell into Britain's hands in 1704. It still calls itself 'Gibraltar in Exile' and, as it has nothing to offer the sightseer, we turn off on to C333 before reaching it. The road to Ronda, which we are now taking, is well known to the British of Gibraltar, but less so to the average tourist. The first visit could be to **Castellar de la Frontera**, which is reached by a left fork at about 10 kilometres from the turning off N340; the sign-post is apt to be hidden under the leafy branches of a huge tree and is easily missed. The ascent to the castle is steep, and having seen so many castles already, there might at first seem to be little object in visiting yet another one; it is when you enter, however, that its peculiarity becomes apparent, for the whole interior is now a village, crammed with tiny, whitewashed houses and meandering, cobbled streets, with only an occasional glimpse of the encircling, battlemented walls. Reminiscent of Split or the Krak des Chevaliers, it is difficult to distinguish the few shops that modestly hide their purpose behind a normal house-front, with the usual *rejas* and flower-pots; one of them makes the town's sole concession to tourism by selling postcards. No one, not even the Mayor, knows the history of castle or town, both of which belong to the widow, *en secondes noces*, of the late Duke of Medinaceli. It may be inferred that neither the shopping nor the night-life of Castellar are its main attractions; these must be found in the surprise of discovering a village where you expected a bare castle interior, the view westward over the still waters of the Pantano del Guadarranque, and the little *mirador*, or belvedere, from which one may have another, but more distant, view of the Straits of Gibraltar.

Another secondary road enables you to rejoin C333 where it crosses the River Hozgarganta, which you follow upstream for a further 13 kilometres to **Jimena de la Frontera**. Driving as far as you can up the steep streets, you have to climb the last stretch to the Castle on foot—a good fitness test. The inhabitants think nothing of it and old women toil to the top in order to fill their water-jars for, as they readily explain, water from the itinerant vendor costs 10 pesetas a *jarra*. The huge castle displays its history for those who can read it. There is a triple, horseshoe-arched gateway, in which Roman tombstones have been used as building blocks, and inside is the vast area where refugees with their flocks and herds would mingle with the garrison in time of war. The underground store-rooms are now partially laid bare, revealing the parallel barrel-vaulted sections supported by piers and arches. At the north end is the municipal cemetery, a common way of using up the waste space inside huge castle precincts, where the dead rest in greater state than ever they did during life. To the west there is a wild panorama of grey granite breaking through the cork forests and at the south end, from a circular tower whose platform projects like the bows of a ship, is another view of Gibraltar and North Africa.

Leaving Jimena we take the right-hand fork on to C341 and arrive at **Gaucín** after 15 kilometres. The town is known chiefly for the fact that Guzmán el Bueno died here of wounds received in a minor border affray, allegedly shot by an arquebus. As this weapon was still to be invented in 1305 one assumes that the usual confusion with arbalest, or crossbow, has crept in. From here we get our last view of Africa and then continue to climb over successive waves of mountain ranges until we surmount the Serranía de Ronda and see the town rising from the centre of its fertile plain.

CHAPTER THIRTEEN

Ronda and its Surroundings

Ronda—Álora—El Chorro—Bobastro—Teba—Olvera—Zahara de los Membrillos—Cueva de la Pileta

The Serranía de Ronda is so called from the *sierras* which surround the enclosed plateau in whose centre is perched the town of **Ronda**. As *sierra* means 'saw', lengthy description is unnecessary. The *pinsapo* flourishes in the eastern part of the range, the Sierra de las Nieves, and is the sole remnant in Europe of a prehistoric tree. The animal counterpart, also found hereabouts, is the timid *capra hispanica* or *pyrenaica* whose destruction requires a licence, much energy and little courage.

We approach Ronda through the suburb of San Francisco, said to have been built, like the Mercadillo, in order to avoid city tolls. This is understandable, for a large amount of dutiable goods passed this way from Gibraltar, the stations on this 'underground' continuing westward through Montejaque and Benaoján, then north to the Sierra Morena. Montejaque is famous for its snow-cured ham, as are many sierras of Southern Spain, from here to the Alpujarras; the consequence, of course, is that all ham is *serrano*, just as all duckling in England is 'Aylesbury'. Ronda can be readily pictured as a setting for *Carmen* in which the smugglers Dancairo and Remendado take the parts of Flores Arrocha, Pasos Largos (Long Strides) and El Tempranillo (the Early One), and Escamillo that of Pedro Romero.

Ronda stands on a tilted plateau, roughly heart-shaped with the southern tip separated from the larger Mercadillo by a fearsome chasm, the Tajo. This part, the old Ciudad, is so isolated by its sheer sides that capture by assault was impossible. Your first sight of it is a stretch of the city wall across the only accessible sector; here is the Puerta de Almocabar, with a horseshoe arch between restored bastions and a later, Baroque gateway at the western flank.

It was through the original gate that Ferdinand the Catholic entered to take possession of the Moorish Ciudad after the siege of 1485, ordering the procedure which became routine during the years of the Reconquest. First the standard of the Cross, a present from Pope Sixtus IV, was hoisted on the highest tower, while the host knelt and priests sang the *Te Deum*; then the ensign of St. James was displayed, and finally the banner of the sovereigns, whereupon the whole army shouted, 'Castile, Castile!' The liberation of the Christian captives followed; the fetters and manacles of which they were relieved were sent from Ronda to Toledo, where they still hang on the outside of the apse of the Church of San Juan de los Reyes. The church had been built specially as a mausoleum for Isabel and Ferdinand, and only the capture of Granada altered their sepulchral dispositions. The purification of the chief mosque followed, with its conversion to a Christian church. In Ronda a new church was also built hard by the Almocabar gate, the first stone being laid by the Catholic Sovereigns on 22nd May, 1486, the Feast of the Holy Ghost, whence the church takes its name, *Santo Espiritu*. It has little of interest, being yet another example of Spanish late Gothic with overdone rib patterns in the ceiling.

Ronda has several adequate hotels, but for two generations the favourite has been the Reina Victoria. It was built by an Englishman, it has always been the Ronda home of the British, especially those from Gibraltar, and it is named after an English woman, Queen Victoria Eugenia, who stayed here with her husband Alfonso XIII. It stands away from the road, in magnificent grounds, and commands a superb view over the western plateau and the jagged sierra. Among the hotel's famous guests was the Austrian poet, Rainer Maria Rilke (1875–1926). His room, with a few volumes and other mementoes, is still preserved, and his statue stands in the garden. He died of tuberculosis and the statue accentuates the wasting of the disease and does nothing to make him look distinguished. He stands where he would probably have liked to stand, backed by roses and palm trees, looking towards the twin peaks of the Dos Hermanas, alone in his *mirador* or, as he would have put it in his poetic German, his *Aussichtspunkt*.

The chief sights of Ronda can be seen in a day, beginning from the Reina Victoria. Going south along the Calle de Jerez, we pass the Iglesia de la Merced and immediately come to the Alameda or public gardens, on the right, that originally had the same name. Today they are called after José Antonio Primo de Rivera. Among the rose bushes and flowering shrubs are cassias, chestnuts and cedars and from the railings at the cliff edge one may enjoy the same view as the hotel guests. A little farther and we come to the famous bull-ring of Ronda, built in 1785. The **Plaza de Toros** is thus one of the oldest in Spain and was built by the local equestrian society, or *maestranza*, as a show ring; attached to it is the *Picadero de Maestranza*, originally for schooling horses, now for shoeing them. The ring, said to be the largest in Spain, is built of grey stone, with two rows of Doric columns, and is unique in having two storeys, each with its roof. In no other bull-ring is the gate of the *toril* below the President's box, instead of opposite, and it is so narrow that one wonders how a well-horned bull can get out. Within living memory the local clergy had their private box adjoining the President's, for their use after the usual service attended by the toreros. A chapel is an obligatory part of the bull ring; in the official rules it is neatly sandwiched between the butcher's shop and the bar.

Ronda upholds its claim to be the home of the *corrida* by reminding the visitor that it was the cradle of the modern fashion of fighting bulls unmounted. Until the end of the eighteenth century, as we have seen, bulls were loosed into a public square and fought from horseback by members of the upper classes. Then, when royal favour was withdrawn from the sport, a Rondeño named Pedro Romero saved it from oblivion and paradoxically saved the breed of fighting bulls from extinction by killing them on foot. He was only one of a large family of toreros, notable alike for their skill and longevity, the latter no doubt being dependent on the former. Pedro staged the first unmounted corrida in 1786, when he was thirty-two, and went on to kill more than 5,000 bulls without injury to himself, winding up his career at the age of eighty by killing a bull at a benefit performance in Madrid. His was the aphorism, 'For bullfighting you need a man and fear gives more wounds than bulls'; his statue stands in the Alameda and they say that all the small houses in this part of the town that have a cross on the stone lintel were his property. Official homage takes the form of a memorial corrida on the 9th September, when the participants dress in the costumes used at the beginning of the last century, and pictured by Goya.

Among other members of the remarkable Romero family were Pedro's son Juan who died at the age of a hundred and two, and José, who retired in 1803 but came back like an ageing opera singer to kill his last four bulls at the age of 73. For some this bull-ring will be doubly hallowed by the fact that Hemingway was a regular visitor, often accompanied by his friend Antonio Ordóñez the celebrated torero. As you leave the bull-ring you should look back at the monumental Baroque façade with its bulging balcony sporting wrought-iron bulls' heads among its curlicues.

The next building is the Teatro Espinel, noteworthy for its associations rather than its architecture. Vicente Espinel was born in Ronda in 1551 and is wrongly credited with having added a fifth string to the guitar. At the time of his birth it had four, increased to five by an unknown musician, and since then to six. But even if he did not improve the instrument, Espinel composed music for it in addition to his other activities. These included the professions of soldier, priest, poet, author—his *Adventures of Marcos Obregón* were the original of Le Sage's *Gil Blas*—and Latin scholar. He conformed to local custom by living to a ripe old age.

The Street—it changes its name to Virgen de la Paz at the public gardens—now leads into the Plaza de España, and to the **Puente Nuevo**, a remarkable piece of engineering of the eighteenth century. It spans the 400-foot deep Tajo, whose sides are so sheer that the piers of the bridge had to be built up from foundations in the bed of the River Guadalevín, which winds along the bottom of the chasm. The architect, an Aragonese named José Martín de Aldehuela, fell and was killed when the bridge was practically complete. The view from the bridge is magnificent. To the east the gorge narrows until it takes a sharp turn; to the west it broadens gradually and on the southern slope one can distinguish an old gate with a horseshoe arch and the ruins of the old Arab mills. The waterfall, about which Ford was so enthusiastic—'and like Wilson at the Falls of Terni, we can only exclaim, "Well done, rock and water, by Heavens!" '—functions but rarely, for the main stream has been tamed, led through a tunnel and made to drive the turbines of the power station.

Inside the bridge and reached by a stairway at the side of the Ayuntamiento is an old prison, now converted into a *mesón típico*, an old-time restaurant with conscious charm. The ceiling is barrel vaulted and a great *puchero*, or stewpot, hangs in the fireplace. The food is of the best, with no concession to foreigners' tastes, and the *serrano* ham is carved before you in the traditional way, from the haunch whose leg still keeps hair and hoof. Ham and eggs feature largely in Spanish country meals and it has even been said that this estimable combination first came about in Spain and was brought to England by survivors of the Black Prince's army.

Leaving the Mercadillo we cross the bridge and enter the old Ciudad of the Moslems, which had to surrender to Ferdinand after a week's bombardment from the other side of the gorge. Iron cannon balls were used, perhaps for the first time, and primitive grenades, made of tow, pitch, oil and gunpowder, transformed the small, crowded town into a furnace. This is one reason why little remains of the buildings of those days, but the streets, if we except the windows, are still typically African; the doors are noted for the infinite variety of ornamental studs which decorate them.

Turning right we soon reach the Plaza del Campillo, a quiet garden perched on the cliff edge, from which the valley of the Guadalevín can be seen very clearly, separating us from the sheer side of the Mercadillo. We can descend by a footpath, but the archway, the mills and the power station situated in the lush valley, can be reached more easily by road, from the point where we first saw the Almocabar gate; the view of the Tajo and bridge from below alone makes the trip worth while. At the back of the Plaza del Campillo is the Convent of Santa Teresa, where the French garrison held out in 1812, after Soult had withdrawn from Andalucía. There were no survivors.

A few steps to the south is the Mondragón Palace, originally built for the first Arab governor in the eighth century and later restored for the use of the Catholic Sovereigns; it has a poorly preserved Arab patio. A finer one can be seen at the *Casa del Gigante*—no one knows why it is so called—where horseshoe arches, large stretches of Arabesque stucco and an *artesonado* have survived. Some relics of mosaic *azulejo*, the oldest kind, have been framed and hung on the walls. This is the only house in Ronda where something of the Moslem atmosphere can be recaptured. A cellar has recently been found underneath the back yard; entered with some difficulty, it contains the stone couch, manacles and fetters of a long-forgotten prisoner and a stuffed vulture of more recent date.

Turning over the accumulated rubbish in this part of the town, one finds broken pieces of tiles of every epoch, mediaeval bricks and even fragments of Roman mosaic. It is usual to give tips at all private houses, assuming that it is a servant, and not the owner, who shows you round.

Distances are negligible in Old Ronda and the Plaza de Trinidad Scholtz, formerly de la Duquesa de Parcent, is only a few yards away. The square was named after the enlightened duchess who did much restoration in the town, and contains a statue of Vicente Espinel. On the north side is the **Collegiate Church of Santa María la Mayor**, originally the chief mosque and thus the first to be Christianised. The bell tower is adapted from the original minaret, square below and with an octagonal second storey, plain with round arches over the windows; the top is not unlike that of the Giralda. The façade is improved by an unexpected addition, a double gallery built into the wall, probably for watching bullfights in the old days. The inside is another example of indecision, being a blend of Gothic and Renaissance. At the west end is a gilt retablo from which the unwary are apt to recoil, as its Salomonic columns are so encrusted with carved vegetable matter that they might have been dredged up after years at the bottom of the sea. The best part is the *mihrab*, discovered by the present sacristan a few years ago. It has a horseshoe arch, of course, and the decoration in the intrados reminds one of the coiled fern pattern of the old synagogue, Santa María la Blanca, at Toledo. There is delicate Arabesque stucco, *naskhi* writing and two consoles shaped like capitals, their carving reminiscent of the Abbassid style. It is interesting to note the Ionic volutes and to remember once more that they were originally Oriental and pre-Greek. It is a pity that much of the decoration has been limewashed and that no further exploration is contemplated, but one should also remember that for many people a church is a place for prayer and not for archaeological research.

Turning east we quickly come to the *Alminar*, the minaret of a mosque which was later transformed into the Church of San Sebastián and is now a block of houses. The lower part, of stone, has been well restored and shows the 'keyhole' door, *alfiz* and fan-shaped decoration with remains of *azulejos* among the ribs; the upper part is of weathered brick and has no features of interest beyond an ornamental frieze.

Going north we soon come to the Casa del Marqués de Salvatierra, a late imitation of the Plateresque style built in 1786. The grotesque figures on the front—of the pair on the left only the man shields the genitals, on the right only the woman—are said to be Aztec and, like the florid wrought-iron balcony, are supposed to come from Mexico. The palace has a handsome patio, a marble staircase of alternate white, red and black steps and a collection of paintings whose general interest outweighs their artistry. There is the unfortunate Aldehuela, who built the bridge, and a copy of a portrait of Vicente Espinel, with moustache and goatee; it is easy to imagine him as the hero of his own picaresque novel.

Almost next door is the **Casa del Rey Moro**, the House of the

Moorish king, and the showplace of Ronda. It is said to have been built in 1042, but many believe that the present building is a new construction on the old site; it was admirably restored by the Duchess of Parcent. Tradition makes it the palace of Badis, king of the *taifa* of Tacorona (Ronda), a monster of lust and cruelty; others, led by the unreliable Conde, say it was built by 'Almonated', who may have been Al-Mutadid, ruler of Seville. It matters little who it was; the story that you have to hear from your guide is that the king used to drink out of the jewel-encrusted skulls of his victims. Badis, like other royal villains, showed symptoms of insanity; he tore wives away from their husbands and daughters from their parents, invaded harems and then slept with his aunt.

The interior contains little of interest, but there are some good ceramic tiles in the floors and ceilings and some old Ronda carpets in which you can still trace patterns that originated across the Caspian. The garden is perched on the edge of the Tajo, nearly 500 feet above the river; on the far side of the chasm the bare rock wall is covered by a mantle of vegetation in its upper part, grass and prickly pear studded with poppies. The outer portico has a horseshoe arch and others are visible in the neighbouring houses, overlooking the Tajo. The garden is closely set with laurels, fig trees and palms, and wisteria adds charm in its season. There is a marble fountain in which papyrus grows, though not the Egyptian variety; it has an octagonal base and a centre shaped like a pierced lantern, the whole decorated with Cufic script and designs reminiscent of the caskets of Córdoba.

Here you will find the entrance to the Mina de Ronda, a staircase cut inside the solid rock and leading to a backwater of the river in which the queen is said to have bathed. If she did so she was certainly energetic, for there are over three hundred steps, their average height being at least 18 inches. The work of excavation was done by Christian slaves and the Staircase's main use was to enable them to bring water up from the river, whence the expression, *Dios me guarde del zaque de Ronda*, 'God keep me from the water-jars of Ronda'. It is said that the siege of 1485 owed its success to another tunnel bored by the Christian besiegers to intercept this staircase and so cut off the water supply; it is a good story, but the tunnel has yet to be found.

The road to the east of the Casa del Rey Moro winds steeply down, passing a rude stone bench called, for no known reason, *el sillón del Moro*, the Moor's Seat. Next to it is the so-called 'Roman Arch', an early eighteenth-century gateway, and immediately below it the Capilla de San Miguel, believed to have been the old synagogue and now a collecting station for museum pieces. From here we can see two old bridges, the Roman one on the left (it is certainly built on Roman foundations) and the Arab bridge with its horseshoe arch on the right. The upper levels of this one, too, have been greatly restored. The great cleft has a certain fascination about it, with the dark stream winding among the rocks below, the rough, bulging walls of brown and purple shadows and the tawny bridges. The nearer one can be seen again from the Arab baths at the riverside, a recent discovery situated in a wild garden where cypresses rise from among roses, lilac and iris, and the almond trees bear pink and white blossoms till well on in May.

Looking up at the Ciudad you can now see the ancient walls and some of their towers, mostly of rubble and brick, with horseshoe arches; one of them, though it is of the same shape, size and colour, contrasts with the rest by its pure Roman masonry of squared stone. The baths consist of a large chamber of three naves, divided by octagonal brick columns that support sixteen horseshoe arches. The hollow floor has been removed in parts to show how the hot air coming from the adjoining furnace passed through. The naves are barrel-vaulted with the star-shaped vents for smoke and steam that are traditional in the eastern *hammam*, and in places some of the original woodwork still survives, with the reddish tinge of *pinsapo* discernible among it. Along the side of the garden is a rough, overgrown wall that leads to a deep well on the bank of the river; in this was an Archimedean screw, turned by animals or slaves, which raised water some thirty feet and discharged it into the gutter which still runs along the top of the wall and brings it to the baths.

To return to your starting point you cross the Roman bridge, the Puente Viejo, take the left fork and come upon the façade of the *Posada de las Ánimas*, the first inn built here, and which numbered Cervantes among its guests. It was built in 1500 and still received custom in 1845, when Ford's book was published, but had apparently gone out of business by 1882 when he wrote *Murray's Handbook*. There is nothing behind the façade, which is not a distinguished one, but the mounting block still stands in the archway, appreciated no doubt after the heavy meals of other days. The name is puzzling, and in her book Miss Epton suggests it may be related to the Chapel of the Virgen de los Dolores further down the street, whose outside columns are carved in the semblance of hanged, half-human creatures. But the eighteenth-century picture nearer the inn, showing the redemption of souls in Purgatory, suggests a more likely explanation; the word *ánima* is used particularly for a soul in Purgatory and prayers for their redemption are supposed to be offered at 8.30 every night when the appropriate bell tolls. This bell is called *Las Ánimas* and, like the Angelus, is used to denote the time, so that a Spaniard can say, 'I only got home at Ánimas.' Remember, too, that travellers in olden days would entrust their safety from robbers to the Holy Souls (*Las Ánimas*).

The road I mentioned earlier, past the ruined, brick-built Arco Arabe, sole relic of a defensive wall, and the crumbling Arab mills, takes us to a different Guadalevín, flowing between grassy banks, over miniature waterfalls and against the stepping stones. Rejoined by the water that has been through the turbines it becomes a sizeable stream; soon it will be the Guadiaro that eventually opens into the sea near Gibraltar, marking the extreme western end of the Costa del Sol. As it leaves Ronda it can look back on an eventful past; it has provided steam for the Arab baths, a bathing pool for a queen, contributed water for Christian slaves to carry up those terrible steps, turned the millwheels for grinding corn and finally provided power for the modern town. But looking down, 'and dizzy 'tis to cast one's eyes so low', one sees only a tiny thread that winds between its rocky walls, under the bridge where Aldehuela triumphed and died.

Numerous excursions can be made from Ronda and nearly all have one thing in common, that you are liable to encounter sections of atrocious road. These vary from time to time, so that it is useless to detail them; earth roads can be smoothed out quickly and can deteriorate with equal speed in a season of storms. Ancient Ronda, Ronda la Vieja, contains the remains of the original Roman town of Acinipo, itself built over the foundations of Iberian and Phoenician settlements, destroyed by the Vandals and used as a quarry by the Moslems. It lies about 12 kilometres north-west of Ronda, in the rugged sierra, and the remains of a theatre hardly make the trip worth while.

A very full day can be spent in the country east of Ronda. The route described here is a circular one, but part of it may be covered on the way to Málaga, and another part on a journey to Granada through Antequera. It is only fair to add that no place of first importance lies on the route; its chief interest lies in a glimpse of the hinterland of Andalucía, a region that for a thousand years has been the stronghold of smugglers, bandits and rebels. Two kilometres along C344 is an old aqueduct, intact except where small sections have been removed to let road and railway through; though it is called Roman, the arches are of horseshoe pattern and therefore presumably built by the Moslems. The road now climbs the sierra to the Puerto del Viento, at a height of 4,000 feet and rightly named the 'Windy Pass', and after 25 kilometres we reach El Burgo, possibly the remains of an Arab fortress. Among its white houses the walled perimeter can still be distinguished, with its round and square towers. Over another pass, *Las Abejas* or 'The Bees', and we drop sharply to Yunquera at 34 kilometres from Ronda. A watch tower or *atalaya* on our right would have served to give warning of raiders coming over the mountains. At Alozaina you have the choice of a leisurely drive to Coín, Alhaurín el Grande, Cártama, with its Phoenician name, and Pizarra. On the other hand you may take a good, unnumbered road direct to Pizarra, whence C337 takes you north to Álora after 7 kilometres. The longer route has scenic charm and attractive villages, but is hardly worth the extra distance if the circular route is to be completed in a day.

Álora was originally another Alhaurín and has flourished because of its luxurious vegetation and summer freshness; if you have taken the longer route, Álora will be the climax of a tour where every hillside is an olive grove and every valley an orchard, always with the great, grey craggy cliffs in the background. The town is built in the saddle that unites a low hill to the mountain range and on the hill is an imposing castle—now the municipal cemetery, a sensible arrangement found also at Jimena. The *alcalde* counts the reception of visitors among his mayoral duties, and in his office is a parchment of 1566, the *privilegio* that conferred on Álora the right to administer justice independently of Málaga. There are beautifully coloured illuminations, including the portrait of Philip II so admired by Miss Epton. It is true that it shows him with a quizzical expression, at variance with our preconceived idea of a stern, bigoted tyrant.

El Chorro is a railway station 12 kilometres north-west on a road that at least starts well. Beyond the station is the huge mass of rock that stretches across the valley. Through the rock is a cleft, the Hoyo, that reduces the Tajo of Ronda to a ditch; and yet this mass of rock has been tunnelled for the railway, and trains cross branch ravines on bridges hundreds of feet above the water. There is also a catwalk for pedestrians, if they are not afraid of heights or distances. In the cleft runs the infant Guadalhorce, released by the sluice gates of the reservoir destined to irrigate fields and crops before it reaches the Mediterranean between Málaga and Torremolinos.

On the mountain to the left is the almost inaccessible site of **Bobastro**. Although a new road is being laid no one should attempt the climb without the help of a guide, for when I last visited it, the road finished on the brink of a precipice without the suspicion of a warning. The guide should be engaged at Álora, for those who live within sight of the ruined stronghold either know nothing of it or are ignorant of how it should be climbed. The steep, barren slopes, that can barely support a scattered herd of goats, have their own beauty. The monotony of grey and brown is relieved by the bright yellow flowers and the fern-like foliage of the wild fennel that grows so luxuriantly where nothing else survives.

The ruined town and fortress have little to offer, but there is one of the only two Mozarabic churches left in Spain; by this is meant churches built by the Christians who remained under Moslem rule and not those who fled north during various eras of persecution and built similar churches in Christian territory. Its remains are strictly for those who have an unflinching enthusiasm for early church architecture. The importance of this eagle's nest is rarely stressed in travel books, but it is the visible reminder of an insurrection, perhaps better called an independent state, that plagued the emirate of Córdoba for half a century. One of the greatest weaknesses of Moslem rule in Spain was the exclusiveness of a ruling caste of Arabs, Syrian, Iraqui and Yemenite, whose disdain for, and exactions from Berbers and *muladíes* caused widespread discontent. The reverse was the case eight centuries later when the Old Christians (Sancho Panza was one) looked down on the converted Moors and Jews. The *muladíes* were Christians who had embraced Islam and their descendants were in many cases sincere Moslems; the Berbers had been converted only a few years longer.

Omar Ibn Hafsun was the son of a landed proprietor near Ronda, whose surname Hafs had been given importance by the addition of the Spanish augmentative ending -*ón*; it is found in the names of many Spanish Moslems, changed to -*un*, such as Ibn Jaldun, one of Omar's biographers. His great-grandfather had been converted to Islam and the family was said to have been descended from a Visigothic count named Alfonso. All that need be told here of his theatrical career is that he was a leader of rebels, true to the Iberian tradition of *guerilleros* that began in Roman days with Viriatus. He changed sides when it suited him and gave hostages when he did so, subsequently sacrificing them without scruple when he changed sides again. At the height of his power his rule extended over most of Andalucía, including the cities of Jaén and Écija. His generalship was poor and his sense of statesmanship worse, for his decline began when he resumed the religion of his forefathers, alienating the many Moslems in his army.

He died a rebel in 917, passing his last days in the Church of Bobastro, near which he was buried in the Christian manner, supine, with his arms crossed and his face turned to the east. His sons continued the struggle for another ten years, but the menace had departed from Bobastro and the emir Abderrahman III was able to turn his attention to outside enemies and to declare himself caliph, successor of the Prophet. He did not, however, omit to occupy Bobastro in order to gloat over the fall of his dynasty's greatest threat, and he had Omar's body and that of his son, also buried in the Christian manner, exhumed and taken to Córdoba, where they were exposed on gibbets. Only the Mozarabs mourned his death and from them arose the legend of the champion of Christianity, only partly true at the best. It has even been said that the Reconquest would have been advanced six hundred years had Alfonso III of León accepted Omar's proposal of an alliance. But Alfonso, surnamed The Great, must have known enough about Omar's history of opportunism and unreliability.

What should interest us today is the comparison between Omar Ibn Hafsun and José María *el Tempranillo*, mentioned earlier among the famous bandits and smugglers. He lived for only 28 years, but in that time he had become so successful as an outlaw that a royal pardon, negotiated in 1832, was the only way of stopping his activities, just as happened to Omar. Both of them on occasion enrolled in the ranks of authority. El Tempranillo is still celebrated in the *coplas* of this region, one of which runs:

> *Por la Sierra Morena*
> *va una partía,*
> *Y al capitán le llaman*
> *José María.*

'A band goes through the Sierra Morena,
and they call the captain José María.'

That was in the 1830s; the tradition lasted until the Civil War and there are still old men who wistfully talk of the days 'when

Gibraltar belonged to us', by which they mean the years before 1936, when they bought their contraband in the free port of Gibraltar.

The Church of Bobastro suffers from two defects; it was never finished and it has largely tumbled down. Nevertheless, the rock-hewn building of three naves with horseshoe arches, and an apse with a horseshoe ground plan, is a fair example of the Visigothic basilica; the Mozarabs obstinately retained the lay-out that their ancestors took from the Romans, and the horseshoe arch which the Moslem builders probably took from them and subsequently modified. A few yards away is a square hole in the ground, allegedly the grave of Omar, desecrated by the authorities whom he had so successfully defied.

From El Chorro the all-weather road—meaning that it is execrable in any weather—continues to a junction, whence the right fork leads to the reservoir or *pantano* of the Guadalhorce and the left to Ardales, past the newer and larger reservoir. From here those who want a sulphur bath can easily reach Carratraca, 6 kilometres away. Eleven kilometres north, in the opposite direction, lies Peñarrubia, where we meet C341 and turn left for Ronda. Five kilometres later the road dips to cross the Almargen and immediately thereafter, at the side of a farm-house on the right, an excellent but unobtrusive road takes us to **Teba**. The ruined castle is perched on a low hill, an outlying spur of the mountain range, and looks down on the undulant, fertile plain; it may be visited, but only on foot, and is hardly worth the trouble. It was from this village that the Empress Eugenia of France took one of her titles, Countess of Teba; we shall hear more about her in Málaga.

On the plain below Teba took place the engagement in which the Black Douglas met a hero's death. Robert Bruce, on his death-bed, had asked Lord James of Douglas to carry out the project he had so often planned for himself, to make the Jerusalem pilgrimage. He begged him to take with him his king's heart and bury it in the Holy Land. James accordingly set out with a con-tingent of Scottish nobles and the heart of Bruce, the latter in its silver case suspended round his neck. Hearing of the endless war against the infidels of Spain, he put in at Seville and joined the army of Alfonso XI; it must be remembered that dying in a crusade automatically cancelled sins and, in fact, was tantamount to 'pratique' for Paradise. The same belief was held in the *jehad* of the Moslems, so that a good fight could always be expected.

Either because the Scots had insufficient knowledge of the

Moslems' methods of fighting, or because they misunderstood the Spaniards' trumpet signals, they found themselves hemmed in by a superior force. It is said that James Douglas might even then have saved himself, had he not seen Sir William St. Clair of Roslyn sorely beset and gone to his aid. When he too found himself hopelessly outnumbered, he took the casket from his neck, said to it, 'Pass first in fight, as thou wast wont to do, and Douglas will follow thee or die', and hurled the heart of Bruce into the ranks of the enemy. After the battle the survivors found the body of James lying over the heart of Bruce, and took both back to Scotland. Few visitors come to this spot, where only the castle ruins recall that summer's day in 1330.

Another excursion from Ronda, shorter and less tiring, starts on C341, but you almost immediately turn left for **Setenil**. The usual warning about the state of the road is given, with the encouragement that upkeep is better in the Province of Cádiz which we enter 5 kilometres before Setenil. This picturesque town is built along the river of the same name and many of its houses are in the shelter of a vast overhanging rock, so that in some cases no proper roof is needed. The town is otherwise undistinguished and it is as well to know how to leave. After crossing the river, you climb the steep, narrow main street to the square at the top of the hill, where cars may be parked to enable visitors to see the remains of the castle. On a busy day as many as six laden mules may climb the road, encouraged by their attendants who still use the Arabic *arré!* for 'gee-up'. Pass through the deep arch, turn left immediately and a fair road brings you to a junction, where a right (north) turn takes you to **Olvera** after 11 kilometres.

One curiosity is worth a glance at about 9 kilometres from Setenil: a village called Torre-Alháquime built on so steep a hill that only the remains of the old walls seem to stop it from slipping down into the River Guadalporcuna.

The best view of Olvera is had from the Puerta Cabañas, before entering the town. From here you may see the parish church and the ruins of the castle on their crag and, facing them on a twin peak, a more recent shrine. Even among so many snow-white towns, Olvera deserves to be mentioned for its charm. The crag with its fragment of keep, wall and sentry tower watches over the rows of low houses, roofed with an infinite variety of Arab tiles, light and dark and tawny. The house-fronts are un-compromisingly black and white, with balconies and street-lamps breaking the severity of the rectangular pattern of door and window spaces. Somewhat unfairly, Olvera's fame rests on its traditional opposition to the law; it could have been a station on the old smugglers' route from Ronda, in the chain whose next link was Morón de la Frontera, of similar repute. The proverb goes, *Mata al hombre y vete a Olvera*, 'kill your man and flee to Olvera', and in the Peninsular War it became a byword to the French among a hundred other hostile towns. On one occasion, when rations had been requisitioned by the occupying detachment, asses' meat was provided in the guise of veal, and thereafter a common reproach in Napoleon's army was *Vous avez mangé de l'âne à Olvera*. John Rocca recounts this story in his reminiscences of the war in Spain; his own experiences here were far from happy and his encounter with a guerrilla band resulted in his having to use a crutch for the rest of his life.

Olvera is on a national road and we follow N342 through cornfields and olive groves to Algodonales where cotton was grown in the days of Moslem rule. A sharp turn on to C339 leads to the banks of the Guadalete, the river that separates us from the hill on which is perched **Zahara de los Membrillos**. 'Flower of the Quinces'—a beautiful name for a beautiful town, you might say, but the word is seemingly the Arabic *sakhr*, a rock, which we saw earlier in the form *sahra* for a fortress. But it is still a beautiful town, with its castle on the usual steep rock, a climb of 20 minutes. The remaining walls show the alternating courses of shaped stone and brick that the Moslems got from the Byzantines and handed on to the Mudéjars. There is one tower left, partly restored but retaining an interesting crossing of ogival arches. The view is of course superb, with the winding river, meadows, fields of corn and olive groves in the foreground. Away to the east the landscape is grimmer, the horizon bounded with the stark, jagged peaks of the Sierra de Grazalema.

Though it is small and rarely visited, Zahara is an instructive little town, with more than a hint of an important past. Alfonso X, the Learned, came here in 1282 to beg the King of Granada for help against his rebellious son Sancho el Bravo. In 1481 Zahara, now a Christian frontier post, was seized in a surprise night attack and the Christian inhabitants either butchered or deported under appalling conditions. Treacherous it may have been, but it is likely that the Moslems had information regarding a request from the Catholic Sovereigns to the Pope that a renewed war against Granada be officially labelled a crusade. It is usually said that the capture of Zahara provoked the capture of Alhama by the Christians, and this in turn sparked off the final

Reconquest that ended with the capture of Granada in 1492. It is, however, unlikely that the Moslems were the sole aggressors. They were the losers, and that is bad enough. The recapture in 1483 by Rodrigo Ponce de León was rewarded by the addition of Marqués de Zahara to his other titles, and the city arms, a castle and a ladder, recall the difficult feat of rock-climbing that the deed entailed.

The Ayuntamiento preserves the Moslem standard, red silk with ornamental Cufic lettering, that was said to have been flying over the castle at the time of the Reconquest. The Parish Church of Santa María de la Mesa is the work of Leonardo Figueroa's nephew, Antonio Matías, and contains treasures that are both rich and gaudy, in spite of two burglaries. The Feast of Corpus Christi is celebrated here with special fervour, the whole town being decorated with trees and branches brought from the surrounding countryside. It appears to be a survival of the summer worship of vegetation divinities, similar to the Jewish Feast of Tabernacles.

Ronda is only 37 kilometres away, along C339, and there are two visits to the south which are rewarding. The first is to **Grazalema** and **Ubrique**, and it is as well to enquire about the state of the road (C344). Even if it is passable for buses it may not be pleasant for small cars. The former town is noted for its woven materials, and the *mantas* of Grazalema, used either as a shawl or as a ceremonial bed-cover, are much in evidence at local weddings, some of them with patterns still used by the Berbers in Morocco. It is, of course, obvious that this type of weaving, like pottery, tile making and leatherware, was inherited from the Moslems. The last is the chief industry of Ubrique, where a good version of Morocco leather can be seen and bought. The industry is now so firmly established that skins are imported, including that of the crocodile. There is little advantage in buying local products on the spot, for they can be obtained in Ronda at very little extra cost.

Now return to C339, if you made the digression, and continue until 25 kilometres from Zahara where you will find a turning to the right which leads through the old smuggler haunts of Montejaque and Benaoján to the **Cueva de la Pileta**. The road is passable, if rough, when there is no snow about, and forks after 14 kilometres, the right branch taking you to a dead end. The drill now is to turn your car and sound the hooter; down in the valley a tiny figure will detach itself and one of the three brothers who own the farmhouse will climb the steep slope towards you, arriving in a quarter of an hour. He will take you up some stone steps and into a vast cave where Palaeolithic man lived some 25,000 years ago, pointing out the drawings, nothing as impressive as Altamira of course, made with a mixture of ochre and animal fat. As usual, animals feature prominently and we can admire our ancestors' powers of observation, memory and reproduction. There is a stallion, easily recognisable by his neck, a mare in foal and bulls fighting. More difficult to explain are the series of upright and horizontal lines, arrows and other primitive patterns. You will have the opportunity, too, to admire the stalactites and stalagmites and to reflect that they were old when the cave-dwellers settled here.

In Ronda and its surroundings we can retrace many of the steps in Spain's progress from early in geological time to the present day: the convulsions of nature left their mark in the Tajo and el Chorro; Prehistoric man in the Cave of La Pileta; Iberians, Phoenicians and Romans at Acinipo, destroyed by the first Germanic invaders. There is plenty to remind us of Moslem rule, and of the Reconquest too; music and poetry, the mysticism of Ibn Abbad which linked the Sufis with St. John of the Cross, Cervantes, the origin of the modern corrida, freedom fighters and smugglers.

CHAPTER FOURTEEN

Ronda to Málaga and Granada

✤

San Pedro de Alcántara—The Costa del Sol—Basilica of Vega del Mar—Estepona—Marbella—Torremolinos—Málaga—Antequera—Loja—Nerja—Vélez-Málaga—Alhama de Granada—Láchar—Santafé

We leave Ronda by C339 and after what seems an interminable climb cross the Sierra Bermeja, the red mountains. They are not red, but grey and bare, except where afforestation has succeeded in planting pine trees on the steep slopes, and where these have so tenaciously seeded themselves, they even grow out of cracks in the rock. It is an excellent road, a notable feat of engineering, and after 28 kilometres the sea comes into sight far below and, incredibly, part of the African coast. We reach **San Pedro de Alcántara** at 52 kilometres and turn right along N340, the main road of the **Costa del Sol**. Once a series of fishing villages, with only Málaga and Almeria ranking as important towns, it is now the playground of Spaniards and foreigners.

The Sun Coast is a lusty child of less than fifteen years' growth. From a succession of beaches, separated by rocky headlands whose only landmarks were the old watch towers, it has become a chain of urbanisation schemes, of hotels and apartment blocks, restaurants and souvenir shops, that eclipses the feeble efforts of the French and Italian Rivieras. Roadside advertisements find limited space between the encroaching, towering flats, until these become continuous and we have the modern equivalent of a gold-rush town, incorporating the leading features of Blackpool and the Copacabana Beach, neither of which are to everyone's taste. On the other hand, most holiday makers are gregarious and the supply is merely trying to keep up with the demand of increasing millions; if they all sought seclusion the Sahara would hardly accommodate them.

The quality of the beaches varies from one to another and even from time to time, when one remembers that golden sand is being imported for one of them, as are flowers from Holland for a promenade. There are still large stretches free from over-

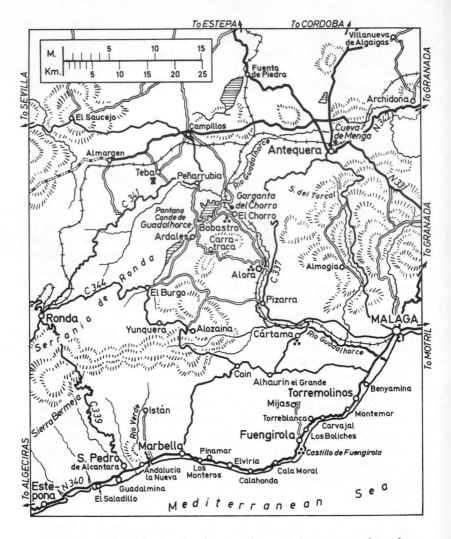

crowding and yet in reach of entertainment, but at any time they
may be absorbed in the giant complex of motels, camping sites,
French restaurants, American bars, cocktail bars, snack bars,
apartment blocks and hotels. Bingo parlours may confidently
be expected, but even now there is an air of excitement as the
cars dash back and forth along N340, as bullfights are staged on
Sundays every few miles (so much for the Northerners' disgust
at cruelty) and hides are tanned daily. But with all this it is
probably the best value for money that the holiday maker can

find, with its almost guaranteed fine weather, safe bathing, impressive landscape, sea-food and passable wine. For the comfort of foreigners, there are English bars for Britons, German restaurants and Swedish cafés for members of those countries and even an occasional tavern for Spaniards and South Americans. *Caelum non animam mutant, qui trans mare currunt.*

It only remains to say that the majority of Spaniards enjoy the cosmopolitan invasion, not for its pecuniary advantages but for the illusion of sophistication and modernity that it brings. Also, the standard of honesty is high, as elsewhere in Spain, and though prices are naturally a little inflated during the holiday season, the visitor is spared the shameless rapacity that he may meet with in some countries.

But for the stranger whose tastes are more discriminating, there are several interesting places to visit. Arriving at San Pedro de Alcántara and turning right along N340, we soon come, through an entrance on the left, to two urbanisation projects named 'Linda Vista' and, *horribile dictu*, 'Play Boy', pronounced *Ply bo-ee*. In a eucalyptus grove, next to the seashore, are the remains of the palaeo-Christian **Basilica of Vega del Mar**, with walls standing about 3 feet high. It is dated to the second half of the fourth century and therefore existed during the last epoch of Roman rule. Its chief interest lies in the ground plan, which includes an apse at each end; European examples of this layout are limited to a tiny chapel at Alcaracejos, north of the Sierra Morena, and one church each at Salonika and Grado. But there are many in North Africa and it serves to remind us of the part played in the development of Christianity by Clement of Alexandria, Tertullian, Donatus, St. Augustine and many others who had their origin there. Even our word 'pope' comes from Carthage, for the local priests were called *papa*, and Tertullian. the first to apply it to St. Peter's heirs, refers to it as *haec Africana vox*.

The church was destroyed by a tidal wave in AD 365, rebuilt and again destroyed by a tidal wave in 526. Thereafter it was used by the Visigoths as a necropolis and their shallow graves are arranged in and around the basilica in any order, the majority naturally at the south-east end nearest to the altar, for the early Christians competed for *post mortem* proximity to holy relics, just as the Jews did for six feet of ground near the Temple. The grave goods are scattered among various museums and one wonders how long this ancient monument itself will survive unspoiled among the bungalows that are springing up around it. At the other end from the altar is the baptistery, with the original cruciform font preserved, and steps leading into it from two sides, as total immersion was practised; near it there is a tiny square font for infants.

Following the shore-line westward for about 200 yards brings us to the barracks of the Guardia Civil, with an *atalaya* next to it, just one of the hundreds of watch towers with which the coast is studded. The next enclosure, the large grounds of a fine mansion, contains the surviving remains of the Roman baths, now an attractive grotto. In spite of being on private property it is classed as a national monument. A hundred yards farther, careful search in the grass reveals a square well-head and the foundations of buildings, the only other remains of the Roman town of Silniana. Mosaics, iron vessels and Roman coins were found here; the latter were no later in date than the reigns of Valens and Valentinian I (321–375), supporting the theory that the town was destroyed in the tidal wave of 365. It may be of interest that Valens was killed near Constantinople by the Visigoths, who later came all the way here to live and die.

To the west the main road to **Estepona** passes numerous beaches; those of Estepona are good compared with the majority, which in this area tend to be pebbly. Note that 'coarse sand' in the brochures may be a euphemism for pebbles as big as a hen's egg. Estepona marks the effective, if not the geographical western end of the Costa del Sol and will probably remain outside the zone of intensive gaiety for some time to come. Its fishing-village nucleus still functions and the ships bring back their gleaming mounds of sardines, *boquerones* and *chanquetes*. The first are traditionally eaten grilled on spits, on the sands at night; the wine that accompanies them puts you in the mood for the soft notes of a guitar and a whispered *malagueña*, until a platform top appears from nowhere and the dancing begins, certainly as good as anything you will see in the advertised night-clubs, or *salas de fiesta*. *Boquerones* are anchovies and can be eaten fresh, though they are not as tasty as the sardines. *Chanquetes* would defy description, were they not the nearest approach to whitebait, fried to the same dry crispness and nowadays served in every bar where preprandial *tapas* are provided. History preserves but one anecdote from Estepona's past: it was raided in 1630 and succeeded in repelling the Moors, the casualties comprising only one Spaniard who, believing the town to be lost, had disguised himself as a Moor.

Pursuing our way east to Marbella, we soon cross the Arroyo

de Nagüeles, which is spanned by what was once a Roman bridge on the left, and within 5 kilometres reach our destination. **Marbella** is more than a holiday resort, for it exudes traditional and tangible history. The name is said to derive from Queen Isabel's remark *Que mar tan bella!* on first seeing it, and the reply of the courtier Vigil de Quiñones, 'Madam, from this moment the town will be called Marbella.' With the inevitable fate of such facile attributions, it is not surprising to learn that it was called Marbella in the days of Moslem domination, centuries earlier.

Marbella still preserves parts of the old town wall and a large section of the powerful castle, built in 960 under the caliphate. This makes it coeval with the Castle of Tarifa, as both were built to combat the menace of the Egyptian Fatimid dynasty. The visitor will see the alternation of stone and brick courses, the poverty of the mortar which has washed away through the ages, and the use of Roman stones and even Ionic capitals. Some of the stone courses of the original Roman building can be made out, with the pincer slots in the upper half, just as they were lowered into position. Others have the slots at the side or bottom, showing that the stones were moved from their original position and used again by the Arabs. The *soga y tizón* work is also evident in the proportion of one header to one stretcher, thus dating the ruin fairly accurately for, as we have seen, the use of two or more headers to one stretcher came in at the end of the tenth century.

The old town has not allowed the tourist industry to spoil its atmosphere and still prides itself on its antiquities as much as on its novelties. In spite of the urbanisation schemes that are being hatched, notably Andalucía la Nueva, Marbella will long remain an agreeable headquarters for the discerning holiday maker, with its easy access to Málaga, Ronda and other places described in the last chapter. Many visitors will find enough entertainment in wandering through the narrow, typically Andalucian streets; others will admire the fountain of 1504 outside the Ayuntamiento, and the Cruz del Humilladero, both relics of the Reconquest. The Cross marks the act of submissiveness often performed by the Catholic Sovereigns at the capture of a town, a notable example being Granada. Inside the Ayuntamiento, on the first floor, are interesting frescoes that remained covered with limewash, and hence preserved, for centuries. They comprise a Crucifixion, in which the Catholic Sovereigns appear as spectators, the royal arms and St. Justa and St. Rufina who, being patrons of Seville, have the NO 8 DO rebus appended.

Continuing towards Málaga we pass numerous pretty beaches,

though not of the finest sand, where the pinewoods come down to the shore. There are short branch roads leading to parking areas and the prospect of comparative privacy except, perhaps, at the height of the season. At 30 kilometres we arrive at Fuengirola: here an old castle at the roadside is surrounded by the usual modern additions, and the promenade looks down on to a stony beach, where the visitors lie with the stoicism of fakirs. Just as most foreign residents and visitors at Marbella were British, so those at Fuengirola are German and Scandinavian. A road of 7 kilometres takes us inland to Mijas, past fields where female workers adopt every expedient to avoid a sun tan. The village is a showplace and knows it, being eminently adapted to those who like their grapes peeled, or have no time to look for less self-conscious examples of typical Andalucía.

We are now in a built-up area, which continues until we arrive at Málaga; on the way we pass through **Torremolinos**, once a fishing village, with a good beach, a D.G.T. Parador and a golf course. There are few Spanish towns in which the enquiring traveller cannot find something of interest. Torremolinos is one of them. But it is only fair to add that it suits the taste and purse of the majority of visitors and is still a favourite summer resort for Spaniards.

Málaga has long been a popular city for holiday makers and for retired or invalid Britons. The climate is equable except—there is always an 'except' in Southern Europe—when the *Terral* blows through a funnel in the mountains that protect the city from the worst of the weather. It blows hot in summer and cold in winter, but only rarely and for a short time. It has snowed twice in a hundred years. Augustus Hare called Málaga 'the dearest place in Spain, being the most Anglicised', but neither part of the statement is true today. It is still, however, one of the most typical of Andalucian towns in the private life that goes on behind the hotel–motor coach–night-club façade. The Andalucian laughs at the idea of the nobility of labour; work is something to be kept secret. Thus, says Fernández del Valle, he often conceals his handicraft in the depths of his patio, as the Moors hid their wives in the harem. Leisure takes precedence over business, but it is the leisure of a gentleman, even when the itinerant vendor of shoe-laces takes time off for a drink. It is rarely that this integrity of the spirit appears on the surface; but deep in his consciousness is the knowledge that León-Felipe expressed so happily:

Para cada hombre guarda
un rayo nuevo de luz el sol . . .
y un camino virgen
Dios.

For every man the sun keeps a new ray of light, and God an untrodden path.

The worst that can happen to a visitor is for him to take serious notice of a leaflet that claims to outline the city's attractions. 'Wine, bulls and olé' are advertised; he will be taken round the haunts of spontaneous exuberance, to experience the bubbling spirits, the grace, the *duende* of Andalucía; he will even be entitled without extra charge to two drinks and, if he wishes, a diploma as matador. But he will do far better, even if he knows no Spanish, to go for a shave or haircut to a barber near the business centre at about half past nine any morning. There is a babel of voices, barbers and customers competing to make themselves heard, the latter feverishly blowing the lather from their lips when it impedes their delivery; the financier, the civil servant and the man with the razor, all must have their say. And what are the subjects of this verbal storm? Mostly football, sometimes the bulls, a spontaneous joke, for there is always a licensed jester; never women and politics for, as they say, *con la política va la alegría*, 'enter politics, exit fun'. As long as the Andaluz has enough work to provide bread, wine and oil he regards politics as a bore.

At the entrance to the harbour, where the liners almost enter the main street, is the Plaza de Queipo de Llano. On one side stretches the park and on the other, to the west, the Alameda del Generalísimo leads to the River Guadalmedina which runs through the town as an undistinguished stream or torrent, according to the season. It has no ancestry and hence has to be called 'the river of the town'. Before this a turning to the right takes you to the principal market (there are four others), whose entrance was once that of the dockyards, the *atarazana*. It is a great square building of white marble with communicating horse-shoe arches; on either side are tiny windows of the same pattern, with engaged supporting columns. The dockyard was built in the first half of the fourteenth century for Yusuf I, King of Granada, and consequently has the crest and motto of his dynasty in the *enjutas* of the *alfiz*. There is a pavement café opposite, where one may sit and admire the Nasrid monument,

and watch the kerb-side vendors of fruit and vegetables over-
flowing from the precincts of the market.

If you turn east and follow the Calle Martínez back to your
starting point, then skirt the pavement cafés on the north side of
the Plaza de Queipo de Llano, and turn left, you will see the
Cathedral before you. Note that for most of the way you have
been walking on marble pavements and that even in the back-
streets, where funds would not run to marble slabs, the kerb
stones at least flaunt their aristocratic descent. The story of the
building of the Cathedral is one of confusion, irresolution and,
probably, lack of funds. It began with designs by the great
masters, for Pedro López, Enrique Egas, Diego de Siloé and
Diego de Vergara followed each other in rapid succession. But
it took nearly two hundred years before the western end and the
twin towers were begun, and even then only the north one was
finished, the other remaining a pathetic stump, hence the local
name *La Manquita*, the missing one.

Inside, the plan of a hall church with ambulatory seems to have
been the inspiration for both Granada and Cádiz, though it is
difficult to say how much all three owe to Toledo. It is customary
to pass over the architecture with a reference to the Greco-
Roman flavour of its Renaissance inspiration, and to concen-
trate the attention on the *coro* that occupies the usual site in the
centre of the nave. Of its 103 stalls some forty were the work of
Pedro de Mena, the favourite pupil of Alonso Cano, who deputed
the work to him with the exception of one figure, San Juan de
Dios, near the south-west corner. It is worth noting that the
works of Cano and his pupil can be distinguished from those of
their less gifted colleagues, Luis Ortiz and José Micael, competent as they are, even by the least-informed amateur.

The student of religious iconography may also enjoy identify-
ing the various saints and their attributes, that form the chief
decoration of the choir stalls. The second from the altar, on the
left, shows Santiago or St. James, in his role of pilgrim with
broad hat, staff and scallop shells. The seventeenth is St. Anthony
Abbott, about whose attributes there is much irresponsible
writing; he has the letter 'T' on his cloak, which is said to represent the first letter of *Theos*, God. No Greek scholar, knowing
that 'th' is a single letter, would support this solecism; it is
actually a crutch, for the monks who lived under his rule in the
Middle Ages were hospitallers. The pig and bell became his
emblem under curious circumstances, when King Philip Augustus
and local authorities allowed the hogs of the Antonines to

scavenge in the streets of French towns, a privilege withheld from those of the laity of whatever degree. The pigs wore bells to ensure that they would be treated with proper respect, and St. Anthony often carries flames to commemorate his superiority to temptation. No. 25 is San Roque or St. Roch, who devoted his life to the care of sufferers from the plague. Here we see him when he was smitten with the disease and retired to a wood to die, only to be kept alive by his faithful dog bringing him his daily bread—a sensitive portrayal of the sort of legend that one longs to believe. These are only a few of the carvings which repay study and a slight knowledge of the saints' lives. Apart from this, the costumes of the seventeenth century are so accurately reproduced that they have been of use to the social historian. The woods include cedar, larch, walnut and American *granadillo*, whose reddish colour made it a favourite with woodworkers.

The first chapel on the right in the ambulatory contains a Virgin said to have been carried by Ferdinand the Catholic in battle; as it stands about three feet high we wonder just how he managed the hand-to-hand fighting. On either side are the kneeling figures of the Catholic Sovereigns, variously attributed to Pedro de Mena and José de Mora; it matters little, for the subjects had been dead for a century and a half when their effigies were carved. Whoever the sculptor was, he made the mistake of giving Queen Isabel black hair, whereas hers was red-gold like that of so many members of the royal house of Castile.

Leaving the Cathedral, you may like to glance at the Isabelline north door, permanently closed, a survivor from the Gothic church which was built on the site of the mosque. The Calle San Augustíne leads to the Palacio de Buenavista, usually described as Mudéjar but possibly dating from before the Reconquest. Here is housed the **Museo Provincial de Bellas Artes**; for the visitor who limits his stay to Málaga and the Costa del Sol, there is enough in it to provide a fair introduction to the art of Spain. In the first room there are a *Dolorosa* and an *Ecce Homo* by Morales, in both of which the transcendent quality of the early master's art is apparent. He is, perhaps, not highly enough regarded today and relegated to the position of 'just another of the Mannerists'. The unprejudiced observer will, however, discern more than superficial virtues in the works of *El Divino*. We know little about him, but it seems that he had a gift of repartee; at his first meeting with Philip II, the King reproved him for the richness of his garments, upon which Morales explained that he had spent all his money in order to be worthy of the audience. In his old age, when he was living in extreme poverty, the King saw him again at Badajoz, his home town. The King therefore ordered an annual pension of 200 ducats 'for his dinner', only to be asked: 'and for supper, sire?' Philip obviously had a sense of humour—which one might suspect on seeing his miniature portrait of Álora—and added a hundred ducats.

In these canvases one sees the forerunners of El Greco's elongated figures and the religious fervour that was to lose itself in High Baroque. Morales' subjects may show one curious feature, the ears are reproduced in profile while the head is full face. This is actually an archaism that goes back to consular diptychs of the later Roman Empire and subsequent Christian ivory carvings, and reappears in our own day as an early manifestation of Picasso's attempts to portray his characters simultaneously from several angles. In Room IV the *Adoration of the Shepherds* by Antonio de Castillo may be compared with the same subject that we saw in the Córdoba Museum by José Sarabia, remembering that both artists were pupils of Zurbarán. The inevitable lesson, I believe, is that environment, or education, plays a greater part than heredity, or natural talent in painting, as in other manifestations of the human soul. A *St. Francis* by Murillo again features the dark brown pigment made from the bones of the stew-pot, and a *St. John the Evangelist* by Alonso Cano is dressed in a robe of rose-violet that reminds you of one of El Greco's favourite colours. Works by Ribera and Zurbarán are shown in Rooms V and VI.

The stairway which leads to the exhibition of moderns has a beautiful *artesonado*, and the gallery round the patio has a similar, but restored ceiling. On the walls of this 'Arabic' patio gallery is a series of paintings of the *romería del Rocío* by G. Bilbao of Seville, which tell you more about this picturesque festival than any amount of description. Many of the moderns repay examination and I particularly recommend the works of J. Nogales, the flower painter, in Room XI. Most of the upper storey is devoted to Málaga's pride in Picasso, who was born at No. 6, Plaza de la Merced, in 1881. Had he taken his father's surname in the usual way, we would know him as Ruiz, but Spaniards are at liberty to take the surnames of their mothers or even maternal grandmothers; and that is why we speak of Velázquez instead of Da Silva and Murillo rather than Esteban or even Pérez.

The furniture of the Picasso house has been installed in a special room here, looking Victorian and uncomfortable. Room

XIV is reserved for the works of Muñoz Degrain, who is not always given due credit for having been Picasso's teacher in the 1890s. He deserves, however, to be known for his own achievements and is noted in Spain for his mastery of light and colour. Some of his work is impressionistic and a strong vein of fantasy runs through it, notably in *The Valkyries*. The climax of the visit is the Picasso Room (XV), which contains about 25 sketches and autographs. Some of the drawings and a portrait of his master with dedication were done when Picasso was aged fourteen. The latter is indeed a finished work of art and we can understand the artist's claim that at twelve he drew like Raphael, though it would have been more in character had he said, 'better than Raphael'. On the way out there are Roman mosaics to be admired in a patio, all very much in the usual tradition.

The Calle de la Victoria, with the somewhat squalid gypsy quarter on the right, leads to the **Church of Santa Maria de la Victoria**, built on the site of the tent of King Ferdinand during the siege of Málaga in 1487. The Moslems' defence was so stubborn that the siege was nearly raised and perhaps for this reason the terms of surrender were made unduly harsh. So exorbitant indeed was the sum demanded for the ransoming of the inhabitants that only a proportion of it could be raised by the unfortunate Moslems. The Catholic Sovereigns coolly pocketed as much as had been collected and then enslaved all the inhabitants because the full ransom had not been paid. It is comforting to know, however, that the entry into the captured city was made under divine protection, with the usual *Te Deum*, the statue of the Virgin of Victory and Queen Isabel with bare feet. The retablo shows scenes from the life of St. Francis of Paola, whose order of the Minims used to live next door in what is now the military hospital.

The *camarín*, a high chamber behind the altar, housing the church's patron, is profusely decorated with stucco work, little cherubs and superfluous ornament; we shall see only one worse, at Priego de Córdoba. The Madonna has been described as a Dolorosa, difficult to explain as she is holding an Infant; elsewhere this work is compared to a hunger-stricken peasant, but the ordinary observer would say she is just a buxom young woman with a microscopic child. She had been presented to the royal couple, whom she preceded into Málaga in solemn procession, by the Archduke Maximilian of Austria; his son Philip the Fair was destined to marry the daughter of Ferdinand and Isabel, Juana the Mad. This image therefore foreshadows a union that gave Spain two centuries of Hapsburg rule. The crypt does nothing to raise the tone of the church. Designed for the Buenavista family, it has a frieze of skulls and crossbones and a ceiling with the same decoration, more suitable for a pirate ship. If time is limited the Church of La Victoria can well be omitted; even the *rejas*, said to be made from the chains of Christian captives liberated in 1487, are without artistic merit.

The Gibralfaro is a good starting point for a tour of the rest of Málaga, whether or not you lunched at the Hostería. The name means 'Hill of the Lighthouse', for the Island of Pharos off Alexandria was transformed into a lighthouse by the second Ptolemy and became one of the wonders of the world. The word was current not only among the Arabs, but in all the Romance languages, where it also does duty for motorcar headlights. A good way to begin is by bus or taxi up the hill, after which the rest of the visit is downhill or on the level. The castle itself succeeded Phoenician, Greek and Roman structures and took its present form under Yusuf I, the Nasrid king for whom the dockyard entrance was built. The huge walls still stand, in many parts adorned with their pyramidal merlons, and from them a bird's-eye view of the whole district can be had. To the north is a plain, on which the city is rapidly encroaching, bounded by the abrupt sierra that fills the horizon and explains why this fortunate part of Spain is relatively immune from the cold north winds. To the south-west lies Torremolinos, now continuous with the city by means of the industrial area, then come the complicated harbours, inner and outer, with a liner or two looking as though they are moored in the park that extends along the waterfront. Nearer again are the hanging gardens and the Alcazaba, with the solitary tower of the Cathedral rising behind it. Directly south, the bull-ring is a prominent landmark, and from there the fashionable suburbs of El Palo and El Limonar show their roofs among the trees that stretch away to the east, until the various headlands and beaches on the way to Motril lead the eye to the far horizon.

A double wall formerly enclosed a path to the **Alcazaba**, but it can no longer be negotiated, though the twin walls still exist. However, a pleasant path winds down outside the south wall, through the pine woods that now clothe the whole hillside, and between thickets of acanthus. You pass the hanging gardens and turn to the entrance of the Alcazaba, from where the fortress rises in an impressive jumble of cube upon cube of wall and tower. Outside the entrance stands a Roman column, from whose capital spring an iron cross and four street-lamps, a typically

Spanish touch. Immediately to the north of the entrance is a small ornamental garden along the street called Alcazabilla, and where it ends modern excavation has revealed part of a Roman theatre —the remainder of it under the foundations of an office block. Its depth shows how much the city has risen in two thousand years, just as the sea has receded from the Alcazaba and the dockyard we saw at the market.

There is no doubt that successive waves of conquerors built their fortresses on this site, and in caliphal times it was a solid governor's residence. It was restored and largely rebuilt under the Nasrids and then allowed to decay until 1933, when hardly anything recognisable remained in the massive heap of ruins. Thorough restoration, some say it is excessive, was then begun by Ricardo de Orueta and today we can recapture the atmosphere with which the old citadel was endowed. The Arco del Cristo, a horseshoe with mixed stone and brickwork, leads to a maze of moss-covered brick paths, past Roman marble columns, a tombstone or two, a prehistoric Iberian boar or a palaeo-Christian font. Hedges of myrtle or cypress surround the various patios on the way up, and the splash of fountains adds to the charm of the roses, vines, jasmine and honeysuckle. The top patio reveals a horseshoe arcade resting on caliphal capitals, and is the site of the eighth-century mosque founded by a Syrian friend of Abderrahman I. The plaster *mihrab* is still standing but, as though to ensure that its capacity for evil cannot revive, it now contains a ceramic jar bearing a cross and the apotropaic letters IHS. There is a small archaeological museum, with objects recovered from the Cueva de la Pilata and from the dolmens of Antequera, as well as photographic reproductions of many Roman mosaics found in the province.

From the Alcazaba we make our way between the imposing Customs House and the Post Office to the Parque, where some of Málaga's two thousand species of plant grow luxuriantly. A broad pavement of black, white and red marble in geometric patterns is kept clean and shining, giant plane trees raise their heads above the palms and bamboos, and kiosks with iron chairs and tables stand under the trees and among the flower-beds. There is an aviary and a swan pool, though not as attractive as the one at Lisbon, and at the east end is the fountain brought by Charles V from Genoa and intended for his unfinished palace at Granada.

The foreign colony of Málaga must have been a large one. A guidebook of 1882 mentions the boarding-house run by a Mrs.

Walsall and adds that Málaga is supplied with first-rate bottled ale by Mr. Hodgson, at whose establishment English goods and provisions of all kinds can be obtained. The wine trade was obviously the lure and the wine merchants of those days included Scholtz, Crooke, Loring, Clemens and John Mark, who was also British vice-consul and presumably the son of William Mark. William Mark came to Málaga in 1816, became British consul and after endless negotiations and disappointments succeeded in establishing a Protestant cemetery. This had been lacking in spite of the commercial treaty negotiated between Cromwell and Philip IV, in which article 35 provided for '. . . a decent and convenient burial place'. Previously an exception had been made for a page of our King Charles I when he was visiting Spain as heir-apparent in search of a bride. Subsequently, the treaty was ignored and Protestants had to be buried upright in the sand below high-water mark, an unsatisfactory arrangement on a practically tideless coast infested with hungry dogs. The whole story is competently told by Marjorie Grice-Hutchinson in a booklet which is on sale in the chapel just inside the gate.

There is a monument to Robert Boyd, an ex-officer from India, 'who died in the sacred cause of liberty'. His grave is not known but is certainly here, for William Mark took the body to his own house on the day Boyd was executed and buried it in his new cemetery the next day. Boyd was a collaborator of General Torrijos and the Spanish liberals, who used London and Gibraltar as their headquarters in plotting the overthrow of Ferdinand VII, much to the annoyance of the British government which in those days did not concern itself with the ethics of the politics of foreign countries. At the third attempt Boyd, Torrijos and fifty others landed at Fuengirola, marched inland, found the Spanish peasant perfectly satisfied with his tyrannical government, and were captured by the authorities. After consultation with Madrid, the local governor General Moreno had the conspirators shot on the sands of Málaga. Even after a hundred and forty years the mysterious Viriato arouses our interest. Letters from this anonymous patriot who used a false name—Viriatus was a freedom fighter in Roman days—were responsible for deciding the time and place of the landing and it is thought that they may have emanated from a Government source, perhaps from General Moreno himself. Historical research has been based on less promising material.

Another foreigner in Málaga's history is a shadowy figure of the nineteenth century. A Kirkpatrick of Closeburn, either a Scot

Above left, Arcos de la Frontera; *right*, Castellar de la Frontera – the town inside a castle. *Below*, Medina Sidonia, Arco de la Pastora.

Ronda, the Puente Nuevo.

or of Scottish descent, combined the functions of wine merchant and United States consul in Málaga. He married a Spanish woman and their daughter, María Manuela, married a grandee of Spain, Don Cipriano Guzmán y Portocarrero, Duke of Peñaranda, Count of Teba and subsequently Count of Montijo. There is only malice to support the tale that María Manuela served wine to her father's customers and caught Don Cipriano in his cups; no true aristocrat would remember an unsuitable proposal on the morning after.

An interesting aspect of the Peninsular War is afforded by the fact that Don Cipriano had fought on the French side; we are rarely told, and only too apt to forget, that a number of Spanish aristocrats, whom we should call Quislings today, supported Joseph Bonaparte. María Manuela produced a daughter whom they named Eugenia María, born in Granada in 1826. As a child she had listened to Stendhal's reminiscences of Napoleon and as a girl she was much in the company of Prosper Mérimée, the French writer who himself was much influenced by Stendhal. He had attached himself to María Manuela and her daughter Eugenia Montijo, who now called herself Countess of Teba, and it is said that he heard the story of the Andalucian gypsy Carmen from the former. Possibly at Mérimée's suggestion the family moved to Paris and, again with his help, Eugenia married the Emperor Napoleon III in Notre Dame Cathedral in 1853. Shortly afterwards Prosper Mérimée was made a senator; with his usual luck he died before France fell to the Prussians and before his *Carmen* was made into an opera and rejected by the Paris audience.

From now on the wine merchant's granddaughter played her part in world affairs. She supported, probably even inspired, French military aid to the Papal states against Garibaldi and the Risorgimento. To symbolise Napoleonic interest in Egypt, as though the dreams of glory of 1798 had never vanished with the dawn, Eugénie, as she was now called, sailed up the newly opened Suez Canal with the first convoy and from Ismailia went on to Cairo. She acted as regent of France on several occasions, settled in Chiselhurst with her husband after the disaster of Sedan and died in Madrid at the age of 94, while on a visit to her goddaughter, Victoria Eugenia of Battenberg, last Queen of Spain.

A circular route of less than 100 miles over excellent roads enables us to visit Antequera and Loja, and allows us later to take a less-known route to Granada. We leave Málaga by N321 and soon after Colmenar take the fork (N331) to **Antequera**, a total of 55 kilometres. Immediately before entering the town the road takes us past two of the famous *dolmens*, megalithic collective tombs; a third, the Romeral, lies farther back along the road and is less easily reached. For those without special knowledge or interest in prehistory, the Cueva de Menga gives a good idea of the astonishing results achieved by the chalcolithic builders over 4,000 years ago. It is essentially a passage, broadening at the far end, and composed entirely of fitted stone slabs, of which the five that form the flat roof and which are partly supported by stone pillars, average 180 tons in weight. Perhaps the most interesting feature is that this type of passage-grave can be traced to Spain from the Eastern Mediterranean, and from here to Brittany and the western parts of the British Isles. There seems little doubt that the Bronze Age builders made the hazardous journeys by sea, probably in coracles, an adventure which makes Columbus' journey a comparative picnic.

Antequera preserves but little of its past, if we except history and legend. It was taken from the Moslems as early as 1410 after a siege in which—though the story is told of other sieges—gunpowder was supposedly used for the first time. The conqueror was the Infante Ferdinand of Castile, who was later elected King of Aragón and given the nickname *El de Antequera*. The siege was complicated by an attempted relief expedition from Granada, but this was defeated and the keys handed over by the *wali*, Al-Karmen. The city's emblem, a jar of lilies, is said to be taken from an attribute of the Blessed Virgin; it is, but through an interesting deviation, for the *terraza* was the badge of the Infante's military order, the oldest in Spain.

The lower town has little of interest; its Collegiate Church of San Sebastián has one of the more elegant Baroque towers, on which is a weathervane in the shape of a trumpeter. The relics of St. Euphemia are said to be suspended here, but all recollection of them has been lost. Inside is the tomb of Rodrigo de Narváez, celebrated governor of the town shortly after its capture. Condé devotes four pages to a 'singular anecdote' told about him. His men captured a young Moslem aristocrat who was on his way to claim his bride; Narváez accepted the Moslem's parole and later, when the couple had surrendered themselves as promised, released them and sent them home with presents and an escort.

Love, directly or indirectly, plays a large part in the history of Antequera. There is an old hermitage of St. Zoilus, whose construction was ordered by the Catholic Sovereigns under strange circumstances. Their only son Juan died six months after his wedding, from a fever which the experts attributed to excessive performance of his marital duties. Others, however, including the Prince himself, diagnosed a kidney ailment and invoked St. Zoilus, who specialised in renal disorders. But the young man died all the same, leaving a bequest which his parents used to build the hermitage referred to. It is interesting to note also that the Roman town of Nescania near by was noted for its Fons Divinus, whose waters were good for stone and the gravel. St. Zoilus was an early Christian martyr whose kidneys had been thrown into a well at Córdoba, hence water from this well worked wonders. The painter Ruiz de Iglesias sent for a supply which promptly cured his nephritis; the water then became so popular that further supplies were brought to satisfy the demand in Madrid. Tasting a sample of this, Ruiz detected the flavour of ambergris, and on making enquiries discovered that a careless carrier had dropped the jar of St. Zoilus kidney-water and substituted a similar one of so-called 'amber-water'.

The Castle has one tower and parts of two walls. The former is called the Torre Mocha, or 'stumpy' though it now has a Baroque bell tower to top it, and is better known as Papabellotas, because its construction is said to have absorbed the sale price of a grove of mountain oaks (*bellota*—acorn). Others give the name to the big bronze bell that hangs inside; its mechanism is below and it is supposed to strike the quarter hours with a large hammer, but doesn't. From here you can see the castle precinct sown with wheat, among which poppies grow, and on the other side the tawny roofs of the lower town, where Pedro Roldán was born in 1624. Here, too, lived Dr. Solano, who initiated a new concept in medicine by predicting the exact time of the crisis of an illness from study of the pulse, so that the life-giving phlebotomy or enema could be performed at, literally, *le moment critique*. To the north-east a great crag stands in the plain, like a second Gibraltar; it is called the *Peña de los Enamorados*, or 'Sweethearts' Peak'. Several legends exist to explain the name, the usual one being that recounted in Southey's poem, *Leila and Manuel*; a Christian knight and a Moorish maiden pursued by her father's troops, locked themselves in a last embrace and jumped off the cliff.

Leaving the castle through the Arco de Gigantes, where we entered, and turning east, we soon find the Church of El Carmen, with a fine *artesonado*, perhaps the best thing in Antequera. It may be only an odd coincidence that the Virgen del Carmen presides over the parish that includes the castle whose governor was named Al-Karmen. The name is usually shrugged off as a corruption of Carmel, but I feel there must be a better explanation. Going the other way, that is to the west, we come out at the back of the hill, where the old Arab Puerta de Málaga, with its horseshoe arch, is now the Ermita de la Virgen de la Espera. About 12 kilometres south of Antequera is the region of *El Torcal*, an immense accumulation of red limestone blocks of the weirdest shapes. Like stalactite caves, waterfalls and other natural phenomena, this extensive jumble of weird patterns appeals to only a few.

Leaving Antequera by N342, we soon see Archidona on the left, with its girdle of mediaeval walls surrounding the highest peak, on which stand the ruins of the old castle. After 34 kilometres we reach **Loja**, whose white houses rise on a gentle slope above the Genil, then suddenly part to allow the castle-crowned rock to emerge. Here Gonzalo de Córdoba, cheated and rejected by Ferdinand the Catholic, passed his last years in the splendid state of a great gentleman. Unruffled by his master's ingratitude he held court and cared for his dependents, mostly old soldiers broken in the wars; no one who had served under him in the days of his glory was ever turned away.

There is little to see in Loja, but much to remember. The Churches of Santa María (with a Baroque face-lift) and San Gabriel are of the sixteenth century, the latter with a good *artesonado*. Below the town is the gorge through which the river forces its way, rather fancifully called *Los Infiernos*. In a square near Santa María is a statue of General Narváez, who steered the wilful and promiscuous Isabel II through Carlist Wars and domestic crises. This 'Big Sword of Loja', as they called him, had to be fairly ruthless to hold the kingdom together, and he once explained the prudence of his policy as, 'I shot some and I hanged others'. He died in 1868 and a few months later Isabel abdicated. By a strange chance she had recently taken as a lover a beefy Italian actor, son of a cook, as a change from her usual young officers, and conferred on him the title of Marquis of Loja. Loja was captured in 1486, six years before the fall of Granada, and among the victorious besiegers was a contingent of English archers under a man whom the historians impartially call Lord Rivers and Lord Scales. He was, in fact, Sir Edward Woodville (or Wydville), fourth son of the first Earl Rivers; Edward's eldest brother naturally became the second Earl Rivers, and also inherited the title of Baron Scales from his mother. Edward therefore had no right to either title and got his knighthood only when his sister Elizabeth married Edward IV in 1464. Washington Irving dates the siege as 1488, which makes Edward's presence improbable, and has him labelled as brother-in-law to Henry VII, whereas it was his niece who married that king. It would have been impossible for Edward Woodville to have been injured at the siege of Loja and get to Brittany where he was killed at the battle of St Aubin du Cormier on 28th July, 1488. His injury consisted in having some front teeth knocked out by a stone; so gallantly had he borne himself that the King and Queen themselves came to his tent to commiserate. 'It is little,' he is reported to have said, 'to lose a few teeth in the service of Him who has given me all. Our Lord,' he added, 'who reared this fabric, has only opened a window, in order to discern more readily what passes within.' This speech gave their Royal Highnesses great pleasure and deserves all praise, in view of the knight's disability.

The obvious way to Granada from Loja is to follow N342 through the fertile plain of the Genil. Here, however, you have the alternative of setting out from Málaga, seeing more of the Costa del Sol and travelling to Granada by an excellent, interesting and less frequented road. We therefore leave Málaga by the coastal N340, on which we shall continue for some 50 kilometres. Now is the time to revise one's verdict on the Costa del Sol, for we have left the crowded and sometimes vulgar resorts behind and a continuous succession of promontories and coves lies ahead, the former crowned with their *atalayas*, the latter in most cases having the picturesque features of a fishing village. From here to Almeria one can enjoy blue skies and bluer seas, away from artificial aids to pleasure but still not divorced from comfort. Behind this chain of promontories and bays rise the hills and mountains that shelter this delightful coast, some cultivated, most bare and rugged.

Arabic influence can be deduced from the names of the villages along the coastal route, Cala del Moral (Cala, as I have mentioned before, is an anchorage); the diminutive La Caleta just past Torre del Mar, and the doubly diminutive La Caletilla, at Nerja, which is as far as this digression takes us. For those who are in a hurry to get to Granada, the turn-off (C335) at Torre del Mar goes to Vélez-Málaga; for others, the coastal strip as far as Nerja, a distance of 21 kilometres, is well worth

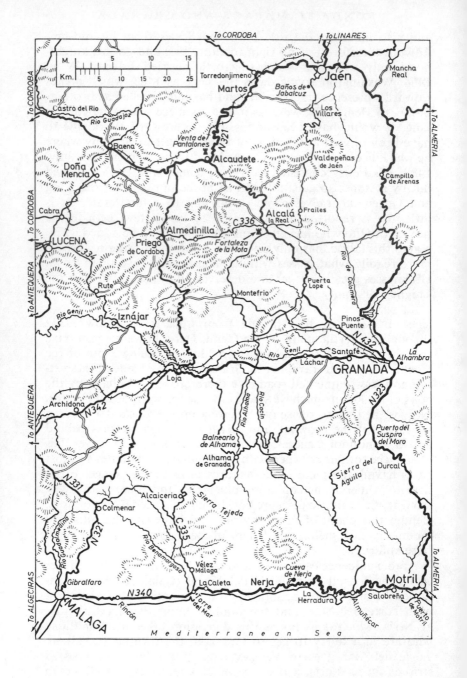

the double journey. The town is built high up and an arcaded, whitewashed shelter among the palms gives a magnificent view of the coast. Among the hotels is a D.G.T. Parador.

There is nothing remarkable about the history of Nerja, which followed a common pattern of Oriental civilisation, with the cultivation of mulberries for the silkworms; vines, whose produce was called *zabib* (raisins) by the wily Moslem instead of *hamra*, or wine; figs and sugar-canes. A bloodless surrender during the Reconquest was followed by the usual breach of treaty and the forced conversion or emigration of most of the Moslem inhabitants and repopulation from the north. The town contains nothing of an earlier date than the eighteenth century, except a sudden leap backwards of several tens of millennia to a recently discovered Cave, in which early palaeolithic paintings of the same epoch as Cueva de la Pileta and Altamira rival the stalactite attractions. There is a small museum and the specialist will find much to interest him, while the casual visitor is conducted through the cavern to the strains of classical music, at least one step up from the Offenbach 'Barcarolle' that they play in the Mallorca caves.

We now return to Torre del Mar and go inland on C335, arriving at **Vélez-Málaga** after 4 kilometres. It is an old-fashioned and conservative town, and Townsend reported that as late as the end of the eighteenth century they were still saying *Vaya Usted con la Virgen* instead of the universal 'Go with God'. It has not, however, shed the once obligatory call at the front door, enquiring whether anyone is at home, of *Ave Maria purísima*, and the appropriate reply, instead of 'come in', *sin pecado concebida*. But more of this a little later.

Opposite the Convent of the Carmelites a right fork past a small square leads up the hill to the Plaza de España, in which stands the Parish Church of St. John the Baptist (*San Juan Bautista*). It is a late Gothic building, with some excellent polychrome statues by Pedro de Mena who, you will remember, carved the beautiful choir stalls in Málaga. The guidebooks also tell you that the church houses the celebrated Cáliz de las Esmeraldas, a chalice set with 365 precious stones. It is here only at Corpus Christi, and for the rest of the year it is kept in the Carmelite Convent we saw on the main road, and as this is *in clausura* some finesse is needed in getting to see it. It is of gold and stands about 6 inches high; the jewels are emeralds and rubies, considerably less than a hundred, and their faceting dates the chalice to the seventeenth century at the earliest.

You should leave the Plaza de España under an arch built in the 1590s (the last figure of the date inscription is obliterated) and reached by climbing stone stairs at whose head is a shrine to the Virgin put up after the Civil War. She is officially called *La Virgen de los Combatientes*, but known locally as *La Virgen de los Mamparados*—the stay-at-homes. Pass through into the upper town, on the way to the other parish church. Upper towns are usually poor, the houses mere cabins without patios, but here the streets are clean, the glaring whitewash hurts the eyes and the daily round goes on at its own slow pace.

At the top of the steep ascent is the **Parish Church of La Encarnación**, or simply Santa María, its walls resting on brick and stone courses, and with an arcade of horseshoe style on octagonal brick columns of Mudéjar origin. The ceilings should be examined carefully, as they are excellent examples of Mudéjar work, especially the *alfarje* of the octagonal covering to the sanctuary, with its central *racimo*, a boss with stalactite divisions. The rest of the interior is plain and lime-washed and the sacramental plate, if it exists still, is not produced as readily as the chalice. It is said to have belonged to Ferdinand the Catholic and to have been presented by him after his capture of the town. During the fight he himself slew a Moor and presented the town with its crest, a picture of the event. The body at the horse's feet, however, is not that of the Moor, but of the King's faithful groom, who gave his life shielding his master. The Ermita de San Sebastián, where the hero is buried, was erected to commemorate his devotion.

It is easy to believe that this old church, now threatened with reconstruction, was once the chief mosque of the town, though it seems as though the Oriental characters we have seen were all the work of Mudéjars after the Reconquest. For the rest, Vélez-Málaga has for centuries been a sugar producer, and the industry, which almost died of neglect after the expulsion of the Moriscos, was rescued by a Frenchman called De Valois, who also pioneered the manufacture of an excellent rum. This otherwise conservative town has unfortunately given this up and a substitute is made, as we saw, in Rute.

From Vélez-Málaga we follow the course of the River Vélez, climbing steadily until we reach the summit of the Sierra Tejeda. Pink oleanders grow on the river-banks, Spanish broom makes golden splashes on the hillsides and, on a warm day, perfumes the air. The inhabitants have planted marguerites and geraniums, which grow in profusion, without any thought of attracting tourists, for this delightful road is rarely used. After the tiny hamlet of Alcaicería, the 'Silk Bazaar', watch out for kilometre stone 37 and draw in at the roadside at the next turn. Walking through the fragrant pine wood on the right you emerge on a crest from which to get your first and best view of the Sierra Nevada, Spain's only range to be crowned with perpetual snow. With its huge length, in the clarity of the morning sun, forming a backdrop to the vast plains of olive trees, it is a sight as thrilling as any that the Costa del Sol can offer.

At the provincial boundary between Málaga and Granada the road changes its number and becomes C340, but remains good as far as, and beyond, **Alhama de Granada**. The name is derived from the Arabic *hammam*, hot baths, an institution that the Romans took from the Greeks, handed back to the Byzantines and through them to the Arabs, who took to them with such enthusiasm that a visit to the *hammam* became a part of the normal day's activities as well as a ceremonial occasion. From the Arabs it passed to the Turks, after whom we have named our Turkish baths. Very few were left in Spain at the Reconquest, for it was generally held that uncleanliness was next to godliness and that hot baths smacked of apostasy. It is believed by many that Queen Isabel the Catholic made a vow not to change her shift until Granada had been captured, and that she had to wear the same garment for the ten years of the war. The story is incorrect, for it refers to a different Isabel, daughter of Philip II and therefore, great-great-granddaughter of the Catholic Sovereign. The siege was that of Ostende and the duration only two and a half years, while perfumes were readily obtainable and baths still unfashionable. The feat was nevertheless considered noteworthy and the French have adopted *couleur Isabelle* for a dull grey, whether in dress material or horses.

Alhama's fame rests mainly on its capture by Rodrigo Ponce de León, later Duke of Cádiz, who subsequently recaptured Zahara de los Membrillos. The surprise assault on this stronghold by the Moslems, without declaration of war, amply justified the Marquis in his bold and successful counter-attack on Alhama, one of the keys in the defence of Granada.

The town is romantically situated on the edge of a *tajo*, recalling that of Ronda in miniature, where the River Marchan finds its way round three sides of the town in a cleft that is broad enough to shelter olive groves. A *mirador* can be found not far from the Parish Church. Although Enrique de Egas and the Younger Siloé had a hand in its construction, the result is unharmonious, the most awkward feature being a classical Renaissance south portal built a few feet in front of a perfectly good late Gothic one. The interior has a simple but good *artesonado* with sunken panels, and *lazos* of eight limbs and—a modern improvement at the time of building—a raised *coro* on low arches over the western entrance. In the sacristy are vestments beautifully embroidered with scenes from the Bible; these are attributed to the Catholic Queen herself, and it is known that her relaxations included this type of work.

The **Baths** from which the town takes its name are along a small road in the gorge of the river. Some attempt has been made to construct an alameda and there are charming views from the bridge and the banks. At one spot the cold, swiftly flowing stream is augmented by a gushing hot spring that appeared after the destructive earthquake of 1884, responsible for the disappearance of the old aqueduct and other scanty mediaeval remains. One of the few picturesque local sights is that of women bringing their amphora-shaped *cántaros*, nowadays too often replaced by hideous plastic buckets, to fetch hot water for the family laundry. The Arab baths have now been incorporated in a new hotel, in whose cellar stand two horseshoe arches with their feet in warm water. The older establishment, believed to be of Roman origin, is a little distance away and will in all probability be closed permanently, perhaps in order to divert custom to the new hotel.

From Alhama an excellent road leads north to join N342 just west of **Láchar**. This tiny village is distinguished by possessing a dream palace of uncertain date; as you approach it from the west it offers a fine castellated appearance, and as you enter from the left side of the main road you come to a courtyard where a palm tree rises between two horseshoe arches, with two more on your right. At a glance it is obvious that the ground level has risen some five feet since the castle was built, and this usually means a break of several centuries in occupation. Creepers spread themselves on the side-walls, there are arched windows on all sides, the walls are crenellated, and the merlons topped with truncated pyramids. Everything is plastered and washed with a coloured lime that is somewhere between ochre and maroon, rarely seen except in Rome.

The entrance-hall contains a tablet giving the alleged history of the castle, from its foundation by Count Julian as a retreat for his daughter Florinda—the story is encountered in the least-expected places, including *Don Quixote*—to the various aristocrats who owned it after the *repartamiento*. This was the distribution of properties to those who distinguished themselves during the Reconquest; Spaniards of course, for foreigners expected to be rewarded with loot or, in the case of the Swiss, hard cash.

The building is difficult to date, for it was captured and burnt by the Constable Álvaro de Luna before the battle of Higuerela in 1430, a prelude to the final campaign of the Catholic Sovereigns. It is interesting to see that the castle is called *Alachar*, Arabic for 'The Refuge'. The interior has been left in a sad state of neglect, and several years ago the floors were piled high with the beautiful Cuenca tiles that had fallen from the walls. They have now been collected and moved to Granada. The Cuenca tiles could not have been put there before 1550, when this method of stamping and baking was introduced, while the *azulejo* frieze in some of the rooms, with the Nasrid Inscription 'There is no conqueror but Allah', should not have been later than 1492, when Granada fell. Of course, we must always remember that decorations do not date a wall and that horseshoe arches, like the Nasrid motto, can be of recent date, as in the Sanctuary of Utrera. Half the building is used as accommodation for employees of the Ministry of Agriculture, whose camp beds look incongruous against the huge pointed arches of the fireplaces and the Arabic script round the windows. I agree with Miss Epton, who discovered this delightful spot independently, that it ought to be made into an *Hostal*.

We continue east over the level, fertile plain with the great curtain of the snow-capped Sierra Nevada before us until, after about 10 kilometres, the road enters **Santafé**. One of the few in the world to be built according to the plan of the ancient Roman camp or settlement, and to have preserved its lay-out unaltered through the centuries, it is a square town built on a chessboard pattern. The main roads (*decumanus* and *cardo maximus*) intersect at the church and from their crossing you can see all four gates, three of them still crowned with their chapel. The town was built during the siege of Granada after the tented headquarters of the Catholic Sovereigns had been burned down, the fire started by a candle left in the draught near the hangings of the Queen's pavilion. This would have been the ideal time for the besieged Moslems to make a sortie and cause unimaginable damage, but they suspected that the fire was a trap, and shortly after, a force of 3,000 Christian cavalry was organised to guard the plain between Santafé and Granada. With characteristic energy a permanent camp was built in eighty days, and this is what we see today.

The Parish Church of Santa María de la Encarnación stands at the cross-roads and carries an interesting reminder of the dramatic days of the siege. Rising from the roof over the west entrance is a wrought-iron lance, supported by two feathers that are joined by a strip of parchment, the whole resting on a turbaned head. If travellers stop here at all, which is rare, they seldom look high enough to see, or read deeply enough to understand this strange combination, whose story follows.

Ferdinand had decided that Granada was to be taken not by storm but by siege and by allowing the internal dissensions of the Moslems to do the besiegers' work. Single combat, the result of challenges issued by the chivalry of both sides, was a daily occurrence and did not advance the army's object; it was therefore forbidden by the King. The Moslems, whose code of chivalry was that of the Christians—and indeed in time of peace Christian youths were often sent to Moslem courts to complete their education—could not understand their challenges being ignored. They therefore acquired the habit of galloping up and hurling their spears, with taunts and challenges attached, into the encampment. A certain giant named Atarfe went one better, jumped his horse over the perimeter of the camp (this was before the fire and rebuilding of Santafé), and hurled his lance into the ground before the royal pavilions. To the annoyance of the court, the label attached to the lance bore the name of the Queen.

Hernán Pérez del Pulgar, generally called *el de las hazañas*, 'he of the exploits', was now to undertake his most ambitious exploit He first swore an oath that he would set fire to the Alcaiceria of Granada, the Silk Market, and formally take possession of the chief mosque as the future cathedral. He then provided himself with a large parchment, on which were written an Ave Maria, a Paternoster, a Credo and a Salve; a store of impregnated, inflammable tow, a slow match and fifteen bold companions. Among these was a Granadine Moslem whom Hernán had captured, freed, converted to Christianity, baptised Pedro Pulgar and made his companion. Under the guidance of the renegade the sixteen entered the town along the bed of the River Darro as far as the last bridge, where they divided, some to look after the horses and the rest to steal through the silent streets to the mosque. There the parchment was fixed with a dagger to the main door, at the site of the present entrance to the Capilla Real. The inflammable materials were distributed through the Silk Market—and then it was found that one of them had left the slow match at the mosque. The great fire did not therefore take place for another three and a half centuries. At least they all got away safely.

The next round occurred when the Queen somewhat incautiously determined to have a view of Granada, which she did from the village of Zubia, some five miles south of the town. A large force went with her and she reluctantly witnessed a pitched battle on the plain; this was precipitated by a challenge which the Christians could not resist, though they had steadfastly refused to be drawn by the usual taunts. The huge, armoured figure of Atarfe issued from the Moslem ranks amid shouts of laughter, and paraded slowly in front of the Christian line, so that all could see Pulgar's Ave Maria parchment attached to his horse's tail. Garcilaso de la Vega, presumably father of the famous warrior-poet, begged permission to punish this insolence and after an exciting exhibition of sword-play, succeeded in killing his opponent in a final grapple. The group over the Church is thus explained: the head and the lance of Atarfe, the parchment with Ave Maria, and the pens with which it was inscribed.

Santafé was also the scene of the signing of the capitulation of Granada, a lengthy document of forty-seven clauses, and a secret codicil of sixteen further items, including a payment to the Moslem King of 30,000 gold pieces. Boabdil, the King of Granada, should have known better than to trust a pledge signed in the shadow of Santafé, the Holy Faith, for nearly all the sixty-three clauses were scandalously ignored and he was short-changed on the money. Here, too, the Catholic Sovereigns signed the contract, also broken, that enabled Columbus to discover the New World, according to a plaque affixed to the same church.

CHAPTER FIFTEEN

Granada—The Southern City

❧

Puerta Real—Plaza Nueva—Casa del Carbón—Casa de los Tiros—Antequeruela—Cuarto Real de Santo Domingo—Alcázar Genil

*Quien no ha visto Granada,
No ha visto nada.*

Whoever has not seen Granada has seen nothing.

Thus do the proud inheritors of the last Moslem kingdom of Spain reply to their rival's boast, which rhymes *Sevilla* with *maravilla*. To most visitors Granada represents little more than the Alhambra, and certainly to visit one without seeing the other is like going to Athens and leaving out the Acropolis. Granada is an essential part of every visit to the South of Spain, though hotel accommodation, except for members of package tours, is apt to be hazardous; if you cannot book accommodation in the D.G.T. Parador on the Alhambra, you will do best to seek a room in a pension that is too small to house a package tour.

As regards Granada's history, only a skeleton is required here; as we wander about we shall pick up enough meat to clothe the bare bones. The city began as a refuge for inhabitants of neighbouring towns, especially the now lost Elvira. When St. Ferdinand took Baeza in 1227, the refugees were received in Granada. In 1410 Antequera fell, and many of its citizens went to swell the numbers in Granada, which was by then regarded as the last stronghold of Islam in Spain. The population was, therefore, mainly the basic Hispano-Roman stock of Al-Andulus, with traces of Visigoth, of Berber and of Arab. They should not by rights have been called Moors, though they had Moorish allies, the Marinids, whom they played off against the Castilians in a risky game of power politics.

After Las Navas de Tolosa, when Southern Spain was freed

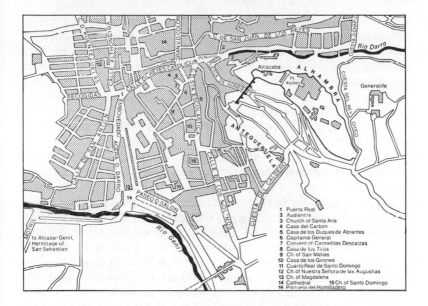

1 Puerta Real
2 Audiencia
3 Church of Santa Ana
4 Casa del Carbon
5 Casa de los Duques de Abrantes
6 Capitania General
7 Convent of Carmelitas Descalzas
8 Casa de los Tiros
9 Ch. of San Matias
10 Casa de los Girones
11 Cuarto Real de Santo Domingo
12 Ch. of Nuestra Señora de las Augustias
13 Ch. of Magdalena
14 Cathedral   15 Ch. of Santo Domingo
16 Plazuela del Humilladero

from Moroccan rule, the Christians moved in. St. Ferdinand was besieging Jaén in 1246 when its somewhat obscure Arab ruler came from Arjona and offered himself and his people as vassals of the Crown of Castile. In accepting, Ferdinand closed a bolt-hole to the rebellious nobles of Castile and created the powerful state of Granada under Mohamed Ibn Annasir Alahmar, founder of the Nasrid dynasty. It was to last until 1492, when the fall of the city marked the climax of the Reconquest. We are apt to forget that the Kingdom of Granada was in feudal subjection to the kings of Castile; the first duty demanded of Ibn Alahmar, the 'son of the red man', was assistance in the conquest of Seville. Returning from this successful mission he found the streets of Granada decorated and a cheering mob greeting him with the title *ghalib*, the Conqueror. He no doubt sadly reflected on how circumstances had forced him to help the Christian subdue his fellow-Moslem; *wala ghalib il 'Allah* he is said to have muttered, thus giving birth to the motto of the Nasrids: 'There is no conqueror but Allah'.

The city is bounded on the south by the River Genil. On the east are three hills, of which the two larger ones are separated by the River Darro, that nowadays pursues its course under main streets to join the Genil. As it enters the city it runs from east to west, under the Calle de los Reyes Católicos, and this forms a convenient northern boundary to the first section of the city to be examined. The second quarter comprises everything north of this, except the Alhambra and the Albaicín, which will be dealt with separately. The first two quarters are relatively flat and comparatively modern; nevertheless they contain more than a vestige of Moslem days, for the wealthy Granadines before the Reconquest had their palaces extending from the foot of the Alhambra to the fertile, irrigated *vega*, the plain through which the Genil winds its way.

Many local writers have tried to summarise the soul of Granada, with varied results; one can only conclude that these attempts are made in an excess of parochial patriotism. There is, let us accept it, no longer one Granada. There are Renaissance and Baroque Granadas, there is the secretive Albaicín of narrow, winding streets and walled gardens, there is the Alhambra and there is even the quarter of the gypsy cave-dwellers on the road to the Sacromonte. The only thing they have in common, and one which you would be well advised to stop and look for frequently, is the massive Sierra Nevada to the south-east, with the white peaks of Mulhacen and La Veleta. From that quarter comes a cooler air, sometimes faintly perfumed with pine or myrtle. Ibn Zamrak, whom we shall meet again, gives us the essence of Granada as it was in the fourteenth century and as it is today.

> . . . and look around you;
> The city is a lady whose husband is the mountain.
> The river's girdle clasps her, and the flowers
> Smile like the jewels that twinkle at her throat.

Granada smiles at any time of year, and during the torrid days of July and August is a refreshing contrast to the oppressive heat of Córdoba. The best time for a visit is from September to November, but spring has its enchantment too, and the festival of music and ballet presented in June provides nights of unforgettable beauty in the gardens of the Generalife.

The **Puerta Real** is a good place to begin our first tour, through the southern city. It is the noisiest spot in Granada and marks the point where the Darro changes its subterranean course; having come so far under the Calle Reyes Católicos, it now turns sharply south under the Embovedado, 'the roofed-in', and the Acera del Darro until it joins the Genil. Like so many *puertas* it has no gate today, and its birth and death took place after the Christian

Above, a village near Motril on the Costa del Sol.   *Below*, landscape near Murcia, with valley and terrace cultivation.

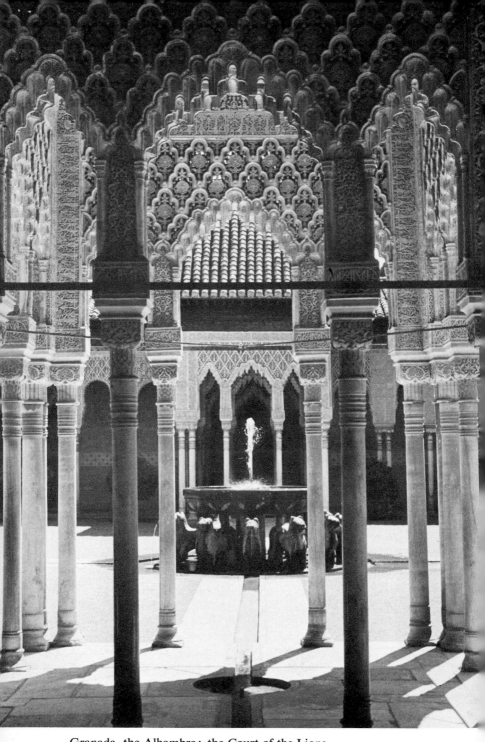

Granada, the Alhambra: the Court of the Lions.

occupation. It was during the sixteenth century that a new suburb sprang up hereabouts, and a protective wall was built to contain it. The area had previously been the 'flea market', *el rastro*, and hence its new gate was first called *Puerta del Rastro* and renamed Puerta Real only in 1624, when Philip IV entered the city through it. Only the name now reminds us of its past, and of its reconstruction in 1610, the year that saw the expulsion of the Moriscos. Here hung the head of Ibn Abu, leader of the last Morisco revolt against their masters, and here, too, was a small oratory of 1640 that enabled travellers to say a prayer on entering or leaving the city. Its image of the Saviour has been moved to the Hospital of St. John of God.

Reyes Católicos is simply a main street and shopping centre, much improved since it lost its tramcars. Half-way up on the left, or north, side, the broad Gran Via de Colón cuts through what was once a picturesque and unhygienic jumble of streets. Where the two main streets meet is an open space, said to mark the centre of the city. A comparatively modern (1892) bronze group of Isabel the Catholic accepting the project of Columbus has recently been brought here from its original site near the river, and is appropriate for the junction of thoroughfares that bear the names of the protagonists. The group, as well as the bas-reliefs on the massive plinth, was the work of Mariano Benlliure during his stay in Rome, and is a good example of the pictorial style of sculpture that marked the close of the nineteenth century. It makes a useful landmark on walks through the city.

The Calle Reyes Católicos, followed eastward, opens into the **Plaza Nueva** which, centuries ago, was used for the running of bulls, the peculiar 'Moorish' type of jousting called the game of *cañas*, the execution of criminals and other diversions. A small oratory near the gallows platform contained a painting of Christ at the Column and no doubt served as the criminals' passport office into the next world. Though greatly changed, the Plaza Nueva still carries the stamp of the past, exemplified in the dignity of the Audiencia, the Court of Appeal, formerly the Chancellery. On the right is the steep ascent to the Alhambra, called the Cuesta de Gomeres, an unimpressive entrance to Fairyland. The Plaza Nueva, which took the place of bridges over the Darro, was extended eastward in the last century as the Plaza de Santa Ana and thus brings one to the Church of Santa Ana. Somehow the front of this church embodies the spirit of Granada and bridges the transition between Moslem and Renaissance styles. The main west entrance is Plateresque, surmounted by saints in their niches

C.G.S.S.   S while the neat brick courses and the tower, with its *ajimez*, *alfices* and projecting eaves of a flattish roof, provide an Oriental touch. Rising from behind cypresses and a cluster of street-lamps, Santa Ana has a simple beauty devoid of ostentation. The touches of white and blue *azulejo* enhance the impression of restraint, the hall-mark of great artists; this building bears the stamp of Diego de Siloé and of one of Alonso Cano's pupils, José de Mora. The latter also carved a Dolorosa in one of the chapels, and a St. Pantaleon, commissioned by the local College of Physicians and Surgeons.

Behind the Church of Santa Ana is the tunnel into which the Darro disappears. The river, which rises in the Sierra Nevada, has for centuries been a centre for alluvial gold seekers and was formerly crossed by many elaborate bridges, those of Moslem days being furnished with shops like old London Bridge or the Ponte Vecchio in Florence. In addition, its waters were used for irrigating gardens and for turning mill-wheels. The amount of metal recovered must have been considerable, and when Charles V visited Granada in 1526 he was given a crown made of the local alluvial gold. There was even a false etymology of the river's name (which comes from the Arabic *Hodarro*) from *dat aurum*, 'gives gold'. The Moslems called it the 'Earthly Paradise', a term afterwards used for the West Indies that Columbus' men plundered so shamefully, and even in the eighteenth century it was still called Valparaiso, which needs no translation. It was an Arab poet who said that the three sweetest musical notes are the voice of the beloved, the splash of water, and the chink of gold.

Turning back to the Reyes Católicos, we pass a fountain, or *pilar*, called *del Toro*, from the centrally placed bull's head which emits jets of water through its nostrils; further additions come from jars poised on the shoulders of scantily dressed youths. It is said to be the last work of the Renaissance architect, Diego de Siloé, to whom Granada owes so many of its fine buildings, including the Church of Santa Ana. Passing the Cuesta de Gomeres, the next opening on our left is the Calle de Cuchilleros, the Street of the Knife Makers, in which the Casa de los Pinedas has a portal which is also the work of Siloé. The street itself was the original path leading to the Alhambra.

A hundred yards west of the intersection of the Gran Via de Colón, on Reyes Católicos, a passage of a few paces leads south and brings you to the **Casa del Carbón**, directly across the small street named after Mariana Pineda. The inhabitants are fond of saying, 'nothing is impossible in Granada', and here we have an example of an old caravanserai, *khan* or *fonduk* set down in the middle of the modern city. The *Alhondiga gidida*, or 'new store' of the Arabs, was built in the 1330s and is the only complete example left in Spain. It was originally the primitive depository, as I have mentioned earlier, where travelling merchants could store their goods and at the same time find shelter for themselves and their animals. At the Reconquest the Catholic Sovereigns gave it to Sancho de Arana, their *mozo de espuelas*, the servant whose function it was to take a walking part in processions, leading the Queen's horse by the bridle. He is often pictured in paintings that purport to show the handing over of the keys of Granada. Arana left no heirs and the property then became the home of the charcoal burners, whose produce was weighed on the official scales next door. In the sixteenth century it became a theatre, for which it is well suited, and some of Lope de Rueda's plays were performed here. Still later it degenerated into a tenement dwelling until acquired by the State in 1933 and restored by Torres Balbás, an architect to whom Granada and the world will always be indebted for a multitude of intelligent renovations.

The entrance is through an imposing porch, behind a great horseshoe arch of brick, with *alfiz*, *ataurique* and a Cufic inscription; from this one can deduce an apprehensive rejection of Christianity, for it reads, 'God is unique, God is alone. He was not begotten, nor did He beget, nor has He any companion.' Above the porch is a twin window flanked by blind pointed arches and reticulated tracery. There is another *ajimez* inside the porch and a plain doorway with lintel leading into the courtyard; the roof is of stalactite work and the sides have carved stone benches. The courtyard is square and consists of a lower arcade surmounted by two galleries, all supported on brick pillars. There is a trough in the centre, where you can readily imagine the merchants' mules being watered, and there are enough shrubs and creepers to provide an atmosphere of dignified neglect.

Only a few yards east from the Casa del Carbón is the Casa de los Duques de Abrantes, of the early sixteenth century. In spite of its Gothic overlay it preserves traces of Arab workmanship in the doors of interlacing woodwork and the *alfarje* over the staircase. The dukedom of Abrantes, by the way, was created for General Junot, whom Wellington defeated at Vimeiro; he was one of Napoleon's scapegoats after the Russian catastrophe and finally blew out his brains. Returning to the plaza in which stands Benlliure's monument, you find the Calle San Matías running south-west between the Capitanía General and the Convent of the Carmelitas Descalzas, the reformed Carmelites founded by St. Teresa. This building occupies the site of the house of Gonzalo de Córdoba, in which he died on the 2nd December, 1515. At the scene of his passing there remains only a plaque on the convent wall, commemorating '. . . the Christian hero, glorious conqueror of Moors, French and Turks, to whose illustrious memory the Commission of Historic Monuments of the Province of Granada has placed this inscription. 1874.'

On the other side of the Capitanía is the **Casa de los Tiros**, so called from the muzzles of muskets that project between the merlons. It was originally a fortress incorporated in the walls that encircled the *barrio de los Alfareros*, the Potters' Quarter. It has been much changed since then, as can be appreciated by standing back in the little square that faces it. You can see the nineteenth-century additions above the battlements, and the five statues placed on the wall, arranged like the pips of a playing card. They represent Hercules, Theseus, Jason, Hector and Mercury, dressed as a herald and with the arms of the Venegas on his surcoat. The family was descended from the marriage of the daughter of a Spanish hidalgo, Commander of Monticl, to the grandson of the Arab Sidi Yahya, and the house remained their property until it was made over to the Spanish government in 1921. Their motto, with several unimportant variations, is as trite as most, proclaiming, *el corazón manda*, 'The heart commands'.

Inside are the local offices of the Department of Tourism, as efficient as all the branches of that excellent organisation, and a museum of local art and industry. A disproportionately small patio preserves a few traces of Arab columns and capitals on the staircase, rescued from neglect and decay in the present century. The only original hall is on the second floor and has a ceiling divided into panels, some of which are occupied by crudely carved and painted 'portraits' of Spanish heroes, and the others by an account of their deeds; each of these begins with the formula, '[Name], among many other exploits which he performed . . .' The characters range from Alaric the Goth, called a Spaniard here, to the wife of the governor of Martos who, with her attendant ladies, defended the town for three days. The ceiling can be dated to before 1539, as one of the texts refers to the Empress Isabel, wife of Charles V, as living, and we know that she died in that year.

Among the many exhibitions here are rooms dedicated to

Washington Irving, the illustrious American 'discoverer' of the Alhambra and later United States ambassador, and to the Empress Eugenia, who was born in Granada. The floor of this latter room was brought from the Generalife and consists of a perfect Arab composition, a geometric *enlaceria* with a central many-pointed star. Until the house was ceded to the Spanish Government, one of its finest treasures was a richly ornamented Arab sword, alleged to have belonged to Boabdil but actually the property of the Moslem princes of Almeria. It is now in Italy, but a similar weapon, also said to have belonged to Boabdil, may be seen in the Museum of San Sebastián. The collection of paintings, pottery and engravings is patchy, but contains much of interest, including some early etchings by Lewis and others. One of the most interesting exhibits is a photograph of the Old Mint at Seville, which was destroyed in 1843. The Fox Talbot method of photography was invented only in 1841, so that this picture, which is not a daguerreotype, must have been an extremely early example. Additional interest is contributed by a panel over the door in the photograph which has the stylised Cufic inscription that can be seen over the entrance to the Alcázar of Seville. This by no means exhausts the attractions of the Casa de los Tiros, which is an excellent place to pass a rainy hour—though these are infrequent during the tourist season.

Passing through the Plaza del Padre Suárez opposite, you can easily find the way to the Church of San Matías (St. Matthew), which contains a redoubtable if not frankly intimidating example of Granadine Baroque in its retablo. Among the sculptured figures, however, is an excellent *San Juan de Dios* by José Risueño, who combined some of Alonso Cano's methods with Flemish traits, though the period in which he worked, covering parts of the seventeenth and eighteenth century, sacrificed realism to Baroque exaggeration.

As it is on the way, though hardly worth a longer digression, you might like to stop in the Ancha de Santo Domingo to see the Casa de Los Girones; so named because it belonged to the famous family of Tellez Girón, of which the Dukes of Villena and of Osuna represent branches (see Ch. 4). The present building is all that is left of an Arab palace that belonged to a sister of Boabdil. A single hall preserves stucco work with Cufic inscriptions of the 'God bless our home' kind, and niches in the door-jambs, with original *azulejos* in the floor of one. The most interesting detail is that traces of red and blue paint survive on the ground work of some of the arabesques, which is quite a rarity.

The end of the street opens on to the Plaza de Santo Domingo, in which stands the bronze statue of the Dominican Fray Luis de Granada. The **Church of Santo Domingo**, which originally belonged to the Monastery of Santa Cruz la Real, was founded by the Catholic Sovereigns. Both monastery and church have had their vicissitudes and were originally built on ground partly acquired from Boabdil's mother, variously called Aisha, Fatima and La Horra. This was part of the old Potters' Quarter, which extended roughly from the Casa de los Tiros and southwards to the Bib Alachar of Moslem days. The church has an attractive portal of three arches on simple, slender columns, and bears the royal yoke and arrows and initials of the founders in the spandrels. In the narthex are some faded frescoes, and the interior bursts upon you as the apotheosis of Granadine Baroque. Even Gautier, who was reasonably tough, was moved to write that it is 'decorated with an incomprehensible superabundance of useless ornaments, gilt and gewgaws ... everything that the tortured taste of the eighteenth century and the horror of the straight line can produce in the way of the most disorderly, artificial, twisted and Baroque.'

We are now in the heart of the **Antequeruela**, the district populated by the Moslems who left Antequera when it fell to the Infante Fernando in 1410. So far we have only passed through streets, many of them mean, none of them spacious; but to the east and south on the hill slopes are the quiet walled gardens, or *cármenes* as they are called in Granada, a name said to derive from the Arabic. One of them belonged to Manuel de Falla, whose grave is in Cádiz Cathedral; it is not difficult to infer where he got his inspiration for *Nights in the Gardens of Spain*. The house, where everything was neat and in miniature, welcomed some of the great artists and thinkers of this century. Zuloaga, whose famous portrait of Falla brings out the musician's hidden mental conflict, Gallego Burín, García Gómez and Bermúdez Pareja, historians and orientalists may have met here as well as in one of the rooms of the Casa de los Tiros.

It is certainly easy enough to fall in love with the Antequeruela, for it conceals its treasures jealously and touring coaches are never seen. Baron Davilier wrote a book on Spain which would long ago have been forgotten, along with its author, had it not been illustrated by over three hundred etchings by Gustave Doré. Among them is one entitled *Une soirèe prés de l'Antequeruela*, a group of women in mantillas listening to a guitar player. The background is nothing like Antequeruela but those who know maintain that Doré succeeded, where few have even tried, in picturing the spirit of this corner of Granada.

The most attractive visit in the Antequeruela is to the **Cuarto Real de Santo Domingo**, a palace to which the Moslem kings are said to have retired during the month of Ramadan; unkind people will suspect that it was for the purpose of eating in secret. The Catholic Sovereigns bought it from the Moslem queens, it became a convent and then, during the nineteenth century, the property of the Ponce de León family. Of the old palace a single tower remains; the rest of the building is modern, and the whole stands in extensive, enchanting grounds. The great hall on the ground floor of the tower is entered through a magnificent arch, with arabesques on the intrados, and ancient tile dadoes on the jambs. Cufic and Naskhi texts succeed each other, and inside the room, which measures over twenty feet square, are lustred tiles with foliate patterns. These are white, blue and gold, for the Arabs found that black, green and yellow, their favourite colours, proved unsatisfactory in the lustre process. There are alcoves with arches, panels of mosaic tiles and of intricately worked stucco above them, and over them a row of twenty small horse-shoe-arched windows with pierced jalousies. Three balconies open at the far end, fitted with doors of complicated wooden lacery, repeated again in the wonderful *alfarje* ceiling.

The furnishings are as precious and as tasteful as the room itself, the whole being quite unforgettable. An interesting point is that none of the Arabic inscriptions contain the *wala ghalib* motto, and it is therefore safe to say that the building dates from before the middle of the thirteenth century. In one respect it is superior to the Alhambra, for it has never needed restoration and one therefore sees a rare example of original Arab decoration in Europe. The palace is private property and not always available to visitors, but when the family is not in residence it is likely that small parties, exercising tact, would be allowed to see this room. A finishing touch is provided by the gate-posts, if you did not notice them on entering. Each one bears an inscribed tile, the one on the right having *Cuarto Real*, or Royal Apartment, and the other saying the same thing in Arabic script, *Dar al-melek*.

It is but a short distance from here to the Paseo del Salon, part of the Alameda on the north bank of the Genil, and we follow this westward till we reach the Puente Genil, which we are to cross. The space in front of the bridge is the Plaza del Humill-adero, where the sovereigns and their escort sank to their knees on the 2nd January, 1422, when they saw the Christian Cross and standards unfurled on the summit of the Torre de Vela on the Alhambra. Crossing the Puente Genil we turn right over waste ground and follow the Motril road, in places signposted to Armilla, for 500 yards; here the road bends to the left, while on the right is a large tree under which goats usually seek the shade.

Below is the tiny Hermitage of San Sebastián, where Boabdil handed over the keys of Granada to King Ferdinand. The building is square and has a horseshoe arch, for it was a *Murabit*, or Moslem oratory. The word, often spelled 'Marabout', is applied either to a Moslem saint or his tomb, and gave rise in Morocco to a cult of fanatical warriors, counterparts of the Crusaders, called Almoravids. The inside is whitewashed and has a circular dome, ornamented with Oriental intersecting ribs and supported on reinforced squinches. An inscription round the walls records a restoration of 1615. The marble plaque commemorating the handing over the the keys of Granada is on the outside wall, to the right.

A hundred yards farther, on the right, is a country house which was once the sumptuous **Alcázar Genil**, another of the properties of Boabdil's mother Aisha and sold by her to the Catholic Sovereigns. Inside there is an original hall of the fourteenth century, which has twin arches with the usual *ataurique* in the *alfices*, and stalactites in a frieze round the walls, supporting an *artesonado*. The porch is of more recent date and the original ponds, on one of which aquatic displays used to be performed, have been much altered. The house is usually open after 4 pm, and for this reason it is better to visit towards the end of this route.

We now turn back, cross the Puente Genil again and walk up the broad Acera del Darro, which eventually meets the Calle de los Reyes Católicos and similarly serves the function of roofing the River Darro. The street of San Isidoro runs almost parallel on the left, and a tablet at No. 7 commemorates the birth of Mariano Álvarez de Castro, the heroic defender of Gerona in 1809, an example of courage and endurance not exceeded even by Zaragoza. I have remarked how Spain adopted the Arab custom of conferring titles on her towns; most of them are 'very loyal', or 'twice heroic' and some have five or six such qualifications. Gerona has but one: 'Immortal'.

On the other side of the Acera is the Church of Nuestra Señora de las Angustias, a title which is expressed in Italian by *Pietà*. Among all the Granadine Baroque, only the central figure of the retablo has an interesting past. It was originally made as a

Soledad, a figure standing upright, with forearms crossed over the breasts; the figure of the Virgin Mother, alleged to have been made in Toledo, was brought to Granada by persons unknown and her arrival soon attained the status of a miracle. As time went on, the dead Saviour was laid before her, a cross erected at the back, arms cut off, blue tunic covered with white and a jewelled pectoral, embroidered gown and golden crown added. Duque Cornejo did the surgery and Archbishop Rios y Guzmán donated the jewels. One can examine the figure closely from inside the *camarín*, even during divine service, without being seen. The face, for once, is that of an aging woman and the expression is suitable for the occasion, but the *camarín*, decorated with local marble in all colours, shapes and sizes, is overwhelming.

If you do not want to look at every retablo, you should pass up the Calle de San Antón without entering the Convent of the Guardian Angel, who failed to protect the sisters against a law-suit, two changes of residence, theft of all their valuables by the French and final occupation of a building for which the Bank of Spain had no further use. You can also pass by the Church of St. Anthony Abbas, most of whose treasures bear the implausible 'attributed to' or 'the school of'. Round the corner was a home for fallen women and female criminals, among whom was numbered the unfortunate Mariana Pineda, who was executed for having in her possession an embroidered banner belonging to the liberal movement—an example of Bourbon justice. The street is called Recogidas, or 'redeemed' and is joined by another called Magdalena, in case there should be any doubt. It is quite near the centre of the town and it may have been hereabouts that Dumas saw the street-walkers light their candles at the Virgin's shrine, with the prayer that she would see to their business being brisk.

A short digression down the Calle Recogidas and a right turn into Magdalena takes you to the Church of that name at the corner of the Calle de Gracia. The façade reminds one of Alonso Cano, with its triple arch, but there are so many windows of the square pattern seen in private houses that it hardly suggests a church. It was built from 1677 to 1694, so that Cano, who died 10 years before the work began, could have done no more than make the design. Inside, as is usual in the churches of Granada, there is a wealth of art, most of it appealing more to the devout than the artistic. There are, however, a few works of Pedro de Mena, including an early *St. John the Evangelist* from San Antón. La Magdalena only assumed its present function of parish church in the middle of the last century. Its predecessor saw the baptism of the local artist Juan de Sevilla, in 1643, and of the Empress Eugenia in 1826. Her house is almost immediately opposite, at No. 12, Calle de Gracia, and has the usual flat-faced oriel window and plain grilles of middle-class homes. It bears the plaque announcing its distinction, erected while Eugenia was still Empress of the French, some medallions and much-faded frescoes. This is worth a comment, for Victor Hugo described the extensive painting of house-fronts in Granada, with columns, volutes, garlands and other pseudo-classical motifs, always including attempts at *trompe l'œil*.

The first turning from the Calle de Gracia is the Calle Párraga, where Gautier lodged at No. 3 in a room that opened on a patio, with balconies supported by white marble columns and Moorish capitals. From here it is only a step to the Puerta Real, where we started our tour. Since Gautier's day avenues have been cut through the warrens of winding alleys, the Darro has been roofed as far as the Plaza Santa Ana, the picturesque costumes and mantillas have disappeared, but the Albaicín and the Alhambra, the dark cypresses and the snow-capped mountains still remain unchanged.

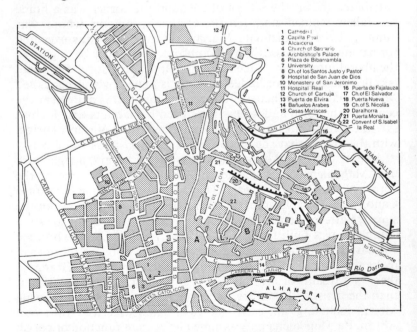

1 Cathedral
2 Capilla Real
3 Alcaicería
4 Church of Sagrario
5 Archbishop's Palace
6 Plaza de Bibarrambla
7 University
8 Ch. of los Santos Justo y Pastor
9 Hospital de San Juan de Dios
10 Monastery of San Jeronimo
11 Hospital Real
12 Church of Cartuja
13 Puerta de Elvira
14 Bañuelos Arabes
15 Casas Moriscas
16 Puerta de Fajalauza
17 Ch. of El Salvador
18 Puerta Nueva
19 Ch. of S. Nicolas
20 Daralhorra
21 Puerta Monaita
22 Convent of S. Isabel la Real

NORTH-WESTERN GRANADA

CHAPTER SIXTEEN

Granada—The North-Western City

✣

The Capilla Real—The Alcaicería—The Cathedral—Plaza de Bibarrambla—Hospital de San Juan de Dios—Monastery of San Jerónimo—Hospital Real—La Cartuja—Puerta de Elvira

The western angle of the area between the Gran Via de Colón and Reyes Católicos contains the Cathedral and a jumble of narrow streets. It is one of the oldest parts of the city, having originally consisted of bazaars grouped round the chief mosque, and preserves in its street-names some of the various trades once carried on there. The second turning to the left, that is, on the west side of the Gran Via de Colón, takes you through an opening in a railing and past the great octagonal apse of the Cathedral. On your left is the old Chapter House, later the Ayuntamiento and one day to be a college for history students. Before the Reconquest it was the *madrasseh*, or religious school attached to the mosque, and until recently preserved an original room with *alfarje* ceiling.

On your right as you proceed along the Calle de los Oficios, is the bulk of the Cathedral, and a small open space giving on to the Gothic front of the Capilla Real. The west side of the little square is formed by the old Lonja, the Exchange designed by Enrique Egas and put up by a Genoese banking firm. Each of the two floors presents four arches supported by columns with spiral carving, the effect of those on the lower floor prejudiced by a vulgar balustrade. The building was soon found to be too small and the door is now the entrance to the ticket office for visitors to the Royal Chapel, the upper floor being the Chapter House.

Northern influence is very marked hereabouts. It was at about the middle of the fifteenth century that Jan van der Eycken of Brussels joined the stream of foreign artists coming to work in Spain. His name became Anequin de Egas and his son Enrique, following his father's profession of architect, became the more famous of the two. He not only designed the Royal Chapel and the Lonja, but probably the Gothic part of Granada Cathedral, subsequently taken over by Diego de Siloé who, you remember, was another son of a foreigner.

The **Capilla Real**, seen from the Plazuela de la Lonja, has a Plateresque doorway, opened in this wall some years after the completion of the Chapel, as the old ingress from the Cathedral side was less practical. The upper part remains as designed by García de Pradas, but the lower is a bad restoration of 1733. The portal and the neighbouring Lonja contrast with the flamboyant Gothic plan and decoration of the rest of the façade; the royal initials, Y and F, that appear over and over again in the ornamental stone filigree balustrades, the gargoyles and the miniature pinnacles with their crockets. It was twelve years after their conquest of Granada that the Catholic Sovereigns ordered the construction of this building as a mausoleum for themselves and their family, previously destined for San Juan de los Reyes at Toledo. The Queen died two months after the mandate was given, but with her usual attention to detail had directed that her body should rest temporarily in the Convent of San Francisco on the Alhambra, until such time as the Royal Chapel should be ready to receive her.

The original entrance is inside the Cathedral, on the right where a transept would normally be placed. It is a fine example, and most appropriate, of Isabelline Gothic. On either side is one of the two patrons of the Chapel, SS. John the Baptist and Evangelist, and there is a profusion of royal crests and initials, with crowned yoke and arrows, apt to appear wherever the royal initials are used. Much of the ornament is repeated inside, and there are four side chapels containing paintings and sculpture; two of them are closed by *rejas* of the early sixteenth century, fine enough in their fashion, but severely handicapped by the presence, dividing the Chapel into two, of the finest *reja* in the whole of Spain, which is to say, in the world. It stretches its golden web across the nave before the crossing and is therefore farther forward than an ordinary rood-screen. It serves to close off the royal sepulchral monuments from the nave—the simple coffins are in the crypt below—but the central panel is left open for us to pass through. Made of wrought iron, richly gilded and artistically coloured, it consists of three storeys. The lowest, whose bars are joined by an ornamental network, has Corinthian columns supporting an ornamental frieze; the centre of the second level has the royal arms with lions as supporters, angels and foliage in a tasteful medley; and above the third rises the masterpiece of sculpture in iron, ten episodes from the life of Christ, the martyrdoms of the two Johns and, in the centre, where it towers above all, the Crucifixion. Some of the *reja*'s splendour is possibly due to the juxtaposition of straight lines, vertical and horizontal, and to intricate patterns recalling the *ataurique* and *sebka* of the Moslems. The masterpiece is signed on the right side of the frieze, below the statue of St. Peter, *Maestre Bartolome me fecit*. It is unpleasant to recall that the same artist, some of whose work we also saw in Andújar and Seville Cathedral, had to petition Charles V for 1600 ducats, because the clergy had gone back on their bargain and he and his family were in want. Round the walls of this gorgeous chapel runs a eulogy in golden Gothic characters on a blue band, too long to repeat here but containing the boast that the Catholic Sovereigns had expelled the Moors. The treaty to which they put their royal signatures, *Yo el Rey* and *Yo la Reina*, specified the properties in Spain which were made over to the Moslems, 'and to their sons and grandsons and great-grandsons and heirs and successors, by law of succession for evermore . . .' To Machiavelli, Ferdinand the Catholic represented a praiseworthy example of the triumph of opportunism over morality, especially in the use he made of religion in the pursuit of his temporal aims. But perhaps we should not judge them too harshly simply because they achieved greater success than most by their perfidy; popes in those days were just as mercenary and dishonest.

The tomb of the Catholic Sovereigns with their effigies is in Carrara marble, and was made in Genoa by Fancelli. Many have believed that they are the work of a Spaniard, partly because the words of the Venetian ambassador Navagiero, who patronisingly wrote: . . . *assai belle per Spagna*, 'very beautiful for Spain'. It was to compete for this commission that Torrigiani, who had been so successful with the tomb of Henry VII, came to Spain and to meet his eventual death in the dungeons of the Inquisition. The faces of the recumbent figures are slightly turned away from each other; Isabel wears the cross of Santiago, Ferdinand the collar and George the Order of the Garter. It will be appreciated that the sculpture was done before his daughter Catherine of Aragón had been repudiated by Henry VIII.

The other tomb, made in similar style, is the memorial to their successor, in name only, Juana la Loca, or, as Ford calls her, Crazy Jane, and her husband, Philip the Fair of Burgundy. The sculptor was Bartolomé Ordóñez, a Spaniard, who died at Carrara when the work was almost completed, where he had no doubt gone in order to match the marble. It is strange that Charles V, their son and ruler of Spain during his mad mother's lifetime, should order their tomb in 1519, when his mother still had thirty-six years of life before her.

The great retablo is the work of Felipe de Vigarni, as his name is spelled in Spanish, a Burgundian from Langres. Although classed as transitional, Vigarni's work, as in this example, eventually became entirely Renaissance. All the subjects are competently carved and coloured, but three compartments reward closer examination. At bench height there is an *Adoration of the Magi* in the centre and it has been remarked that the youngest king is remarkably like Charles V. Still more exciting is the bas-relief on the right below the bench, which shows the forcible conversion of Moslems, a measure introduced while both signatories to the treaty of surrender were still alive. Note how the women are wearing long robes—the effect of drapery is beautifully reproduced—which they pull up to cover the lower face and usually one eye. It is to be noted that, while the veils that were once worn at Véjer de la Frontera and Mojácar are no longer to be seen, this habit, of covering all but one eye, is still practised in some backward regions of the South.

At the sides of the retablo are the Catholic Sovereigns *orantes*, a somewhat idealised but technically excellent work of Diego de Siloé. The significance of the figures is enhanced by the reliefs of their patrons, St. George and St. James, whose decorations we saw on their recumbent effigies, and by the fact that Ferdinand is placed next to the panel of the surrender of Granada and Isabel to the conversion of the Moors. The Chapel and its sacristy are a picture-gallery of works of varying merit, but before examining the paintings we should notice the Isabelline doorway leading from one to the other, by Jacobo Florentino l'Indaco, said to have been a pupil of Michelangelo. The delicate rib pattern of the roof is also admirable, especially in comparison with the many inferior examples to be seen elsewhere. The Queen had a special liking for painters of the Flemish school which flourished during the fifteenth century; Rogier van der Weyden here represents the first half of the century and the influence of the van Eycks (not to be confused with the Egas family), and his successors Dirk Bouts and Hans Memlinc both left notable works that can be seen here.

The gem of the collection is undoubtedly Bouts' *Triptych of the Passion*, a Descent from the Cross flanked by a Crucifixion and a Resurrection. This is sometimes confused with the triptych which the pious Queen carried about with her during her incessant travels, along with the silver-gilt reliquary, erroneously pointed out as the case for the jewels she is falsely alleged to have

pawned to finance Columbus' first voyage. Of the portable triptych only the centre piece, an *Adoration of the Kings*, remains;
its authorship is unknown. In addition, there is a Van der
Weyden Nativity and a *Pietà*, two leaves of a triptych, of which
the third is in the New York Metropolitan Museum; Bouts' Head
of Christ and a Virgin with Child and Angels; two examples of
the same subject by Memlinc, one with saints and one without,
also a Nativity, a Descent, Three Holy Women, a *Pietà* and an
attributed John the Baptist.

There are numerous anonymous works of the Flemish School,
some of them as pleasing as those of the famous masters, as well as
less successful attempts by Spaniards to copy their style and
methods. Pedro Berruguete, however, spent years in Italy, working
for part of the time under Justus of Ghent (Joos van Wassenhove),
and his St. John in Patmos that hangs here shows a marked contrast to the efforts of the untravelled. The Italians are represented
by a Perugino, Christ before the Sepulchre, and Botticelli's Geth-
semane. It is instructive to compare the naivety of this undoubted
masterpiece with the dramatic rendering of the same subject a
century later by El Greco, at Andújar. A wry smile may be
extracted by Juan de Sevilla's painting of the embrace of Boabdil
and King Ferdinand; the sub-title *Kiss of Judas* is missing.

Reliquaries in the Chapel contain a piece of the True Cross
and the right arm of John the Baptist. The Treasury's most
precious pieces, historically speaking, are the crown and sceptre
of Isabel and the sword of Ferdinand. The Queen's mirror, converted into a custodial, is also here, and the royal banners, with
their individual designs, are of great value. Embroidered vestments and an illuminated missal of 1496 complete the list of outstanding works of art; you will readily appreciate that a single
visit to this treasure-house is inadequate.

Directly opposite the Royal Chapel, two small passages lead
to the Reyes Católicos. In one of them the Restaurant Sevilla
upholds its excellent reputation for local dishes. Not far away, in
the Placeta de Silleria, there is a maker of guitars, one of the
crafts that is threatened with mechanised extinction. The process
is more complicated than the production of violins in Cremona
and the kinds of wood used vary with the type of instrument.

The **Alcaicería** stands on the site of the old silk bazaar and
resembles a narrow Oriental street, with marble columns dividing
the shop-fronts every few feet. Entrances to the shops are through
horseshoe arches, each surmounted by an *ajimez*. There is
Arabesque in stucco, while latticed windows and shutters of

alfarje succeed each other on both sides, and in the centre lamps and bowls of flowers are suspended about every three paces. It is all a bit too good to be true, and it transpires that the tidy little quarter of today was built after 1843, when the old bazaar, still Oriental in flavour, was completely destroyed by a fire that started in a match factory. The name Alcaicería is used for silk bazaars throughout the Moslem world and is said to be derived from the word Caesar; one explanation makes him the Emperor Justinian, who contrived to corner the silk market and subsequently, it is said, allowed certain Arabs to manufacture silken textiles.

From almost any street corner in the bazaar, you can see the Cathedral, and making your way there you will emerge in the irregular Plaza de Alonso Cano and see the entrances to the Church of Sagrario on your right, and the Cathedral itself on the left, as you face them. In front of the former is the bronze statue of Alonso Cano. He was born in 1601 and therefore aged twenty-nine when he finished his first major work, now at Lebrija. A native of Granada, he studied in Seville, as a fellow apprentice of Pacheco along with Velázquez, and then under Martínez Montañés. In contrast with his serene portraits, on canvas or in the round, Alonso's temperament and career were stormy and more in keeping with the features of the statue we are inspecting. When thirty-six he fought a duel, whose cause has long been forgotten, with an amiable painter, Sebastián de Llanos y Valdés. After wounding him severely he fled to Madrid, where he was protected by Velázquez and the all-powerful Olivares, minister of Philip IV, whose portrait by Velázquez hangs in the Prado. One night Alonso arrived home, to find the body of his wife, killed by dagger thrusts. This was his story and he stuck to it when suspicion fell on him. Judicially examined he pleaded successfully that, as an artist, his right hand should be exempted from the torture. He came through the ordeal and was discharged for want of evidence. Later the King made him a minor canon of the Cathedral, which provided him with a small competence and his keep; hence the incumbent was known as *racionero*; his workroom on the first floor of the Cathedral tower may still be seen.

His stormy temperament fits his self-portrait, which used to hang in the Louvre—the aquiline nose and sunken eyes, and the wasp, representing some temporary enemy, buzzing near his ear. His was nevertheless a charitable nature and if a beggar approached him when he himself had no money, which was usually

Decoration in the Alhambra, Granada. *Above*, the Nasrid motto,
"There is no conqueror but Allah", as a "bend dexter" on a Christian type
shield. *Below*, "ataurique" stucco work in the Court of the Lions.

The Alhambra, Granada. *Above left*, stalactite arches; *right*, the Puerto del Vino. *Below*, an ablution tank from caliphate Córdoba with later inscription in praise of the King of Granada.

the case, he would go into the nearest shop, make a sketch and give it to the beggar, telling him where and for how much to sell it. His other redeeming virtue, as a man, was his sense of humour. Once, when Málaga was threatened by a flood, the Bishop took refuge in the organ loft, saying it was better to be crushed than drowned. Said Alonso, 'If we are to perish like eggs it matters little whether we are poached [*estrellados*, also meaning battered] or boiled [*pasados por agua*, also meaning immersed].' To crown his gifts, Alonso was a teacher and the members of his school achieved renown for their sculpture; among them I have mentioned Pedro de Mena, his favourite, and others included José de Mora, Pedro Antanasio Bocanegra and Juan de Sevilla. His influence lasted, at second hand, well into the eighteenth century.

The **Cathedral** was originally consecrated in the chief mosque, of which Hernán Pérez de Pulgar had taken possession in the dramatic fashion related in Chapter 14. When the building became too small the Cathedral was built in continuity, the old mosque being rebuilt as the Sagrario, outside whose portal is the statue of Alonso Cano. The original plan was drawn up, we do not know precisely by whom, in 1518 and Enrique Egas took charge of the work in 1521. He was soon replaced by Diego de Siloé, who continued until his death in 1563, when he was succeeded by a selection of others. Here is another example of a Gothic plan ending up as a Renaissance church with ambulatory. Harvey has called this enormous building an architectural tragedy, and it is true that the design of the piers, with the clumsy pedestals of the upper pilasters, is unattractive. The replacement of an apse by a dome, so that the light falls on the altar, is nothing new to us for much the same plan can be seen in Cádiz and Málaga, but it is criticised more on technical than aesthetic grounds. The five broad aisles and the roomy circular sanctuary do nothing to evoke that feeling of pious awe for which many people prefer a chilly gloom. The limewash, which was formerly glaring white, has now been toned to a pale cream and takes away some of the starkness of which writers have complained.

There is a Plateresque portal of Siloé on the north side, with his initial at the foot of one of the niches; the undoubtedly noble proportions of this Puerta del Perdón are spoiled for some by the reclining figures of Faith and Justice above the arch. The main, or west portal was designed by Alonso Cano and shows much originality; its form is roughly that of the Roman triumphal arch with its high, central entrance flanked by a smaller one on each side. For Baroque architecture it is singularly free from useless ornament and its well-proportioned masses stand out boldly, giving the chiaroscuro effect that Alonso achieved so often with the brush. One small detail here is as good as Alonso's signature, the substitution of medallions bearing reliefs for the usual capitals of the pilasters. His pupils continued the practice, and one may verify it on the front of La Magdalena. The assorted sculpture is mostly by Verdiguier—some of whose work is in Córdoba Cathedral—and his son.

The most striking feature in the interior is the great **Capilla Mayor**, the circular structure housing the high altar, and communicating with the ambulatory by seven openings between the piers, themselves pierced by passages that run parallel with the ambulatory. Above the pulpits on either side are the kneeling figures of the Catholic Sovereigns (the Cathedral contains three sets of these) by Pedro de Mena. Higher up, in niches, are the celebrated busts of Adam and Eve by Alonso Cano, painted after his death by Juan Vélez de Ulloa, the only exceptions to Cano's insistence that he must colour his own sculpture. The faces are noteworthy in showing many features of the Italian *cinquecento* and have often been likened to Michelangelo's representations of Renaissance youth. The interior of the Capilla Mayor ascends in storeys, of which the second contains seven paintings by Alonso Cano of episodes from the life of the Virgin. Above are stained-glass windows, fourteen of them from Flanders painted by Theodore of Holland, and others designed though not executed by Diego de Siloé. The choir has been accommodated in this altar chapel since 1926, when it was moved from the usual position in the central nave; there it was more suitable for worship than sightseeing.

In making a tour of the side chapels and annexes, I intend to select only such works of art as could hold their own in the best company, apart from those that have an interesting history. This account is, therefore, by no means a catalogue. Beginning on the right of the entrance is the small Cathedral Museum, containing many works which, though excellent, do not fulfil these requirements. The third opening on the right is the entrance to the Sagrario, that is, the church in which the sacraments are kept and which ranks as the parish church of the area. It occupies the exact site of the mosque to which Hernán Pérez de Pulgar affixed his Ave Maria, and for this reason Charles V granted a burial chapel to the hero of the exploit. This may be found on the left, in a passage that was built to communicate with the Capilla

Real, and is only one of the rewards earned on the night of the 18th December, 1490. The other privileges granted to Pérez Pulgar and his family were those of sitting in the choir and, some say, of wearing their hats in the Cathedral. The other item of interest in the Sagrario is a fine marble font of 1522, from Italy. As the 18th December is the Feast Day of Santa María de La O (whose strange title I have already discussed), the Sagrario is dedicated to her.

Next comes the Capilla de la Trinidad, in which the central painting of the retablo, a Trinity of course, is by Alonso Cano. It was only the preliminary sketch for a much larger work that was bought by the Monastery of San Antón, taken over by the Provincial Museum on the dissolution in 1836 and promptly stolen. This, which amounts only to a preview of a picture that will probably never be shown, is called the *chanfaines*, a stew made from lights, best rendered as 'chitterlings'. It is said that Alonso exchanged this version of the picture for a dish of them.

Then follows the tasteless Baroque retablo of the Altar of Jesus of Nazareth, which contains four canvases by Alonso, an alleged El Greco and four by Ribera, an Infant Jesus appearing to St. Anthony, a Magdalen, a Martyrdom of St. Lawrence and a Head of St. Peter. The companion St. Paul was stolen in 1844. Granada has always been known for its discriminating art collectors.

The closed door to the Capilla Real has already been noticed and after it comes the Altar of Santiago. The main piece is an equestrian statue of St. James which Cean Bermúdez, the great art historian, attributed to Alonso de Mena, father of the more famous Pedro. The horse is good. There is also a small picture of the Virgin, given to Isabel the Catholic in 1491 by Pope Innocent VIII along with the Order of the Golden Rose. The picture was used as an altar-piece during the first mass said in the newly captured Alhambra.

We are now in the ambulatory and enter the Sacristy on the right. Here are a fine Crucifixion by Martínez Montañés, a painting of the Annunciation by Alonso Cano and—possibly the most appealing work of art in the Cathedral—a miniature carved *Inmaculada* by the same genius. It was originally made to stand on the lectern in the choir, but rightly considered too good to be exposed to possible injury. Even those who disliked painted wooden statues, which is after all the norm of sculpture in these parts, will be enchanted by the tenderness of this little work, which arouses the same emotions as the *Cieguecita* of Montañés in Seville Cathedral (see Ch. 5).

Continuing round the ambulatory we come to the Chapel of Santa Ana, which has a variant of the older theme: the Infant Jesus seated on the Virgin's knee, and the Virgin on St. Anne's. Here St. Anne has her daughter on one knee and her grandson on the other. The Chapel of St. Lucy shows the saint in the traditional, unappetising way with her eyes on a plate. Her attribute, and the fact that she is often invoked in diseases of the eye, is derived from the resemblance of her name to the Latin *lux, lucis* for light.

In the Capilla de la Antigua is a restored Gothic Virgin and Child, quite an exception in this Cathedral, said to have been brought from Germany by troops taking part in the Conquest of Granada. It was presented, presumably to the original cathedral, which was in the mosque where the Sagrario now stands, by the Catholic Sovereigns. The statue is now in the centre of a large and delirious retablo in what the Germans so aptly call *blühendes Barock*, 'blooming Baroque'. Coming back along the left aisle we finish at the steps that lead to the solitary tower. Next to them is the entrance to the Treasury, formerly the Chapter House, in which the last two of Alonso Cano's sculptures can be admired, the Virgin of Bethlehem (*La Virgen de Belén*) and a more than life-size bust of St. Paul, surprisingly well thatched for one who is traditionally bald in mediaeval art.

Facing the main entrance to the Cathedral is the Archbishop's palace, and behind this the **Plaza de Bibarrambla**. The name, *Bab ar-raml*, means the Sand Gate, and the Plaza is situated over what was once the bank of the River Darro. Such riverain strips of sand, or the dry beds of winter torrents, were used as promenades, hence the common Spanish name *Rambla*. The gate itself was in the city wall a few yards to the west, but was pulled down in the last century. By a curious feat of salvage, it was taken away and the pieces stored in the Archaeological Museum until 1935, when Torres Balbás rebuilt it near the approach to the Alhambra. The common name for the gate was *Orejas*, or 'ears', and there is an incredible tale that it was so called because a platform in the Plaza de Bibarrambla collapsed during a fiesta in 1621 and the mob seized the opportunity to cut off the ladies' ears in order to steal their earrings. Though frequently repeated, the story can be proved to be worthless; first, it was called *Puerta de la Orejas* in the century before the alleged episode; secondly, an alternative name was *Puerta de las Manos* (Hands) and there is documentary evidence that the hands or ears of punished malefactors were exposed here. The legend was probably composed to fit yet another name, *Puerta de Cuchillos*, Gate of Knives, but this was only because the *cuchillería*, or knife-makers' quarter was here.

The Plaza itself is an oblong space with trees and a grotesque Neptune fountain. At one time it was used as the arena for bull-fights and other fiestas, including the burning of priceless Arabic manuscripts by Cardinal Jiménez de Cisneros, better known as the founder of the University of Alcalá de Henares. In spite of the fact that it has gone down in the world, the Plaza is still a pleasant spot for a stroll, with its flower-stalls along one side adding a touch of colour. On the 3rd May every year the whole of Granada competes in a festival in which each parish produces a cross of flowers; at the same time the house-fronts are hung with the best rugs, cushions, shawls and flower arrangements that can be produced and almost every man and woman wears Andalucian dress. This area and the Albaicín are particularly rewarding to the sightseer.

All around are reminders of the past; on the west side is the small Calle de Cucharas, recalling the arch of that name, meaning 'spoons', because here were the booths where the poor could buy their wooden spoons. Off the north-west corner there have traditionally been meat and fish markets, and although changes have been made from time to time, the present fish market cannot be far from the pre-Conquest one.

At No. 34 of the Calle Lucena, which is also here, San Juan de Dios established his first hospital with the money that he earned chiefly by begging, but sometimes as a wood merchant. A true Christian, he incurred the enmity of the authorities for sheltering vagabonds and prostitutes and seems to have been somewhat excitable, so that for a time he was locked up as a lunatic.

Returning to the Cathedral, a few yards away, we find the Calle de la Carcel and, at the end opposite the Cathedral tower, the Colegio de Niñas Nobles, a school for girls of aristocratic parentage, originally limited to the founders' families. The Plateresque door and one window repay detailed examination. Going north, we come to the Calle de Santa Paula; a plaque on No. 10 informs us that Alonso Cano died here, after occupying the house from 1663 to 1667.

Most of the University buildings are about a hundred yards to the west, and it is best to start at the Plaza de la Universidad, where a statue of Charles V, a copy of one in Madrid, stands on a massive plinth. The area and some of its buildings have seen

many changes since the Emperor originally founded the Imperial
College to train workers for their task of converting the Moslems,
or rather the Moriscos, who were officially Christian. The work
was later taken over by the Jesuits, who built their Church of
St. Justus and St. Pastor on one side of the plaza; when they
were expelled in 1767, the buildings were partly demolished in
order to make a small botanical garden, and partly converted into
the present University.

The Church, La Iglesia de los Santos Justo y Pastor, shows the
features typical of Jesuit churches throughout Spain, heaviness,
exaggerated volutes and a multitude of finials. The main portal
gives the impression of a retablo applied to a blank surface, as
does the east entrance too; this in some respects recalls the
Sevillian Baroque of the Figueroas. The interior has reticulated
or stuccoed barrel vaults, fluted and Salomonic columns, a large
dome with light pouring in through the windows of its drum,
statues, paintings and a feeling of restlessness. This is so applicable to many other churches of the Baroque period that only the
expert will miss an itemised description.

Following the Calle de San Jerónimo, we pass the typical
Granadine façade of the Faculty of Pharmacy on the right, to
find the **Hospital de San Juan de Dios** facing us. This was the
first one belonging to his Order of Hospitallers, his own hospitals
in a series of private houses proving inadequate for the care of
the sick and destitute. There is much of interest in the life and
works of St. John of God. His youth was passed as a shepherd,
a soldier, a herdsman and an itinerant bookseller. He came from
Portugal and went as far as Hungary in the army that was
intended to repel the Turks of Suliman the Magnificent. He
settled near the Puerta de Elvira here in Granada, where he
continued to sell books, but reading works of devotion had the
same effect on him as reading the romances of chivalry had on
Don Quixote. He and his followers always travelled with a
shepherd's crook and a basket; whence they became known as
the 'Brothers of the Basket'. The expenses of their establishments
were provided by begging, the saint's formula finally being incorporated in the emblem of the Order. *Quién hace bien para sí
mismo?*, he would ask, 'Who wants to do himself a bit of good?'
The virtue of almsgiving is, of course, one of the five precepts of
Islam and still persists in Spain. The building itself has a fine
Renaissance courtyard and a dado of Valencian tiles; a small
chapel inside the entrance houses the effigy of Christ removed
from the Puerta Real, and the staircase still has its original *alfarje*

ceiling and some less attractive, later improvements. It was built at the beginning of the sixteenth century to house the Hieronymite monks, and the Catholic Sovereigns issued a decree that the stone of the Arab Gate of Elvira should be devoted to that purpose; in a short time, however, the monastery moved to its present site.

One could continue the round of Renaissance and Baroque churches, without the relief of interesting associations, but only two remain to be described. We follow the Calle del Gran Capitán for one block and turn right into the Calle Rector López Argüeta; on the opposite side is the entrance to what was the **Monastery of San Jerónimo.** First degraded and plundered by the French, then neglected since the time of the dissolution, the grounds were a cavalry barracks and manège until recently. A first attempt at restoration was made in 1916, and recently more elaborate work has been resumed, paid for, it is said, by the Mother Superior of the Hieronymite nuns in the Convent of Santa Paula, Seville. This lady, who doubles the parts of Abbess and Good Fairy to Granada, is the daughter of the Duke of Infantado; one of her properties, generously made accessible to the public, is the Carmen de los Mártires near the Alhambra.

The smaller patio of the monastery has lost its upper storey and will one day be restored to its former elegance; Queen Isabel, wife of Charles V, lived here for a while, finding the situation more to her liking than her husband's apartments in the Alhambra Palace, though not before she had conceived the future Philip II.

The main patio is a superb construction. It has thirty-six arches in its lower cloister walk and seven magnificent doorways of carved stone, the work of Diego de Siloé. The upper gallery has a Gothic stone balustrade, and everywhere are the initials of the Catholic Sovereigns, and coats of arms, including those of the kindly Hernando de Talavera, first archbishop of Granada. His sympathetic efforts to convert the Moslems met with scant success and the task was handed over to the more formidable Cardinal Jiménez, he who burnt the Arabic books in the Bibarrambla. Talavera also wished to translate the Bible into Arabic but was overruled by the Cardinal, or so says Augustus Hare, Jiménez adding that 'Hebrew, Greek and Latin were the only languages in which the word of God ought to be used.' This is manifestly absurd, for his great polyglot Bible, the *Complutensis*, included a Chaldaean (Aramaic) version as well. The centre of the patio is a dense thicket of orange trees and there is a wonderful view upwards from one corner that enables you to see both rows of arches, surmounted by a quaint wooden gallery and the massive upper structure of the old stone church.

The Church of San Jerónimo is no longer used and is not of itself a thing of beauty, though it may appeal to some. Its better features, the arched entrances to the chapels and the low curvature that supports the *coro en alto*, are offset by the usual ceiling ribs and the rather inferior frescoes that cover every available inch of wall space. The stone carving and most of the numerous statues are by Jacobo Florentino l'Indaco and Diego de Siloé; the former, whose entrance to the Royal Chapel we have seen, will be met with again at the Cathedral of Murcia. The great retablo is an imposing sight, and its transition from Renaissance to Baroque, during a period consumed by endless squabbles over the payment of the artists, is quite obvious. The authorship of the various parts has never been decided, so many contracts for sculpture, painting and gilding being made and broken over so many years; but the retablo contains a précis of the Christian religion, effigies and episodes, various virtues and selected saints.

The ceiling of the transepts is decorated in high relief with the figures of Caesar, Hannibal, Pompey and other heroes of antiquity, as well as Judith, Deborah, Penelope and assorted heroines. All these are featured as a compliment to the Great Captain, Gonzalo Fernández de Córdoba, and his second wife, Doña María Manrique. The Church is, in fact, nothing else but a memorial to the great soldier, whom we have now followed faithfully from his birthplace at Montilla. His kneeling, armoured statue in polychrome wood is on the left of the sanctuary, that of his widow on the right; his features are idealised and bear no resemblance to the few portraits that survive from his lifetime. It is remarkable that the statues still exist, for Gonzalo's remains were desecrated by Napoleon's troops, perhaps because he was so often described on commemorative tablets as 'the terror of the French and Turks'. His sword was stolen, apparently for the few shillings that the silver work would fetch, and, of course, all other portable treasures disappeared at the same time, while the beautiful *rejas* were melted down for munitions.

His adventures did not cease with his death. The scattered remains were preserved in various places until, by order of Isabel II, they were returned to Granada. In 1870 it was decided to build a national pantheon in Madrid and the bones of the Great Captain were sent for. However, his remains were soon restored to Granada and now rest in the crypt of this church, while a marble tablet at the foot of the altar steps declares that he earned for himself the name of *Magni Ducis*, the Great Captain. Here we take our leave of him.

The Calle de San Juan de Dios takes us north-east to a small park in which the *Monumento a la Inmaculada* or *Virgen del Triunfo* rises from among the roses. The fight for the doctrine of the Immaculate Conception reached the stage, in 1617, when the Pope, while not committing the Church to accepting it, at least prohibited the publication of any contrary opinion. This monument was put up in the following year, and special medals were also struck to commemorate the pontifical ruling. There is a less noticeable monument here too, a column and cross dedicated to Mariana Pineda who, you will remember, was shot as a traitress. It is now generally believed that she was embroidering the fatal banner of liberty, though at one time there was a strong rumour that it had been 'planted' in her house by a rejected suitor.

The **Hospital Real** is here, a fine building begun by Enrique Egas, and very similar to the contemporary hospitals at Toledo and Santiago de Compostela. Being of the early sixteenth century they embody the best features of Plateresque, the classical severity of the Renaissance relieved by the beautiful decoration round doors and windows. Here, the main entrance is Baroque of a far later date. The plan of the three hospitals is identical, a Greek cross inscribed in a square, with a patio between each pair of arms; in this one, however, three of the four patios were never completed. The interior, though bare, is impressive, and the upper storey has particularly fine Mudéjar ceilings to each wing. The altar was intended for the crossing under the dome lights, so that it could be seen by patients in every part. At the time of writing all is bare, except that the wooden cage in which San Juan de Dios was locked still stands, containing a small shrine and a statue of him holding a crucifix. The contents of the Archaeological Museum are being transferred here gradually, and almost enough has arrived to start a lapidary museum comprising Roman, palaeo-Christian, Visigothic, Moslem and later exhibits. In the solitary completed patio, built in the style of the Italian Renaissance, the royal initials and crests are everywhere; note that the latter is without the chain, the emblem of Navarre, which would agree with the date of 1511 given for the commencement of building, as that kingdom was not incorporated into Spain until 1515.

The museum will be the latest of many functions that the old building has exercised; it was first founded for the care of pilgrims and the indigent sick. Soon it combined with this the work of another hospital, on the Alhambra, for traumatic surgery, and yet another established by Charles V for the care of lunatics and the feeble-minded. Still later it specialised in syphilis and cases from every part of Spain were brought to it, while under the Bourbons it took on the additional duty of an orphanage. It continued to house lunatics until last century and sustained the high reputation of Spain in this branch of charity. There seems no doubt that the sympathetic care of the insane originated in the East and was practised by the Moslems before it was known in Christian Europe; we shall see evidence of this in the Alhambra Museum. Whether or not it was due to the interchange of ideas between Christian and Moslem Spain is an undecided question; it is, however, remarkable that the first asylum in Christendom was founded in 1409 by the monk Joffre in Valencia, and was followed in the same century by those of Zaragoza, Seville, Valladolid and Toledo.

La Cartuja is usually regarded as a necessary part of the visitor's tour of Granada, but I would say that, if time is short, this is one of the easily spared sights. The buildings are of the sixteenth century and not remarkable architecturally, but the interior of the church, the Sagrario and the sacristy remind one of the combined efforts of extravagant Baroque builders and a gang of crazed pastrycooks. Between the white, stucco-encrusted engaged piers are presses fantastically inlaid with ebony, ivory and tortoiseshell, and a three-foot dado of veined brown marble contributes to the extravagance.

A greater attraction in the Cartuja is the collection of paintings by Fray Juan Sánchez Cotán, and even this statement requires qualification. He was a pioneer, junior to El Greco but a generation before Zurbarán and Velázquez, and excelled in his mastery of the *bodegón*, or still life. His most famous one, at San Diego in California, puts more expression into a cabbage than is shown by the saints of many another artist. In the Church of the Cartuja, a screen across the nave divides the places allotted to the monks from those of the lay brothers. On it hang two of Sánchez Cotán's paintings, one of them his well-known Flight into Egypt. Mary, Joseph and the Infant Jesus are sitting under a tree, angels hover above them and their simple luncheon is laid on a white cloth over a rock. However much the figures and the background may be praised, however competent the lighting and the composition, it is my opinion that the bread and cheese show the true artist. Though he became a Carthusian only late in life, Sánchez Cotán was of blameless character, and as proof of this it was said that the Virgin herself came down from Heaven to give him a sitting. His speciality here is the series of pictures portraying the Catholic martyrs of England, in which his religious zeal tends to outrun his artistic sensibilities. They used to hang in the attractive patio, spoiling the pleasure of the squeamish, especially British, visitor who perhaps imagined that the Catholics themselves held the monopoly of torture and barbarous execution.

Other interesting paintings by Sánchez Cotán, apart from more directly religious subjects, include a retablo in one of the halls and four canvases in the apse. The two other artists who are well represented are Bocanegra, of the school of Alonso Cano, and Vicente Carducho. The latter was an Italian whose father had been summoned by Philip II during the building of the Escorial, and who became court painter immediately before Velázquez. The history of the Carthusian Order was his particular interest and here he competes with Sánchez Cotán in portraying, literally, the trials and tribulations of the monks. Carducho had come to Granada especially to meet Sánchez Cotán, whose paintings he greatly admired, and at once recognised him by the resemblance between the man and his works. It is true that Cotán's benevolent face reflected the inner glow of his spiritualism, but it is not generally known that he was a useful man to have about a monastery, being a skilled clock repairer and plumber. An interesting feature in the presbytery is a Head of Christ that is recognisable in an instant as the work of Morales but is thought to have been painted by an unknown artist in his style. Below it is a Virgin of the Rosary by Bocanegra, which could easily be a Murillo of the first period, *estilo frio*.

Returning along the Calle Real de Cartuja we reach the **Puerta de Elvira**, originally the most important gate of the Moslem city. Its name is derived from Medina Elvira, the city built by the Arab invaders on the ruins of the Roman town of Iliberis, which required little distortion to become Elvira. Of the massive structure, with towers and barbican, there remains today only a huge horseshoe arch crowned with battlements. The rest was demolished, first to build the Hospital of St. John of God, then because *norias* in the vicinity were damaging the foundations, later because the buildings provided cover for footpads, again during the French occupation, and finally, for no clear reason, by the Ayuntamiento in 1879. As you look at the towering fragment that remains, little imagination is required to estimate the size of the original gate complex, a fortress in itself.

A short distance to the south-west there used to be another gate called *Bab Alkuhl*, from the Arabic *kohl*, the antimony eye powder inherited from the Egyptians of Pharaonic days. The word came to mean any refined essence, and the gate was named after the lead sulphide which was brought through here to the *alfarería* (Arabic *fakhari*, a potter), where it was used as a glaze for the baked clay.

In the Calle de Elvira was the famous *pozo Ayron*, a shaft sunk by the Arabs to allow air to escape from the bowels of the earth and thus diminish the frequency of earth tremors. Granada lies in the earthquake belt, a fact which was said to account for the wife of Charles V leaving the Alhambra for sturdier quarters. About half-way along the street is the Church of Santiago, in which Pedro de Mena was baptised and Diego de Siloé buried. The latter's skull was 'rescued' in the last century and given by Jiménez Serrano, author of an artists' guide, to his friend Enríquez Ferrer, who decorated the coffin of Mariana Pineda. Artistic appreciation will really have reached its zenith when fragments of painters fetch as much as those of saints. The headquarters of the Inquisition were in the warren of streets west of the church, swept away when the Gran Via de Colón was constructed. On the abolition of the Inquisition in 1830, its archives were burned in the patio of the Convent of San Augustín, now across the Gran Via. And so the circle, that began with the burning of Arabic manuscripts in the Plaza de Bibarrambla, was finally completed.

CHAPTER SEVENTEEN

Granada – The Alhambra

'There is no conqueror but Allah'

The hill that rises south of the Darro, on the eastern side of the city, has taken the name of the fortress-palace that crowns it. It is wedge-shaped, and its point lies between the Darro valley and another called the Assabica. On the south side of this rises the Mauror, on which stand the Torres Bermejas. The base of the wedge is formed by rising ground on which are the Generalife gardens, and behind that again is the Cuesta del Rey Chico, the 'Hill of the Little King'. On it is the Silla del Moro, the fort where King Boabdil, *El Rey Chico*, was said to have sat brooding over his rebellious city. Fortunately it is not necessary to know more than a few facts about the politics of the Moslem kingdom, for they are complicated and unedifying; the little that is needed to illustrate a visit to the Alhambra can be brought in as we go along.

To most people, and especially those who have been taken on a single conducted tour, the word Alhambra is synonymous with the palace; admittedly this is the most impressive part of the area, but there is much else that should not be missed. The fortifications, for instance; why are they called 'red'? the name Alhambra is simply *al-hamra*, the red, in Arabic and one is tempted to link it with the Nasrids who built the palace and were descended from Ibn Alahmar, the 'Son of the Red Man'. But there is evidence that the fortress of the Alhambra was so named long before the days of the Nasrids, unless indeed the ancient historian was referring to the Torres Bermejas, or Red Towers.

It is a help to think of the Alhambra as consisting of three parts, the oldest, or Alcazaba, on the tip of the wedge, then the royal palace, and the *población*, or township, at the base of the wedge. When we visit this complex of architectural growth and decay, we must remember that restoration has alternated with destruction for hundreds of years. The constant civil wars of Moslem days had already left their mark of neglect on the fortress

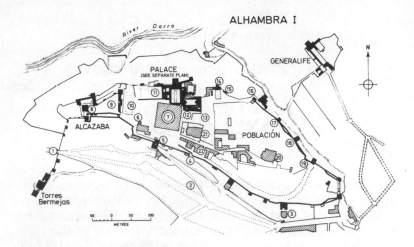

If following the text, the visitor must change to *Alhambra Palace II* after item 11

1. Puerta de las Granadas
2. Reconstructed gate of Bibarrambla
3. Torre de Siete Suelos
4. Puerta de los carros
5. Puerta de la Justicia
6. Puerta del Viño
7. Palace of Charles V
8. Torre de la Vela
9. Plaza de Armas
10. Plaza de los Aljibes
11. Patio de Machuca
12. Rauda
13. Partal Gardens
14. Torre de las Damas
15. Torre del Mihrab
16. Torre de los Picos
17. Torre del Cadí
18. Torre de la Cautiva
19. Torre de las Infantes
20. D. G. T. Parador
21. Santa Maria la Real
22. Shops and restaurant

when the Catholic Sovereigns took Granada; they, as well as their grandson, Charles V, did their best to preserve and embellish this superb monument and it remained the pride of the Spanish monarchs for two centuries. The second period of neglect came with the Bourbons, for Philip V dismissed the hereditary governor, the descendant of the Count of Tendilla, for having taken the wrong side in the War of the Spanish Succession. Destruction was added to negligence when the French under Sebastiani blew up a part of the fortifications after Wellington's victory at Salamanca had forced them to leave.

Restoration, often of an unskilful type, was begun during the 1820s, partly stimulated by the publicity given to the incomparable palace by Washington Irving in his *Tales of the Alhambra*.

It is, however, only fair to add that work had been begun a year before his arrival. It continues still, and each year more of the ancient beauties emerge under the expert direction of antiquarians, artists, and architects. There is nothing static about the Alhambra; it has its flowering and its withering, but never did it flower in the last six centuries as it does today for our fortunate generation.

Access has recently been made easier, and compound tickets are available, so that you can see every part in turn, the custodian detaching his portion as you enter each section. It is therefore as well to finish one part thoroughly before leaving it for the next, as the authorities prefer well-drilled sightseers who do not try to return against the stream. Hours are from 10 am to 8.30 pm daily and the main parts of the Palace are illuminated until midnight on Tuesdays, Thursdays and Saturdays. Apart from these evenings, the best time for visiting the palace in comparative seclusion is between 1.30 and 3.30 pm.

Start at the Plaza Nueva, where the Cuesta de Gomeres, named after a famous Moslem family, leaves it on the east side. A car is useful and saves time, but many prefer to make the steep ascent on foot, in order to enjoy the peaceful atmosphere of the woods as well as to escape the restrictions imposed by one-way roads. After a 200-yard climb the road passes through an arch called the Puerta de las Granadas, which takes the place of an older gate in the wall that used to connect the Torres Bermejas on your right with the Alcazaba of the Alhambra on your left. It is a Renaissance construction, heavily rusticated, and carries three pomegranates above, opened to show their seeds. Pedro Machuca, who was responsible for much that we shall see, built the gate in 1536; like most of his work, it does not harmonise with the earlier buildings.

Beyond the gate the road forks into three; the right branch should be taken by cars or if you want to see the Torres Bermejas, which you reach by turning back at an acute angle to the right at the first opportunity. The towers are being rebuilt and are not very thrilling, but the basement contains a Roman drain and arches. It would be surprising if a strategically placed hill like the Mauror had not been used as a Roman fort. What remains of the Arab *tapia* walls is red, hence the name *bermejas* or vermilion, and the bricks with which it is being rebuilt are made of the same clay and are redder still.

Following the central path your way lies through the elm plantation that clothes the southern slopes, a delightful place to wander on a hot day. The great elms were planted by the Duke of

Wellington, or so runs the tale that is repeated in one English
account after another. It seems to have started in *Murray's
Guide*, where Ford stated that the trees were sent from England
to the Governor of the Alhambra in 1812; as the French left only
in September of that year and Wellington was campaigning in
perilous circumstances until mid-November, the story can hardly
be true. Then one must consider the fact that Bertaut in 1659
and the Rev. Joseph Townsend in 1786 admired the groves of
elms on the way up to the Alhambra. The most reliable account
credits the Marquis of Mondéjar with the replanting of the old
Arab garden in 1625–41. Walking on up the central path you
pass, on your left, the rebuilt Gate of Bibarrambla, overlooked
by most passers-by as it stands among the trees. It is a fine example
of a town gate that needed little restoration; note the scallop
shells above the inner arch, the badge of Spain's patron saint but
used by Moslems, Romans and Greeks as an emblem of fertility.

Where the three paths meet again is the station for the half-
hourly bus to town, a useful thing to know, and the Hotel
Washington Irving, which cannot be far off its centenary.
Opposite is the Torre de Siete Suelos, which will be described
later. Here the walls rise above you in all their impressive bulk,
only a few yards from the road, and if you turn west they follow
at your right hand. Shortly the road forks, the right branch
going to the comparatively modern Puerta de los Carros through
which, so they say, the great stones were brought in during the
building of the Palace of Charles V. The slightly longer left fork
takes you to the **Puerta de la Justicia**, the traditional entrance;
you have a view of its massive proportions from the bend in the
road and can leave a car parked here if you prefer not to take it
through the Puerta de los Carros. Immediately below, on the
left, is the Pilar de Carlos Quinto, the ornamental fountain
planned by Machuca and executed by others. It perhaps embodies too much classical allegory for the tastes of today but
might be considered beautiful in any other setting.

As you face the Puerta de la Justicia you see an open level
clearing on your left, a comparatively modern gun emplacement.
On your right is a recent addition to the scene, a fountain built
in 1959 to commemorate the centenary of the death of Washington Irving. Possessing a rare blend of romanticism and delicacy
of feeling, he left a magical tissue of history and fantasy that
stimulated further interest in saving the Alhambra from ruin.
He may be compared to his advantage, with the other romantics
of his time who scribbled their names on the sixteenth-century

Above, palm grove at Elche. *Below*, the great wheel of La Ñora, near Murcia.

Murcia, the Cathedral façade.   Note the resemblance to a domed mosque and minaret.

frescoes. The space in front of the gate was formerly an occasional place of execution and the *cadi* would receive petitioners on the Fridays when the king himself was not performing that office in the Mexuar. There has been much restoration to both brick- and stonework, but the visitor may from now on take that for granted. The portal is imposing, with the usual horseshoe arch in a plain *alfiz* and a tiny keyhole window at each upper corner. On the keystone of the arch an open hand is engraved, probably the universal talisman for averting the Evil Eye.

The entrance leads into a square chamber and facing you is another horseshoe arch with various Arabic inscriptions, including one which dates the *Bab Asshariya*, the Gate of Justice, to 1348. Above this arch is carved a key, with hanging cord, its significance not properly understood, but apparently a symbol confined to the kingdom of Granada. An old belief has to be quoted, that when the hand grasps the key the Moslem empire in Spain will perish (one version), and the other that the Nasrids will return. You may take your choice. Above the interior arch is a niche containing a Virgin and Child, flanked by the yoke and arrows, proof that it was commissioned by the Catholic Sovereigns. Below it there is a band of excellent *azulejos*, in blue and green, after a style seen mainly in Persia.

Inside the tower the passage makes four right-angled turns before opening into the grounds of the Alhambra. The outer doors are under the second arch and keep their original pivots, bolts, iron sheathing and studs; if these fell in an assault there would still be opportunities for defence at each of the sharp turns. In the last chamber is an inscription in Gothic lettering, probably brought from elsewhere, commemorating the appointment of the Count of Tendilla as first military governor. You may notice that the name of the sultan is given as Muley Hassan instead of his son, Muley Abu Abdallah (Boabdil), and that the plaque was intended for a well. Next to it is a closed altar, where a service used to be held every 2nd January, the anniversary of the surrender of Granada.

Leaving the Puerta de la Justicia you follow a path on the inside of the perimeter; the wall on the left is a reconstruction that has utilised Moslem gravestones from the abandoned cemetery in the Assabica valley, up which you came. You soon turn to the right and come out next to the Puerta del Vino, which you can examine after buying tickets at the great Renaiss..nce Palace of Charles V. With it behind you, look west to the massive towers of the Alcazaba, and make your way there past the Puerta del Vino. Before reaching it you will see, on an ivy-covered wall on the left, the marble tablet that commemorates the heroism of José García, head of the military pensioners, who risked his life to cut the fuse that the French had laid round the fortifications when they had to retire in 1812. One has only to see the remains of the towers that they did succeed in blowing up to realise how much we owe to José García.

The **Puerta del Vino** is basically one of the oldest buildings of the Alhambra, though its façades are later additions. Nevertheless, the east one, which you approach, contains an inscription in honour of Mohamed V who, you may remember, was the ally of Pedro the Cruel and reigned from 1354–91. The gate, now detached from the wall that used to subdivide the area, has almost everything that the memory retains of Moslem Spain—the horseshoe arch, the engraved key, the *alfiz*, the splayed panels above, the Arabic inscription and, under the tiled eaves, an *ajimez*. Inside there is a second arch on which the doors are hung, then follows a square guard chamber with lateral recesses, and finally the western arch. This has much the same plan, but is notable for the precious *cuerda seca* tiles in the *enjutas*, with rosettes and non-geometric patterns. With their flower-like Arabesques in soft tones of green, blue and yellow, it is not too fanciful to compare them with some of the earlier Isnik ware from Asia Minor (Nicaea).

The name 'Wine Gate' has a strange sound for a Moslem citadel, even though we know that the Spanish Arabs flagrantly disobeyed the Prophet's prohibition of alcohol. Some believe that the name originated after the Reconquest, and there are documents listing the privileges of local wine growers and their exemption from excise. Others, however, draw attention to earlier mention of a *Bab Alhamra* ('bib' seems to be a local usage), and this could well have been called the Gate of the Alhambra. In written Arabic the words 'red', *hamra*, and 'wine', *khamra* are distinguished only by a dot, or diacritical point; by a very slight change in pronunciation and writing, therefore, the Wine Gate could have been produced from the Alhambra Gate.

As you go westward, the open space on the right is the Patio de los Aljibes, named after the cisterns that were installed after the Reconquest; previously the main road leading to the Palace of the Alhambra ran at a lower level. Before you the three eastern towers of the **Alcazaba** are lined up with their curtain wall; that on the right is the keep, or Tower of Homage. Nearer is the lower *antemuro*, as we saw in the Almohad defences of Seville, evidence of the age of the Alcazaba and the fact that it preceded the Nasrid dynasty. The entrance is on the left at the end of a path bordered by acanthus, and leads immediately into the garden of the *adarves*, the battlement walk. This is a long and narrow ledge, adorned with box and myrtle hedges, flower-beds and a fountain, with a precipice on the left and the sheer walls of the fortress, now pleasantly clothed with jasmine and honeysuckle, on the right. The fountain has curious reliefs round its rim, reminiscent of the capitals in the Palace and not unlike some of those of the much earlier Abbasid period in Iraq.

The view is, of course, magnificent, but there is an even better one when you climb higher. From here, however, you can see the Torres Bermejas on the Mauror hill and the arches of the ridge that runs east, possibly the wall of the underground food-stores of Moslem days. It is easy to trace the line of the wall that ran down into the Assabica valley to join the Torres Bermejas to the Alcazaba, pierced at its lowest point by the Puerta de las Granadas, through which we came.

Tempting though it is to stay in this hanging garden, breathing the scent of the myrtle and listening to the water about to take its final plunge through the elm woods, there is so much of interest to come that only those with weeks to spare can indulge themselves. At the end of the garden is the Torre de Pólvora, on its wall a *copla* by the Mexican poet Icaza:

> *Dale limosna, mujer,*
> *que no hay en la vida nada*
> *como la pena de ser*
> *ciego en Granada.*

Spare him a penny, woman,
For I cannot call to mind
A sadder fate for a human
Than to be in Granada—and blind.

After this it is unnecessary for me to praise the panorama.

Of the other five towers of the Alcazaba, most visitors are content with climbing the next and highest, the **Torre de la Vela**, the Watch Tower. Crowning it is the modern housing of the great bell, moved to its present site after the last one was struck by lightning in 1882. The bell was cast in 1773 and has served since then to regulate the irrigation of the *vega* during the night, when water is diverted to new channels at regular intervals. There is a whole code of signals, beginning with the *toque de* *ánimas* at 8 pm and finishing with the *toque de modorra*, which corresponds to the nautical eight bells in the middle watch when sleep is supposed to be most profound. The bell is also rung on 7th October, commemorating the Battle of Lepanto, and all day on 2nd January, the anniversary of the surrender of Granada to the Catholic Sovereigns.

From the *adarve* garden, turning sharply to the left, you will find a green wicket-gate that may be open; if it is not, the custodian of the garden will be glad to open it for you and receive a tip with the promptness of practice and the gravity of a gentleman. The entrance opens on to the **Plaza de Armas**, a parade ground that was built over Moslem houses and baths; their foundations and lower courses have been laid bare by the archaeologist. Immediately on the right are the bottle-neck openings of the *mazmorras*, the dungeons into which Christian slaves were lowered at night by ropes and hauled out again in the morning to work under the overseer's whip. Terrible tales are told of their sufferings, while the captive Moslems in Christian hands were comparatively, but only comparatively, well treated. The reason was that most of the Moslems had skills which were useful to their new masters, while the reverse was not the case.

In the far corner on the right a horseshoe arch leads to a passage through the Torre de las Armas and out to the steep hillside through the Puerta de las Armas, one of the oldest and formerly busiest of the entrances to the Alhambra. From here a zigzag path led down through the woods to the Cadi's bridge across the Darro. Looking back along the northern wall you can see the *cubo*, another semicircular gun emplacement which is built round one of the original square towers. It is reached by the protected walk in the Alcazaba walls that continues round the whole perimeter, and allowed the garrison to move rapidly from one part to another. What we have seen so far serves to emphasise that only constant vigilance and impregnable walls enabled the Nasrids to rule, in ever-quickening decadence, for two and a half centuries.

In crossing the Plaza de los Aljibes from south to north we unconsciously follow the sunken road that used to connect the entrance at the Puerta de la Justicia with the **Royal Palace**. Two towers face you; the one on the left (Torre de Mohamed or las Gallinas) has the original entrance to the Palace in front of it, and here our road used to join that from the Puerta de las Armas. The other, Torre de Machuca, is named after Pedro and Luis,

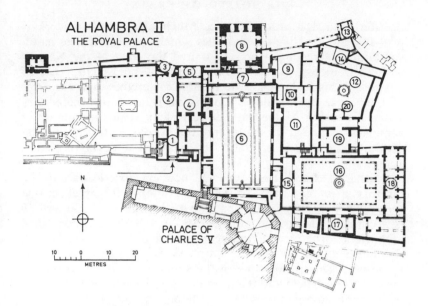

ALHAMBRA II
THE ROYAL PALACE

PALACE OF
CHARLES V

METRES

1. Present entrance
2. The Mexuar
3. Moslem Oratory
4. Patio del Mexuar
5. Cuarto Dorado
6. Patio de los Arrayanes
7. Sala de la Barca
8. Sala de Embajadores
9. Patio de los Cipreses
10. Sala de Camas
11. Baths

12. Patio de Daraxa
13. Tocador de la Reina
14. Apartments of Charles V and
    Washington Irving
15. Sala de los Mocárabes
16. Patio de los Leones
17. Sala de los Abencerrajes
18. Sala de los Reyes
19. Sala de Dos Hermanas
20. Mirador de Lindaraxa

father and son, who were the architects of the great Palace of
Emperor Charles V, where you began your visit by buying tickets.
Opposite the Palace's north-west corner is a stone coping and
if you lean over it you get the best view of the Patio de Machuca,
sadly fallen from its former grandeur but still preserving the
charm of only partial care. Round a central fountain are the low
box hedges, then the orange trees and the taller hedges of cypress.
It is not usually open and is off the track of conducted tours.

The entrance to the Palace is now farther to the right, through
a passage that leads directly into the **Mexuar**. This represents the
old audience hall, but was so radically altered during the addition
of a second storey in about 1840 that little of the original pro-

portions and decoration remain. Much of the stucco work is post-Reconquest, like the wall tiles which are nevertheless handsome and interesting. Here are united the crest of the Nasrids with their motto, 'There is no conqueror but Allah', that of Charles V, his badge with the Pillars of Hercules, and the arms of the López de Mendoza, Counts of Tendilla and hereditary governors of the Alhambra. The rest of the dado is made up of geometric Mudéjar *azulejos* and the whole, dating from the sixteenth century, is probably the work of a Sevillian potter, Juan Pulido.

At the far end of the Mexuar a new entrance leads into the Oratory, a small, narrow room whose outer wall is in effect one long balcony, though divided into twin windows. The *mihrab* is accurately placed and points ESE; it is built as a horseshoe arch, richly ornamented, and bears Arabic inscriptions, of which the aptest is that which says, 'Don't be one of the remiss. Come to prayer.' This is only one of the spots from which a glorious view of the Albaicín and the mountains can be enjoyed, though a wider panorama will present itself later.

From the Mexuar you enter the Patio del Mexuar, small and plain and quite unrecognisable as the spot illustrated in Washington Irving's *Tales of the Alhambra*. The brickwork is again decently hidden, the shanty and balcony removed and the mule drivers replaced by official guides. Geometric tile mosaics clothe the lower walls and patterned ones surround the rectangular doorways. The one leading into the Cuarto Dorado is a dentate horseshoe, on slender columns with stalactite (*mocárabe*) imposts. The upper windows are once more partly *ajimez*, with wooden jalousies, while here and there curtains of gay colours woven in the Alpujarras relieve the predominant pale cream and lilac. The floor is laid with white marble slabs and a low, shallow fountain of darker marble in the form of a scalloped bowl plays in the centre. It is an exact copy of the original one, that has been incorporated in the taller fountain of the Patio de Lindaraja. To the north is the Cuarto Dorado, a small room entered through a series of three arches; it is practically in line with the Oratory, at the back of the *mihrab* in fact, and thus blessed with the same glorious view from its windows.

We take the left of the two square doors from the Patio del Mexuar, and turning two right-angled corners, enter the **Patio de los Arrayanes**, 'of the Myrtles', also called de la Alberca, 'of the Pool'. In the narrow passage through which you pass, a new ceiling has been made in Arab style, using the correct woods, joinery and colours; seeing it, you may well doubt whether the artisans of today are in any way inferior to those of the Moslem kingdom. In the patio, the marble floor with low myrtle hedges and the orange trees on either side of the shallow goldfish pond, enable you for the first time to recapture something of the authentic atmosphere of the Palace. It is true that each constituent can be seen in one of the other rooms, but the elegant composition that they make when harmoniously combined is first experienced here. There is space and air, cooled by the twin fountains, with the soft blue sky above. The light brown side-walls have their doors and windows in *alfices* and contrast with the arcades at either end, with their slender columns of white marble, capitals carved in low relief, stalactites and ornamental Arabic writing alternating with the *ataurique* and *sebka* designs that cover the façades and interiors. Letting your gaze wander over the tile dadoes, the frieze of Arabic writing in stucco, and the infinite patterns that the artist produced on walls and ceilings, you will begin to understand the old Lancashire dame, wheezing determinedly at the tail of the tour, 'Ee-e-e, but they couldn't leave nothing oondecorated, could they?'

The Alhambra Palace represents the final stage of a decadent art; it is the Rococo of the Hispano-Moresque, the decorations of both being the expression of *horror vacui*. Behind massive walls, protected by their Negro bodyguard and freed from the menace of Castile by the civil wars of Pedro the Cruel and their chaotic consequences, the last Sultans of Granada lived their sensual lives. In an earthly paradise that more than reproduced what was promised to the true believer in the life to come, they hunted and hawked, feasted and fornicated, surrounded by poets, musicians and acrobats. Of the poets, Ibn Zamrak, vizier of Mohamed V, was the last of a great line and, in the memorable phrase of García Gómez, his works were published in the most sumptuous edition the world has ever seen, the walls of the Alhambra Palaces. For much of the decorative Arabic in the Patio de los Arrayanes is one of Ibn Zamrak's poems, interspersed (sometimes interpolated by careless restorers) with the praises of Allah, Koranic texts, the Nasrid motto and pious wishes for the health of various sultans. The south-west corner of the patio used to give access to a part of the Palace destroyed when Charles V built his own. However, the damage was not so extensive as we used to believe, and there is no truth in the story that the winter palace of the Moslem kings was sacrificed; today you can enter the crypt of the Renaissance palace through the same opening.

A gallery above the south arcade gives a wonderful view of the patio and the massive tower which rises behind the northern end, the *Torre de Comares*.

The arch in the centre of the northern wall leads into the **Sala de la Barca**, said to have been so named because the *artesonado* is shaped like an inverted boat, but more likely to be a corruption of the Arabic *baraka*, blessing. The word appears several times on the walls, along with the Nasrid motto in the royal crest. In the door-jambs at the entrance are confronting niches, walled with tiles, in which flowers or incense burners would stand; there is no support for the belief that visitors to the throne-room beyond would take off their shoes and place them there, so the name *babucheros* sometimes used for the niches is quite inaccurate. The ceiling is the chief glory of this room, with its rounded corners supported on intricate squinches of aggregated stalactites. It is difficult to believe that the whole of this room was burnt out in 1890 and that restoration was completed only in the present decade.

The entrance into the **Salon de Embajadores**, occupying the whole of the ground floor of the Torre de Comares, is through a double arch. The most massive of all the Palace towers, it takes its name from the coloured glass that was used in the windows in Moslem days and is still called *kumariyya* in eastern countries. Between the two arches on the left is the entrance to the upper rooms, which contain nothing of interest, and on the right what was once a private oratory of the sultans. The usual niches occupy the jambs of the second arch and are surrounded by interesting instructions, 'Deliver Yusuf from all danger of the Evil Eye with five words,—Say: "I take refuge in the Lord of the dawn. Thanks be to Allah" . . .' The Sala de la Barca has been well named 'The anteroom to Heaven', for the Hall of the Ambassadors, like that in the Alcázar of Seville, is the richest in the palace. It is about 35 feet square and 60 feet high, so that it occupies nearly half of the space inside the tower. In each of the three outside walls are three alcoves with windows, the middle one an *ajimez*; the one facing the entrance was occupied by the royal throne and is even more richly decorated than the others. In its *alfiz* runs an inscription, 'Help me Allah who repels the Devil . . . Deliver me from the wrath of Allah and from the Devil who allows Hell to gape . . .' You begin to wonder how secure the tyrants felt, even when they had taken every precaution against mortal enemies.

The floor of the hall, which was once covered with marble, is now laid with brick. The walls, with their intricacies of arabesque, *ataurique*, Naskhi and Cufic script, *sebka* and geometric lace-work, tinted with shades of blue and red, and all rising above the dado panels of tile mosaic, defy detailed description. High up, between two rows of inscription, runs a band of endless lines that repeat the 'sunburst' pattern of the *lazo de doce*, a figure with twelve rays, whose outlines are indefinitely prolonged, cornering and interlacing but never terminating. It has been said that this Oriental maze illustrates the difference between the philosophies—I use the word to include sciences—of East and West. As the eye and the mind lose themselves in its intricacies, one can compare the limitless desert with the compact *polis* of ancient Greece, and the concept of infinity in Arabic algebra with the closed figures of Greek geometry.

Notice the pierced, patterned stucco windows in each alcove, and high up the frieze of red and blue wooden *mocárabes* that supports the ceiling. The stalactite pattern that we see on every side characterises Nasrid decoration in Spain, and is not found in the earlier Omayyad or Almohad buildings. It appears to have originated in Asia Minor and was a favourite device of the Western Seljuk Turks, though they may have acquired it else-where. Certainly they were using it extensively in the thirteenth century, before stalactites had appeared in the Mosques of Cairo (Sultan Hassan and Kait-Bey). Thus the alleged derivation of the ornament from the subconscious associations in the minds of desert nomads in North Africa falls away. The ceiling itself is one of the most beautiful in the world of eastern art, with its delicately interlaced panels of cypress, whose hollows are filled with mother-of-pearl in starry patterns, a device that recalls the seven heavens of antiquity. It stresses the importance of looking up in every part of the Palace, for it is only recently that we have forgotten that ceilings, as much as floors and walls, require decoration.

In the days when the Hall of the Ambassadors justified the boast inscribed on one of its walls—'I am the heart of the palace among all its other members'—one stood inside a cube whose six sides, without exception, delighted the eye. The floor was white marble covered with precious rugs; the ceiling outrivalled the night sky with its pattern of glittering stars. Through the door-way a vista of three decorated arches frames the Patio of the Myrtles and the further arcade, more unsubstantial than ever, reflected in the quiet pool. As the tower is a bastion each of the other sides has its own view. From the western windows, now protected by glass panels for the comfort of winter visitors, you

can see the sheer north wall, with the towers of Machuca and
Las Gallinas, then those of the Alcazaba, and beyond them the
distant city as far as the Hospital Real, though the Cathedral is
just out of sight. In the opposite direction rises the Tower of
Abul Hachach, with the delicate columns of the balcony of the
Queen's dressing-room and beyond it the wooded slopes that
lead to the Generalife.

From the bay where the throne stood you see the whole hill of
the Albaicín spread out before you, its bell towers and cypresses
breaking the horizontal pattern of the roofs, while farther to the
right the outer Arab wall runs down from the Chapel of San
Miguel. Even from this distance you can see the road to the
Sacromonte and distinguish the whitened doors and windows of
the gypsy caves, among the thickets of aloe and prickly pear.
Charles V is said to have looked long at this same view and then
remarked, 'Ill-fated was the man who lost all this', adding that
Boabdil should rather have fought to the death to preserve his
reign.

Among the events which are said to have taken place in this
hall, the imprisonment of Boabdil and his mother is the most
dramatic and the least likely. The ageing king, Muley Hassan,
had taken another wife, Isabel de Solis, daughter of the Spanish
governor of the captured town of Martos. The child captive had
been brought up as a Moslem and, probably because of her outstanding beauty (did she really have a face like the full moon, a
body like a willow branch and hips like a mountain of sand?)
was given the name Zoraya. Palace intrigues were the rule in
Granada and Zoraya succeeded in making her old husband afraid
of Aisha, the chief wife, and her son Boabdil. They were imprisoned in the Torre de Comares, from which Boabdil was
lowered to safety in a basket suspended by the knotted scarves
of his mother and her ladies. The story, if true, would account
for Boabdil later deposing his father and for much of the civil
war that hastened the end of Moslem Spain far more than did
the armies of the Catholic Sovereigns.

Other anecdotes relate that the final council to decide the
surrender of the city took place here; and that Aisha led her son
to one of the windows and said, 'Look at what you are surrendering and remember that all your ancestors died kings of
Granada.' And finally that it was in this hall that the Catholic
Sovereigns commissioned the expedition of Columbus—we have
already seen the same deed commemorated in Santafé. A still
more unlikely tale runs that it was here that Isabel offered to

pawn her jewels to finance the expedition; the total expense was 70,000 florins, far less than the sum which had been extorted from the unfortunate inhabitants of Málaga alone.

At the south-east corner of the Salón de Embajadores an opening enables you to visit the lower level. A short passage whose marble columns have capitals dating from earliest Nasrid times opens into the **Patio de los Cipreses**, or **de la Reja**, a somewhat sombre one in which four cypresses grow. From here various passages lead to the cellars of the surrounding buildings and also provide access to the gallery that follows the whole perimeter, part of which we saw in the Alcazaba. To the south lie the baths, modelled on the classical lay-out of the Roman ones, and the first part that you enter is the **Sala de Camas**. The most colourful of all the apartments, it reiterates the dominant theme of all these buildings, the piling up of light, fragile-looking structures on slim, marble columns. The centre of the floor, constructed of ornamental mosaic tile, has a low fountain, and the gallery that surrounds the apartment, supported by four slender columns, painted and gilded dosserets and crobels, is framed in a wealth of gold and white stucco, that repeats the Nasrid motto over and over again. At either end are deep tiled recesses, in which the bathers could recline after the rigours of the bath; these and the floor are clothed with the oldest tiles, and all the rest of the decoration is post-Reconquest. This need not worry you, for you may well consider that if it did not look like this, it could hardly have improved on the restoration.

The upper passage was formerly closed in with wooden lattice screens, and one side formed a musicians' gallery. From another the Sultan was alleged to inspect the bathers, for you are now in the *harem*, or private section of the Palace. The word is akin to *haram* and has the various meanings of holy, untouchable and taboo. Münzer, who visited only two years after the conquest of Granada, was told by the governor that from this gallery the Sultan used to throw an apple to the woman he selected for the night. This was one way of preserving a high standard of marksmanship in the royal family, for the slightest inaccuracy could have landed him with one of his mothers-in-law.

The **Baths** (*Baños*) are entered through an archway and are simple but pleasing. The tiles are mostly eighteenth century, as may be deduced from the upper frieze, whose 'PV' lettering takes us to the reign of Philip V. His stay, along with his beautiful wife, Elizabeth of Parma, seems to have been the last occasion on which the Alhambra was spruced up for royalty. Today its maintenance benefits package tours, which are perhaps of far more value to the country. Note the star-shaped vents in the roof, allegedly once filled with coloured glass, in which case they could hardly allow the escape of steam. In an adjoining room are the two large tanks for the cold plunge and a hole in the wall through which the heating apparatus can be seen.

Back in the Sala de Camas there is a small door in each corner; you enter through one, another leads up to the Patio of the Myrtles, a third, now locked, gave access to a latrine, and you now pass through the fourth, on the east side, to reach the **Patio de Daraxa,** or Garden of Lindaraja. The patio is limited to the south by the Hall of the Two Sisters, above which is the *mirador* of Daraxa. On the north side are the buildings constructed by Charles V which effectively screen the rolling landscape beyond the walls from those using the *mirador*.

Here it is as well to enlighten the newcomer regarding the identity of the beautiful Lindaraxa (the spelling is immaterial). The apartments to the south were the residence of the sultana, *dar Aisha* (some say that this name was given to the favourite wife because the Prophet's wife was so called), which became Daraxa. The *mirador* was *al ain dar Aisha*, 'the eye of the house of Aisha'; so poor Lindaraxa and her adventures were created only to fit a name. It is a beautifully quiet garden, with box hedges and citrus trees, cypresses and acacias that surround the pillar on which the bowl of the fountain rests. The support is of the seventeenth century and the bowl is the original one from the Patio del Mexuar, of which we saw the exact copy. And yet it is not quite exact, for the rim of this one is incised with one of Ibn Zamrak's poems, a paean of self-praise by the fountain and therefore indirectly of the king who ordered it.

Below the *mirador* is one of the cellars of the Sala de dos Hermanas, which I shall describe later, called the Sala de los Secretos; it has no artistic claim to your attention and is simply shown as an example of an echo. If you stand in one corner a whisper from the opposite side comes through quite clearly, though it is inaudible to anyone standing in the centre. The effect is fortuitous and the only secrets originally preserved here are said to have been the bathers' clothes.

You now have to return through the Patio de los Cipreses, up the steps and along the gallery constructed by Charles V, adorned with columns and Arab capitals, leading to the **Tocador** (or Mirador or Peinador) **de la Reina**. The dressing-room prepared for the Empress Isabel, wife of Charles V, was simply built on top of the existing Tower of Abul Hachach, and is remarkable for the fine colonnade of the surrounding gallery, with its magnificent views, and for the frescoes of the sixteenth century. In the floor on the right of the entrance is a marble slab with 16 perforations, an Arab luxury that allowed perfumes to percolate into the chamber from below. The walls are covered with frescoes, the best being the series portraying Charles' successful expedition against Tunis. Unfortunately they have for centuries been 'scrawled over with the insignificant names of aspiring travellers', as Washington Irving wrote. Of all the romantics who visited the Alhambra he stayed the longest and spoiled the least. Here you could once find the names of Chateaubriand, Byron and Victor Hugo, alleged creators of beauty but too preoccupied with their own importance to mind defacing it. The earliest vandal advertised his bad breeding in 1664 and an officer of the 'Hundred Thousand Sons of St. Louis' added his name in 1823. These priceless frescoes are now being restored by a team of artists, equipped with modern aids such as the infra-red lamp, and it is thrilling to see how they can bring the old paintings to life and consign the vulgar scribblings to oblivion. You can now pass through the Apartments of Charles V, which the Emperor never occupied, though Washington Irving did, and then return to the Patio of the Myrtles.

The rest of the Alhambra Palace belongs to a different complex. It is difficult to visualise as one walks round, losing all sense of time and direction, that there are three different palaces; the Mexuar is the administrative building, and the Cuarto de Comares was the palace largely constructed by Yusuf I. In this was included everything we saw after the Mexuar, except of course the apartments of Charles V. When Mohamed V came to the throne (1354) he not only completed his father's work in the Comares section, but built an entirely new palace, the Cuarto de los Leones, whose main axis, the patio, runs at right angles to the Patio of the Myrtles. This is where you should begin again, for near its south-eastern corner is the modern passage that connects the two complexes. We enter the narrow Sala de los Mocárabes, the simplest of all the rooms in this highly ornate palace, but partly destroyed in the great explosion of 1590. Half the ceiling is original and there are three arches of stalactites with hanging *racimos*, resting on engaged columns with inscribed capitals.

This is a poor introduction to the Cuarto de los Leones, which represents the climax of Nasrid art, exceeding both in beauty and in decadence everything that had gone before. In contrast to the abstract and somewhat mathematical spirit underlying the Cuarto de Comares, that of the Leones casts away its inhibitions and relies on nature as much as art. The slender columns to which one becomes accustomed now take on the appearance of a forest; stucco becomes diaphanous and every effect is set against a background of blue sky, landscape or at least an ornamental façade.

The centre of this dream of beauty is the **Patio de los Leones**, a court arcaded like a classical peristyle, and when they first see it visitors are apt to run out of superlatives. Today we are at least partly prepared by the cinema and the travel agent's leaflets, but nothing can make the reality anything but dramatic. How shall we replace the debased adjectives glorious, and gorgeous, fabulous and fantastic? How does one describe the permutations of a hundred and twenty-four slender columns, single and double, in groups of three or four, that make the arcade and support the projecting pavilion at either end? And the final boldness that placed the basin of the central fountain on the backs of twelve stylised lions? We do not need Ibn Zamrak's adulatory poem carved round its rim to tell us that this garden offers a work whose beauty Allah did not wish to equal. Groping for the right words and not finding them, we can only fall back on Dumas and repeat, '. . . a dream petrified by the wand of a magician.'

You should circle the patio in an anti-clockwise direction. Half-way down the right side are fine double doors and one turns in through two arches—notice the tiled niches in the jambs of the first—to the **Sala de los Abencerrajes**. We met the Banu Sarraj in Andújar and noted that the once powerful tribe turned Christian and allied itself with the Catholic Sovereigns. The reason was that their leaders were beheaded in this room by order of the Sultan, having been called in one by one. Apart from the fact that we do not know why, when and by whom the leaders were killed, the story is a good one and the credulous may see the rust marks in the basin of the fountain, confidently pointed out as the blood of the Abencerrajes. The original story was that Boabdil, who gets the blame for everything, stumbled over his favourite wife, Morayma, in a tryst with the Abencerraje chief, Hamet, under the Cipres de la Sultana. The bloody revenge is unlike what we know of Boabdil, who is far more likely to have apologised for intruding. Two more versions are based on the feud between the Abencerrajes and the Zegris. The latter being in the ascendancy, the King, who was either Mohamed the Lame

or Muley Hassan, father of Boabdil, ordered the execution with
the same Oriental perfidy that Bertrand du Guesclin and Henry
of Trastamara employed in killing Pedro the Cruel.

Though the *azulejos* and the stucco are of the sixteenth century,
they have largely been based on older examples, even copying
part of one of Ibn Zamrak's poems from another hall. The
capitals are among the finest in the Alhambra and their imposts
bear the text, 'There is no greater aid than that which comes
from Allah, the merciful and compassionate'. The domed ceiling
is the true glory of this room, supported on an eight-pointed star
which rests on stalactite squinches; each ray has a pierced stucco
window on either side, so that sixteen of them send down a
diffused light. The interior of the dome is simply a mass of
stalactite niches, thrown in relief by the lighting and resembling
a giant honeycomb. Above the Sala de los Abencerrajes are the
few remains of the *harem* living-quarters, whose unique feature
is the use of black marble capitals of the style used in Almansor's
addition to the Mosque of Córdoba, and therefore probably of
the eleventh century. They were obviously obtained elsewhere.

Continuing the circuit you find that the whole east side of the
Patio de los Leones is occupied by the long, shallow **Sala de los
Reyes**, sometimes called de la Justicia. As the rooms are in the
private quarters of the king, these late names refer only to
worthless legends or to one of the paintings you can see. The
entrances, one to each division, and the communicating passages
are all contrived in arches of stalactites. (There is a limit to the
number of times one can repeat the formula—the tile dado, the
sebka, the inscriptions, the arches and the capitals with their
strange imposts.) But the greatest wonder of all is apt to strike you
when the endless repetition of honeycomb and filigree threatens
a surfeit; namely, that all of this was made for one man only,
for it would be rarely indeed that another would be invited into
the *harem*, even when the women had been veiled or locked away.
Perhaps this accounts for the generally superficial level of the
poetry that one reads on the walls, adulation, descriptions of the
beauty of the sultan's possessions, more adulation and some
routine piety.

The Sala de los Reyes has a feature that is unique in Moslem
Spain. In three alcoves at the back are paintings on leather let
into the ceilings. They are certainly strange and no one has yet
solved their mystery, though it is fairly obvious that they were the
work of a Christian and, from their resemblance to paintings in
a palace in Florence, possibly a Tuscan. There are hunting scenes

with backgrounds of frankly western architecture, and one where a horseman is spearing a woodwose, or wild man of the woods, holding a damsel who in turn has a sleeping lion on a chain. The central one shows ten Moslems, who are believed to be the ten Nasrid kings (excluding two usurpers) who had ruled up to about AD 1400. Some have red beards, the rest black, but no conclusions can be drawn from this as beards were frequently dyed either red with henna or black to make them more imposing. Boabdil, for instance, is shown with a blond beard in one portrait, and black in others. The capitals in this hall are worth a second look as you leave, for most of them show traces of the blue paint with which they were intricately adorned. Note also how the lead which was used to bind column and capital has been squeezed out round the edges of the joint. Unsubstantial though they may look, the superstructures are heavy enough to produce some strange effects; in one doorway a marble jamb had become noticeably bent, and when the thousandth visitor asked the custodian how it had happened, he was told, 'because they cut it green'.

On the north side of the Patio is the **Sala de dos Hermanas**, the 'Two Sisters' being enormous slabs of white marble forming part of the floor. Just as in the Sala de los Abencerrajes opposite, there is a central fountain with a drain running into the courtyard, but here the honeycomb cupola is even more magnificent. There is one original wooden jalousie, and a whole poem of Ibn Zamrak forms a frieze above the tile dado. The sentiments are trite but the technique is in parts excellent; '. . . for he who serves the glorious one, himself acquires glory', is one of the more sycophantic phrases. Poor fellow, all he received was a knife in the ribs at the orders of one of his glorious master's successors. The entrance to the hall has the usual double arch, with a passage between; the one on the left leads to a latrine which is worth inspecting to appreciate the use which was made of running water to fulfil ritual requirements. The passage to the right leads to a stair and to the upper rooms. As the Sala de dos Hermanas was the residence of the Sultana Aisha, and there is good evidence for this, her companions and maidservants would occupy these rooms.

Opposite the entrance is the archway leading to the Sala de los Ajimeces, named after the twin windows looking north. Between them is the entrance to a worthy end to an enchanting tour, the bay that is known as the **Mirador de Lindaraja**. Is it surprising that tales have been conjured up to add the illusion of romance to this poetic name? Everything described before is reproduced here in miniature, with a tile dado of black, white and yellow that surpasses in beauty any that we have seen. Through the windows your gaze is held by the graceful movement of the tree-tops in the Garden of Daraxa; the buildings on the farther side should never have been placed where the foothills and mountains once made their dramatic back-drop to the view. They were not there in Moslem days, when the fierce Sultan could yield to the tranquil scene, and when that palled, to the verses that adorn the walls. One line is enough to explain *al ain dar Aisha*, 'I am an eye full of joy in this garden.'

CHAPTER EIGHTEEN

The Alhambra Circuit, The Generalife, The Albaicín and Alcazaba

✣

The Partal Gardens—Towers of the Circuit Wall—The Palace of Charles V—The Archaeological Museum—The Museum of Fine Arts—The Generalife—La Silla del Moro—The Albaicín—The Old Alcazaba

A door in the south-east corner of the Court of the Lions leads to a brick tower, usually called the Torre de la Rauda and once thought to have been the sepulchre of several kings of Granada. It is possible that it guarded the entrance to the royal cemetery, which lay behind the Sala de los Abencerrajes and whose remains can be inspected. They consist chiefly of foundations, among which you can make out the coffin-shaped graves, so orientated that a body lying on its right side would have its face turned towards Mecca. The name of *Rauda*, which it has retained from the sixteenth century, is taken from the garden which apparently surrounded it.

From here, or from an exit in the Garden of Daraxa, you can make your way into the **Partal Gardens** (Jardines del Partal). Myrtles, cypresses and laurels, roses, carnations and violets rise in tier upon tier, framed in mossy or ivy-covered walls, and everywhere there is water. The present gardens are all that remains of the extensive ones that used to surround the royal palaces and continued as the Garden of Daraxa. Most will have heard of the worship of water by the desert-dwellers who settled in Spain, and it is too easy to fall into the habit of picturing the Moslems of Spain as anchored Bedouin. By now it ought to be clear that there was very little Arab blood left among them, and that the Moorish contribution came from the inhabitants of an African country which complains of too much rain in its northern part. There is nothing exceptional in liking fountains and runnels during an Andalucian summer. But Spaniard and Moor show exceptional affection for flowers; in Spain old men may sit for hours in the April sun, with a rose held between their teeth, and in the Moroccan War of 1860 Alarcón made a significant observation. Just as in Spain, he wrote, we stop a stranger in the street to get a light for our cigarette, so the Moors will go up to anyone who is carrying a bunch of flowers, smell them and go on without a word.

It is not difficult to picture the area in its great days when the mansions of wealthy court officials dotted the slopes where the great garden flourished. One of them is still there, the **Torre de las Damas**, built on to the fortress wall. Before it is a large, rectangular pool of the usual type, which mirrors the imposing front of the house with its great portico of five arches. It is this feature which gave its name to the gardens, for *partal* is the Arabic adaptation of 'portal'. Cypress hedges surround the pool and palm trees rustle pleasantly. At the far corners are a pair of stone lions, originally intended for the Maristan, or lunatic asylum; their dedicatory tablet is in the Alhambra Museum. The chief interest of the Torre de las Damas is not so much in the main building, with its fine decoration and spacious views, as in the humble Arab houses that adjoin it. Nevertheless, there is one curiosity in the *azulejo* work of the hall: whereas the usual tile mosaic of the 'lozenge' type consists of white strips that cross to make the pattern, in this case of blue and green diamonds, near the door one panel reverses the colours and has white diamonds in a coloured grill. The arrangement must be extremely rare, even if you take into account the many examples of the lozenge pattern that have survived.

The small Arab houses with keyhole windows that are built on to the mansion are the relics of at least a dozen that used to house the servants. In the upstairs room of the nearest are the remains of a 'fresco', one of the rare survivors of pictorial art among the Moslems of Spain. The method used was to reproduce main outlines by stencil, whence the repetitive effect, and then to colour with the use of egg-yolk as a medium. There are three bands of episodes, hunting, music and singing, and a warlike expedition with camels and horses. The discovery of a Marinid banner suggests that this could have been the household of a Moroccan chief on pilgrimage to Mecca. Of great importance is the fact that we have here an authentic fourteenth-century Moslem painting, once more demonstrating that the prohibition against the portrayal of the human figure was not a part of the Islamic religion, at least so far as the Koran goes. The *hadith*, or commentaries, have less force. Perhaps one may speculate that the Semites, who discouraged pictorial art so strongly, lacked the necessary artistic gifts. Looking at the cavaliers in these paintings in distemper one is reminded of the figures in Persian miniatures of the thirteenth century, and wonders whether itinerant artists might not have painted them.

If you now continue round the inside of the walls in a clockwise direction, you find the Torre del Mihrab a few yards away, a private chapel used by the owners of the Torre de las Damas. The decoration is of the style to which we are now accustomed, with the *mihrab* resembling some contemporary ones in North Africa. The next tower is the **Torre de los Picos**, so called after the pyramidal merlons which crown it; many details of its internal structure suggest Gothic influence and it has been suggested that it was the work of a Christian, possibly captive, architect. The tower's purpose was to guard the entrance from the Generalife, the Puerta del Arrabal, and a rough path leads down to a horseshoe-arched gate and adjacent quarters for the guard. It is now kept closed permanently. The next tower is that usually called del Candil, but more properly **Torre del Cadi**, the only one in which the battlement walk passes through instead of behind the building. It was the command post and served to check sentries and possible enemies who might have gained access to the battlements. Inside the wall there is a sunken road, along which cavalry or large bodies of troops could hurry to a threatened area; in peacetime it was used by officials and residents on their way to and from the Palaces.

The **Torre de la Cautiva** is next along the wall, the name of 'captive' being derived from the popular but unsupported belief that Isabel de Solis, wife of Muley Hassan and enemy of Aisha, lived here. The tiny patio contains attractive stucco and stalactite work and it is the only tower which, except for the ceilings and floor, is entirely authentic. The disappearance of these must be blamed on the French troops. Their loss is made all the more deplorable by one of the many eulogistic poems that cover the walls: 'This work has come to bedeck the Alhambra. It is a dwelling place for the peace-loving and for warriors . . . You can say, when you see it, "behold a fortress, or maybe a pleasure house". In this castle there glow with equal beauty, the ceiling, the floor and the four walls. The stucco and the tiles are exquisite, but the carved woodwork of the ceiling surpasses them in elegance . . .' The dado of mosaic tiles achieves fresh beauty, though you would think that every combination had by now been seen. First, each panel forms an isolated composition, grouped about a centre-piece, like the patterns of some Oriental textile; and secondly we again have something unique here, a colour between rose and lilac among the mosaic tiles.

At the eastern tip of the perimeter is the **Torre de las Infantas**, described as the perfect model of a dignified Arab house. On it is based an old legend, retold by Washington Irving under the title *The Three Beautiful Princesses*. To anyone who has seen these enchanting places, the story of Zayda, Zorayda and Zorahayda and their Christian lovers revives memories on every page. At one point the cavaliers are prisoners in the Vermilion Towers, and then they are working in the deep ravine which still lies at the foot of the Tower of the Princesses. One can even borrow from Irving's description of this, the most aristocratic of all towers: 'The interior of the tower was divided into small, fairy apartments, beautifully ornamented in the light Arabian style, surrounding a lofty hall, the vaulted roof of which rose almost to the summit of the tower. The walls and ceiling of the hall were adorned with arabesques and fretwork, sparkling with gold and with brilliant pencilling. In the centre of the marble pavement was an alabaster fountain, set round with aromatic shrubs and flowers, and throwing up a jet of water that cooled the whole edifice, and had a lulling sound.'

The next tower, or rather its ruins, used to stand at the end of the main street of the Alhambra, as it ran alongside the principal water supply. Somewhere in this area José García cut the fuse that would have destroyed all the rest of the Alhambra, most of the towers of the south wall having already been blown up.

You have probably been aware of the Palace and gardens of the Generalife on the hillside on your left, rising from among the woods, and you now come to the highest point of the Alhambra hill, where the water from the Generalife is brought across the ravine in the body of a modern footbridge. Standing on it you can even feel the rush of water beneath your feet and on the far side is one of those vaulted *aljibes*, or cisterns, in which various streams are brought together before being launched into the Alhambra. Even if the passage into the Generalife were permitted, I would still advise continuing the circuit. Looking back over what was once the *población*, the third fraction into which we divided the Alhambra, you can see how much of it is ruin, with bare foundations as featureless to the amateur as the remains of a Neolithic settlement.

The rest of the perimeter is, however, just as dull, and there is no need to visit the sad ruins left by the French, not even the **Torre de los Siete Suelos**, the Tower of the Seven Floors, built underground by the way. Legend has it that it was through this gate that Boabdil quitted the Alhambra on his way to hand over the keys. It is said that he asked for it to be walled up afterwards, and certainly a sixteenth-century engraving pictures it with the title *Porta castri granatensis semper clausa*. In Moslem days it was the main entrance to the Alhambra, more important even than the Puerta de Justicia; destroyed by the French, it is only now being restored. The story of the seven underground levels is, of course, pure fantasy, but it gave rise to legends such as the one of the *belludo*. This phantom was said to live in the tower, guarding the treasure of a Moorish king. At night, and for reasons best known to itself, it would pass through Granada in the guise of a headless horse, followed by six hounds.

We now leave the walls and go due west among the ruins of the *población*. The first building of any size is the former Convent of San Francisco, now the Parador Nacional of the D.G.T. and the best value of any hotel in Granada. It was originally a Moslem palace, but there is little of this left, and the rest of the building is too recent and has suffered too many vicissitudes to preserve more than one item of interest. The north-west portion has a little *mirador* in which the Catholic Sovereigns were buried until the Capilla Real had been finished, in accordance with the Queen's wish. A simple marble slab marks the spot.

Going west you find yourself in the Alhambra's only street, the Calle Real, with souvenir shops and a modest restaurant on the left. They are good and the owners are not grasping; the restaurant has a pleasant patio, part of which used to be beneath a fig tree, until the day that a ripe fig dropped into a tourist's soup. Opposite is the Church of Santa María de la Alhambra, occupying the site of the former mosque, and before it a stone column commemorating the incredible bravery of two Franciscan friars, Pedro de Dueñas and Juan de Cetina, who took advantage of the peace that officially existed between Christian and Moslem to go and preach on the steps of the Mosque, where they promptly achieved martyrdom. The treasures of the Church consist of a marble font which has obviously done previous service in an Arab fountain, and three statues by Alonso de Mena. The Visigothic tablet that used to stand over the door of the sacristy is now in the Museum of the Alhambra, where we shall shortly follow it.

The **Palace of Charles V** is one of the finest secular Renaissance buildings in the world, and certainly without a rival in Spain. It reminds one vaguely, however, of the remark made by Bourgoing about Columbus' son: that he would have been a great man had he not been the son of a greater father. Had this palace been needed in Madrid, or even in the town of Granada, it would have done very nicely, but to have placed it contiguous with the Palace of the Alhambra was to invite comparison and at the height of the Renaissance it never occurred to artists that Oriental architecture might rival, let alone outclass, theirs. Not that most of us would like to see this great building disappear, for it too is a work of art.

We should first dispose of some common inaccuracies. You may be told that the Palace was abandoned because the earth tremors made the Alhambra hill unsafe, or for various other reasons. The project was not abandoned, though money was wanting for much of the time (Charles V and his son Philip II presided over the most splendid bankruptcies that the world had yet seen), but building proceeded at a snail's pace through reign after reign and, according to the latest accounts, was finally completed in 1957. I can only say that in 1968 they were still putting a ceiling into the upper gallery. Then there is a story, a favourite among the guides, that the palace was built for receptions and as administrative headquarters only, and was never intended to be a residence. This also appears to be a fallacy, for the chronicles state that Charles, needing a royal residence for his periodic visits to the Province of Granada, found the Alhambra Palace too cramped and cold, in spite of the apartments that were put up for him. One can well understand that a young man brought up in the massive castles of Flanders and Burgundy, with their gaping fireplaces, should find the shelter of the Moslem Palace, with its tile and marble, inadequate; and the Arab method of getting warm, the *brasero* under the table and the *camilla* draped over the knees, quite intolerable. It was also for this reason that Charles' bride took up her residence in the Monastery of San Jerónimo during the honeymoon.

The project was begun in 1526, when the Governor of the Alhambra, the Count of Tendilla, put forward a member of his retinue, Pedro Machuca, as a candidate for the post of architect. His training had been in Italy under Michelangelo and, some say, Raphael, and he was engaged in painting and in carving retablos at the time. Not only is it fairly certain that Tendilla nominated the artist, but it is likely that the excessive emphasis on mythological subjects in the decoration is not entirely due to contemporary Italian taste, but to the fact that Tendilla's brother, Diego Hurtado de Mendoza, member of a family already distinguished in art and literature, was one of the great humanists of the age. He was obviously conversant with the classics, translated and commented on Aristotle's works, and wrote a fine history of the Conquest of Granada.

Pedro Machuca, a gentleman of Toledo, was gifted with the usual Renaissance attribute of versatility and may well have been influenced by Hurtado de Mendoza. In addition to this palace, he designed the Puerta de la Granada and the Pillar of Charles V, both of which we saw before entering the Alhambra. He was also a painter of some note; one of his pictures is in the Capilla Real, where it is overshadowed by finer works, but a Deposition in the Prado can hold its own in any company. The cost of the Palace was supposed to be partly defrayed by increasing the tax paid by the Moslems, an exaction forbidden by the Treaty of Surrender signed at Santafé. However, it is usually said to have been a voluntary payment in return for permission to wear the turban; this is difficult to believe, as the turban had fallen into disuse at the time of the fall of Granada, being retained chiefly by *cadis* and *alfaquis*.

The Palace is imposing enough, with its lower level of rusticated stone, and pilasters in which bronze hitching rings suspended from lions' and eagles' heads imitate the Florentine style. The windows are severely classical, each one surmounted by a circular light. The doorways have Ionic and Corinthian columns on the south side, and plain Doric on the principal, west front. The circular courtyard, a surprise after the square exterior, has a row of Doric columns to each of its galleries. The columns were originally intended to be of marble, but the burden of empire compelled the builders to use a conglomerate stone which, though highly polished, looks like a dish that they would dare to serve only to prisoners or schoolboys. It has the delightful Spanish name of *piedra pudinga*, which is how 'pudding stone' has survived translation.

The only use to which the palace was put during its first two centuries appears to have been for entertainments, especially bullfighting; the Moslems had staged the same 'sport' before the conquest, even to the refinement of tiring the bull by baiting it with hounds before its human opponents risked their lives. Moors were, it seems, among the best toreros and, according to Goya, took up bullfighting when they came to Spain, and were credited with inventing *banderillas*. Goya's series of plates in the British Museum are worth studying and include an impression of

Charles V spearing a bull at Valladolid. But you may hear it strenuously denied that the palace was ever used for this purpose and it is a fact that the circular patio was not completed during the reign of Charles V. There is similar lack of precise information about the sculptured bulls' heads round the gallery; were they simply a revival of the old Iberian totem?

At the risk of straying too far from the Alhambra I must here mention the surviving village processions on St. Mark's day, when a garlanded bull is blessed by the priest, caressed by the women and sometimes subsequently killed by amateur toreros. The bull of St. Mark, of course unconnected with the saint's emblem which is a winged lion, is simply the old fertility rite, the relic of the prehistoric spring festival that figured in Ancient Egypt and, perhaps, in Crete.

The Palace houses two museums of more than ordinary merit. That on the ground floor, approached from the patio and opened on request, is the **Museo Nacional de Arte Hispano-Musulman**; its Director is a well-known scholar, Señor Don Jesús Bermúdez Pareja. Though small, there is an astonishing amount of good material collected in the museum, but it is preferable that one should know what to ask for; the usual custodian is well-informed and most helpful. Immediately inside and to the right are two inscribed plaques; the smaller is the Visigothic tablet of dedication that used to be seen above the sacristy entrance of Santa María de la Alhambra. Badly weathered though it is, you can still make out the names of Gudila, the noble founder, and of three saints, Stephen, John and Vincent. Near the end one may read, '*SANCTO PAULO ACCITANO PONTF...*'; by the use of the ablative one may guess that the original dedication was performed by a sainted Bishop Paul of Guadix. The plaque, which was found in the foundations of the mosque when the present church was built, suggests that, as usual, the Arabs had chosen the site of a Visigothic church for their own mosque. Here, too, is a marble plaque with an inscription inside a horseshoe arch, which was placed over the door of the Maristan in 1367. The inscription, after briefly mentioning the purpose for which the building was opened (we note that it was for Moslem lunatics), is simply a genealogical tree and eulogy of Mohamed V. As he was an ally of Pedro the Cruel and a witness of the state to which Castile was being reduced by its senseless civil wars, he was probably sympathetic towards the mentally afflicted.

Small though the floor space of the Museum appears, it contains a surprising amount of interesting material; there are royal

Moslem tombstones, pottery, glassware, carved and gilded woodwork, Arab braziers in stone and marble, ancestors of those still in use, specimens of metal ornament, and stucco and carved capitals from the eleventh to the thirteenth centuries. The average visitor will want to see only the showpieces, of which there are three. An oil painting, apparently of the fifteenth century, shows two knights in Christian armour (though this was also used by the Moslems, according to a poem by Ibn Al-Khatib) engaged in combat, and round the edge the repeated Nasrid motto *in Spanish, Solo Dios es vencedor.* Why this should be in Spanish remains an unsolved mystery. Secondly, there is a great marble ablution tank, on whose front are four lions devouring four stags, and on the sides a heraldic eagle with various animals. All the carvings are characteristic of the style of the later Omayyad days of Córdoba, while the inscription is in much later Arabic characters and is in praise of Mohamed III of Granada. The conclusion is that the exhibit was brought here from Córdoba some time after the fall of the Caliphate and the inscription altered at the beginning of the fourteenth century.

The last item is the famous Alhambra vase, an unrivalled example of Granadine workmanship. Along with others, it was found in the Palace precincts—according to popular belief, filled with gold—and as late as the seventeenth century they were on view in the Adarve garden of the Alcazaba. One was broken and the pieces were carried off by souvenir-hunting tourists; another just disappeared without the formality of first being reduced to fragments. This one, though lacking a handle, is a beautiful example of fourteenth-century Hispano-Moresque work, whose nearest rival is the one, probably made in Málaga, now in the National Gallery of Sicily. Here we have an unequalled combination of form, design and colour. One can almost conjure up the Arab's sex symbol in the willowy neck of the jar, rising from the generously curved body that narrows at the foot like the old amphora that used to be thrust into the earth to stand upright. The design is of stylised leaves in blue and pale gold on a white background and the surface is matt rather than lustrous; gazelles appear among the foliage and an inscription is repeated endlessly round the belly. It helps us to bring the Palace of the Sultans a little nearer; we know that furniture was limited to a bare minimum, a chest and a low table, carpets, curtains and cushions (as late as the eighteenth-century Spanish women might still sit on cushions, cross-legged, to drink their coffee or chocolate from low tables). So we can readily picture the artistic effect of decorative jars, lamps and incense burners.

To some, the following items may also be of interest: a restored hand and forearm of the type we saw over the Puerta de la Justicia, but with the key engraved on the forearm itself; a copy of the sword of Boabdil, of which the original is in the Museo de San Telmo in San Sebastián; hollow copper balls strung on a pole, from a minaret in Granada, and of the same pattern as those formerly on the Giralda and still to be seen in Morocco; and stocks with variously sized apertures, the larger for both feet, the smaller for one only. It is economically made to accommodate several occupants, provided they alternately face their neighbours.

Upstairs is the **Museo de Bellas Artes**, devoted chiefly to works of local artists, including those who lived here, though born elsewhere, such as Pedro Machuca and Sánchez Cotán. The latter's Adoration of the Shepherds, facing you as you enter the vestibule, is noted for the masterly treatment of a lamb in the foreground. I have previously remarked that this painter is best known for his still life while his portrayal of humans is less successful. In Hall I is the magnificent *Triptych of the Gran Capitán*, a superb example of Limoges enamel and the work of Nardon Penicaud. There are six compartments, the central one a Crucifixion and the two larger side-pieces a Road to Calvary and a *Pietà*. Apart from its artistic merits, which are too obvious to require further elaboration, minor points are revealed by closer study; in the small Last Judgment all the figures have gilt hair, except St. Peter at the top left, though we do not know why. The gaping jaws of Leviathan on the right, which is the side of the damned, are easily accounted for, since the monster has been equated with Satan since the days of St. Gregory. A humorous touch is added by the presence of two tonsured priests, one among the saved and the other among the damned.

Then there is an outstanding sculptured Entombment at the end of the hall, the work of Jacobo Florentino l'Indaco, from the cloister of San Jerónimo and designed for the tomb of the Gran Capitán. It was originally intended to bury him in the cloister, and the group's surround is a copy of the one which remains at the Monastery. In the same hall are a fine German Gothic Virgin, which used to stand above the inner gate of the Puerta de la Justicia, and a bas-relief in wood by Diego de Siloé, a Virgin and Child; the expressions are portrayed in a masterly fashion. In passing to the next hall you see the reconstructed portal of the vanished Church of San Gil, by Diego de Siloé and his school; inside there are the choir stalls from the former Convent of Santa Cruz la Real, of which Nos. 1–16, by Juan de Orea, are of great delicacy.

Hall III is for the admirer of Sánchez Cotán and gives the visitor every chance of comparing his figures and still lifes. His Vision of St. Hugo representing the celestial builders of a monastery with an audience of Carthusians, is said to foreshadow the art of Zurbarán. If this is the case, then the shadow is long and thin. There will not, however, be two opinions about his masterly *bodegón del cardo*, which ranks as one of his best still lifes.

In Hall V Alonso Cano is well represented, with and without the assistance of Pedro de Mena, and again we see the tenderness which he was able to infuse in his painted figures. His pupil Pedro Atanasio Bocanegra has an insipid *Inmaculada* here and a Crucifixion in Hall VII. This aggressive, boastful painter got on his colleagues' nerves to such an extent that he was twice challenged to a duel with paint brushes; he evaded the first but was forced to accept the second, with Teodoro Ardemans. The contest was to take the form of each party painting the other's portrait; Ardemans finished his in an hour and Bocanegra floundered on for longer and then produced a worthless daub. Ardemans' picture now hangs in the Archbishop's palace; Bocanegra died soon after, of spleen no doubt.

The moderns and not-so-moderns are well displayed and repay study. Impressionists of the Spanish school, romantics and exponents of Art Nouveau are cheek by jowl and though there are many excellent works, only two well-known names, Mariano Fortuny and Muñoz Degrain, are found. The former's Swordsmith of Toledo is a fine example of late Baroque. This does not mean that one should ignore the works of others. On the contrary, there are dozens of Spanish artists who are unknown outside their own country and sometimes even at home, but whose work is highly regarded by visiting experts. Daniel Vázquez Díaz is one, and his pencil portraits here consist of Gómez-Moreno the archaeologist and art historian, Manuel de Falla and García Lorca, perhaps the three most famous Granadines since Boabdil.

The **Generalife** is approached along the road that leads past the Washington Irving Hotel, and you can gain admission with a portion of the inclusive ticket, or by paying five pesetas. It was the summer garden of the kings of Granada, private and personal, and therefore in complete contrast to the type of palace garden exemplified by Versailles, a thinly disguised form of showing-off. What then did the kings of Granada desire when they retired to their garden? Solitude, flowers, perfumes and the sound of water. García Gómez—one cannot write for long about Granada without introducing the name of this great man—quotes a poem by Ibn Luyun, who may have been of Spanish descent, if Luyun means León. The theme is the construction of a garden, and the Generalife seems to have been built in accordance with the plan advised. The pavilion with its views, the trees, the flower-beds, the aqueduct, ponds and fountains are all there. García Gómez compares it with others still existing in Morocco. Nevertheless, even if it is Oriental in concept, it is not foreign to the Spanish temperament, the patio mentality inherited perhaps from the Romans with their atrium.

The Generalife (*Gennat Alarif*, the Garden of the Architect) lies on the slopes of the Cerro del Sol, behind and above the Alhambra, of which it commands a magnificent view, as well as of the Darro valley and the Albaicín. It is approached through avenues of cypresses and, if you take the upper, right-hand path, under arches of trained oleanders. Almost the first sight is of the open-air theatre, a recent construction which is used each June to stage the best in music and ballet. The auditorium is divided into stages by low box hedges and is small enough to retain much of the intimacy that chamber music demands. I cannot hope to convey the soothing quality of the performances on summer nights. *La música, para quien la entienda* runs the proverb, 'music is for him who understands it', and to many the setting itself cannot be improved by the performance. Said Ibn Zamrak, 'Granada is a bride whose crown and jewels and robes are flowers; her tunic is the Generalife . . . her pendants the clusters of the morning dew.'

The central pool is fed from either side with the feathery spray of a score of fountains, the cypress hedges form arches, and paths run between the beds of roses; on the outer path, the seats and the view invite rest and contemplation, and everywhere there is shade and the sound of water.

For those who wish for more solitude and less contrived beauty, the Carmen de los Mártires marks the site of former food-stores and dungeons of Moslem days, as well as the field where tournaments and parades were held. The park is open to visitors during the same hours as the Alhambra and its mansion is used as a restaurant during the summer months. There are fine groves of trees, among which there used to be an oak said to have been planted by St. Teresa, though she was never in Granada, and there still exists a cypress which was allegedly planted by St. John of the Cross. Behind the house is a natural park with a very wide variety of trees: chestnut, magnolia, plane, poplar, cypress, oak, elm, lime, laurel, palm and pine, any of which may be shrouded by climbing ivy. Water, brought by an old Arab aqueduct, cascades down mossy rockeries and runs between box and myrtle hedges. This is another property that belonged to the Mother Superior of the Convent of Santa Paula in Seville and was presented by her to the Municipality.

Farther up the hill is the **Silla del Moro**, mentioned earlier, where the old castle is being reconstructed. From the drive in front of it there is a view of every part of Granada, with the exception of the Generalife, which is hidden by trees. One can even pick out the individual churches on the Albaicín and, on the extreme right, the Collegiate Church of San Cecilio on the Sacromonte, near the cave where the leaden documents were found in 1594. There were in all twenty-five sheets inscribed in Arabic and Spanish giving details of martyrdoms. Controversy raged over their authenticity for centuries, but the abbey church had been built and its museum stocked. There seems to be no doubt that the 'documents' were forgeries, and that their discovery was conveyed to the archbishop by the forgers themselves. San Cecilio was alleged to have had his sight restored by wiping his eyes with the Virgin's handkerchief, a relic sent for by Philip II during an illness. The seventeenth-century etymologist, Bernardo Alderete, was nearly condemned to the stake for pointing out that the Spanish language did not exist in the first century; his hurried explanation that San Cecilio wrote in Castilian because he foresaw that it would be in use when his tablets were discovered, was accepted.

Slightly to the left, we see the outer Arab wall of the Albaicín descending the bare hillside, and among the houses on the hill farther in is the Church of El Salvador. To the left again is the Darro valley and across it rise the sheer walls and towers of the Alhambra. With field glasses you can even see the luncheon tables laid on the terrace of the former Convent of San Francisco, now the D.G.T. Parador. One higher point remains, the Parque de Invierno or del Llano de la Perdiz. In its bare central plateau, where nothing resembling a park can be seen, are a sundial and an orientated circle which enables the visitor to pick out mountain peaks and other places of interest. A journey there is not really necessary.

From the Alhambra we had several views of a parallel hill, running east and west, on the other side of the Darro. It has been loosely called the Albaicín whereas, in fact, only the east or right side is properly so called. The rest is the **Alcazaba**, whose name I purposely withheld to avoid confusion with the other Alcazaba on the tip of the Alhambra hill. This one, which might be called the eastern Alcazaba, is believed to be the oldest inhabited part of Granada and is certainly one of the most interesting. It was completely walled and later suburbs, including the **Albaicín**, were built outside and then protected by their own walls. Like the settlers in the Antequeruela, the inhabitants of the Albaicín were refugees; they came from Baeza and migrated to Granada in 1239, when St. Ferdinand captured their home town. The name of this suburb, therefore, is simply a corruption of the Arabic *Rabad Al-Baezin*, the 'Quarter of the Men of Baeza'.

With their customary industry the new settlers re-established their trades and in two at least, pottery and dyes, they achieved fame. These arts continued after the Reconquest, and dyed velvet was mentioned by Lope de Vega, *Para vos me dió Granada el mas fino carmesí*, 'Granada gave me the finest carmine for you', and his contemporary Cervantes writes of '. . . the clear dawn, when it comes up enmeshed in the colour of the papers of Granada.' The paper was a speciality called *salud de Granada* or *papel de arrebol*, the latter a word which signifies the rosy clouds at sunset. It was as highly esteemed by poets as Tyrian purple by the ancients.

Today Alcazaba and Albaicín can be treated as a single entity, a district of quiet, narrow, cobbled streets and ancient white-washed houses of high walls surrounding extensive gardens, of cypresses and poplars. Córdoba gave us an idea of Moslem worship; the Alhambra of how the rich lived. Here we have the best chance of recapturing something of the atmosphere of a Moslem town. For this reason there will be little emphasis on churches and their artistic treasures, of which the best examples have already been described. Thus, in true Andalucian style, we shall avoid *soso y aburto*, the flat boredom which is so foreign to the local temperament.

The commonest fallacy about the Albaicín is the belief, re-peated by writers, that it is a gypsy quarter. There is actually one small area inhabited by gypsies, but it is out of sight on the north of the hill; the gypsy caves that you are dragged to are on the road to Sacromonte, on the east, beyond the boundary of the Albaicín. Its wall is best seen from the Alhambra, as a continuous line from the Hermitage of San Miguel, formerly a defensive tower, to the Darro valley. On its right, farther to the east, are the whitewashed entrances to the gypsy caves, cool in summer and warm in winter, often furnished with surprising luxury. The owners' main source of income appears to be the performance of so-called flamenco for parties of tourists; admittedly many of the best performers, especially of the *zapateados*, an elaborate form of tap-dancing, are gypsies, but you don't see them here. The *canasteros* or 'hawkers' dances' will not be found here either, though they are the nearest thing to a pure gypsy dance. What is presented nowadays, in the quaint atmosphere of whitewashed stone walls hung with copper pans, telephones and television sets discreetly covered with Spanish shawls, is the *zambra*. This is a dance of uncertain origin—the name possibly comes from the Arabic for a piper—and consists of castanets, handclapping, tap-dancing, mock passion and especially pirouettes that make the flounced skirts rise to reveal slim legs (not so exciting as it was last century), all forming a mixture impossible to classify. But it is well received by the customers, who particularly appreciate the free glass of wine that is served.

The Albaicín is a tour best done on foot, as the streets are tortuous and may even end in a flight of steps; a guide is a great help as no map can take you to every place of interest. But much can also be achieved by asking passers-by (those in uniform are the most reliable) or engaging an intelligent child, who usually knows the shortest way from point to point. We start at the Plaza de Santa Ana (see Ch. 15) where, on the left, you will see the house in which San Juan de Dios looked after his unfortunates, and in which he died in 1550. The Casa de los Pisas is still the headquarters of the Order of Hospitallers he founded, and the room in which the saint died has been converted into an oratory that can be entered from the Calle del Aire, next to the Audiencia. The continuation of the Plaza is the Carrera de Darro, one of the oldest and most picturesque streets in Granada, with colourful houses on the left and, on the right, the narrow channel of the river with its succession of stone footbridges, and then the towering cliff on which stands the Alcazaba of the Alhambra. You may remember that when I described this, I mentioned a path leading down from the Puerta de las Armas. It used to cross the Darro a few yards farther on and on the other side you can still see the spring of a horseshoe arch, the original Puente del Cadí of the eleventh century.

Opposite the broken arch, at No. 37, Carrera de Darro, is the

Bañuelo, one of the best-preserved Arab baths in Spain. The various rooms have been only slightly restored, for they were well preserved by being filled with earth and debris over the centuries, while a house was built above. The most important items are the horseshoe arches of brick, supported by marble columns with a wide variety of capitals, among which can be distinguished two Roman, one Visigothic and a few caliphal examples. In the barrel vaults of the ceiling are the usual octagonal and star-shaped vents, and at one end is the space for the heating arrangements. Behind the baths is the Convento de la Concepción. The plaza in front of it was first the site of the Maristan, whose dedicatory inscription can be seen in the Alhambra Museum, and later of the mint founded by the Catholic Sovereigns.

At the next corner of the Carrera de Darro is the **Casa de Castril**, named after one of the fiefs of the descendants of Hernando de Zafra, whose signature as secretary follows those of his sovereigns in both the public and private versions of the terms of surrender of Granada. It is a corner house with a fine Plateresque front; amid the rather aimless jumble of sculpture is a reproduction of the Tower of Comares, granted to Hernando as an addition to his arms in recognition of his assistance at the drafting of the treaty.

The corner balcony of the upper storey is of a type that is also to be found in Úbeda, in which a slender marble column is substituted for the quoin. Over it, in large Roman letters, is the announcement, *Esperándola del cielo.* A mistranslation is responsible for two versions of one legend. It seems that one of the Zafras discovered a page in the bedroom of his daughter. In vain did the unfortunate young man plead that her outcry had brought him to her help. About to be hanged from the balcony he asked for mercy and was relentlessly told, 'Hope for it in Heaven'. You would have thought that the daughter could have thrown some light on the identity of the would-be ravisher, but apparently she did not. However, the more grammatical explanation is that the youth's penultimate words were, 'I am expecting it from Heaven' and, when asked for an explanation, added, 'the justice that is denied me on earth.'

The mansion was at one time well known, for it housed both the Archaeological and Fine Arts Museums of Granada. The former is to be installed in the Hospital Real while the latter is now in the Palace of Charles V. All that is left inside are pleasant patios, in the second of which are some good carved wooden columns.

C.G.S.S.   Y

A memory of old days clings to the name of the **Church of** **San Juan de los Reyes**. It is reached by the Calle de Zafra, on the left, and was the first church to be dedicated in Granada, on 5th January, 1492, by order of Ferdinand and Isabel. It was originally a thirteenth-century mosque, patronised exclusively by renegade Christians, and the choice of title reminds us of the church of the same name built in Toledo as a mausoleum for the Catholic Sovereigns. Presumably it reflects their gratitude at the prospect of being buried in Granada. The bell tower still incorporates most of the minaret and is reminiscent of the Giralda in its blind arcades, *sebka* work and spiral ramp instead of stairs. Under the convent behind the church was found a section of a Roman road and other remains, including graves, and portions of the fortifications of the Alcazaba also came to light here.

A little higher up the hill to the north is the **Aljibe del Trillo**, a cistern that is famous in a district where old Arab *aljibes* are seen in quantity. The façade is of brick, and the *enjutas* of the horse-shoe arch have modern *azulejos* in place of the antique ones. As well as being of archaeological interest many of the old cisterns still form part of the regular water supply and have been fitted with incongruous brass taps.

If you return to the Darro and continue east you may notice street names such as Horno de Vidrio or del Oro, where the trades of glass making and gold refining were carried on. At the last bridge, where a road leads to the Generalife in the forest above, you turn left up the Cuesta del Chapiz, which roughly marks the limit of the Albaicín. The Peso de la Harina marks the spot where flour was officially weighed in the seventeenth century, and on the right, in an attractive garden, are the Casas del Chapiz. These joined Arab palaces are named after one of their proprietors, a Morisco called Lorenzo el Chapiz, instead of by the old name *Dar Albaida*, the White House; presumably they were the largest buildings in this quarter, Rabad Albaida. They have been carefully restored and are now admirably suited for their present function as a School of Arabic Studies and an extra-mural part of the University of Granada. García Gómez, one of the founders, has described how they brought a wealth of enthusiasm and a dearth of money to the project, how Torres Balbás saved the buildings from ruin, how the gardens were replanted with cypress and myrtle, the pomegranates pruned, the walls whitewashed. The result of all this labour is an important nucleus of Hispano-Arab studies, as well as the more easily appreciated rooms and courtyards in Morisco style.

The road leads on to the Plaza Albaida, where a branch to the right threads its way among the caves to meet the Camino del Sacromonte that turned off at the Casa del Chapiz. At the Plaza Albaida you are in reach of several **Casas Moriscas**, by which is meant the original houses of the Moslems, and not, as the name would have you believe, necessarily converted ones. The road continues as the Calle de San Luis, where No. 27 preserves some remains of its past architecture, with its galleries supported on wooden corbels, fine *alfarje* over passages and one room, and wall paintings of birds and animals interspersed with the more usual decorations, the only examples extant in a private house. Another attractive house is No. 2 Calle de Yanguas, off the Calle San Martín round the corner. There is a small central well with geometric tiles, and two original sides to the courtyard, whose ground-level galleries, known locally as *cenadores*, have their own *aljibe* with a horseshoe arch. There is also a quantity of Oriental decoration, tile work and painting.

The energetic may now take the road to the **Puerta de Fajalauza**, less than half a mile farther, where a tunnel-like gate with ogiavl ceiling, the whole surmounted with battlements, passes through the outer walls to the old potters' quarter. The blue and white Fajalauza ware is still made and seems to have been produced without interruption since the Reconquest, judging by the examples one sees in museums. Some in the Archaeological Museum of Madrid have the double-headed eagle of the Hapsburgs displayed on pieces made long after their day. The outer defences take a large bend to the south from here, and it is these that can be seen from the Alhambra. This stretch of wall is the **Cerca de Don Gonzalo**, named after Gonzalo de Zúñiga, Bishop of Jaén, who is said to have had it built as the price of his ransom. The more likely story is that an earlier bishop, St. Pedro Pascual, had the wall built as the price of *his* ransom, but changed his mind when the time came and chose to purchase the liberty of 300 Christian captives of lesser degree, while he himself died in captivity in 1300. Bishops came expensive in those days.

Returning from the Puerta de Fajalauza, or more directly from the Calle de San Luis if you have omitted it, you reach the **Casa de los Mascarones**, so called from the two grotesque stone faces which decorate the walls. It was the house of a poet of whom we are not likely to hear, though he is mentioned by Gerald Brenan. Pedro Soto de Rojas was simply one of those who followed Góngora, just as dozens of painters emulated Velázquez, Zurbarán and Murillo. He was a canon of the nearby

Church of El Salvador, where he is buried, and his best-known poem is based on the subject of his beautiful garden *Paraiso cerrado para muchos, jardines abiertos para pocos*. Today, the property is the barracks of the Guardia Civil and few would think of it as a paradise closed to many, a garden open to few.

The Calle del Pardo is at the back of the next block, and at No. 32 is another **Casa Morisca**. It is almost complete and must be as much like a pre-Reconquest house as it would be possible to find. There are friezes of geometric tiles, lobulated arches and arabesque stucco work. On the walls of the patio, which has the usual central fountain of the wealthy, are ornaments of wrought iron and tiles of many kinds, including the easily recognisable Fajalauza ware. The entrance arch to each room has the tiny niche in each jamb for incense or flowers, like those in the Alhambra Palaces. The ceilings are particularly fine examples of *alfarje*. Recent excavations have revealed the original system of water-pipes that supplied the house from the Sierra Alfácar, and a tunnel that was probably for escape in the troubled times towards the end of the Nasrid reign, and may have led to the nearby Calle de Minas (*mina* means tunnel).

The **Church of El Salvador** occupies the site of the great mosque of the Albaicín, whose patio it preserves, with its central *aljibe* now sealed but the brick arcades surviving, and with the original double row of pointed arches on two of the sides. There is nothing to see inside the church, which was damaged by an earthquake and burned out in the troubles of 1936. The only interest attached to it is the recollection that it was once one of the two churches of Granada with the right of asylum.

The Calle de Panaderos leads to the Plaza Larga, in which you will find the **Puerta Nueva**, with the usual horseshoe arch and an angled passage for defence. To the west run the remains of the massive walls of the Alcazaba, built in the thirteenth century on the foundations of older ones, and so dating to Roman days, when this ridge formed the northern boundary of Iliberis. The Puerta Nueva is also called Puerta de las Pesas, because the country folk used to bring their produce here, and one of the market master's duties was to see that the weights used were correct, and not adjusted to fleece the innocent farmer. Defective weights were nailed above the gate—some are still there—and presumably the merchant was lucky if his hand was not put on show too. The market master was a high official and in caliphate Córdoba had at one time been given power of mutilation or execution on the cross, without appeal to higher authority. Al-

Khushani cites the case of a man unjustly executed by the Sahib Al-suk, or in the nearest Spanish, *zabazoque*.

Once inside the gate, you climb some steps and turn sharp left into the Callejón de San Cecilio. The whitewashed oratory of this martyr is among the houses on the left side of the street. Its construction in a massive piece of masonry makes one suspect that here are the remains of a very old gate called the Hizna Román, the Roman fort, though some say the name was only a corruption of Hernan Román, owner of an adjacent orchard. At the end of the street is the broad plaza of the Church of San Nicolás. The building itself is a recent one, for its sixteenth-century predecessor was burnt down in the disturbances of 1932, but the digression is worth while, to see both the large *aljibe*, and particularly the magnificent view from the terrace to the south. From it one can enjoy a panorama that is bounded to the right by the *vega* beyond the city, includes the Alhambra and Generalife spread out in front, and finishes on the left with the snows of the Sierra Nevada.

At the bottom of the street, which winds down between typical *carmines*, is the Cuesta de María de la Miel. It practically traces the eastern line of the Roman settlement's forum and basilica, which occupied the area bounded by the walls, from the Puerta Nueva as far west as the Church of San Miguel. Excavation in the eighteenth century was prejudiced by the 'planting' of spurious Roman remains, so that even the genuine finds were discredited. The tunnels made by explorers were responsible for the name of the Placeta de las Minas, which is our next objective. The street of María de la Miel is related to the *aljibe* whose water was so sweet and clear that the Arabs called it the 'honey well', translated literally by the Christian conquerors. Near by are the remains of an aqueduct, originally put up in the reign of the last Zirid king, bringing the water of Alfácar to the western part of the Alcazaba. It has been identified by some with the Ain Al-adamar, the Fountain of Tears, of the Arabs.

We turn right along the Cuesta de María de la Miel until we reach the Placeta de las Minas, just inside the Puerta Nueva, whence a street to the left leads westwards along the inside of the walls of the Alcazaba. Random exploration here is rewarding; one path leads along a mule track through what may once have been a postern in the great mass of masonry; another to a corner where No. 15 Carmen del Aljibe del Rey is actually an orchard built on top of the battlements, from which you have a magnificent view of the whole stretch of wall. Still farther to the west, the Callejón del Ladrón del Agua—the Street of the Water Thief conjures up a vision of strange crimes—passes the **Daralhorra Palace**, another residence of Boabdil's mother who was also called La Horra, the Chaste. It is a part of the Convent of Santa Isabel la Real, which will be described from its other side, and contains much of the original construction of the fifteenth century. Note especially the decorative arches that open between the rooms, and the painted wooden ceilings, particularly those of the patio arcades.

This is the heart of the oldest part of Granada, for the palace is built over the foundations of the great castle of Badis, the Zirid king, which remained the only fortified residence in Granada until Mohamed Ibn Alahmar began building on the Alhambra two centuries later. The whole of this area has the air of aristocratic calm that one associates with the surroundings of a royal palace, heightened by the secrecy of high walls and the view of tree-tops above them.

If we follow the walls westward, we soon come to the Puerta Monaita, a corrupt rendering of Bibabonaidar, the Gate of the Threshing Floor. Hence its other name, Puerta de la Era (from the Latin *area*, a threshing floor) is still used, and in Ford's day the district was called *las eras de Cristo*, the holy name being also given to an adjacent tavern. The gate is worth studying, for the small guard-room which it contains is the first of which we know in Spain of the type that uses a right-angled turn for defence. We make our way back to the Callejón del Gallo, where one of the surviving towers of the Alcázar of Badis remained until Christian times, when it received the name La Casa del Gallo. The cock in question was a weathervane in the shape of a bronze Moor on horseback, with lance and shield, and an Arabic rhymed inscription, translated into Spanish as:

> *Dijo Badis Aben Habus,*
> *Así ha de ser el guardián del Andalus .*

The version of the story given by Washington Irving states that old King Badis, harassed by the fear of invasions from every quarter, took advice from an Arabian astrologer. The latter told him of a weathervane he had seen in Egypt, which was composed of a bronze ram and cock; on the approach of an enemy the cock would crow to give warning of the danger, and the ram would turn to indicate its direction. Alas, the old king and the older magician fell out over a woman; the magician won, for he caused the earth to open and disappeared into the ground along with the girl, where he had previously built a magic tower. On this were the talismans of a hand and a key—need I add that the whole legend is an economical way of explaining both the weather-vane of Badis, 'the guardian of Al-Andalus', and the Torre de la Justicia of the Alhambra? Badis was of course, a historic character, even if the astrologer was imaginary, and grandfather of the last of the Zirids, Boloquin, whose quarrel with the Jews of Lucena has already been noted.

We emerge in the pretty Plaza de San Miguel where, as usual in the South of Spain, the maximum dramatic effect is extracted from a crucifix and some street-lamps. On the east side there is a walled-up *aljibe* with horseshoe arch, actually forming a part of the Church wall. The building itself is permanently closed and contains nothing of interest, unless, that is, you count the site of Bocanegra's baptism. So far as we know, the southern boundary of the Roman forum passed through this square and there are traces of the earlier Moslem castle.

Behind the church, on the left of the street, running west, is the **Convento de Santa Isabel la Real**. Even the story of its founda-tion is interesting, for the Catholic Queen had issued a decree that it should be established on the Alhambra. Difficulties arose and made this impossible, so Queen Isabel ordered its transfer to the present site, an old palace of the Moslem kings of Granada. This had already been promised to Secretary Hernando de Zafra, so he had to be compensated with another mansion, the one on the bank of the Darro, with *Esperándola del cielo* painted over the balcony. The back of the Convent incorporates the Daralhorra Palace.

The convent church is approached through a quiet, cobbled courtyard shaded by cassias and black poplars. Its doorway is one of the finest Isabelline examples we shall see, reminiscent in many ways of San Jacinto in Córdoba; the insignia of yoke and arrows are carved in relief in the *enjutas* to great advantage. The nave has a remarkably attractive Mudéjar *artesonado* and the chapel of the high altar has a rather later, but equally attractive ceiling with pendants recalling the Decorated style of English Gothic. The large chapel on the left has an inscription of 1628, announcing that it is reserved as a sepulchre to Pedro de la Calle, *beinte y cuatro desta ciudad* and his heirs; the quaint title 'twenty-four of this city' refers to the office of chief of the city council.

The large building across the road was part of the inheritance which Pedro de la Calle left to his son José. He, in turn, founded a hospital for ringworm sufferers (*Hospital de la Tiña*) in what had once been an Arab royal palace and is now the **Orfelinato de Nuestra Señora del Pilar**. It was here that Boabdil, whose reign was a succession of troubles at home and abroad, was for the second time accepted as king when he came to the Alcazaba for refuge from his father Muley Hassan. In the civil war between father and son, which did so much to hasten the end of the Moslem kingdom, the Albaicín and the Alcazaba next to it were strong partisans of *El Rey Chico* (Boabdil). There are traces of the building's aristocratic past in one of its halls, where some stucco ornament and a dado of old *azulejos* remains; with the Alhambra only a few minutes away it is hardly worth the trouble of examining them. But a Latin injunction over the door recalls the time when the palace that had sheltered royalty redeemed itself; it commands those who enter to care for the sick and poor and not to be disgusted at *scabiosi* or *leprosi*. You should enter the patio, built up from the salvage of the Arab palace, and see the orphans playing among the marble columns with their Nasrid capitals. Diseases come and go but orphans remain, and in few western countries do Church and State combine so dutifully in the care of these children, with almost Oriental diligence.

The **Church of San José** was consecrated on the 7th January, 1492, and therefore without any waste of time. It had been the mosque of the *marabouts*, that strange sect of fighting hermits that many believe to have been the forerunners of the Templars and other combatant religious orders. The lower part of the minaret is all that is left of the ninth-century building, and is claimed to be the only one surviving from before the Almoravid invasion of the eleventh century. Córdoba, with its Alminar de San Juan, will vigorously contest this assertion. The minaret is worth climbing to see the horseshoe arch in the south wall, from which the muezzin may have called the faithful to prayer. There is an *aljibe* at its foot, no doubt a part of the water supply for ritual ablution. The mudéjar ceiling over the high altar, an octagonal dome of gilt *alfarje*, is one of the treasures of the church, the other being a Crucifixion by José de Mora, considered the best in the whole of Andalucía—a bold statement in view of the number of competitors.

From here you can descend either south or westward, to the Plaza Nueva or Gran Via de Colón respectively. The road is winding, along streets that zigzag round the slope on which the Alcazaba was built. Along one you skirt the abandoned Church of San Gregorio Bético and cross the Calderería Vieja, where the cauldron makers used to work. Other street names mention an old and a new prison; another is the Street of the Negroes; were these the Sultan's African bodyguard? Certainly the adjoining Calle del Zenete refers to the quarters of a Berber tribe who provided the palace guard for King Badis. From these the title eventually passed to the marquisate bestowed on one of the Mendozas.

CHAPTER NINETEEN

Granada to Alicante

El Puerto del Suspiro—Almuñécar—Salobreña—Motril—Almería —Níjar—Mojácar—Cartagena—Alicante—La Santa Faz—Villajoyosa—Benidorm—Villena—Alcoy

The coastal route which we shall take has many scenic surprises but, it must be confessed, less than usual of historic or artistic interest. It enables us to complete the Costa del Sol to just beyond Almería and then to continue along the Costa Blanca. Holiday resorts are springing up everywhere and, regardless of the quality of bathing, can practically guarantee fine weather for at least six months in the year. As the number of visitors is increasing every year, it is impossible to discuss hotel and other amenities, but the number of camping sites marked on travel folders is in direct ratio to the quality of the beaches. The countryside becomes more and more desolate between the irrigated river valleys and, as you go eastward to Almería and beyond, vaguely familiar. The reason is that it is in great demand for cinema films that need a desert background. But the journey is a fascinating one and a very fair imitation of the North African coast; it finishes at a delightful town, beloved by the sophisticated holiday maker.

We leave Granada by N323, which climbs over the western shoulder of the Sierra Nevada to make its way to the coast. *At 15 kilometres we reach the **Puerto del Suspiro**, also known as 'The Moor's Last Sigh', *el ultimo suspiro del Moro*. The road has followed the footsteps of Boabdil from the Ermita de San Sebastián, where he handed over the keys of Granada, and here he and his companions are said to have turned for their last look at the city they loved so well. So overwrought were they that all the men burst into tears. The oft-repeated story, at least in the more reliable version, tells us that Aisha said, 'It is right that the King and his knights should weep like women, since they did not fight like soldiers.'

Y mirando colérico a Granada,
huyo vencida, pero no domada.

* See map on p. 260.

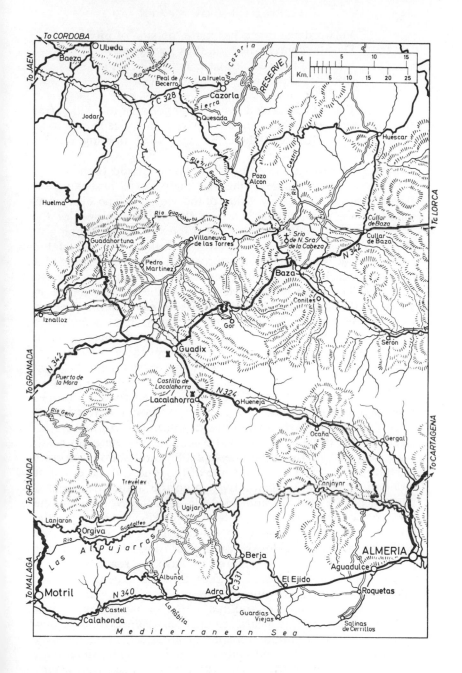

Forward she urged her mare, no sign of pity
Did she concede her son thus shamed;
Her scornful gaze she cast upon the city,
Conquered perhaps, but never tamed.

We know that Boabdil ruled his little kingdom of the Alpujarras for a few years and then, cheated of part of the price he was to be paid, left for Morocco where he later died fighting for his Moslem friends.

If you want to see the Alpujarras, where Gerald Brenan lived for years, you continue along the main road, branching off beyond Durcal, the Happy Valley of the Moslems. The Alpujarras comprise the mountainous area on the southern slopes of the Sierra Nevada, primitive and of great interest to the ethnologist. Brenan's *South from Granada* gives a faithful account of life there. Órgiva is an important source of iron and the ore is sent to Motril, whence it goes by coaster to Bilbao and from there to England. The countryside is fertile and the climate alpine in parts, so that almonds blossom as late as April, while pigs are fattened on acorns and chestnuts and their ham is cured in snow chambers up the mountain. Unfortunately there is not a single item of cultural interest, if you except the generous wine, the *vino de la costa*, which grows in the narrow zone between snow and the tropic coast. A final word to those who propose doing the round trip over the Sierra, the highest road in Europe; it is open only from July to September, and even then it is wise to confirm that it is passable on the day of the expedition.

The most attractive route to the coast leaves the main road, branching to the right at the Puerto del Suspiro, and then crosses the Sierra del Águila through some of the loneliest and grandest mountain country in Spain. Even here the authorities keep a benevolent eye on you, and roadside signs tell you where the best scenic photographs can be taken. Passing through the Cazula Estate it is possible to catch a glimpse of the *Capra hispanica*, which is jealously preserved; possible, though not probable, unless you are prepared to leave the road. Suddenly, as you round the hundredth bend, with pines soaring on either side and asphodels growing on the grassy banks, you see the Mediterranean below you, and in a matter of minutes find yourself among the prickly pears, citrus, date palms, loquats and sugar-cane. Then the poor remains of an aqueduct accompany the road for a few yards and quite suddenly you are in **Almuñécar**. This is the epitome of Mediterranean fishing villages, with whitewashed houses climbing the cliff, good hotels, a nearby estate, the Punta de la Mona, with its magnificent gardens, and several beaches. Some will consider the Hotel Sexi a misnomer, until they learn that this was the Phoenician name for Almuñécar; others, who have been looking forward to fine sand, will feel that the Gritti Palace should be here rather than in Venice. But apart from these disappointments, the holidaymaker will enjoy this town at least as much as the more publicised resorts on the western Costa del Sol.

Almuñécar occupies an important place in Spanish history, for it was here that in 755 Abderrahman was welcomed by Omayyad supporters and the Yemenite Arabs, whom they had been shrewd enough to enlist on their side. Thus was the emirate of Córdoba founded and one of the great cultural advances in the history of Europe inaugurated. The town stands at the edge of the fertile river valley and a promontory reaches out to sea. On the first of its humps squats the castle, with a round tower at each corner, except for the one that has been removed to make the entrance to the cemetery—the castle's present function.

Going east along N340, which we left after visiting Nerja, we come to **Salobreña** after 15 kilometres. Once just another fishing village with the usual Arab castle, the inhabitants, like those in so many other coastal villages, have become fishers of men and tourists come every year, attracted by the picturesque huddle of houses climbing the hill to the castle, and separated from the sea by about half a mile of cultivated land.

The next town is **Motril**, important for its sugar factories and the port, which lies some distance along a branch road. It is not one of the more picturesque places and the sea-front is not recommended as it consists of a stony beach backed by a shanty town. Its function is that of a collecting post for iron ore and the sugar cane grown along the coast and in the irrigated hinterland, and brought in by picturesque mule and donkey trains.

For over 60 kilometres the road follows every curve of the coast, with perpetually changing views of bay and headland, the latter typically crowned with their old *atalayas*. The first can be seen at Torrenueva which, like so many other unspectacular villages, has a *playa*. You will find other beaches at Calahonda, where a line of boarding houses and apartment blocks has already sprung up, and at Castell de Ferro, which differs from the others only by having the remains of a castle on the hill. At **La Rábita** we find something different at last. The beach is no better than the others, but the village itself, with its tiny, flat-topped houses haphazardly arranged, is typically North African, and the fishing industry spreads itself quite unselfconsciously along the water-front.

Shortly after Adra, from which Boabdil sailed into exile, C331 leads to Berja, a small town which may be regarded as the southern entrance to the Alpujarras and retains many of the primitive customs for which this region is noted. Its fertility and its delightful situation prompted the Arabic verse, quoted by J. B. Trend:

> He who comes to Berja,
> On the road to Almería,
> Has no remedy but to stop there
> And give up the journey.
> For the houses and gardens
> Are so many paradises;
> But the roads that lead to them
> Are so many hells.

The coast road leaves the sea to cut across the base of an uninteresting bulge of land, studded with salt-pans. Passing El Ejido you see the landscape change to the light, sandy earth that you will find throughout the remainder of Southern Spain, studded with sparse scrub, thickets of prickly pear and cane brakes where the river valleys permit cultivation. You find the sea again at Aguadulce and after another 11 kilometres enter Almería through the picturesque fishing quarter of La Chanca, named after the nets still used in tunny-fishing, possibly the Arabic *shabka*. Cave-dwellings are interspersed among the little shacks and the limewash varies capriciously among the pastel shades.

The history of **Almería** loses itself in the mists of antiquity. Archaeologists have established the existence of a typical neolithic culture, which seems to have spread northward beyond the Pyrenees and eventually to Britain. So much has been found in the way of artefacts that we know more about Stone and Bronze Age Almerians than we do about their successors for a thousand years. There is evidence of direct contact with North Africa and the Near East in the discovery of hippopotamus ivory and ostrich egg shells, and in the change from primitive trench-graves to corbelled tombs with passages, equivalent to those we saw at Antequera.

After the Carthaginians came the Romans, for whom Almería was *portus magnus*, the main harbour for trade with Italy and the East. Under the Visigoths it lost importance and only gained it again under the Moslems by a fortunate accident. The important town in Omayyad times was Pechina, 10 kilometres up the river, and in the ninth century Almería was represented by a watch tower and a small settlement. In 955 Abderrahman III raised its status to that of a town, naming it 'The Watch Tower', *Al-Mariyya*. It sat astride the road that led from Pechina to the sea and which entered the new town by the Gate of Pechina, *Bab Bashana*. Today the central square of Almería is called Puerta de Purchena, named, they will tell you, after a town forty miles to the north, but you now know better.

The area became a maritime republic with colonies in North Africa, the joint enterprise of Berbers and Yemenite Arabs. In Pechina one of the town gates—here is an odd piece of information—had to be decorated with a statue of the Virgin, in imitation of the Puerta del Puente in Córdoba where the same totem had been inherited from the Visigoths. Though it has been suggested that this un-Islamic addition argues the presence of Christians among the men of Pechina, I prefer to think of them as a crowd of snobs imitating the ways of the metropolis. Almería was taken from the Moslems in 1488, and in 1522 a disastrous earthquake finally ruined it.

Travellers tell of the former prosperity of Almería, derived chiefly from its home-produced silks and imported textiles. It was through this port that Europe acquired words that are now in daily use, *iskalaton* (scarlet), *attabi* (a striped taffeta made in a quarter of Baghdad so named, hence our 'tabby' cat), and 'buckram' from Bokhara. Clothes made in Almería were highly thought of. The *aljofar* work, ornamentation of garments with seed pearls, was another speciality and, with the inevitable arrogance induced by prosperity, the inhabitants used to boast,

> *Cuando Almería era Almería*
> *Granada era su alquería.*

When Almería was Almería, Granada was merely its farm.

You will thus realise, as you walk through Almería, that its past has more importance than its present and that, with the exception of the much-restored Alcazaba, very little remains of the former. The fortress-palace must be one of the largest in Spain and, because of its recent restoration, one of the most complete and therefore best adapted to the cinema. There are extensive gardens and easy access to the battlements with their pyramidal merlons, from which you see a rich variety of scenery lying at your feet.

To the north and west are the rolling, scrubby, tawny hills that give the area a deceptively barren appearance, deceptive because the fertility of the irrigated valleys out of sight more than makes up for the barren uplands. To the south, you overlook the port and the deep blue of the Mediterranean, a colour that never ceases to astonish. The city lies on the east, and a double curtain wall of *hormigón*, the rough concrete of the Arabs, plunges into the terraced valley and up the slope of San Cristóbal, the Arab *Laham*, where it is lost to sight. With its nine square towers set against the hill slope it gives as good an idea of an Arab city wall as you are likely to get. For the film producer it is as well to add that an expert can date the landscape by the pyramidal battlements, which are Almohad, and the prickly pear, which is sixteenth century at the earliest. Turn and look inside the castle grounds, a park in miniature with palms rising above the oleanders and hibiscus; this is the perfect setting for the annual summer festivals of music and art. On the debit side, the old mosque at the top scarcely shows a trace of its former function, and has now been converted into the Chapel of San Juan, with Gothic overtones.

The Cathedral, of the usual Gothic plan with Renaissance trimmings, occupies the site of the chief mosque, which was taken over within a short time of the capture of Almería in 1488. When Münzer visited it, in 1494, there had recently been an earthquake, but nevertheless the former mosque still had its 800 columns; it finally fell to ruin in another, greater earthquake of 1522, after which the present building was begun. Münzer showed special interest in Moslem practices, and in the Province of Granada, where respect for the religion of the conquered still persisted two years after their defeat, he tells how the muezzin, calling the faithful to prayer, would insert his right forefinger in his right ear. This practice, which is permissible but not obligatory, is mentioned in the *Sunna*, one of the commentaries on the Koran. It also lays down that the muezzin must go around the minaret in a clockwise direction, relic of a prehistoric superstition that survives in the drinking of port wine.

The Cathedral is said to have been built like a fortress in order to provide a refuge during pirate raids. The plans were drawn by Diego de Siloé, as were those of Granada Cathedral, but here we lack the genius of Alonso Cano in the façade. The portal is Renaissance with Corinthian and Ionic columns, and is flanked by buttresses. There are corner turrets and a high tower that might, and probably did, serve as a look-out against the threat

Above, semi-desert near Vélez Rubio – typical of large areas east of Granada. *Below*, countryside near Ecija, between Córdoba and Seville, one of the most fertile regions of Spain.

Rock dwellings.   *Above*, houses built into an overhanging cliff at Setenil, near Ronda.   *Below*, cave dwellings in the barrio de Santiago, Guadix.

of corsairs. Cannons are said to have been placed high up to combat the same menace. Inside, the Cathedral has some fine, alabaster carvings by Alonso Cano on the high altar, and more on the altar of the second chapel on the right. Like other places that are off the regular tourist route, its inhabitants try to make the most of what they have; in this case, of eight dingy canvases high up in the sanctuary, variously ascribed to Ribera and Murillo. The choir stalls of carved walnut are by Juan de Orea and not, in my opinion, as good as those he made for the Convento de la Santa Cruz and now in the Alhambra Museum of Fine Arts.

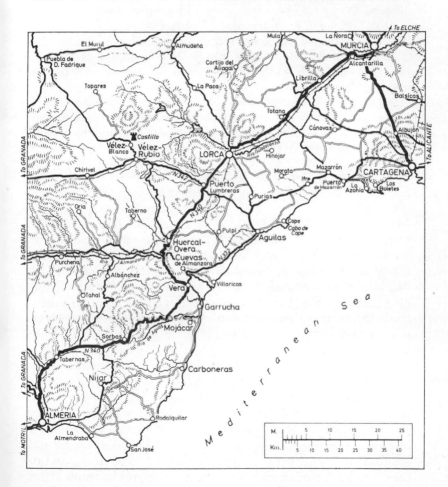

A change from N340 may be had by taking a secondary road due east, to **Níjar**, a typical Andalucian town on a hill. At the foot is a fountain with 12 spouts, where the surrender of the town to the emissary of the Catholic Sovereigns, Garcilaso de la Vega, is said to have taken place. Níjar is famous for its pottery and lies at the southern edge of a zone whose clay is particularly well suited to this craft; we shall pass pottery displays along almost the whole length of our road back from Alicante to Granada. The decoration of the pottery here is individual, the usual patterns being tiger stripes and splashes, with the colours allowed to run. These are brown and yellow, made from iron oxides, and green from copper, all obtainable locally. The blue has to be imported, by some from as far as Germany, and is also a mineral colour, being made of a ground stone, the same technique, in fact, that was originally used by mediaeval artists in making ultramarine from powdered lapis lazuli.

An earth road now takes us back to the coast at Carboneras, and as we go north, the shingly beaches gradually give way to sand, while flat-roofed cottages with small square windows dot the arid landscape. At **Mojácar**, which is $2\frac{1}{2}$ kilometres inland, the same cottages were piled up the hillside, a cubist's dream. I say 'were' advisedly, for today Mojácar has become a tourist haunt and the population is cashing in on the craze by pulling down all the picturesque streets and building pensions. It is said of Mojácar, as it was of Véjer de la Frontera, that the women wore veils within living memory; they are probably referring to a very old man with a very long memory. It is most unlikely that it represented the customs retained by descendants of the Moriscos for over three centuries; as elsewhere, it was probably an attempt by the dark-skinned peasantry to acquire an aristocratic pallor. It is significant that in every part where women are said to have retained the yashmak, the men wear the *calañés*, in this region made of palm leaves.

The road continues along the coast as far as the uninteresting town of Garrucha, where it turns inland to Vera. It now forks and we take the right branch (N332) to Cuevas de Almanzora, one of Spain's richest areas for prehistoric research. Crossing from Andalucía to Murcia and regaining the coast at Águilas, a picturesque harbour, we follow N332 to **Cartagena**. Its natural advantages as a sheltered port made this the chief stronghold of the Carthaginians, from whom it of course derives its name. It has had an eventful history; Scipio Africanus captured it in the

Second Punic War, and earned a reputation for generosity by freeing a Carthaginian captive damsel who was betrothed to a native Spaniard, giving her the ransom as her dowry. Judging by accounts of the riches that were found in the city he could well afford to purchase the good will of the Iberians. It became a bishopric under the Visigoths and was the home of the four saintly sibs of whom Isidore was the youngest. It is not, however, true that he was born in Cartagena, but rather in Seville. The family had moved there when the coastal strip was sold or given to the Byzantines who, under Belisarius, had wiped out the Vandals of North Africa and were on their way to defeat the Ostrogoths in Italy. The only remarkable legend attached to those times was that a swarm of bees was seen issuing out of baby Isidore's mouth, an omen of his future powers of oratory. But now that we know he was never in Cartagena as a child it is quite possible that the bee story is exaggerated.

From Roman times the city has been the main centre for the export of *spartum*, esparto grass, and in the little archaeological museum one may see woven esparto of those days. When the Moslems came they adapted the old name *spartaria* for the Cartagena district to *Kartachannat al-halfa*, i.e. Cartagena alfalfa, which was the name of esparto grass before it became applied to lucerne. The city's further adventures include a raid by Drake, during which the harbour's guns were carried off, an attempt at autonomy by Communists in 1873—note again how seaports tend to be anti-conservative in Spain—and the embarcation of Alfonso XIII for exile in 1931. As everywhere along this coast one eats well, and Cartagena has a reputation which it has sustained since the days of the Roman *garum* paste of mackerel. Today's best-known dish is also for the masses, *molcones blancos*, a delicious sausage.

It is best to get one's bearings by first climbing to the Parque de las Torres, a pretty and well cared-for garden in which rises the Castillo de la Concepción. It is said to be the successor of Carthaginian, Roman and Arab fortresses, and a bust of Hasdrubal commemorates the alleged founder of the first. Roman inscriptions found here support the second claim. We look out over an almost completely landlocked harbour, ideal for its role as one of Spain's chief naval bases. It is also a busy mercantile port and the rich lead ores of the interior are shipped here for export, along with manufactured goods and, of course, esparto grass. So old is this trade that we are told of its use in making the ropes that moored the barges when Xerxes crossed the Hellespont. In Herodotus' account, however, only flax and papyrus are mentioned.

Charles V's admiral, Andrea Doria the Genoese, said he knew of only three safe anchorages in the Mediterranean, June, July and Cartagena, and we can well believe him when we survey the port. It is a pity that Charles didn't believe it, for he launched his attack on Algiers in October 1541 and lost most of his fleet.

Near the foot of the Castillo is the ruined Church of Santa María la Vieja, possibly the only one in Southern Spain to have a Romanesque portal (even this is in an *alfiz*) and corbel table. Time and the Civil War have done their worst and there is little left of what is said to have been the first basilica in Spain. There are one or two Roman columns, a Byzantine one and the well which St. Isidore used to point a moral. Observing the grooves that the ropes had cut into the marble well-head in the course of years, he moralised on the advantages of perseverance; his lesson was at least successful enough for it to be quoted here, fourteen hundred years later. It is quite possible, by the way, that St. Isidore *was* in Cartagena at some point, for his support of the Orthodox against the King's Arian creed led to his exile from Seville from 580 to 585. Santa María de Gracia is not far away; it is of the late eighteenth century and its attraction is the group of four statues, the Saints Leander, Fulgentius, Florentina and Isidore, carved and painted by Salzillo of Murcia.

At the north-west end of the town is the little Archaeological Museum, with odd relics of the various civilisations that flourished here and, as something unique, an exhibition of Roman mining equipment. On the west of the main quay, near the yacht club, is the memorial to the seamen who lost their lives at Cavite, in the Philippines, during the Spanish–American war of 1898. There is also an early submarine here, suitably displayed and claimed to be the first ever invented, by the New Carthaginian, Isaac Peral , in 1887. According to standard authorities he was about ten years too late to be given priority. That, apart from the plinth of a Roman monument, the Torre Ciega, a little way out of town, completes the attractions of Cartagena.

We are now at a part of the Mediterranean coast whose equable temperature, dry climate and excellent beaches make it a target for the investor. Grandiose plans are made, and have in some cases been carried out, for building private cottages, chalets and apartment blocks; the latter are inevitable and can be found disfiguring any bay which has the prospect of becoming a holiday resort. Mazarrón and its port are on the fringe of one of these development areas; north of Cartagena there is another and more ambitious one. The Mar Menor is a lagoon separated from the open sea by a strip of dun-coloured land, La Manga, on which hotels and private residences are being built at great speed; the inhabitants can then choose whether their day will be spent on the shore of the Mediterranean, or that of the lagoon. The towns of Murcia, Alicante, Orihuela and Elche are all within 100 kilometres, the first at less than half that distance. N332 takes us north, in sight of the sea for nearly the whole 100 kilometres of our next stage.

Alicante is a seaside town and seaport of great beauty, though

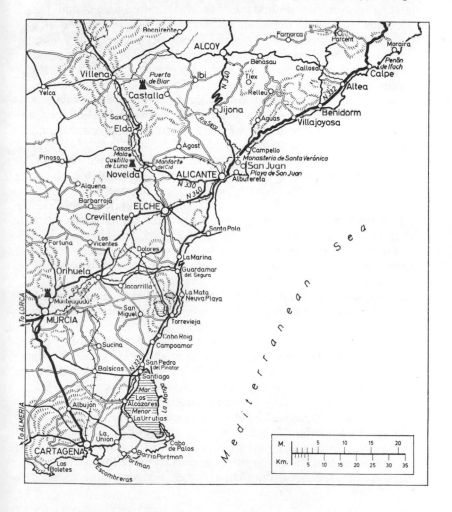

situated in the unpromising surroundings of tawny earth and
bare hills; these last ensure an equable winter climate, but some
find the summer heat occasionally oppressive. Augustus Hare
loathed the place, in spite of the hospitality of the English
colony, and described it as 'miserably abject and squalid'. No
one would agree with him today, and the Spaniard describes this
sparkling, clean town as *preciosa*. For centuries it exported the
strong wine named after it, and which was highly thought of for
its medicinal properties. Louis XIV took it in doses of 10 drops
during his last illness but the effect was disappointing, for it did
nothing to arrest the gangrene that killed him. Seventy years
later, however, its reputation was still undiminished and the
Marquis de Langle deplored the fact that '. . . a hundred sick
people die for lack of a spoonful of wine of Alicante.'

The holiday maker's Alicante centres on the magnificent
Esplanade, with its four rows of date palms, some of them with
multiple trunks, and its broad walk of tricolour mosaic paving,
laid in waves so that with a little concentration you can imagine
yourself walking on a corrugated path between bushes, canes
and creepers. The palm trees extend in both directions, beyond
the limits of the ornamental paving, to the west past the yacht
club, and to the east, after running along the inner harbour,
beyond the entrance to the mole, whence passengers embark for
the Balearic Islands, North Africa, the Canaries and South
America. Here is the first of the excellent bathing beaches of this
coast, with fine, golden sand, no dangerous sudden slope from
shallow to deep water, and plenty of room, even on Sundays
when the crowds gather at the nearest point. Those who are
spending more than a few days here would be well advised to
buy a light deck-chair or inflatable mattress; the chairs that you
can hire are small, made of wooden slats, and have straight backs.
They are fine for the hardy Spaniard, who has yet to learn the
art of lounging, but hardly the thing for the English.

From the centre of the Esplanade runs the broad and busy
Rambla de Méndez Núñez, a convenient shopping street. On its
right, that is to the east, the Calle Mayor leads to the Co-
Cathedral of San Nicolás of Bari, a solidly built edifice of the
seventeenth century, rebuilt since its destruction in 1936. A little
farther is the Church of Santa María de la Asunción, with an
attractive façade but little else to remind one of its past history.
It was practically destroyed by a fire in 1484 and the miracle in
this case was that the corporals were burned while the sacraments
they enwrapped were untouched. When we get to the tobacco

factory we shall have the opportunity of comparing the relative potency of their respective tutelars. The miracle is commemorated on a plaque at the end of the left aisle, near the entrance to the sacristy, where there is also a wheel of bells. From here it is a few yards to the Plateresque Ayuntamiento, a particularly fine example of this style. There is an interesting chapel upstairs, with some original floor tiles and modern paintings. On the staircase hangs a marble plaque with red letters, a copy of the original town charter given by Ferdinand the Catholic in 1490. Note that it begins, *en el nombre de Dios*, the exact translation of the usual Arabic introduction, *Bismillah*, 'in the Name of God'. The city crest has the rebus $^{AL}_{LA}$, the first line standing for *Acra leuka*, white headland, the Greek name, and the second for *Lucentum*, the Latin name, and Alicante. Thus *Costa blanca* is an old Greek name for this coast, and not an advertising slogan.

On the north side of the Ayuntamiento is the quiet Plaza de Santa Faz, where you can have a good outdoor luncheon at the Mesón de Sancho Panza. Farther north you pass through a region of squalid back streets and soon emerge in the higher, picturesque Barrio de Santa Cruz, where once more whitewash, grilles and flower-pots have taken over. At 21 Calle de Toledo is the Museo de Cerámica Levantina, a private collection made by Don Ramón Quiles. The ceramics range from Greek and Roman amphorae, *azulejos* of ever. style and period, bleeding and shaving bowls, to clay teapots like those still used in North Africa. Among the many other exhibits that make this a museum of folklore, and one that is not to be missed, is a spinning-wheel of the type still used in Morocco. When you leave, going east, the analogy is maintained by the blue outlines of doors and windows and by the door knockers in the shape of hands, all North African talismans against the Evil Eye.

The Fábrica de Tabacos used to be one of the sights of Alicante and is still opened to the public on one day a year, the 20th May, when a religious service is held. This is the anniversary of a fire which raged through the factory when, thanks to the invocation of the Santa Faz (which we shall see) no one was injured. There is a curious air of secrecy about the factory, which was inspected by Richard Ford, among others, over a century ago. Access is today impossible and one has memories of another factory, where the best customer arrived without warning and asked to be taken through it. Arriving at the blending room he stared with interest at the conveyor belt, on which alternate spadefuls of tobacco and horse manure were being heaped. Later, when the management was resigned to the loss of their most valuable order, the visitor said that he would double it. Astonishment, shock, relief; then, when the contract was signed, 'But didn't you see what was going on in the blending room?' 'Oh yes, that's why I've doubled my order. I had thought that it was all horse manure.'

The Diputación, the Chamber of Deputies, is at the other end of the town, in the Avenida General Mola, and houses a good Archaeological Museum. Thanks to the foresight of a committee of experts, the exhibits are arranged in chronological order, so that one can follow the development of man and his arts from paleolithic to modern days. Among the relics of the Stone Age, along with the earliest pottery and bracelets made of bone, are skulls whose molar teeth are ground flat in the same way as those of primitive tribes today who live on coarse cereals. There are Iberian stone bulls, Carthaginian figurines, most of them of the goddess Tanit, Greek and Roman lamps and vessels, sepulchres and millstones, with special exhibits of the complete finds in Carthaginian, Greek and Roman towns that have been excavated in this province. An interesting case of adaptation is seen among the Arabic pottery, some of the vases being painted with manganese in imitation of the indigenous Iberian method. You will remember that the same black pigment was used much later in the manufacture of *Cuerda seca* tiles.

Before leaving Alicante we have to see the Castle of Santa Bárbara, which hangs over the town on a bare brown rock. The name is said to have been given to it because of its occupation by the Christians on the saint's day, 4th December, but it is more likely that she was made guardian of the castle, a tower being her attribute. A number of saints are venerated here; St. Mary of the Assumption, because the wife of Alfonso X was devoted to that mystery, now dogma; St. Nicholas of Bari, possibly because he is patron of sailors; St. Veronica, whose miraculous kerchief we shall see; and finally St. John, whose feast day is celebrated with particular enthusiasm here, as throughout Europe, as it is the pagan midsummer festival when bonfires are lighted and effigies burned.

The Castle of Santa Bárbara may nowadays be visited in great comfort by a lift whose entrance is in the rock face immediately behind the beach. It is a huge work, patched up after the damage sustained at various times, and has monuments to such heroes as Hamilcar Barca and Nicolas Peris, the Castilian seneschal, who died with sword in one hand and keys in the other. He was fighting against the King of Aragón, for we are now in the kingdom of Valencia and therefore between two spheres of influence. You may hire a guide to take you round, and see dungeons, cannon in their embrasures, sick bays, powder magazines and stores. The latter are possibly the most interesting, for one of the doors has a faded announcement, *Repuesto ingles*. As British troops were quartered here both during the War of the Spanish Succession, when they were allowed to march out with the honours of war, and during the Peninsular War, when they helped to keep the French out of Alicante, we cannot say when the food-store was actually in use. Local belief supports the first occasion.

Leaving Alicante on N332 you follow the coast as far as Calpe, our farthest objective. The road passes through bare, rocky, unpleasant country and man seems to have done his best to assist nature's ugliness with crops of roadside advertisements. After 5 kilometres is the village of Santa Faz, where a blue-tiled dome and two towers with bartisan turrets can be glimpsed among the palms. A left fork takes you to the Baroque Convent of Santa Verónica, in which the **Santa Faz** is preserved. The Holy Face is one of the impressions left on St. Veronica's kerchief when she wiped the Saviour's face in the Via Dolorosa. In order to account for the other two examples it is ingeniously maintained that the kerchief was folded into three. The miraculous kerchiefs are now housed at St. Peter's, Rome, the Cathedral of Jaén and here. The Holy Face in the Cathedral of Lucca, which provided William Rufus with his favourite oath, *Per vultum de Lucca* is said to be a *postmortem* portrait begun by Nicodemus and finished by miraculous helpers. The story of Veronica is a late arrival in hagiology and is not accepted wholeheartedly by all Catholics. It has been explained away by the habit of early missionaries in Eastern Europe of handing out paintings of the Saviour on linen, each of which was proclaimed 'a true image', *vera ikon*. From this to Veronica was but a step and it is a poor hagiographer who cannot find a miracle to fit a saint. The authorities at Santa Faz do not insist that the features are a true portrait of Christ; very sensibly they say that the sacred piece of linen bears bloodstains that are roughly the pattern of a face and that the features were added by a pious but inexpert hand.

The holy relic is partly encased in a gold shield, like Byzantine icons, which it probably is too. On the back, but rarely shown, is a Dolorosa. It is perpetually exposed on the high altar or, when the main church is closed, in a chapel off the sacristy. The three kerchiefs have travelled extensively; in 637 they were sent from Jerusalem to Cyprus, on the arrival of the Moslem Arabs, and later from there to Constantinople. Before the Turks captured this city too, the relics were taken to Rome, thence to Venice, back to Rome and finally to their present resting-places. The fame of Veronica's kerchief was such that Elcano, Magellan's lieutenant and the first to circumnavigate the globe, left instructions in his will that an unfulfilled vow of his should be attended to by his heirs. In danger of shipwreck he had vowed to make a pilgrimage to Santa Faz and, when he failed to relieve himself of it, instructed his heirs to visit the shrine and hand over 24 ducats. It is sad to relate that the heirs of this great explorer, who was a favourite of Charles V, could not raise the money. In 1944, however, the Spanish naval authorities decided that it was no use waiting any longer for Elcano's heirs to comply with his request, and in a solemn ceremony themselves fulfilled the explorer's vow.

Three kilometres farther you can turn right to the beautiful sands of the Playa of San Juan. The next stop is at **Villajoyosa,** a town that dispels the gloom which the waste-lands have instilled. All along the coast there have been new settlements, pensions and motels, all looking as naked as cubical architecture, new paint and a complete absence of trees can make them. At Villajoyosa you turn off to the right and descend steeply past the surviving stretch of old town wall, to the unpaved sea-front. Suddenly you feel you have been transported to Portofino or the Venetian lagoon, for the narrow house-fronts, quite unselfconsciously, are painted maroon, orange, yellow, pink, blue and green. Then there are the white rims to doors and windows and the green, roll-up sunblinds draped over the balconies. This is one of the few shingle beaches, but the enchanting town more than makes up for this minor defect.

At the top of the village, where you rejoin the main road, is the Church of Santa María del Carmen, whose gilt Gothic retablo is not improved by Baroque figures stuck on top. The patroness is Santa Marta, whom we all remember as the epitome of housewifely virtues, and who looks after servants in particular. She is usually shown with a ladle or skimmer in her hand, or with a bunch of keys attached to her girdle. This is the only example I know of her carrying a mop and bucket. Villajoyosa differs from the numerous towns hereabouts which have an annual fancy-dress pageant or sham fight entitled 'Moors and Christians', the local version of Cops and Robbers. As this is a fishing village, the contest is aquatic, with the Christians sallying forth to prevent the Moors from landing.

Benidorm is the favourite holiday resort of all the Costa Blanca and of the whole coast of Valencia as well. I cannot refrain from quoting Gabriel Miró, the Alicantian writer, 'This sparkling little village nestles into a backcloth of all shades of blue, where the walls are the hue of wheat stalks and everything is as bright and clean as a new pin. The houses tumble over the lemon-tinted cliffs, houses shaded by the sail cloths of ancient feluccas. A fig tree peeps out from among the stacked oars and piles of nets; it exudes a perfume that is as thick and warm as resin.' It is very different now. The old fishing quarter is on a promontory, the big tree has been mislaid, but you can get books from the English lending library, tea at the 'One for the Pot', bacon and eggs the way mother used to cook them in Stockholm, a Venetian gondolier's hat, a toy Pomeranian or anything else you may have forgotten to pack. I asked for the fishermen, whose labour built the village; four are left, but the fishing boats have all been sold to less fortunate villages. The men themselves have made enough to retire by the sale of their cottages. Five thousand Spaniards have immigrated and pass themselves off as local colour and there are upwards of 50,000 foreign visitors and residents.

If you want to sample the local food, continue along the road for a mile or two until you reach a sign directing you to El Niño. This restaurant is famous for local dishes, best ordered in advance, and the prices are reasonable, as they are everywhere along this coast, even in Benidorm. One of their specialities is *Pebrera tallaet*, made of pimiento, potato and tunny-fish gills; another is *Arroz en Fresols y Nar*, a stewed rice containing bacon and mutton. Rice dishes are the pride of the kingdom of Valencia and every town, indeed every restaurant, claims to be pre-eminent.

When you reach Altea you will be enchanted with your first glimpse of the bell-shaped Valencian church domes, in shiny blue tiles picked out with white patterns. Here a zone of coastal gardens and orchards begins, with bougainvillæa, rambler roses, olive groves and almond trees that blossom in January. The last stop is at Calpe, a picturesque village and bay with the sheer Peña de Ifach rising to form the northern arm, though somewhat spoiled by the apartment blocks that rise from its causeway. The hill can be climbed by first passing through a tunnel and once on top the view is magnificent.

An inland excursion from Alicante begins along N330 to Monforte del Cid, through a countryside where the hills are arid and the river-beds nourish their *huertas* which, with irrigation, more than make up for the waste-land. You pass through Novelda, with its triangular fourteenth-century castle tower at Mola, and see next to it a modern Sanctuary of Mary Magdalen on the brow of a hill that looks down into the River Vinalapó. The architecture is a surprise, for it was built by a pupil of Gaudí with little originality of his own, so that it looks like a miniature Sagrada Familia from Barcelona. We leave the road again to visit Sax, which has a castle under restoration in an almost impregnable position. By remembering that people used to come home from work here every afternoon, you will acquire the determination to get to the top, where the view is rewarding.

Villena is our next stop, one of the lesser known but more rewarding towns in this part of Spain. Overshadowing it is the Castle of the Villenas, so called because it became the property of the Pacheco family, Marquises of Villena, in the fifteenth century. From outside the castle is impressive by virtue of its double walls, each strengthened by semicircular or round towers, and by the massive keep from whose square top spring six bartisan turrets. It is indeed rare to find these so far south, for their origin in the Iberian peninsula is accepted as Portuguese and Castilian. For instance, one finds them on the Torre del Clavero in Salamanca, the Mudéjar castle of Coca and the Tower of Belem in Lisbon; their origin is sometimes said to be Indian. The lower courses of the great keep are still the original ones of the Arab builders, made of *hormigón* and ten feet thick, and the upper ones are Christian additions of shaped masonry. Unique ceilings of the first two floors survive.

The second attraction in Villena is the Church of Santiago, a late Gothic building with polygonal apse, chiefly remarkable for the spiral grooving of its columns. The plain interior, relieved by hanging wrought-iron candelabra and the major part of a fine gilt *reja* of 1553, had a pronounced influence on local architecture, and the anonymous 'Master of Santiago de Villena' is often cited by specialists.

The third visit is to the Palacio Municipal, originally a Renaissance building, of which the entrance and patio are untouched; it was the work of our old friend Jacobo Florentino l'Indaco, whose works we saw in Granada and can be found in Murcia and Jaén as well. The Town Hall houses the Archaeological Museum of José María Soler, named after its founder who is a keen local amateur. It contains exhibits of the uninterrupted history of the region during 50,000 years and is guaranteed to stimulate the imagination of every visitor. Among the exhibits are Bronze Age discoveries of cooked or burned food, with a clove of garlic easily identifiable among them. The pride of the Museum is an amazing treasure of pure gold, discovered by Don José Soler himself in 1963. Dating from about 1000 BC, it consists of a variety of ornaments and utensils which were put in a jar and apparently buried hastily in a dry river-bed. The total weight of the gold objects is about twenty pounds, so that it is smaller than the Carambolo treasure of Seville, but contains a far richer variety of ornaments, rings, bracelets and necklaces, as well as bowls and flasks, many of them with geometric work in repoussé.

We are near the old border of the kingdoms of Castile and Valencia, which accounts for the style of Villena Castle. Going east for 8 kilometres we cross back into the region of Valencian dialect, the *lemosí*, whose descendants include Mallorquín in the Balearic Islands, Catalan, Provençal and even a language spoken on the Ligurian coast of North Italy. It was originally the Langue d'Oc and was spoken in the areas round Toulouse and Limoges, deriving its name from the latter city.

The castle at Biar is similar to the one at Villena, but better preserved; the outer wall with round corner towers is very impressive. The Church of the Assumption is Gothic, with a fine Plateresque portal; it is another of those that are orientated north-south, suggesting that it was built on the foundations of a mosque, which often has its *mihrab* in the long east wall. Churches, on the other hand, have their sanctuary in the narrower side. Elda has only one tower of its castle, and at the next road fork you bear right for Ibi, which also has little of interest, but this route takes you through the terraced, irrigated *huerta* and within sight of Castalla, the most imposing, if least well preserved of the castles. The two ends survive, perched on a sheer rock, with the blue sky as background. All round are olive groves, vines and wheat-fields.

Alcoy caps a steep hill and although an industrial town, has much to recommend it. The Plaza Mayor, on the hilltop, must be entered on foot. It is of the eighteenth-century type that we first saw in Córdoba, but smaller, surrounded by four-storeyed houses and looking in on the two triple street-lamps in the centre. Its size and shape reminds you that it was originally the cloister of an Augustine convent. The steep Calle de San Juan leads down to a large paper factory where cigarette paper, the popular

Bambú, is one of the products, as it was when Ford visited it in or before 1845. As the word 'cigarette' had not yet been coined, he writes of the *papelitos* or 'economical little paper cigars'. To those who were taught that the cigarette came to Britain only after the Crimean War, it comes as something of a surprise to learn that it was ubiquitous in Spain in the late eighteenth century, and well known to our troops at Gibraltar.

Alcoy's other produce of renown is the *peladilla*, praised by Ford and excellent still; these owe their reputation to the quality of the locally grown almonds and the thinness of the sugar coating. A similar, but less-known sweet is made in the same way, using pine seeds. After the other towns we have visited you are apt to miss the whitewash which has become standard elsewhere. As is proper for a manufacturing town the houses are brown and grey, but the inhabitants have the peculiar pride of factory workers, scorn the leisurely courtesies of the countryman and like to refer to their district as the Cataluña of Castile. Their geography is archaic and the claim exaggerated, but at least Alcoy has a long history of industry, forced on her by the paucity of arable land and the latent power of her tumbling streams.

The road back to Alicante, N340, passes through the small town of Jijona, where the poor remains of an Arab castle crown a rock overhanging the road. *Turrones*, a sort of nougat, are manufactured throughout the province, but this is claimed to be their home town and the *torrons de Xixona*, as they are called in the local dialect, are produced at the rate of millions of pounds a year and grace Christmas tables in many parts of Europe and America. During the summer, when production ceases, many men of Jijona wander abroad as sellers of ice-cream and especially *horchata*, a delicious iced 'milk' of tiger nuts. This Valencian speciality is often sold throughout Spain in a type of milk bar, the horchatería, run by natives of Jijona. To reach Alicante we next pass through the town with the sweetly disappointing name of Muchamiel, sweet because the name literally means 'much honey' and disappointing because it is derived from an Arabic word *Mutxamel*, which has nothing to do with honey. In spite of attempts at irrigation the soil here is dry and chalky and supports only almond trees and a few vines. It is now only 10 kilometres to Alicante, which we reach by the coast road, passing the beach of San Juan on our left and the Convent of Santa Verónica on the right.

CHAPTER TWENTY

Alicante to Granada

❧

*Elche—Orihuela—Murcia—Alcantarilla—Vélez Blanco—Baza
—Guadix*

The direct road from Alicante to Granada offers a wealth of
attractions to the enquiring traveller. Too often the temptation
of doing the journey in a day because of the uninteresting landscape allows only a perfunctory stop to see the palm groves of
Elche and another for the cave-dwellings at Guadix. An extra
day will enable you to see everything described here, except of
course certain festivals that have their due season.

Elche lies on N340, 23 kilometres from Alicante. The palm
groves, as you would expect, make the most powerful impression,
grouped as they are round the town and infiltrating between the
buildings. They are irrigated from a lake that has preserved
its exact dimensions since Strabo described it in the first century
A D. The predominantly flat-roofed, whitewashed houses and the
ubiquitous palms contrast with the surrounding arid landscape
and remind one strongly of an African oasis. The old part of the
town lies to the right of the road and the main turning takes you
almost immediately to the large Church of Santa María. Ten
yards before reaching it, however, there is an open space on the
left, where a square house represents the lower storey of an
ancient tower, La Calahorra. The Church of Santa María is
Baroque, built of a rather drab stone, as indeed are many
buildings hereabouts; it has the bell-shaped dome of the Valencian
region but the tiles are new and blue, an unpleasant colour used
since the reconstruction that followed the destructive rioting of
1936. The main portal is by the German sculptor who rejoiced in
the cryptic name of Nicolás de Busi (von Busch?), and the bulging
Salomonic columns somehow remind one of a beer-drinking
German. The church's importance to the visitor lies in the fact
that it is used for the mystery play, half of which is given on
14th August and the rest the next day. To allow tourists to see it
without wasting time, the dress rehearsal on the 13th presents
the whole play.

The origin of the *Misteri* is said to go back to the thirteenth century, but it is more likely that its adaptation as a play is of the sixteenth century. The *Mystery of the Acts of the Apostles*, in which the drama of the Assumption of the Virgin Mary was included, seems to have had its first performance in Paris in 1540, by order of Francis I. But there is evidence that the text of the *Misteri* was written in Catalan in the previous century while the legend was in circulation long before that and was illustrated by miniaturists as early as the tenth century. The music, too, is traditional and Gregorian; some say that parts were taken from the Mozarabic liturgy, not by any means a far-fetched belief.

The drama is, of course, a religious observance, not an entertainment, as it is presented in the church. Elche obtained the rare privilege of continuing its presentation when the Council of Trent forbade the performance of plays in consecrated buildings. Some of the actors are clergy and others, presumably more agile, take the parts which entail being lowered from the cupola, about 100 feet above the stage. The language throughout is Catalan of an archaic kind and similar to the dialects of Valencia. The words are sung throughout and it is therefore not too fanciful to claim this spectacle as the forerunner of Italian grand opera. The action is easy to follow, especially if you know the apocryphal stories of the Dormition, the paralysis and conversion of the impious Jew who touched the Virgin's coffin, and the Assumption.

Opposite the church and a little way north is the old Alcázar, Señoría or Altamira Palace, the remains of a great castle that was incorporated in the city walls and overlooks the now canalised River Vinalapó. It is not impressive seen from the street, but a better view can be had from the bridge on to which the road leads; the square tower and a bartisan turret are seen to advantage from here and of course palm trees form a frame, as they do to almost everything in this town. You reach the other side of the city wall by going south from the church; this brings you to the Plaza Mayor in front of the Ayuntamiento, with its pleasant Renaissance façade and decorative balconies. The clock is a modern one but the striking of the hours is done by two puppets, or *jaquemards*, on the fourteenth-century Torre del Consell. The figures are called 'Calendura' and 'Calendureta' and are not, as elsewhere (in Astorga for instance), on either side of the bell. Instead, each has its own bell, the upper, smaller one housed on top of the dome, the other, in the chamber on which the dome rests.

The palm groves are everywhere and the latest count makes the number of trees 125,000. They are divided into *horts*, the local

Above, Jaén Province, leading producer of olive oil. *Below*, Ubeda, a potter's wares displayed in the old Valencia quarter.

Above, Ubeda: the Renaissance patio in the Casa de las Torres. *Below*, Láchar: the entrance to the castle-palace.

name for *huertos*, or orchards. The most famous is the Hort del Cura, named after Don José Castaño, a priest who was still living in this century. The tree called the Palmera del Cura is at least a hundred years older than the man it is named after, and is better called the Palmera Imperial. It has seven subsidiary trunks that spring out of the main stem and then rise vertically like a giant candelabrum; to imagine it you must add the undergrowth of pomegranates and the flower-beds which have been planted beneath the date palms. When the trenches are flooded by irrigation they remind one more than ever of an oasis where, as the Arabs say, the palms stand with their feet in the water and their heads in the fire of Heaven. Dates are not their chief produce; by tying the leaves up so as to shade the inside ones a specially bleached specimen is produced, suitable for Palm Sunday celebration and subsequent employment as lightning conductors on the front balcony, if suitably blessed.

In this part, near an ornamental pool, is a reproduction of the famous *Dama de Elche*, the stone female head found on a neighbouring hill and now to be seen in the Prado Museum. It is justifiably world famous as an example of Iberian sculpture, owing much to Greek influence, of about 500 B.C. If you look at her face while your hands block out the fantastic headdress, you will find nothing Oriental or voluptuous about the features; you can see the thin lips, low cheek-bones and pinched nose coming out of church any Sunday.

Ten kilometres farther is the little town of **Crevillente**, where it is worth while stopping for a minute to see the Church of Nuestra Señora de Belén, quite without artistic merit but so Moslem in outline that you might imagine yourself in front of a mosque. The tower on the left, as you face it, could be the minaret, the main dome stands a little away from it, and on the right is a smaller dome reminiscent of the madrasseh so often attached to mosques. Crevillente was the birthplace of a little-known Hispano-Arab surgeon, Al-Xafra, whose works have only recently come to light. He was employed in the court of a king, living in Guadix after banishment from Granada, and wrote a treatise on wounds, inflammations and tumours. His case records show a knowledge of anatomy, and his treatment of fractures, with extension of the limb and padded splints or a plaster of bitumen and resin, has not changed much since he described it in the thirteenth century.

Orihuela is not to be missed, for it breathes the quiet aristocracy of a bygone age. In some respects it is like Úbeda, but whereas the latter is a town of Renaissance buildings, Orihuela is made up of the best type of Baroque mansion, with a family crest over the door or on the street corner. The present name perpetuates the Roman Aurariola, which the Moslems eventually changed to Auriwela. By sheer chance the fertile district was first called *Tudmor* or *Tadmir*, a name identical with that of the Syrian oasis-town of Palmyra, in its native form. To complete the resemblance, both districts were noted for their myriad palm trees; but, as I have said, the identity of name was fortuitous. The district of Orihuela was called *Tudmir* by the Arabs, from the fact that it was the semi-independent territory of the Visigoth Theodomir, at the time of the invasion of Tarik and Musa.

Theodomir was the one ruler who kept his realm, though only as a vassal of the Moslems. Various Arabic documents have preserved the text of the negotiated surrender, on much the same terms as those granted to Granada by the Catholic Sovereigns but with better faith on the part of the conquerors. The popular legend has it that the invaders besieged Theodomir and that after a battle in which Gothic casualties were numerous, Theodomir dressed the women in men's clothes and armour, had them tie their hair under their chins to simulate beards, and paraded them on the ramparts. Convinced of the impossibility of conquering this powerful city, Abd Al-Aziz, son of Musa, decided to offer generous terms. We must, however, remember that Abd Al-Aziz and indeed most of the Arab leaders were not evilly disposed towards the Visigoths. The sons of Witiza, who had betrayed Roderick, went to Damascus for an interview and were granted possession of many of their estates. In the same way Abd Al-Aziz himself obtained peaceable ownership of Roderick's land by marrying his widow; and eventually all Christian land passed into Moslem hands by intermarriage as much as by force of arms. It is strange that the same story of the disguised women is told of other towns, such as Murcia and Tortosa, the latter as late as 1149, when the Moors were trying to recapture it. Perhaps it is simply the Spanish version of the geese that saved the Capitol in Rome.

Orihuela lies astride the River Segura and therefore in country well irrigated by its waters. It is said that the Moriscoes were so adept at this farming method that many were concealed by their Christian neighbours at the time of their expulsion in 1609, and that the present fertility of the area is due to this. Certainly nothing but skilled irrigation could make this apparent desert as productive as it is; the negligible rainfall counts for nothing and the old saying is still true today,

Llueva o no llueva,
trigo en Orihuela.

Whether it rains or not,
there is corn in Orihuela.

The second largest date-palm plantation of Spain is here, owing
its existence, like that of Elche, to the skilful employment of its
river.

The Cathedral dates back to the early fourteenth century,
with a transept of a hundred years later. The north portal is
Renaissance, while the other entrances are Gothic. The west,
which is the main one, has lengths of older frieze inset, and a
peculiar dentate arch of which the teeth are lanceolate in Gothic
style and called *caireles*, or tassels. The interior is not particularly
impressive as architecture, but the spirally carved vault ribs of
the transept are obviously inspired by the Church of Santiago
at Villena. The *reja* before the high altar, however, is outstanding
and claimed to be the best in the kingdom of Valencia. At the
top, in the centre, are Adam and Eve and immediately below
them the Annunciation; the juxtaposition is intentional and
frequent in mediaeval iconography, signifying the origins of sin
and redemption. The *coro*, which is placed centrally, has some
wood carving which does not rank with others that we have
seen. The last chapel on the right, from which there is also access
to the Museum, has the famous retablo of Saints Catherine,
Christopher and others, a great work of the early sixteenth
century by a little-known artist of the school of Pablo de San
Leocadio, named Monzo.

The Diocesan Museum contains many works in gold and silver
which are of no special interest, except to looters, and a famous
painting by Velázquez, one of the very few in Southern Spain,
entitled *The Temptation of St. Thomas Aquinas*. Religious subjects
were not this painter's speciality, for which he had the King's
patronage to thank, but here we see what the master could do
with an unpromising subject, for even the angels look human,
which is quite an achievement as more effort is usually expended
on making humans look angelic. The treatment of the saint's
left hand, with its three-dimensional effect, is in a sense the focal
point of the picture, though the composition is obviously aimed
at making his face this—unfortunately precisely in the centre of
the canvas. Of the other paintings, the *Magdalen* of Ribera is
outstanding for the expression and for the moulding of the arms.

There is also the interesting fifteenth-century missal of Pope Calixtus III, uncle and predecessor of the other Borgia pope Alexander VI, with its fine miniatures and marginal designs.

One local custom deserves mention, that of the *caballero cubierto*. By special Papal sanction a gentleman with a University degree is chosen from among the nobility every year, and has the privilege of keeping his hat on in the Cathedral during the processions of Holy Week. The choice can be made from a long list, for in 1437 Alfonso V of Aragón, the Magnanimous, conferred nobility on all the inhabitants of Orihuela. It is not easy to unearth the cause of this unprecented award, for the King was at that time busy in Southern Italy conquering the Kingdom of Naples. Nobility as a routine has now lapsed, but the *caballero cubierto* is still chosen annually and shares his rare distinction with the Seises of Seville and the Pulgar family of Granada.

If you leave the Cathedral by the main, west entrance and follow the south wall, you pass the attractive south portal, its Gothic archivolts occupied by saints and musicians, the latter presumably the four-and-twenty elders of the Book of Revelations. The wooden doors have the ornamental studs which are especially frequent here, as they were in Ronda. At the end of the south wall is a Romanesque Cloister attached to a Gothic cathedral. There is an explanation, of course: it was brought piecemeal after the Civil War from the damaged Convento de la Merced and rebuilt here round the War Memorial, an early Gothic cross much like the village crosses that are still a feature of the English countryside. It is only a small cloister but it has two storeys; the capitals are plain, almost Roman or Visigothic in their simple designs, but everything harmonises and the cypresses, orange trees and hibiscus add the final touch to a unique construction. There is a wall plaque of St. Roch with his dog, as we saw him in Málaga Cathedral; it is carved in a black stone and came from the Convent of San Sebastián, before which it may have been a part of the Puerta de Magastre in the city walls. St. Roch and St. Sebastián were the original patrons of the city, hence their conjunction here; they were superseded by St. Justa and St. Rufina, the church of the former being a little to the west.

The old time University was housed in the huge Seminario or Convent of the Dominicans, usually called Santo Domingo for that very reason; it is off the Calle de San Juan, standing somewhat apart from the other buildings we have seen. The entrance is through the Puerta de la Olma, sole remaining gate in the city

wall, of which there is even less left than there is of the castle
perched above the town. There are two patios, both originally
Renaissance, one in all its pristine magnificence, the other more
attractive by reason of its trees and bird-song. The main staircase is a wonderful piece of construction; it should be examined
from below, when the cunning series of harmonious intersecting
arches that support it can be seen. It deserves to rank with the
Vise at St. Gilles near Arles as a showpiece for students of architecture. Coffered ceilings of the time of Phillip II are everywhere
except in the refectory, where there is a ribbed vault. Here too
are series of *azulejos de montería*, the so-called 'hunting tiles',
which in this case include scenes from country life. As a rule
these degenerate tiles of the eighteenth century come from Seville,
are poorly drawn and may contain a corrupt or stylised version
of the Arabic word *alafiya*, prosperity. The Baroque Church
adjacent to the Convent has the usual dome, Corinthian columns
and a wealth of meaningless adornment, but the effect is nevertheless one of splendour rather than vulgarity. The University
gave many famous graduates to Spain and deserves more than
a hurried glance. There is a playground at the back, and behind
this an old Arab *tapia* wall has recently been discovered.

The Church of Santiago is a handsome structure, but only the
Isabelline-Gothic portal remains of the original building, thanks
to seismic and civic commotions. It is a fine example of the type
we have now seen in various parts, set in the usual *alfiz*, with the
double doors divided by a statue of St. James on a spiral column.
The statue is a replacement since the Civil War. This is the door
which was specially opened in the old church in 1488 for the
entry of the Catholic Sovereigns, who stopped here on the way to
the siege of Baza, on the eastern front of encircled Granada.
Orihuela had, of course, been in Christian hands for two centuries and the royal couple was simply using it as a base. Their
yoke and arrows and the motto *Tanto Monta* flank the carved
arms of Spain. Again one can make a fair guess at its date from
a curious fact: it incorporates the pomegranate of Granada but,
as the conquest was still in the future, the fruit is not opened to
reveal its seeds—in fact it is the only example in Spain of this
heraldic curiosity. Another oddity, of the commoner canting
variety, is the presence of the crowned oriole, with a sword in
one claw, in the municipal crest.

The interior is mostly of the sixteenth century, the western
half Gothic, the remainder severe Renaissance in the style of
Juan de Herrera. The retablo of the high altar has a badly restored

painting by Juan de Juanes, a famous member of the Valencian school and therefore much influenced by Leonardo da Vinci and Raphael; this is a *Last Supper*, its main interest being the chalice in Christ's left hand. This is how Richard Ford described it, whereas the far better-known version by the same painter in the Prado at Madrid shows the chalice standing on the table. As Ford was referring to the Madrid one it seems a curious coincidence that he should have described the Orihuela one. There are also Passion figures by Salzillo, whose main output will be seen at Murcia.

There has been a great deal of moving round in Orihuela and works of art are apt to be found in new premises. One example is to be seen in the Biblioteca pública de Fernando Loaces, named after a sixteenth-century archbishop of Tarragona and Valencia. In a small room off the main library is the *Paso de la Diablesa*, which is paraded through the streets in the Good Friday procession and admired by all. The upper level is a cloud that supports cherubs carrying the instruments of the Passion, grouped round a cross. All this is based on a globe that in its turn rests on a skeleton and a female devil (*La Diablesa*), brown in colour, with bright glass eyes, a pendulous mole on the right cheek, bald except for a tuft of hair between the horns, and wearing nothing above the waist. The group is probably even more horrible than the sculptor intended. The sculptor was our old friend Nic. de Busi. There is also a small archaeological collection, consisting of some prehistoric finds and fragments of late Roman mosaic. The Library contains over 20,000 books, some extremely rare, and is well catalogued and displayed. Here you may discover items of local history, such as the story of the Mozarab Armengola, who brought about the Reconquest by James I of Aragon.

The streets of Orihuela reward the casual stroller with the front of many a Baroque palace and glimpses of fine tile dadoes inside. Though the guide-books speak chiefly of rice dishes and sweet-meats as Orihuela's contributions to science, turkey is the base of her two best dishes. *Guisado de pavo* is a succulent stew of this bird and *arroz con costra* or crusted rice, uses the customary variety of meat, veal, pork, sausage and turkey rather than chicken; there is even a slight flavouring of prawn. Beaten eggs are spread over the surface before cooking and are responsible for the golden crust. A further refinement is contributed by the local wine; we are approaching Murcia, where the red table wine is blessed with a noticeable bouquet, while being light enough not to make you sleepy. It is a pleasant change from the wines of La Mancha, usually served as Valdepeñas, and is obtainable everywhere on draught.

We continue on N340 for the 23 kilometres to **Murcia**, capital of the province, passing Monteagudo on the right just before arriving. The ruins of an Arab castle that replaced a Roman one are perched on the needle point of a freak pinnacle. A Crucifix now towers over it and detracts from its scenic value; to get it there must have been a feat, for the climb on foot is arduous, and unrewarding too. Within a short time we enter the Plaza de Santa Eulalia, where the now-vanished walls were once pierced by an important gate. Even if the remains are few, they should be examined for they are the only remaining portion of the twelfth-century defences and represent the oldest-known part of the city, which is first heard of after the Arab conquest. The foundations, and little more, are of Almohad walls with Mudéjar additions and will interest the archaeologist. The tombs are part of a cemetery that extends under the Plaza and consists of graves that are laid on top of each other to save space. The pottery which was found in them forms the nucleus of a small ceramic museum, where it is interesting again to observe the use of manganese in colouring.

Ibn Arabí of Murcia is cited as an example of the *Sufi* mysticism that has played an important part in the development of religious thought. The word is a simplification of the Arabic for 'spiritual theology', and like most abstract concepts has a concrete foundation. In this instance, the word is taken from *suf*, or camel hair, and refers to the simple clothing worn by the practitioners of the cult. At once we realise that sufism does not stand alone in the developmental line of divine mysticism: it was John the Baptist who wore 'his raiment of camel's hair' and who also tinged religion with poetic imagery. Its earliest expression is the Song of Songs, in which the love of God is given the verbal disguise of carnal love. At least sixteen hundred years later Ibn Arabí used the well-worn oriental criteria of female beauty to express his desire for, and love of, God.

> ... a bright-faced, lissom damsel,

> Swaying drunkenly,
> To and fro
> Like branches, fresh as raw silk,
> Which the winds have bent;

Shaking
Like the hump of a stallion-camel,
Fearsome hips
Huge as sandhills.

There seems little doubt that Ibn Arabí's works, especially those referring to the legend of Mohamed's Night Journey beyond the Tomb, were Dante's inspiration; and there is no doubt whatever that he was the link between sufism and the erotic mysticism of St. John of the Cross, whose path we shall cross later.

The mention of raw silk brings to mind Murcia's place in the development of a trade which is still holding its own against the competition of synthetic fibres, at least in Spain. Silkworms, and the essential mulberry tree, were introduced in the wake of the Moslem conquest and the Province of Murcia became one of the main centres for the production of silk. Both in the country *barracas*, or shacks, and in the houses of the city, silkworms are kept in trays of mulberry leaves—the *barracas* are square buildings with a pointed roof and the door, the only opening, is left open. In town the trays are carried up to the third floor. On the first Friday in March there is a religious ceremony, to which great commercial, if not theological, importance attaches. *La bendición de la simiente del gusano de seda.* This is the blessing of the silkworm eggs, obviously equivalent to the driving out of the devils at seed-time which is practised in India and elsewhere. It is a necessary precaution, for the silkworm is a delicate creature. We can read or see, in a *zarzuela* of Rodríguez de Hita (*Las Labradoras de Murcia*, 1769), how important the silk industry was to the Murcians two centuries ago. According to a local superstition, silkworms will die of fright if they hear the noise of thunder so, in the ceremony, the composer has the chance of bringing all his peasant characters on stage, playing and singing *fortissimo* to drown the peals of thunder. Incidentally, it is a *jota* that they perform, a dance that is found in many regions of Spain, most typically in Aragón. It is entirely different from the flamenco of Andalucía, which is only a matter of fifty miles ahead of us.

A by-product of the industry is losing its market; when the larvae are about three inches long they are put in a vinegar pickle and the gut later pulled out, processed and turned into surgical sutures and fishermen's tackle. Unfortunately nylon thread is proving cheaper and just as good.

The Cathedral is geographically in the centre of the town, its fine façade in the Plaza de Belluga, named after a heroic arch-bishop who, during the War of the Spanish Succession, kept the Austrians at bay by flooding the surrounding fields and enlisting a volunteer force. The west front was built by Jaime Bort y Melia, a Valencian who died in the year of its completion, but the tower is a separate work, in which Jacobo Florentino l'Indaco had a share. It carries out the ideals of Baroque sculpture—for it is sculpture rather than architecture—by its brilliant use of planes, giving the desired chiaroscuro. The curves are also original, so that the highest part, over the portal, is surmounted by convexities. Seen from a distance, the tower on the left and the curved centre again remind you of minaret and mosque, a pattern apparently rooted deeply in the soul of the South.

The interior is cool and pleasant, of a light cream which takes the splashes of colour from the stained-glass windows. The main construction is Gothic, but there are other later periods as well which harmonise adequately. The *reja* before the high altar is very plain, with a row of gilt leaves along the top and in its ogival arch; it is an early example, of 1497. The retablo is of the last century, a Gothic revival piece, and on its left is a shabby-looking urn, said to be the work of Florentino l'Indaco and containing the viscera of Alfonso the Learned. Symmetrically opposite it, another urn holds bits of the four saints of Cartagena; their remains have been fairly widely distributed through Spain. It is difficult to understand why Alfonso should make the bequest to Murcia, whose Moslems had risen against him while his kingdom was being mismanaged in his absence. Perhaps it is true, as Peyron wrote, that Murcia gave him shelter on an earlier occasion, when he came back unsuccessful from his attempt to supplant Richard of Cornwall as Holy Roman Emperor.

The important Chapel of the Vélez is the last on the right. Modelled on the florid Gothic tomb chapels of Álvaro de Luna at Toledo and the Constable of Castile at Burgos, its hexagonal plan and overwhelming decoration date it to the beginning of the sixteenth century. So intricate are its designs and so complex the interlacing strands of stone, that one feels there is more than a hint of Moslem influence. The crest of the Vélez family is displayed abundantly. In a pew high up on the left a stone skeleton stands respectfully at the back. The retablo is a painting of St. Luke with *his* painting of the Virgin and Child, and above it is a Crucifixion with a rhythmic, leafy background; this and the horizontal partitioning of the decoration confirm the earlier impression of the Oriental touch. The other resemblance, supported by the huge carved chain on the outside, is to the Portuguese Manoeline style, as you find, for instance, in the Abbey of Batalha. It is not only chance that they are roughly contemporaneous.

The Cathedral Museum, on the left, contains a mixed bag but a full one. You are first shown a silver custodial of about fourteen hundredweight, that turns automatically to show all its horrors, though one can admire the excellent technique while deploring the taste. There is a late Roman sarcophagus which once served as a retablo, called *Of the Muses*. The figures on the side, however, are clearly those of actors. Three polychrome stone statues of the fourteenth century, including a *Pietà*, give a welcome touch of simplicity to the overpowering collection of jewelled pectorals, crowns and other adornments. There are early charters and a collection of chips of bone, each meticulously labelled, from a host of saints. At one time they would have represented a fortune, but the market has not been active for many years. Among the articles on display are offerings of medals for valour, won by pious warriors, and others awarded to football teams.

Beside the Cathedral the Calle de la Trapería runs north, a pleasant street closed to traffic, as is the Calle de la Platería which turns off to the left. A traditional street of silversmiths, as the name states, it was still used by them earlier in the present century. Here you will find the Casino de Murcia, a fine club well known for its décor. There is something dreamlike about it, a feeling of being transported to the spacious days when the upper classes neither knew nor cared about the workman's problems. It is significant that the 'Let them eat cake' story of Marie Antoinette appears in a book of Spanish proverbs published in 1508, as *A mengua de pan, buenas son tortas*, 'when bread is scarce, cakes are good.' The furniture is excellent, if outdated, the floors are parquet throughout and the great ballroom has five huge crystal chandeliers, and sofas covered in yellow brocade. The lobby is overpowering, being a faithful reproduction of part of the Hall of the Ambassadors in Seville's Alcázar, and guaranteed to tame the brashest guest.

It is convenient to go first to the Archaeological Museum, which is on the left where the Calle de la Trapería has become the broad Gran Vía de Alfonso X el Sabio. Exhibits are well displayed here and there is an excellent collection of ceramics and some Roman, but not Byzantine, mosaics. On the other hand, sculptured fragments from the excavated basilica of Agezares near by are difficult to place. They would agree well with the theory that the church was built during the Byzantine occupation, though some authorities prefer to classify them as Visigothic. The treasure of Finca la Pita consists of Arab gold coins, silver coins of Alfonso X and assorted others.

Finally, there is the Museo de Salzillo, the sculptor whose work is proudly shown throughout the Province of Murcia and beyond. Francisco Salzillo Alcaraz, son of a Capuan sculptor and a Spanish mother, was born in Murcia in 1707. He shines in a century that was generally poor in art and though he shows little originality, his figures are so lifelike that they sometimes remind one of a waxworks. If you have conscientiously followed painted wood sculpture from Martínez Montañés to Busi, then you should take the final step of visiting this museum.

Helped by two brothers and a sister out of the large family that he had supported since he was twenty, Salzillo turned out 1,792 separate works; these are scattered, and rather than spending time in seeing a mere handful at each church, you can see a considerable number here. Murcia, by the way, has adopted the excellent idea of printing a brief trilingual guide on the entrance tickets to her museums, economical of time and money. My own taste prefers the *Belén* above all other works displayed here. It is a collection of the most diverse figures, human and animal, illustrating every episode of the Nativity. Christmas 'cribs' such as these are popular in Sicily and Southern Italy and may reflect the long connection between Spain and those parts. Among the 1,500 figures portrayed here are the anachronistic but invaluable records of the clothing worn in Salzillo's day by poet and peasant. Although every figure is in miniature, their attitudes and expressions are remarkably true and we may be sure that the supreme realist has left us an accurate visual record of his times.

The rest of the museum contains the *pasos* for Holy Week, superb in their technical perfection. The actors in the drama of the Passion look too much like real people for comfort and their expressions are so appropriate that we must once more remind ourselves of their purpose to illustrate a story, not to win prizes at an academy of art. The most elaborate of these works is the Last Supper, whose figures are slightly less than life-size. Here the artist's realism has reached its zenith, every figure appearing to have been arrested in the middle of an action. Judas, in conformity with age-old custom, has been given red hair and beard, no doubt as the direct descendant of the scheming slave in Greek and Roman comedy, who was always presented with a red wig.

Before you leave Murcia, you should see the thirteenth-century

Virgen de la Arrijaca in the Church of San Andrés next door.
From here you may turn west to La Ñora, which entails a short
digression from the main road, or else cross the River Segura by
the Puente Viejo and so continue along N340 to Alcantarilla,
where you meet the country lane from La Ñora. The name is
simply the local form of *noria*, the *nawra* or Arab water-wheel,
and at this village we see our first iron one, still in use and
measuring about 20 feet in diameter. It is set upright in a narrow
channel, down which the irrigation stream is directed at regular
hours. The slope of the channel ensures a fast flow, the paddles
turn the wheel and the pierced compartments in the rims raise
water to the top, where the chamber, now upside down, empties
itself into the aqueduct at the side. From here the water is
led through the fields in its ancient course and helps to make the
huerta of Murcia one of the richest areas in Spain.

It is only a few minutes' drive to **Alcantarilla**, where we join
N340 and almost immediately see a second iron *noria* on the left
of the main road, also in daily use. To see the turning wheel and
listen to the gushing water as it pours into the old aqueduct on its
pointed arcade, is to be taken back to the days of Moslem
domination. The authorities have conveniently set aside an
acre or two behind the wheel as a Museo de la Huerta, where
every detail of the daily life of the Murcian peasant can be studied.
The buildings are typical *barracas* and are used to house the
various exhibits, including the manufacture of the great water-
jars, the *tinajas* and *alcarrazas* seen in Andalucía. A *ventorrillo*, or
local tavern has been reconstructed, with specimens of regional
dishes. The embroidered costumes, which are now worn only on
feast days, are well displayed, and a typical farmhouse is furnished
with locally made chairs, tables, wrought iron, drapes, lace, rugs
and pottery. A tray of mulberry leaves and twigs, with silkworm
cocoons laid on it, has not been forgotten and a rather too loud
gramophone adds a background of local music—a museum to
interest those who avoid museur‚s.

Sixty-four kilometres of uni·.teresting, infertile, inhospitable
country lie between you and L‚rca. A disappointing town on the
whole, for the guidebook attractions never live up to their description. In the lower town, at the corner of the Plaza Vicente, is a
Roman milestone serving as pedestal to St. Vincent Ferrer who,
if he had seen this statue, could pardonably have preached an
impassioned sermon against the sculptor. The Castle on the hill
is imposing, but the square Torre Alfonsina, named after *El
Sabio*, the conqueror of the town, is in bad repair. The Torre de

Espolón, along with the rest of the castle, is so dilapidated as to be past restoration and, in fact, the whole ruin is best seen from a distance.

On the same ridge are the remains of four churches, neither old nor interesting, and the upper town has many patrician house fronts of the Baroque era, whose escutcheons and even studded doors are frequently covered with whitewash or paint. The Ayuntamiento, on the Plaza de España, has a pleasant Renaissance front and is overshadowed by the massive Collegiate Church of San Patricio. This is an example of the worst type of Baroque ornament with an incongruous medley of bishops and *putti*, the whole painted a sickly colour somewhere between pink and yellow. On the way out of Lorca the Casa de Guevara is often pointed out as a fine example of Baroque domestic architecture; the twisted columns and meaningless ornament are a matter for individual appraisal. The Fonda de Madrid opposite, which was once similar, has made way for a perfectly plain house-front, so no time need be lost in looking for it. By and large, Lorca is not to be taken as an obligatory stop.

The same cannot be said about **Vélez Blanco**, which has one of the few interesting Renaissance, Italian-style castles in Spain. It is reached by taking the right fork (N342) at Puerto Lumbreras and continuing as far as Vélez Rubio. The digression south along N340 to see Huércal Overa is not worth the trouble. Both roads take you through lunar landscapes, where the only crops of note appear to be esparto grass and crockery, which is displayed at the roadside in front of small cottages apparently built for the purpose. Vélez Rubio has an eighteenth-century church of red stone and need not detain you; but a good side road takes you to Vélez Blanco 6 kilometres away, and on the left towers the famous castle.

There are several features which distinguish this castle from most others; it is polygonal and is separated from a massive fortification on the left, as you look up, essentially a barbican. In former days mounted visitors and even coaches would ascend a ramp inside this southern portion and cross over the tremendous arch that still connects it with the northern part, the castle itself. In this way the front door, so to speak, was reached by a drawbridge on the first floor and the stables were at the same level. Immediately beyond them is the open space where the white marble patio once stood and on its east side the gallery, or *paseador*, gives a superb view over vineyards and olive groves, or inside, into the patio. The merlons are double, pyramidal, and topped with ornamental 'buttons'. The family crest, of which more will be said later, is prominently displayed, and is the same as that in the Vélez Chapel of Murcia Cathedral. The castle is today entered by a narrow, climbing passage in the northern part, where it is easy to bump your head. The caretaker acts as a guide and will obligingly poke among the rubbish on the floor and show you fragments of marble and *azulejo* from the original patio.

The castle was built for Don Pedro Fajardo y Chacón, first Marquis of Vélez and fifth hereditary *adelantado*, or governor of Murcia. In return for the family possession of Cartagena, which he had to return to the Catholic Sovereigns, he was given land and townships in the Vélez valley, including Beled Albiad, the White Place, whose name was soon changed to Vélez Blanco. The idea of a Renaissance castle may have come from a relative, Don Rodrigo de Vivar y Mendoza, who had the splendid palace-castle of La Calahorra built for him at about the same time, the beginning of the sixteenth century. Fajardo's family became extinct at the end of the seventeenth century and the castle suffered from neglect, which increased in the disorders that followed the Peninsular War; it was eventually used as a shelter for the homeless and even, it is said, as a stable. At the beginning of this century a French dealer was able to acquire the patio and other parts of the castle of which the owners wished to dispose, and in 1913 they were bought by George Blumenthal, the President of the New York Metropolitan Museum, who reconstructed the patio in his house in Park Avenue and willed it to the Museum on his death. It is only in this decade that the splendid patio of white Carrara marble has been erected in the New York Metropolitan Museum, where it is better preserved and more available to lovers of architectural and sculptural beauty than its sister at La Calahorra.[1]

The family crest, which I mentioned earlier, was probably carved along with the other ornamentation in the patio by the Lombard sculptors who had completed their work at La Calahorra. The three nettles on rocks in the sea, in the first and fourth quarters, are those of the Fajardo family, that is of Pedro's mother, who was the last of a line of governors of Murcia. The crest of the Chacóns, his father's family, occupies the second and

1. For those who cannot visit New York an excellent idea of the patio, with its sumptuously carved windows and capitals, can be obtained by writing for the *Bulletin of the Metropolitan Museum of Art*, Fifth Avenue and 82nd Street, New York. N.Y. 10028, *Volume XXIII, Number* **4** of December, 1964.   Price 50 cents.

third quarters and this confirms the fact that Pedro was allowed to use Fajardo as his family name. You have seen the Vélez Chapel in Murcia and the majestic ruins of the Castle of Vélez Blanco, and I can only urge you now to try to see the marvellous patio (or its photographs) with its capitals and window pilasters, the Spanish ceiling tiles in the gallery, the harmony and proportion, secure from the ravages of time and the neglect of man.

The lonely road between the sierras now seems to stretch endlessly ahead and gives one time to think back to the days when the Reverend Joseph Townsend passed in the opposite direction, discovering that the ham he had been given was neither smoked nor boiled and the six bottles of wine he had with him were useless without a corkscrew. If he had more hardships than we are likely to encounter, he also had more time to observe the countryside. The carob trees seem to have been more numerous in 1787 and the herbs, which the Moors came to collect as late as Ford's day, were many and varied, and everywhere was esparto grass, though this has now receded to the hilltops. Here he saw donkeys with their nostrils slit to help their breathing, and donkey drivers sitting at the roadside eating snails and rice. As he approached, one of the diners rose respectfully and asked whether he would care to share their meal, an empty formality which he properly refused with equal gravity.

Cullar de Baza was a miserable hamlet, with several cave-dwellings—we shall meet these along the road from here—and a church which could not accommodate all the villagers on a Sunday, so that some stood in the forecourt during Mass and crossed themselves when they heard the bell ring for the elevation of the Host. This is not too far a cry from the overflow in the Patio de los Naranjos in Córdoba. Nowadays the Venta del Ángel looks after travellers, with clean rooms, excellent food and a host who is knowledgeable about local sights, which are few. On a hill behind the inn is the Sanctuary of the Virgen de la Cabeza, which grew from an *atalaya* of Moslem days. A domed chamber was added in Christian times, so that the whole came to resemble the outline of a mosque, with which you are probably already familiar. The merlons of the tower are also a later addition.

Twenty kilometres farther along N342, during which we pass several more wayside displays, we come to **Baza**. (We can understand Miss Rose Macaulay's hobby of picking up specimens of local pottery in whichever part she happened to be, it does make a delightful and cheap adjunct to a tour.) Baza is a quiet town whose main interest lies in the pleasant alameda on the hill, a shady walk among planes, palms and chestnuts. The cannon used by Isabel la Católica in the siege of 1489 were removed from here after the Civil War and are now in the adjacent garden that surrounds the Cruz de los Caidos, the War Memorial. They make picturesque corner-posts to the central cross. They are iron, with prominent hoops to reinforce the barrel, and have rings at two places along their length, enabling them to be dragged by teams of mules over the slippery mountain tracks in winter. Their bore is over 8 inches and the length of barrel about 4 feet from muzzle to touch-hole.

Below this little park, in Caño Dorado, an interesting fountain of 1607 forms part of the wall of a house, with masks and lions' heads spouting water. The Colegiata is a late Gothic building of grey stone and would give a pleasing impression were it not for the plastered brick tower. The Alcazaba of the Moslems exists only in name, and to look for its ruins is a waste of time; it is the counterpart of the Palacio of Marchena (see Ch. 9) and many another site which preserves the name of a vanished monument.

Guadix is 48 kilometres farther along N342 and lies in the valley of the Rio Verde, a minor tributary of the River Fardes, fed by the snow of the northern slopes of the Sierra Nevada— you should look half left as you enter Guadix, to see the snow-capped ridge. The waters of the Fardes eventually join the Guadalquivir, far to the north, and thus flow to the Atlantic across the breadth of Andalucía. The scenery is certainly strange, the broad, fertile river valley and its reddish cliffs contrasting with the ashen sugar-loaf hills honeycombed with inhabited caves. Guadix has a respectable ancestry and a turbulent past; it was a military settlement in the early days of the Roman empire (a plaque built into the wall of the Cathedral mentions a 'Caesar son of Augustus', and the badly spelled 'Colony of Acci'), and then one of the twenty-one Visigothic dioceses. After the Moslem conquest Acci became Wadi-Ash, the River of Acci, hence the transition to Guadix is easy.

The Cathedral is somewhat forbidding, with its great brown walls and mock cannon peeping over the top; it is another of those Gothic-Renaissance mixtures whose origin can be seen in Málaga, and therefore a cousin of Granada. It is the site rather than the building which holds the interest, for Guadix claims to be the cradle of Christianity in Spain and has records of a very early martyr, St. Torquatus. If, as seems likely, the mosque was built over the Visigothic church, then the present Cathedral also

occupies the historic site, for it is built on the Moslem foundations. This probably accounts for its poor orientation, with the
ornate Baroque front on the south face. The interior was so
much altered in the eighteenth century that it retains nothing to
delay you, for by now you are probably inured to the clustered
Corinthian columns, the dome on its four arches and the func-
tionless pseudo-Gothic vault ribs.

The Plaza de la Paloma, though considerably restored since
the Civil War, preserves its delightful Renaissance atmosphere,
not least in the Ayuntamiento. A harmonious feature, which you
can see elsewhere in the city as well, consists of galleries in the
upper storey, some even taking the form of projecting balconies
which, as always, lend distinction to the plain, whitewashed
walls. A little higher up the hill is the Church of Santiago, with
the typical Andalucian feature of an ornate Baroque portal
against a blank wall, the retablo effect that we first saw in Seville.
It has a superb *artesonado*, with some of the geometric patterns
picked out in gilt. The Alcazaba, originally of the ninth century,
occupies the top of the hill and is normally entered from the
seminary across the street by means of a bridge. It can also be
entered from the back, for it is partly a playground and the
pupils are obliging enough to open a door that leads on to an
unofficial rubbish dump. As the fine for dumping is clearly
announced as 100 pesetas, Guadix must be one of the richest
cities in Spain. Some restoration of the castle has been necessary
but it is inconspicuous, and the precincts, with their double wall
and towers, bring back an echo of the past, of Moslem days and
even earlier.

To the north you can see the opposite wall of the river valley,
studded with caves, such as were dug out of the cliffs of many
riverbeds in prehistoric times. To the south there is bare rock,
and sugar-loaf hills dot a landscape reminiscent of the foothills
of a volcano before vegetation has had time to grow. The scene
is thickly speckled with white dots, which are the limewashed
frames of doors and windows. This is the *barrio de Santiago*,
where the cave-dwellers have congregated most thickly. Take time
to visit them and you will have some preconceived ideas corrected.
Some of the caves are luxurious, with modern furniture, electricity and even the telephone: others, without being luxurious
still have their television set. If it is a hot day, the cave will give
welcome coolness; if cold, you will find warmth inside. Nearly
everywhere you will be invited inside with Spanish courtesy, for
few of the inhabitants here are gypsies. I have not discovered why

it is generally believed, even by Spaniards, that all cave-dwellers
are gypsies; there have been troglodytes in Spain as far back as
records go, as evidenced by Plutarch's account of the method by
which Sertorius overcame the Characitanians in about 77 BC.
These people were cave-dwellers in the caves of a large and
impregnable hill. Sertorius encamped his army beneath this hill
and attempted, though without success, to lay siege to the
stubborn tribe. On reconnoitring the hill one day, he noticed
that a strong northerly wind was whirling up clouds of dust from
the plain and blowing it in the direction of the caves. He immediately ordered his men to gather piles of dust and heap them up
as near the mouths of the caves as possible. The wind did the
rest, helped by the hooves of his cavalry which churned up even
more dust. A few days later the choked and blinded Characitanians were forced to leave their caves and surrender.

From Guadix you can make an excursion for about 15 kilometres on N324 (you can continue to Granada on N342) to see
the Castle of La Calahorra. It is the property of the Duchy of
Infantado and you will remember that the abbess of Santa Paula
in Seville was a member of this ducal family. La Calahorra is not
so readily opened to casual visitors as are her properties, but if
you have the correct introductions you will see an Italian Renaissance patio, the parent of the Vélez Blanco one but far more
orthodox. The architect and sculptor was the Lombard Carlone
and his team contained three other Lombards; the rest, both
men and marble, came from Liguria. Though many Italian
Renaissance patios can be seen in Italy, that of Vélez Blanco
(now in New York) is possibly the only example of a happy
mating with Hispano–Moresque tradition. Returning to Guadix
the road climbs to the Puerto de la Mora and then winds down
to Granada through magnificent scenery. But if you are doing
the journey in winter it is as well to enquire whether the pass is
open.

CHAPTER TWENTY-ONE

Granada to Jaén

✦

Pinos Puente—Alcalá la Real—Priego de Córdoba—Alcaudete—
Martos—Jaén

The old coach road to Córdoba is represented by N432, by which we leave Granada. A tramway accompanies us as far as **Pinos Puente**, where we enter the village on the right and quickly find that the road turns to cross the Rio Cubillas, a tributary of the Genil. Few bother to make the deviation from the excellent main road; if anything attracts them there, it is the anecdote about Columbus; yet the bridge itself has considerable merit, even without its associations. **See Map on page 260.**

The first feature is the chapel which straddles the bridge, the Puente de Pinos, an attractive structure, recalling that of Wakefield in Yorkshire. It was built in the eighteenth century to replace the ruins of a defensive tower destroyed by the artillery of Juan II who, with his favourite Álvaro de Luna, made an incursion into Granadine territory in 1431 (see Láchar, Ch. 14). The bridge itself is built on a large central horseshoe arch and two flanking smaller ones, which has led to the belief that it was of Arab construction; Emilio Camps Cazorla, however, has shown that it is of Visigothic origin,[1] if not earlier. One of its stranger features is the zigzag interlocking of the voussoirs, almost unique in Spain, though a well-known example is the Tomb of Theodoric in Ravenna.

Apart from the fierce battles which were fought here, the bridge is remembered for the Columbus episode. After many years of suspense he thought at last that the Conquest of Granada would allow the Catholic Sovereigns to give his project more attention. Perhaps because his terms were too high, perhaps

---

1. Experts use the extent of the prolongation of the semicircular arch in the horseshoe as one of their criteria. In this case the prolongation measures a fourteenth of a radius in the largest arch, and a sixth and a quarter in the others. Much of the sandstone masonry is in *soga y tizón*, in the ratio of 1:1, a method used by Romans and Visigoths before Moslem times. The last point, emphatically Roman or Visigothic, is the use of round starlings, or cutwaters, as footings to the piers instead of the pointed ones built by the Arabs.

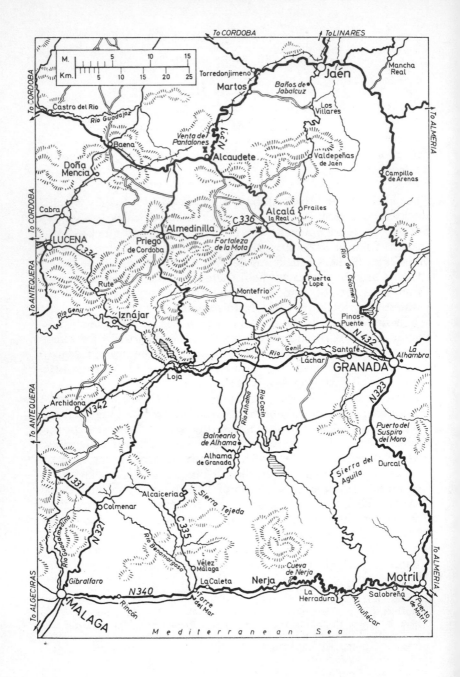

because of the expense of fitting out the expedition, his proposals were once more rejected. This time he determined to offer his idea to France or England, and was riding his mule along the road to Córdoba, when better counsels prevailed. Some say that it was Juan Pérez of La Rábida, who had once been Isabel's confessor, whose pleading turned the scale; perhaps it was simply a case of second thoughts. My own belief is that someone reminded their royal highnesses that the port of Palos had been sentenced to provide two caravels, free of charge, in the Queen's service for the current year; this would, of course, reduce the expenses of the expedition (see Ch. 9).

Alcalá la Real is about 30 kilometres farther, grouped round the steep hill on which stands the Castillo de la Mota. This was the headquarters of the Count of Tendilla, who was in charge of the march between Jaén and Granada, and later Governor of the Alhambra. The Count occupied an impregnable position, and one so near to the city of Granada that escaping Christian captives used to make for Alcalá la Real. In order to prevent the recapture of the fugitives, which occurred frequently, the Count built a watch tower on an adjacent hill and had a fire lit on it every night to serve as a beacon. The country here has many *atalayas*—it is possible to trace one line direct from Alcalá to Jaén—and both Christians and Moslems used them for signalling, smoke by day and blaze by night.

The castle is kept closed except when the bell has to be rung for a feast day or funeral, or when a visitor wishes to look round. The guardian is gouty and delegates a volunteer to take you up the steep lanes, through the outer ring of walls and up the steepest part of the climb to the locked entrance. Inside there is a horseshoe gate, with an adult fig tree growing out of the wall above it. The earliest chapel, a Gothic one of about 1520, still stands but the Church of Santa María de la Mota was allegedly burned down by the French; its ruins are extensive and you can distinguish Gothic and Renaissance remains. The circular stair of the bell tower is an example of fine craftsmanship; there is a ruined keep and a cannon stands upright with its nose in the ground—it is fondly supposed to be 'Moorish' but is indistinguishable from the cannons of the seventeenth century.

The view is what you would expect in this mountainous yet fertile region. Beyond the tawny roofs and whitewashed walls of the town the olive fields reach away into the distance, with parallel lines of trees set at different angles to produce the impression of an intricate set of planes. Three *atalayas* crown nearby hilltops, and far to the south is the white line of the Sierra Nevada. Just below you are the ruins of the Church of Santo Domingo de Silos, whose retablo is now in the Church of Santa María de las Angustias, which stands not far from the Ayuntamiento, in the lower town. The retablo, which is partly in bas-relief, while the rest is made up of paintings by Juan Ramirez, hangs at the side of the presbytery; it is too dirty to allow one to judge its worth. The baptismal font used for the infant Juan Martínez Montañés is of a simple Renaissance type and is kept in a store-room off the sacristy; when I last saw it it was used to hold tins of paint with which the doors and windows were being touched up.

The bronze statue of Martínez Montañés, who was born here in 1568, stands before the Ayuntamiento. We have seen some of his works, notably at Santiponce, and can confirm that he was remarkably restrained for a sculptor of the Age of Baroque. He combined classical balance, realism and humanity and was never other than dignified; his statues' serenity contrasts favourably with the emotional, almost hysterical works of the Castilian school of Juan de Juní and Gregorio Hernández. Those who saw *La Cieguecita* in Seville Cathedral will understand. His portrait by Velázquez hangs in the Prado Museum; it shows a rugged countenance with deepset but thoughtful eyes, and his features, like his hand, suggest strength combined with artistic sensibility. He appears to be making a preliminary sketch for his carving of Philip IV. He was summoned to Madrid, when he was well on in his seventies, to make this as a model for the bronze statue of the monarch by Tacca. Perhaps he valued truth above all things, as he neared the end of a fruitful life; at all events the King was not amused. If you have the chance to compare the Velázquez portrait with that of Gregorio Hernández (or Fernández) in the Biblioteca Nacional of Madrid, you may believe that aristocracy in art accompanies refinement of features.

Instead of continuing on N432 you may now go west along C336 through pretty country given over mainly to olive groves and orchards. At Almedinilla, on the left, a tiny fortified town clings precariously to a slope, a blend of East and West; even the name has a Spanish diminutive tacked on to *al-madina*, the city. We have temporarily left the Province of Jaén and after 30 kilometres reach **Priego de Córdoba**, a town whose spaciousness and repose convey an impression of wealth and distinction. Its wealth is undoubtedly due to the Catalan settlers who came here two centuries ago and founded the flourishing textile industry. To them too can be attributed the ostentatious, but attractive, house-fronts on many of the streets, so different from Córdoba itself where display is largely kept to the privacy of the patio. Your first view is of tightly packed white houses rising above a con-stricting dark wall, and it is therefore surprising to find how roomy the town can be, except in the picturesque Hispano–Moresque quarter.

Beginning from the main square, where the Ayuntamiento stands, we follow the gently rising Calle de los Héroes de Toledo. On either side are house-fronts of different styles, and the two churches are examples of over-decorated Baroque, which is only a foretaste of what is to come. As you continue up the street you may study the beautiful *rejas*, forged in a multiplicity of patterns, and the decorative balconies which are essential ingredients in the Spanish urban scene. At the top are the famous fountains, of which the lower, with its hundred or more jets, is called the *Fuente del Rey*; in the centre is Neptune in his chariot, a smaller edition of the fountain near the Prado Museum in Madrid. The upper is better described as a still, clear pool of cold fresh water; the Virgen de la Salud stands in a niche in the rock face behind. The area is away from the road, and can be reached only by steps; it is shaded by five great plane trees and stone seats invite rest and reflection. When Al-Edrisi passed through in the twelfth century he noticed that water ran down the main street, providing power for mills. The fountains must represent the upper part of the stream, and it is possible that the street you have just ascended was its ancient course. The Heroes of Toledo were, of course, the garrison of the Alcázar in 1936 and it was not difficult to find out the name of the street before the Civil War. It was Calle del Río, River Street.

Returning to the main square, the Calle del General Queipo de Llano leads to a War Memorial standing in a small park. Behind it rises the dark brown stone of the castle walls, fairly well pre-served. A horseshoe arch to the left of the entrance attests its ancestry and the remains of an *ajimez* in the wall of the keep adds the usual touch of interest. In front of the castle is a pretty complex of interleading squares, like miniature parks with fountains, and opposite stands the Church of Santa María de la Asunción, whose bell tower matches those of the castle. Just below it is the plain wrought-iron *cancela* of the west entrance; the rest of the exterior is partly whitewashed and an original note is struck by the assortment of angles made by the various parts of the tiled roof, culminating on the south side in a phallic emblem covered with green and white *azulejos*. This corner is the most attractive in a handsome town.

The inside of the Church is Rococo and has a Sagrario of 1782, a lesson to the unwary. Be prepared for a Ford fricassée of stucco, surrounding a central circular altar piece containing, among other startling ingredients, four lifesized gilt apostles. The introduction of foreign styles such as this is a sure sign of prosperity, unfortunately replacing the older, and to us more interesting, native art. The retablo of the high altar contains paintings by anonymous artists, and polychrome wooden statuary of considerable merit. There is an English grandfather clock here, as in so many Spanish churches and Turkish mosques, but this is an exceptional one which is not only going but registers the correct time and day of the month.

The other churches of Priego try to outdo the Sagrario. Down the Carrera de Álvarez the Chapel of the Aurora has gathered the worst excesses of Baroque flamboyance into the compass of its narrow front; this is but a prelude to the Rococo interior, in which vacuous and anything but angelic faces thrust through the white icing that covers the ceiling. There is also a huge gilt retablo. The Church of San Francisco, a few yards away, follows the same trend, but is redeemed by some fine sculptures of Montañés, especially his *Christ at the Column*. Try to avoid the Capilla del Nazareno, which simply piles on the agony, until you stagger out feeling that you have escaped from the inside of a wedding cake. The church front is rare and pleasing, with a peculiar type of pargetting, a design of joined eight-sided patterns each of which is the exact plan of a palaeo-Christian baptismal font. It is dated 1776. In spite of some of the church interiors, I leave Priego de Córdoba reluctantly, for here as nowhere else can be recalled the spacious days of the earlier, reforming Bourbons, an era of prosperity and the century which saw the birth of Francisco Salzillo and Goya.

Martos is a pleasant town with plenty of tradition. Its history takes it through the usual Roman and Visigothic days, but only becomes interesting when the governor, one Álvar, was called away to Castile with his troops, and Alahmar of Arjona (who founded the Nasrid dynasty in Granada) thought the time ripe for attacking the defenceless town. Álvar's indomitable wife, however, dressed the women in men's clothes and armour and baffled the artless Moslem, one of a race which seems never to learn. Martos is chiefly remembered for the judicial murder of the brothers Juan and Pedro de Carvajal, who were accused of killing Ferdinand IV's favourite, Juan de Benavides. The King sentenced them to be executed by being thrown from the great rock that dominates the town, the Peña. At the last moment the condemned brothers called upon (*emplazar*) the King to appear for judgement in thirty days, and thirty days later he died, thus achieving the title *el emplazado*. It may be suggestive that the first written account of the alleged episode appeared two hundred years later.

Of course, Martos has had other ups and downs; long after this episode, it was captured and sacked by the Moslems of Granada and among their booty was the infant daughter of the governor, Isabel de Solis. I have mentioned how she was brought up as a Moslem and became the favourite wife of Muley Hassan, thus founding an anti-Aisha faction, and possibly contributing to the fall of Granada. I have not recounted the sequel, that Queen Isabel received her with sympathy, persuaded her to return to the faith of her family and ennobled her two half-Arab sons, whose descendants continue to carry the Nasrid motto, 'There is no conqueror but Allah', in their coat-of-arms.

There is little to see in the town. The Church of Santa María de la Villa is next to the remains of the castle on top of the hill (not the Peña de los Carvajales, of course, which is much higher and right out of town); it has recently been restored and contains nothing of interest. The tombs of the Carvajals have been lost; some say they were in the Church of Santa Marta, which has an attractive Isabelline portal, others that they were in Santa María de la Villa. If the former is true, they have been replaced by a plaque; if the latter, then they were blown up during the Civil War. The old prison, which travellers once praised for its sumptuous exterior, is now the Ayuntamiento and has a handsome portal of 1577, its double door adorned with elaborate studs and handsome knockers of the same date.

Jaén is 24 kilometres farther, and before entering the city one should take a right fork (no signpost) leading to *Castillo de Santa Catalina*, now the sumptous D.G.T. Parador.

The view of **Jaén**, with traces of the three walls that used to connect it with the castle, is superb. As a change from the universal whitewash to which we have become accustomed, the predominant colour of roofs and walls is beige, with a golden gleam when the sun strikes at a certain angle. It irritates the *literati* that Manuel Machado, the poet, should have named it *Jaén plateado*, 'silvered Jaén', for they can find no reason for his choice of adjective. Perhaps he just liked the sound of the words, which would efficiently finish a hexameter. Beyond the town are the endless leagues of olive trees that produce the liquid wealth of the province and beget a hundred gems of wisdom among the old wives, such as, *Aceite de oliva, todo mal quita,* 'olive oil removes every ill.' In the evening the air is still and every ridge stands out sharply, while the long shadows of the olive trees look like the teeth of a giant's rasp.

It is believed, but is not certain, that this was the castle of Ibn Alahmar, who came to St. Ferdinand and offered to become his vassal while Jaén was being besieged. It was certainly rebuilt by the saint near the original site, for a plaque over the doorway states that it surrendered on St. Catherine's day, 25th November, 1246. There is a small Gothic oratory in one of the towers on the north side, the ceiling picked out with stars and the vault ribs decorated with the lions and castles of León and Castile. Light enters through hexagonal openings in the sides, closed with blue glass. The keep has a horseshoe entrance and is also reconstructed. Visitors should bear this in mind, for restoration bears the same relation to reconstruction as do cosmetics to plastic surgery. Before leaving, you should see the steep incline leading to a postern, where it is presumed that cavalry and baggage mules would enter and leave.

For two centuries Jaén was called 'the guard and defence of the realm of Castile' and you can still observe the northern colouring of the descendants of Castilians with whom the city was repopulated. Possibly for the same reason you do not quite feel you are in Andalucía, though there is nothing Castilian about the architecture.

The Cathedral is one of the very few in Spain, and possibly the only one in the South, which receives unanimous approval from the experts. There are two reasons for this: first, the building and its decoration are homogeneous, although it replaced a partly built Gothic church begun in 1512; and secondly the proportions are so faultless that the building seems perfectly balanced, whether it is seen from the Castle, from the streets or from inside. The concept needed a genius, and its execution men of skill and, above all, taste. The plan was that of Andrés Vandaelvira, passed over by many art historians, perhaps because his best work lies within the narrow confines of the province. His successors carried out his intentions loyally and that is why we do not see a work which begins in one style and continues in a succession of others, according to prevailing fashions.

Although Jaén Cathedral took 192 years to complete, there is only the slightest touch of Baroque feeling in the west front, introduced by López de Rojas. It is probably quite justified, for the pinnacles moderate a certain squatness which would otherwise result from the tall flanking towers. The creamy stone is, of course, necessary to the design, for one cannot imagine the same satisfactory impression had the stone been that of, say, Úbeda. Other attractive touches are added by the upper gallery of the south transept and the open space before the tall railings, where old people sit among the roses in the spring sunshine. The saints on the balustrade, all by Pedro Roldán, gesticulate in true Italian Renaissance style, but who ever saw an *alfiz* round a Renaissance window outside Spain?

The interior fulfils the expectations aroused outside; the plan, with a lantern supported on round arches and the whole resting on clustered Corinthian columns, recalls Málaga, Granada, Cádiz and Guadix. But none of them have the fine balance of Jaén which, without a trace of Gothic devices, achieves the soaring effect that the others miss. The crest of the Cathedral is reproduced here and there and needs elucidation, consisting as it does of the enthroned Virgin and Child over a dragon. There are several legends, all concerned with the appearance of a dragon, the *lagarto*, at a fountain in the Magdalena district, where the women went for water. According to one version a knight encrusted his armour with mirrors and then slew the dazzled beast. Is it possible that Cervantes drew inspiration for his Knight of the Mirrors from this? The better-known version, however, is that a condemned criminal was offered his life if he slew the beast; he filled a sheep skin with gunpowder (which makes the *lagarto* comparatively modern), attached a fuse and threw the dummy to the dragon, who obediently swallowed it and blew himself to pieces. Since then any loud report here is called 'the explosion of the *lagarto* of La Magdalena'.

The *coro* has some finely carved stalls of the sixteenth century; they impress both individually and in the mass. The wooden canopy has scenes from the Old Testament which foretell those of the New. The upper row of stalls, which is the best, shows scenes from the life of Christ, and the lower an eclectic martyrology. Among the team of artists were a German named Gierero and López de Velasco, father-in-law of Jacobo Florentino l'Indaco. The chapels are copiously decorated with works of art, among which a few are of major interest; the only one that appeals to me is a *Pietà* by José de Mora in the fifth chapel on the right. A pretty detail is the inclusion of two cherubs as 'weepers', howling their little heads off, each with its pocket handkerchief. In the Sala Capitular, or Chapter House, is a fine retablo featuring incidents from the life of San Pedro de Osma, a work of Pedro Machuca who, you will remember, was a painter and retablo maker before he began to build the palace of Charles V on the Alhambra.

The Cathedral Museum contains 97 works of art, most of them by artists of purely local repute, though there are a *St. Matthew* and a *St. James* by Ribera and a *Head of John the Baptist* by Valdés Leal. There are several eighteenth-century works which are, to say the least, bizarre. Among these is a *Last Supper*, in which a whole lamb, still in its skin, sits on the dish while a cat and dog are visible under the table. Another exhibit is an escritoire and reliquary combined, in ivory and gilt, with a miniature orchestra. My favourites are Nos. 88 and 97, a *tenebrario* or fifteen-branched candlestick, and a Pascal candlestick by Bartolomé de Jaén, the master of wrought iron, whose *rejas* we have seen elsewhere.

The Cathedral's pride and joy is the *Cara de Dios*, the Face of God, the second fold of Veronica's kerchief and similar to the Santa Faz in so far as the holy countenance looks out from a golden shield, in the Byzantine style. It was said to have been carried at the head of St. Ferdinand's army when he captured Jaén, or received its negotiated surrender. The relic is exposed on Friday afternoons and at other times is kept securely locked away in a jewelled case in a strong-box behind the high altar. It is stated categorically that Bishop Nicolas de Biedma received it personally from Pope Gregory IX in 1376. There is, however, a school of thought which maintains that the kerchief was a papal gift to a certain St. Euphrasius, one of the first seven evangelists in Spain, whose diocese was Iliturgis, between Bailén and Andújar. The holy man had been asked to come to Rome and liberate the Pope from the temptations of the devil. Fortunately Euphrasius had a captive goblin who, in return for the promised left-overs from his master's supper, agreed to carry him to Rome, a journey which was accomplished in half an hour. All ended happily, with Satan retiring baffled, the saint richer by a kerchief and the goblin feasting on the left-overs.

Opposite the Cathedral is the Ayuntamiento, with its decorative seventeenth-century front, and next to it the Archbishop's Palace with a pleasant loggia below the roof. Leaving this on our left, we go north along a narrow street, Calle del Doctor Martínez Molina, more concisely called La Maestra, one of those which are closed to wheeled traffic and protected by *toldos* in summer. This leads to the northern part of the city, which is also the oldest, though we have to omit the Church of San Ildefonso, a heavy Gothic structure, which lies to the east. All other places of interest can be visited along this route, which is also the most picturesque, with its steep streets intersecting the road as they climb the slope of Santa Catalina. A little way along, on the right, is the Primitivo Club, or casino (No. 22), formerly the fifteenth-century palace of the governor, the Condestable Lucas de Iranzo. In the basement are ceilings commonly called Mudéjar, but actually the work of Moslem craftsmen borrowed from Granada, as Pedro the Cruel did in Seville a century earlier. They are not true *artesonado*, for they are not shaped like inverted troughs, but the wooden painted *enlacería* is there in all its intricacy.

At the next fork, we bear right to the Plaza de San Bartolomé; in the fifteenth-century church here there is a fair *artesonado* and a green ceramic font with Gothic writing in relief. You will remember, from Carmona, how the making of these was prohibited, so that all extant specimens are of considerable age. There is a Montañés *paso* for Holy Week, the *Cristo de la Expiración*, which is too realistic for the sophisticated.

Hereabouts the streets become narrower, steeper and more frequent, and give you glimpses of picturesque corners; the relative absence of trees and whitewash will be noticed, but cobblestones, weathered brick and street-lamps, window grilles and closed-in balconies contribute to the old world atmosphere. Few will remember the craze for a game called *diavolo* at the turn of the century; it consisted of spinning a wooden object, something like a tight-waisted cotton reel, on a string stretching between two sticks. So popular was it that *Punch* even had a drawing that showed the missing arms of the Venus di Milo restored with the hands holding the sticks of the diavolo. Jaén is the game's last outpost, and here you may see staid matrons and perky schoolgirls lounging in doorways or running along the winding streets, spinning their *diavolo* tops. Games are strictly segregated between the sexes; a small boy here would blush to be found practising *diavolo*.

We continue along the streets of San Bartolomé and San Pedro, holding a northward course until we reach the Plaza de los Caños, where a weathered *pilar* of 1648 attempts to imitate Machuca's fountain on the Alhambra. Apart from other differences, this one no longer produces water, but it makes a good receptacle for rubbish. A turn to the east along the Calle de Santa Cruz and a succession of corners bring you to the **Capilla de San Andrés**, perhaps ranking as the high point of this tour. Knock loudly for the caretaker, make sure you tip him and your reward will be prompt. San Andrés is said to have been built on the site of a synagogue, but of this there is no trace today. In the patio is a bust of the founder, Gutierre González Doncel, who was treasurer to the Medici popes, Leo X and Clement VII, in the 1520s. The interior consists of a nave and two aisles, separated by three pointed horseshoe arches on each side. The showpiece is the **Capilla de la Purísima**, in which is a painting of the Florentine School, showing the Virgin with a rayed nimbus of gold, hence her name *la Virgen de la Luz*. The *reja*, by Master Bartolomé, is the glory of the chapel, exquisite and small, and one of the few examples of his art in his own home town. It is of wrought iron, polychrome and gilt, and has the fairly common refinement of figures in mirror image that are welded together to suggest solidarity. The upper part shows the Tree of Jesse; below is the Marriage of the Virgin. Before leaving, ask to be shown the tiny Mudéjar door (*la puerta pequeña*) leading to the pulpit and the tiled stairs on the other side.

On the far side of the next block is the *Internado de Santa Teresa*, a converted Arab palace, in whose basement are the extensive Arab baths. The main structure is still recognisable, but neglect has had its usual effect, and the borrowing of floor and wall tiles has taken away all its charm. Restoration has already begun but in the meantime it is still used as a lumber room. Above, there is a brick patio of Renaissance type, but nothing else of interest. A little farther on the *Monasterio Real de Santo Domingo* has become a boys' school. The nuns who direct it gladly point out what is usually regarded as its major interest, the Plateresque patio with the famous portal of Vandaelvira, dated 1582, on the south side. It has had a colourful past, for it occupies the site of what was first an Arab palace, then the residence of St. Ferdinand, and later the local headquarters of the Inquisition.

The furthest point of the tour is the Church of La Magdalena, presiding over the parish of that name. It occupies the site of a mosque and in the courtyard is the *alberca*, a large Arab rectangular pool, fed by a constant stream and containing goldfish. Apart from this, it represents the ritual ablution site of Moslem days and the wall of lacy brickwork surrounding it is in keeping with its history. The site is one which Ford described as 'the

fountain which bursts from the rock as if struck by the rod of
Moses'; the source is in the neighbouring plaza and the description helps us to understand how the parish got its name. This was
of course the fountain to which the women of Jaén used to
repair until the dragon moved in. The foundation and name go
back to the early days of the Reconquest, when the gush of water
reminded the pious of the tears welling from the eyes of Mary
Magdalen (*John ch. xx, v.* 11). The cloister walk round the pool
has had many Roman tombstones incorporated in its walls,
suggesting that the site was outside the Roman town where
burials would have been prohibited. Recently, when the layers
of limewash were stripped from its walls, Gothic frescoes were
discovered. The interior of the church is of the common Gothic
pattern of the Reconquest; its pride and joy is the famous *Calvary*
of Jacobo Florentino, in polychrome and gilt wood. The expressions of the individual figures are as admirable as the craftsmanship and it is not surprising to learn that it took second prize in a
competition in Seville some forty years ago.

We return at a higher level and pass through the Plaza de San
Juan. The church of that name preserves an old defensive tower,
now called the Council Tower, or Torre del Consejo, where the
city fathers had their first meeting place after the Reconquest.
Continuing along the Calle de Aguilar, with its picturesque, steep
side-streets, you come to the Arco de San Lorenzo, probably
a post-Reconquest, but possibly an even earlier gateway,
now standing isolated in its plaza. A Mudéjar chapel has been
built over it, with a dado of mosaic tiles and a Gothic retablo,
but as it is permanently closed, no further description is called
for.

The Calle Almendros continues to the Church of La Merced,
a relatively modern building, which contains the celebrated figure
of Padre Jesú Nazareno. It is rare enough for Jesus to be called
'Father', but here His popular name, probably expressing still
more devotion, is *abuelo*, grandfather. The seventeenth-century
figure, older than the church, is in a chapel on the right, surrounded by *ex votos*, including even medals, on the plinth. Continuing in the same direction we join the Calle de Juan Montilla,
which leads from the Cathedral round the old city walls; these
are easily recognised, even though houses have been built into
them, for towers stand here and there and the sweep of the
crescent is still that of the old perimeter. On the left of the road,
and below its level, is the Convent of the Carmelitas Descalzas,
the reformed Order founded by St. Teresa. It contains a precious

manuscript, the original *cántico espiritual* of St. John of the Cross, whose life and work illustrate the Spanish temperament so well. It is shown to visitors at 4 pm, a time strictly observed.

Juan de la Cruz was born near Ávila, grew up in poverty, went to Medina del Campo with his widowed mother, became a male nurse and novice at the Carmelite priory, and was sent to Salamanca for a three years' university course. Possibly the most important event in his life took place at this point, for he attended the classes of Fray Luis de León, an Augustinian monk who had recently been appointed lecturer in theology at the University. León was a poet and one of his best-known works was the translation into Spanish of the Song of Solomon; thus Juan de la Cruz (at that time still called Juan de San Matías) met poetry, mysticism and religion in one rich blend. Both he and his teacher were to suffer at the hands of jealous rival orders in the future.

Juan was soon to come under the influence of St. Teresa, herself a mystic, and take part in the founding of the barefoot Carmelites who, by the way, wear sandals. His life was the mirror of his soul, while his poetry attains heights of ecstasy that few have attempted. In his work culminated the image of Divine Love clothed in carnal language, which had its beginnings in the Song of Songs (we shall assume that this was not, as sometimes stated, an Oriental love song included in the Bible by mistake). 'I charge you, O ye daughters of Jerusalem, by the roes, and by the hinds of the field, that ye stir not up, nor awake my love, till he please.' In the *Cántico Espiritual* we have the same imagery, the *ninfas de Judea*, the leaping antelopes and the appeal for silence, 'that the Bride may sleep secure'. And again, *Cogednos las raposas, que está ya florecida nuestra viña* sang Juan—literally, perhaps, for he was fond of singing—'Take for us the foxes, for our vine has now come to flower , . .'; what else is this but, 'Take us the foxes, the little foxes, that spoil the vines . . .'?

To explain Juan's poetry as inspired solely by the fiction of secular love displayed in the Song of Songs would be to ignore another influence, that of sufi mysticism. We met Ibn Abbad at Ronda and Ibn Arabí at Murcia; the latter is universally regarded as a philosophic and poetic genius, and although his speculations on the relationship of God and man may be too refined for our pragmatic age, we can at least sense the identity of Ibn Arabí's 'celestial light' with the 'active intellect' of Aristotle, and Juan's *sumo saber*, the supreme knowledge that is beyond the scholar's grasp. In similar vein Ibn Arabí explains the erotic nature of the paradise promised to the true believer, and himself uses erotic similes, in order to bring the eternal truths within the grasp of the common man. In this climate of emotional mysticism it is surely unnecessary to resort to the psychiatrist for the explanation of the more explicit passages in the poems of St. John of the Cross.

CHAPTER TWENTY-TWO

Baeza, Úbeda and the Sierra de Cazorla

⚜

From Jaén to the Guadalquivir is 35 kilometres on N321. The river is by now fairly broad and spanned by the Puente del Obispo, named after Bishop Alonso Suárez de la Fuente el Sauce of Baeza. He had the bridge built in 1508 as one of his many good works; the modern one, recently completed, is less picturesque but better suited to the volume of traffic it has to carry. The countryside is fair and fertile and, of course, the olive tree provides the main crop; at many a village you catch the scent of freshly pressed oil as you pass the refinery. Once north of the Guadalquivir, although the landscape does not change, you can sense a difference in the towns and villages; in those through which we have passed so far, the appearance of a turbaned Moor would cause little surprise; we now enter a region where the same sense of fitness would greet the vision of an armoured knight. The exploits of the warriors of Baeza, during the days of the Reconquest, earned the city the title of *Nido Real de Gavilanes*, 'Royal Nest of Falcons', and Úbeda was the home of the twelve knights who fought the Moorish champions under the walls of Algeciras.

Baeza is 8 kilometres from the Bishop's Bridge, a town full of interest and, like Úbeda, one where the lover of old stones can profitably pass a day or a week. It has been populated continuously since the Bronze Age and has had its moments of glory and its famous sons, both in peace and war. Few towns were peaceful when the Middle Ages drew to a close and the first task of the Catholic Sovereigns was to infuse a sense of discipline and obedience into the nobles. Among the hundreds of troublesome castles that were ordered to be razed was that of Baeza, whose demolition was ordered by Isabel as early as 1476, that is a year before her throne was made safe by the defeat of her rival, Juana la Beltraneja, at the battle of Toro. Among the noble families who were settled here at the Reconquest, the chief trouble-makers were the Carvajals and the Benavides, mostly originating in Segovia. The earlier inhabitants, as we know, fled to Granada and founded the Albaicín. It was usual for strong points to change hands several times during the Reconquest, and Baeza was no exception. On one occasion, it is said, the retreating knights shod their horses backwards and once more fooled the simple infidel.

Entering from Jaén, the right fork leads immediately to a quiet and charming plaza. On the east side is the **Antigua Carnicería**, the old slaughterhouse and meat market, a Renaissance work of the mid-sixteenth century. Its grilled windows, plain front and carved coat-of-arms of Charles V make it the most attractive slaughterhouse that human eye has ever seen; its function has been transferred to other quarters, and this beautiful building will one day be a museum and library. Facing you is the Audiencia Civil, the Appeal Court, another fine Renaissance building in golden stone, somewhat older than the Carnicería. Its erection was authorised in 1511, 'above the fountain of the said city', and the building had to include a chapel near the Jaén Gate, where the first mass was said after the capture of the city in 1227. The ground floor at the front consists of six entrances between piers above which are seven lions. The entrances were once booths in which public scribes sat, hence the plaza was occasionally called *de los Escribanos*. Today it serves an equally useful function by housing the Tourist Offices and the local Chief of the Fine Arts Ministry, Don José Molina Hipólito, a genial and scholarly authority on the whole district, including Úbeda. His published works include guidebooks to that town as well as Baeza.

At about the time when the Audiencia was built, *La Fuente de los Leones* is thought to have been brought here from the ruins of the Carthaginian, and later Roman, city of Castulo. Its water gushes from the mouths of four weathered, couchant lions with curly manes and collars; this detail suggests that they may have been the lions of Cybele. There is nothing to support this belief in the central female statue, but as she has lost her left hand, we do not know whether she carried a *patera*, drum or drumstick, the usual attributes of the goddess. She also lost her head, quite literally, during the Civil War when she was mistaken for the Virgin Mary, though local tradition has always dubbed her Himilce, whom Hannibal married at Castulo, just north of Linares. A new head has now been made for her and goes well with her classical draperies.

At the south-west corner of the plaza is the Arco de Jaén, to which the Audiencia is joined. A delightful balcony occupies the corner, and a painting of the Virgin used to be housed here, to which the knights would say their prayers before leaving on a foray through the adjacent arch. This arch is not the original one, but a special construction voted by the city council to welcome Charles V during his first visit, as the original arch had been destroyed at his grandmother's orders. Next to it is another, the Arco de Baeza, erected to celebrate the Emperor's victory over the *Comuneros* in 1521; this should evoke a smile, for Baeza was one of the few towns that took the side of the insurgents.

A flight of stone steps takes us past the east side of the Audiencia; we immediately turn left along the cobbled Calle del Beato Juan de Ávila and find on our left the massive building that used to house the University of Baeza, perhaps the least known in Europe. Springing from its corner is the Arco de Barbudo, named after a Master of Alcántara who rode out through this gate in 1394 to meet defeat and death at the hands of the Moslems. Inside the arch is a wall shrine to the Virgin, one of the thousands that are seen throughout Spain. It is not uncommon for them to carry a few lines of doggerel, encouraging the passer-by to offer up a prayer. This is one that may be seen elsewhere, but is relatively unusual.

> *Si quieres que tu tristeza*
> *se convierte en alegría,*
> *no te pases, pecador,*
> *sin saludar a María.*

If to joy you wish to change your woe,
Hail Mary, sinner, ere you go.

The Instituto Nacional de Enseñanza Media, formerly the University and now a high school, is a large but undistinguished building of the usual cream-coloured stone, black with lichen on the north side. The poet Antonio Machado taught French grammar here for seven years, having moved from Soria after the tragic death of his beloved nineteen-year-old wife. An Andalucian by birth, a Castilian in upbringing and residence, he nevertheless managed to combine the colour of the South with the sombre fatalism of Castile; common to both is the flash of reality that underlies all Spanish fantasy, as Sancho Panza alternates with Don Quixote. For example,

> *El ojo que ves no es*
> *ojo porque tu lo veas,*
> *es ojo porque te ve.*

The eye you see is not an eye because you see it;
it is an eye because it sees you.

If it is not the decisive answer to Hume, Bishop Berkeley and
the other Idealists, it is at least as telling, and much more concise
than anything the Realists have thought up.

At the end of the street is the Romanesque portal of the much-
restored Church of Santa Cruz, the only survivor of many
churches built soon after the Reconquest. The original south
portal is at the side; the west, which faces you, was brought
from the ruined church of San Juan. Plaster unfortunately dis-
guises the original masonry and inside the pointed arches are also
relics of the restoration. On the right is a horseshoe arch with
characteristic Visigothic proportions; on the left frescoes of the
fifteenth and sixteenth centuries have been uncovered. Turning,
you can see the **Palacio de Jabalquinto** facing you. The richly
ornamented façade is based on the Isabelline style, with a
Renaissance loggia above. Door and windows are still Gothic,
of a sort, and the *picos*, or diamond studs, are reminiscent of a
building in Segovia. There are also stylised pine cones, floral
designs, stone lacework and the eight heraldic crests of the
founder and his wife. On either side rise cylindrical columns that
splay out into six rows of stalactites; they probably looked more
at home when the balconies they supported were still there.
There is a fine Renaissance patio, with white marble columns, and
a monumental Baroque stair with profuse decoration. The
building is now a seminary, a good thing, for it is kept in repair
and there is no difficulty about seeing the various parts. Perhaps
the best of these is the Salón de Actos or Archives, where six
columns with their Romanesque capitals were placed, after
being saved from the ruined Church of San Juan.

Turn right on leaving and continue uphill for a few yards, and
you emerge in a depressing plaza, where a rather ponderous
arch of triumph with all the medallions and telamons of the
heroic age rises from a fountain. It is not as bad as it sounds,
when reduced to its proper proportions before the **Cathedral**.
This jumble of Gothic, Renaissance and Baroque is not a thing
of beauty, but at the north-west angle a square tower rises on the
lower courses of the previous minaret. The west front, next to it,
contains the Puerta de la Luna, an outstanding example of
Mudéjar work of the thirteenth century. It consists of a cusped
horseshoe arch, similar to those of the Casa de los Caballeros
de Santiago in Córdoba (see Ch. 3), except that this one is made

of stone instead of brick and plaster. To enter the Cathedral you have to send a small boy, with a promise of rich gifts, to find the sacristan's wife, who has the keys.

The Cathedral turns out to be another hybrid of the type that we have seen so often, with Gothic bottom and a Renaissance top. It is, however, cool and roomy. A chapel on the left, that of Santiago, has a relief of St. James the Moor Slayer, obviously modelled on the one at Úbeda, which we shall see shortly. Among the many works of art I prefer the pulpit of 1580 and the *reja* that closes the new *coro* (the old one was in the religiously orthodox but architecturally prejudicial position). The former is hexagonal, repoussé and coloured, and represents a wide variety of subjects, not forgetting the family crest of the canon who paid for it. It is believed to act as a sheath for an older, wooden pulpit that was used by St. Vincent Ferrer in 1410. The *reja* is another of Master Bartholomew's wonderful works, carried out in the early sixteenth century. The bishop at the time was the same Alonso who commissioned the Puente del Obispo, and his coat-of-arms is incorporated in the *reja*. The cloister should also be visited, and especially the Mudéjar (as usual called Mozarabic) chapels, with their horseshoe arches and stucco work.

Go a short distance south from the Cathedral, with as many digressions as you can find, through a quarter of narrow, cobbled winding streets, where the house-fronts are partly stone, partly plaster and whitewash, a compromise between Castile and Andalucía. Doors of once aristocratic houses stand out with their ornaments and *alfices*, and their family crests, often blurred with layers of limewash. Eventually you reach the Paseo del Obispo and, turning left twice, find your way to the Puerta de Úbeda, one of the few reminders of the ancient fortifications. A square tower survives and carries the arms of the Catholic Sovereigns; the arch itself has its beauty enhanced by the street-lamp that hangs from the centre. Part of the old wall runs south from here and finishes at another tower; the only other remnant is west of the Puerta de Jaén.

To the west, on the other side of the Plaza del Generalísimo, are the ruins of the Franciscan Convent and Church, in which much of Vandaelvira's finest work survives on the portal. The Ayuntamiento was formerly the prison and law courts combined and its façade is a jewel of Andalucian Plateresque. It demonstrates what, to my mind at least, is the essence of the style, at its most attractive, with stretches of plain wall between the decorated doors and windows. To most of us it is in better taste than the over-decorated front of the Jabalquinto Palace. The chief exhibit inside is the giant custodial, which should by rights be housed in the Cathedral, but the theft of the first one in 1628 and the loss of the second in the sacristy fire of 1691 persuaded the authorities that divine protection was best reinforced by profane. It is a huge edifice of silver, partly gilt, and offers everything that the most ardent iconolater could desire, if not more.

On the way back to the Plaza de los Leones you pass the Casas Consistoriales Bajas, on a corner of the boulevard, built in such a way that the city fathers could use its balcony to watch bullfights and other spectacles. These would have included the annual procession of the bull of St. Mark, instituted in fulfilment of a vow that caused a plague of locusts to depart. The excuse is immaterial; the old habit persists, with or without the caressing of the symbol of fertility by the women. At one time it was even obligatory for the bull to attend Mass.

After having walked through the oldest part of Baeza you have now returned to your starting point, and across the road is the Plaza de los Leones. You can now drive along the side of the boulevard towards the Plaza del Generalísimo. On the left are the trees of the Alameda, always a welcome feature in Spanish towns; on the right, an arcade with projecting upper storeys supported by wooden posts, and a side-walk and shop-fronts in the dark, cool shadows. It is only to be expected that wooden columns are now being replaced by brick or concrete and that the imposing fronts are drifting towards modern mediocrity. The old city grain-store, once situated inside the barbican, can still be seen about half-way along. Though the Alhóndiga long ago lost its function and much of its beauty, it still presides over the line of shops where the various crafts plied their trade in olden days.

Crossing the Plaza del Generalísimo you enter the Calle de San Pablo, which continues north-west as the road to Úbeda. Once Baeza had no further need of walls the nobles had their mansions built in the suburbs. You pass the imposing fronts that now disguise the modern premises behind them, or the ruthless work of rebuilding. There are the Palacio de los Condes de Garcíez, of which the upper storey still preserves its primitive plan; the Baeza Club, once a castle; the sixteenth-century Casa de los Acuña, with an *alfiz* in its Renaissance front; the darker face of the Casa de los Cabrera, with the brownish tinge that we shall see in Úbeda; and on the left the Parish Church of San Pablo.

The sobriety that characterises the streets of Baeza, always excepting the Palacio de Jabalquinto, is maintained in this church; its treasures are few, but the best are a *Cristo de la Expiración*, attributed to Pedro Roldán, and a triptych, believed to be from the brush of Van Dyck, in the Chapel of Nuestra Señora de Fátima. The name honours a miracle-working Virgin who appeared in the Portuguese village of Fatima in 1917. The local saints are more numerous than those of any other town, for the eleven thousand virgins of Cologne are said to have been born here. Both their number and birthplace are subject to correction, for the claims of Cornwall are stronger, and the earliest reference gives only ten companions who preferred death to dishonour. Ford gives various explanations which might account for the discrepancy and points out that eleven virgins would hardly suffice for the thousands of reliquaries that contain their remains. An even greater mystery is why there is no church in Baeza dedicated to St. Ursula and her companions.

Úbeda is very near, only 8 kilometres away, which gives an indication of the country's fertility. Almost unknown to foreigners today, it was once a city of consequence, a fact which will dawn on you as you pass from one monumental building to another. It is a Renaissance town rising from an Arab street plan, with old walls and towers, historic treasures, imposing views, friendly inhabitants and a magnificent hotel in a sixteenth-century palace. Let us begin there.

The **D.G.T. Parador del Condestable Dávalos** is named after a famous son of Úbeda, but was built and maintained for a time as a residence for the chaplain of the adjacent Church of the Saviour. It is a beautiful building and the weary traveller, looking at its horizontal lines, can begin to feel rested even before he has set foot inside. The two storeys are simple and aristocratic which, in fact, sums up the whole town; attractive grilles and wrought-iron balconies decorate the windows, with red, pink and white flowers cascading from them. Under the roof runs a classical frieze of egg and dart pattern, and a corner balcony has the slender, white marble pillar that is seen here more than in any other town. I need not detail all the interior attractions. The furniture is a compromise between antiquity and comfort; thus the electric bedroom lamps are of a complicated Oriental pattern, like enlarged, glass sea-urchins. The rooms and passages are carpeted with a famous local product, the *ubedies*, which were one of the chief exports of the town in Moslem days. They were woven of esparto grass and, though not brightly coloured, are attractive for the age-old patterns which are woven into them. The waitresses wear local costume—in this they are unique— their dresses being red, blue or green with bright, embroidered flowers, their stockings white and their aprons black. They wear starched white caps and the thongs of their slippers criss-cross up the legs like the *endromides* of the ancient Greeks.

The Constable of Castile, after whom the Parador is named, was the third to hold that office; he assisted at the capture of Arcos de la Frontera, which became a part of his fief. Incidentally, he actually did take part in the capture; the Spanish word *asistir*, simply means to be present at or, in a secondary meaning, to render medical care. The visitor must not, therefore, show astonishment when he reads that St. John of the Cross died in this town, 'assisted by the Ubedan doctor Villaroel'.

In front of the Parador is a spacious square, partly planted with flowering shrubs and trees and surrounded by buildings of the beautiful local stone. This is difficult to describe, being light grey when freshly cut and darkening with age, at the same time acquiring a brown tinge. How much of the colour change is caused by a lichen is difficult to estimate; some of it, however, is undoubtedly due to age. On the left is the imposing façade of La Iglesia de El Salvador, which occupies one of the narrow sides of the oblong Plaza de Vázquez de Molina. It was founded in the mid-sixteenth century, by Francisco de los Cobos y Molina and his wife. They were important people, for he was secretary to Charles V and his wife was a friend of the Empress, Isabel of Portugal. The third pair in this illustrious group were Francisco de Borja, Marqués de Lombay, Duke of Gandía, and his wife Leonor. The Duke is better known today as St. Francis Borgia, great-grandson of Pope Alexander VI and thus great-nephew of Caesar and Lucrezia Borgia. The Cobos crest, five lions *passant regardant*, is on the left side and can be seen on many other buildings in Úbeda. That of his wife, Doña Maria de Mendoza, balances it on the other.

Doña Maria was one of the attendants to the first wife of Prince Philip, and was present at the birth of Charles V's first grandson. Unfortunately, the story goes, she and the other lady-in-waiting went out for a few hours, as girls will, to watch an *auto de fé* at which two heretics were condemned. During their absence the Princess asked for a lemon, which was given her by a serving-maid 'not knowing that it could harm her', the result being her sudden death. The interesting fact that emerges from this tale is that the medical writer who recounts it in 1951 adds how lucky we are today, now that the toxic potential of the lemon is substituted by beneficial vitamins. Others, however, have suspected that her sudden death was due to a pulmonary embolism.

The church was planned by Diego de Siloé and built by Andrés de Vandaelvira, of Flemish origin but born in Spain. Its general outline recalls that of Murcia Cathedral in that the massive building rises gradually to a central apex and is flanked by a tower, reminiscent of the mosque and minaret. The corners are occupied by sturdy cylindrical buttresses and the central panel is a display of fine relief sculpture, biblical and allegorical. The interior has noble proportions, though partly obscured by eighteenth-century ornamentation; there is, however, a fine *reja*, presented by Álvaro de Mendoza, Bishop of Palencia and brother of Doña Maria. The most important artistic work is the Jesus from a group of statues by Alonso Berruguete, probably the only work of this outstanding sculptor to survive in Andalucía. The rest of the retablo was destroyed in the Civil War, which was particularly hard on church treasures in this area. A red crayon sketch of the whole work has been found in the Uffizi Gallery of Florence and shows how the artist projected the subject of the Transfiguration. Another casualty was the statue of St. John the Baptist as a child, a sensitive study in alabaster by Michelangelo, of which only the hand survives. A host of other treasures has just disappeared, but a pretty chalice was saved, originally a favourite goblet of Charles V, which he gave to his secretary. Cobos had the Gothic decoration added round the stem and presented it to the church.

The square contains five other handsome buildings, the Palacio de las Cadenas, now the Ayuntamiento, where the municipal archives are also kept; the Carcel (prison) del Obispo, which was nothing more than a home for women who wished to retire from the world without taking vows, the Palace of the Marqués de Mancera, the present recruiting hall, and lastly the **Church of Santa María de los Reales Alcázares**. A conglomeration of styles from different epochs, this rests on the foundations of the principal mosque and incorporates a few remains of the old citadel, as its name implies. The front is typical of Úbeda; to describe each variant of an art form which you can see in almost every street would be boring. Behind the main portal is a part of the castle wall with a Romanesque doorway, reached from the cloister. This is small, Gothic and crowded, with only three sides surviving. Its most attractive feature is a cypress completely hidden by creepers. It is difficult to make a mental reconstruction of the patio of the mosque, but this is where ritual ablution took place among the orange trees. The western walk of the cloister still shows the *soga y tizón* masonry; elsewhere there are early Christian reliefs on the walls, floral and animal designs, and the earliest-known city arms with the archaic feature of lions with crested manes. The church has three naves, as well as a row of chapels in each side-wall, and an ugly, bright blue ceiling of the seventeenth century replacing the original wooden one. Of the surviving ones, the Gothic Ivy Chapel (Capilla de la Yedra) has another of Master Bartholomew's *rejas*, showing the Tree of Jesse and the Meeting at the Golden Gate. The latter shows two companions of Joachim, one with a sheep draped round his neck, the other with a mediaeval shepherd's crook, which leaves no doubt as to Joachim's profession. Two *rejas* in other chapels are attributed to the same craftsman, but are less impressive.

The typical, narrow street between the Parador and the Church of the Saviour leads past the Palace of the Cobos if you branch right, and otherwise along the Calle Horno del Contador. On the left, at a corner, is a plain mansion whose heraldic crest has woodwoses as supporters; hence it is called La Casa de los Salvajes. We emerge in the large Plaza del Generalísimo Franco, whose previous names include Mercado, Cercado, del Rey and de la Constitución. It had the first of these names in Cervantes' time, and there was an inn at No. 37 in which he is said to have stayed. The centre of the square has a modern statue of St. John of the Cross and facing you is the imposing mass of the **Church of St. Paul** (Iglesia de San Pablo).

It is difficult to picture scenes of violence in the peaceful streets of Úbeda, but as recently as 1936 destruction of church property assumed frightening proportions. Similar destruction took place during the Civil War that finished with the murder of Pedro the Cruel and the triumph of his bastard half-brother, Henry of Trastamara. The city declared for Henry and was sorely damaged by one of the former's supporters, Pedro (or Pero) Gil. Among other punishments, he set fire to the Church of St. Paul and its archives in 1368, but it was not for that reason that he became a favourite character for the story tellers of those days. On one occasion a damsel named Elvira, with whom Pero Gil was in love, was abducted by a Trastamara supporter, Rodrigo Chaves, and brought to Úbeda. Pero, or some say King Pedro as well, found his way into the town and in fact into the Chaves residence, where, with the help of a handy priest, he forced his host to marry the girl. No sooner was her honour thus restored than he

killed the bridegroom and married the girl himself. A busy night
for the priest.

The south front of San Pablo, facing the square, is a fine
example of Gothic architecture and decoration. The *trumeau*
between the studded leaves of the door carries a statue of the
patron saint, with his usual attributes of sword and book. The
tympanum has a relief of the Coronation of the Virgin. On the
left of the portal a railed enclosure, the *tabladillo* of 1610, served
for the reading of municipal edicts, and above it a balcony of
1686 was made so that the dignitaries of the church could watch
bullfights. A similar balcony adorns the upper storey of the
Ayuntamiento, at the west end of the plaza, and was built for
the same purpose. The apse of San Pablo dates from 1380, so
that we may assume it was part of the reconstruction donated by
Henry of Trastamara to the 'loyal' city. Its charm depends on an
entirely extraneous object, the ornamental Renaissance fountain
of 1559, round which there is always a crowd of gossiping women,
children, mules and asses. Seen against the grey stones and white
mortar—another distinctive local feature—it makes what used
to be called 'an artist's bit'.

The interior shows transitional trends, and many of the capitals
have quaint Romanesque figures of men and animals among the
foliage which is so characteristic of the Gothic masons' work.
There are several chapels that deserve more than a passing
glance, two of them with fine *rejas*. Opposite the north entrance,
and easily identified by the skulls above the arch, is the Plateresque
Chapel of the chamberlain Vago, also called the Chapel of the
skulls, *de las calaveras*. Apart from its ornamentation, believed
to be among the first of Vandaelvira's works, its name, La
Capilla del Camarero Vago, gave rise to one of the few misunder-
standings possible in the precise language of Castile. This was
because the high-born and wealthy chamberlain bore the same
title as a waiter, so that a countryman, being shown the grandiose
chapel of *el camarero*, hurried to the nearest tavern to ask for a
job. By a strange chance the last chapel on the right offers another
example of linguistic confusion; you will usually hear it called
the Chapel of the Duke of Alba, whereas its name, La Capilla
del Alba, refers to the first light of dawn (*el alba*) which enters the
church through its window.

Half-way down the east side of the plaza is the narrow Calle
de San Juan de la Cruz, formerly named Callejón de los Toros,
because the bulls for the corrida were herded into the plaza
through here. Its present name derives from the fact that it leads

to the **Oratory of St. John of the Cross**. This is where he died, and the Oratory itself was the first building erected to his memory. A plaque on the small side-door states that he was admitted here to the Convent of the barefoot Carmelites (he was suffering from a 'putrid fever') on the 28th September, 1591, and another on the main entrance that he died here on 14th December. His body has had almost as many adventures dead as alive. We found it being stolen, in the first chapter; it now rests in the Carmelite Convent of Segovia and when last seen, in 1859, was still incorrupt. When I said that his body rests among the Carmelites, I was exaggerating: *some* of it is there, it is too much to expect any saint's remains to be in one piece, for even a finger-nail may perform miracles. In the case of the 'Ecstatic Doctor', as he has been officially entitled, a leg and a hand have been saved for Úbeda and remain in this chapel.

It is not far to the Puerta de Losal which, being a Mudéjar construction of the thirteenth century, is much nearer the pure Oriental type than works done by subject Moslems after the Reconquest was complete. The double horseshoe arch opens sideways from a mean, cobbled street and, as usual, is placed at right-angles to the city wall outside, so that assailants would be exposed to every noxious substance that the defenders could drop on them. Beyond the gate and down the hill to the right is the Valencia quarter, where potters still ply their craft in the old way and produce the single-handled amphora of Moslem days.

The busy east-west Corredera de San Fernando marks the line of the old north wall of the town and the recent demolition of a house has revealed an octagonal tower that was once a part of the defences. Crossing the Corredera into the Plaza de Abastos, and climbing the hill at the far end you arrive at the **Church of San Nicolás**, a notable example of Gothic architecture, originally built in the thirteenth century under St. Ferdinand, but whose present form is that of a hundred years later, with portals of the late Gothic and Renaissance periods. The Gothic portal, which faces you as you climb the street, is fairly simple and anything but typical of the Isabelline style of its time, 1509. It was, like so many other constructions, ordered by Bishop Alonso Suárez, who had the bridge over the Guadalquivir built, and his crests with episcopal hat and tassels are carved above the door. The cornice is based on ball-flower moulding and supports a statue of St. Paul. The west door is by Vandaelvira and dated 1566. The viewer can make up his own mind regarding the respective merits of the styles.

Vandaelvira's work is seen again inside, where the Dean's Chapel, though quite out of harmony with the plain Gothic interior, is a marvel of rich Plateresque decoration; its *reja* is remarkable, enabling you to compare the skill of a local craftsman, Álvarez de Molina, with that of Master Bartholomew, whose works we have seen elsewhere. As with retablos, so with *rejas*; the painting and gilding are by another hand, that of Antonio, son of Julio de Aquilis the Italian painter who helped to decorate the Tocador de la Reina in the Alhambra Palace.

From here you may go south-west, past several Renaissance mansions, to the Plaza del General Saro, situated at what was the north-west corner of the old walled town. It is a pretty square, with a fountain and rose garden (and sometimes a swarm of very tame bees) in the centre. On the side of the old town rises the **Torre del Reloj**, part of the old fortifications, whose line can be followed down the Calle Queipo de Llano southward, where other towers are interspersed with the houses. The tower dates from the thirteenth century and is crowned with a Renaissance housing for the great bell, still used to announce solemn occasions. The clock is, of course, modern, but below it in a shrine, is the *Virgen de los Remedios*. It used to be the custom for kings to swear before this statue that they would uphold the rights and privileges of the town. Among them were Charles V and his son Philip II.

Above and below the clock are the crests of the Hapsburgs and the Town of Úbeda. The latter consists of a golden crown, conceded by Henry of Trastamara, and a border of twelve lions *rampant*, commemorating the Ubedans who accepted the challenge of the Moorish champions during the siege of Algeciras. Some of their names turn up over the centuries, Cobos, Molinas and Cuevas. Among the latter was Beltrán de la Cueva, intimate friend of Enrique IV, *el impotente*, and obviously of his queen, from the fact that her daughter, whose claim to the throne was successfully fought by Isabel the Catholic, was commonly called La Beltraneja.

A digression west takes you along the wide Calle del Obispo Cobos to one of Úbeda's finest buildings, a masterpiece of Vandaelvira, the **Hospital de Santiago.** It stands back from and above the road on the right, its steps flanked by stumpy columns with heraldic lions. The entrance is a round arch in a plain *alfiz*, with voussoirs of the huge dimensions that we see in sixteenth-century buildings throughout central and northern Spain, and even in Sicily, which was at that time a Spanish possession. They are so long as to be almost grotesque, each stone about the length of the radius of the arch. An iron lamp projects from the wall on either side. Above the entrance is a dedication, *Maria sin pecado concebida*, which may strike you as a trifle priggish a little later. Above that again is Vandaelvira's signature tablet, almost a reproduction of the one in Baeza Cathedral and another on the north portal of the Church of the Saviour here. It shows St. James the Moor Slayer on horseback, trampling over the fallen infidel. So far there is nothing remarkable about it; Vandaelvira's quirk is to have the hindquarters of another horse projecting into the composition.

The plan of the building, grouped round its beautiful patio, is satisfying. Compared with El Salvador it is plain and restful, and the creamy stone of the corner turrets sets off their pyramidal steeples set with coloured tiles. From the right side of the patio a monumental stairway leads to the upper floor, its walls and ceiling decorated with *trompe l'oeil*. The frescoes in the coffered ceiling are the original ones, as fresh as the day they were painted. The Chapel was badly damaged in the Civil War, and only its general plan, a *reja* and some ceiling paintings in the sacristy remain.

The hospital is one of several that were built or adapted to a specialised purpose, the treatment of syphilis. Its charter specifies that it was founded for this, 'and for no other disease', and we saw the same use made of the Hospital Real in Granada. In Seville the erudite and kind-hearted priest and poet, Juan de Salinas, was made governor for life of the local Hospital de las Bubas, as the disease was called. No stigma appears to have attached to the disease, for his aristocratic friends contributed impartially to comforts both for the patients and for the nuns of a nearby convent, of which Salinas was confessor.

Back at the Plaza del General Saro, we turn south along the Calle de Queipo de Llano, which continues as Calle de la Cava, with the remains of the town walls on our left, appearing as an occasional tower among the house-fronts. At the end, the old wall reappears and near the south-west corner is a *mirador*, a tiny promontory from which, among the rose bushes, you have the choice of a variety of views. You can now see that the town itself stands on a shelf and the south wall reinforces the protection of the cliff. Here and there splashes of colour show where the curtain wall has been pulled down and the stones used for houses, so that whitewashed fronts, gay with balconies of flowers, are dotted between the towers. At the foot of the cliff are the allotments of the townsfolk, who come out of an evening to till or weed and in due course to gather their harvest, returning home in the twilight with their laden donkeys. From here the tiled roofs are an exact match for the walls and one's first impression is of scattered grey church towers rising from a tawny mass of stone. To the south the fertile valley of the Guadalquivir stretches into the distance, where the purple sierras show as a fringe on the horizon. So flat is the plain that 'The Hills of Úbeda' have become proverbial and to go over the Hills of Úbeda is equivalent to perpetrating a *non sequitur*. The following legend provides the best illustration.

The first objective after the victory of Las Navas de Tolosa in 1212 was Úbeda, and Alfonso VIII was preparing his assault within a few days. He posted one of his commanders, Álvar Fáñez the Younger (*el Mozo*) in the plain to cut off the Moslem retreat at the right moment. But Álvar met a damsel, a Moslem damsel, needless to say, and in a copse; the first meeting was but a prelude and a return match was arranged for the following day. Unfortunately for Alfonso VIII as it turned out, the assault had also been arranged for that day and at the crucial moment Álvar was in the copse and the inhabitants of Úbeda escaped. Naturally he was called on to explain his absence, and was asked by the King where he had been; Álvar, his head still full of romantic memories, waved his hand vaguely in the direction of the vast plain of the Guadalquivir and replied, 'In those hills, Sire.'

In the neighbouring part of the town there are a few more rewarding sights. The gypsy quarter is attractive, and it is common for an artist to settle down at a street corner day after day to attempt his interpretation of a picturesque scene. The Puerta de Granada is on the south side too, leading out on to a steep bank with a winding, neglected path. It is all so dull and commonplace now, a plain arch in an untidy wall, an unpaved street and some simple cottages. Yet it is through this gate that Isabel the Catholic rode out from Úbeda on her way to the front, during the war for Granada.

To the north there is a maze of quiet streets, with the **Casa de las Torres** in one of them. Though largely spoiled by reconstruction—it is now a school—it is still worth seeing for the rich façade between the towers, decorated with everything that a powerful imagination could produce. The voussoirs are, of course, on a majestic scale, medallions and crests abound, wild men support the shields, while friezes of intricate carving, a lavish use of columns, niches, gargoyles, sirens, conch-blowers and dragons elbow each other out of the best places. On the few spaces that were left bare stone scallop shells were placed as a reminder that the owner, a member of the Dávalos family, was a knight of Santiago. Behind and to the right is the Street of the Moon and Sun; the Chinese-sounding name comes from one of the many aristocratic houses, on whose front a sun and moon are carved. To the north is the Church of San Pedro, too often sacked to preserve more than a faint breadth of its Romanesque origin, and a baptismal font possibly of the same epoch or even older. Making for our starting point to the east, we pass two buildings that deserve the name of palace, more generously bestowed in Spain and Italy than elsewhere. One is the four-storeyed tower of the Palacio del Conde de Guadiana, in which one corner balcony over another shows the white marble column. Its top storey, which resembles an Italian loggia, is almost identical with that of the Palacio de Vela de los Cobos, which lies a short way south on the way to the hotel. Both have those corner columns and the look of aloof breeding that characterise Úbeda.

To the east the **Sierra de Cazorla** rises abruptly out of the plain. Scenically it is one of the most attractive parts of Southern Spain and can be recommended to anyone in search of quiet and unspoiled natural beauty. Its landscape varies, for at one moment you may imagine yourself in Switzerland, at another in the Black Forest, and yet again in the Lake District. A delightful coolness is the rule, even at the height of summer, and there are a thousand paths between tall pines, mountain oak and juniper, black poplars and cherry trees. Bracken and ferns provide cover for the busy wildlife that is never far away, and in unsuspected corners you may come upon lilies, jasmine and violets. The latter is a rare species, discovered at the beginning of this century, the *Viola cazorlensis*, or giant violet, found nowhere else in the world. As though this were not enough, there is the D.G.T. Parador del Adelantado, built like an Andalucian *cortijo*; I need not detail its attractions, for the words 'D.G.T. Parador' are synonymous with good taste and comfort.

Cazorla is a game reserve, and the wildlife photographer will come back year after year; the hunter must obtain his permits in Madrid (they are not cheap, for it costs 5,000 pesetas to bag one mountain goat), and learn the local rules by heart. It is best to buy your permit through a travel agent, from the Dirección General de Montes, Caza y Pesca Fluvial. You should really have a guide, for among other pitfalls there is a fine of 3,000 pesetas for killing the female of any species other than the wild boar. The Arabs, who were fooled so often, would become paupers under the existing regulations. Various species of stag, the moufflon or wild sheep, and the wild goat are the chief targets for the individual sportsman, while wild boar are often the victims of a *battue*.

Bird life is varied and picturesque; the Peña de Halcones overshadows the town of Cazorla and lives up to its name, being not only the haunt of falcons but of the royal eagle, which has a wing-span of four feet. This is dwarfed by the rare *quebranta-huesos*, the bone-breaker, a giant with a wing span of 10 feet, comparable only to the lammergeier of Central Europe and the great condor of the Andes. The name is taken from the birds' habit of taking bones with them and dropping them on a rock, which enables them to get at the marrow. It is obvious that the habit was noted from earliest times, for Aeschylus is said to have been killed by a tortoise dropped in this way, the eagle, otherwise noted for its good vision, having mistaken his bald head for a rock.

The drive to **Cazorla** is best made by taking the Jodar road from Úbeda and then turning left on C328 after crossing the Guadalquivir. The lower hills on the left conceal the remains of a Roman, later an Arab town where some excavation has been done. Among them is a shallow cave with traces of the manacles with which a prisoner could be secured in such a way that his head could be fixed beneath a water spout. This Chinese water torture, turning up here, demonstrates how much civilisation had spread in the Dark Ages. Cazorla itself is a small town, whose only remarkable feature is the Puente de las Herrerías, alleged to have been built for Queen Isabel to pass over on her way to the campaign of Granada. This is where you first experience the sense of imminence, the feeling that the great crags which seem to lean over the valleys are about to fall. This is repeated and even intensified at the next village, La Iruela, where the old castle is perched on a narrow, sheer rock that seems to cleave its way through the houses like the prow of a ship in the ocean.

Seven kilometres farther we enter the Reserve, and at the barrier there is a humble but pleasant hotel, El Control, where a large room, private bath, full board and perfect quiet can be had for 200 pesetas a day. From here, roads take you through the various parts of the Coto Nacional de las Sierras de Cazorla y

Segura, to give it its full title. Only 6 kilometres farther there is a *mirador*, from which the young Guadalquivir can be seen winding down the valley like a silver thread, a paradise for the fisherman. The Embalse del Tranco is an artificial lake in the course of the Guadalquivir, fifteen miles of serpentine, placid water that blends with the alpine scenery. For once we admit that man has improved on nature. A little beyond its northern end lies **Segura de la Sierra** with its magnificent, restored castle; apart from the glimpse of Moslem days and the picturesque whitewashed alleys so typical of Andalucía, the town gains interest from the fact that it lies astride the great watershed of the south. To the west, the Guadalquivir collects the autumn rains and the melting snow of spring; eastward, the Segura winds through the Murcian landscape, bringing its waters to the *huertas* where corn and fruit and palm grow in the folds of a desert.

The return journey should follow C328 for 13 kilometres to Peal de Becerro, where an Iberian necropolis will interest some. From there a good country road crosses the Guadalquivir, giving a last glimpse of the famous river. You have now probably seen its source, followed it past Andújar, the Bridge of Alcolea, Córdoba, Seville, through the desolate *marismas* and to its mouth at Sanlúcar de Barrameda. Nutrient, majestic, historic, one leaves it for the last time with a twinge of regret.

Torreperogil is soon reached, but of the castle of Pero Gil himself, one of whose adventures I have recounted, only two towers remain, one of them octagonal. The Gothic-Renaissance church was so thoroughly plundered during the troubles that one must look upwards for anything that was out of reach of the mob. There is an attractive and curious fresco in the ceiling of the sanctuary, whose restrained colours contrast favourably with, for instance, the blue of Santa María de los Reales Alcázares in Úbeda. Torreperogil is near the scene of St. James' first triumph on the field of battle. As I have explained earlier, it was believed for centuries that he came to the rescue of the hard-pressed Spaniards at the Battle of Clavijo; now the battle has disappeared from the record of history and has been placed in the pages of legend. But the legend itself has been transferred from Clavijo to nearby Lentíscar, where a minor skirmish resulted in the defeat of the Moslems after they had burned the Sanctuary of Santiago. The Sanctuary was rebuilt in the eighteenth century and is visited on the saint's feast day, but few know that the patron himself made his first of many appearances near the little town of Torreperogil.

From Úbeda you may return to Bailén through Linares, an

ugly mining town near the Carthaginian and Roman settlement of Castulo. There is a museum of finds from this site, but it is housed in a school and only open for half a day a week, on Tuesdays when I last visited it but now it is quite likely to have changed. To some the town is of importance because Manolete, Prince of Matadors, was killed there on the 28th August, 1947; the date is documented as the traditional day of the autumn fair for at least a century. It is far pleasanter, however, to leave Úbeda by the quiet C3217, passing through olive plantations and over rivers, to meet the main Madrid road at La Carolina. From there you climb the Sierra Morena by the same highway on which you entered; and return to a different Spain, where a palm tree is a prodigy, fertile valleys no longer intersect the barren uplands and harsh extremes of climate replace the languorous southern air.

Chronology

To make it easier to grasp the relationships of time, this brief chronology of men and events is offered. Its scope is limited to people and places described and visited in Southern Spain.

Date	Christian Rulers	Moslem Rulers	Events
700	Witiza Roderick	17 emirs	Expedition of Tarif (710). Invasion of Spain by Tarik and Musa (711) Battle of Covadonga (718)
750		Abderrahman I Hisham I	First part of Córdoba Mosque built
800	Alonso II		
		Abderrahman II	Second part of Córdoba Mosque
	Ramiro I (of Asturias and León)		Discovery of body of St. James Alleged battle of Clavijo Viking raid on Seville
850		Mohamed I Mondhir Abdallah	Rebellion of Omar Ibn Hafsun
900		Abderrahman III	Death of Ibn Hafsun Medina Azzahra begun
950		Hakam II (His Basque concubine, Subh, Hisham II (Almansor virtual ruler)	Third part of Córdoba Mosque Fourth part of Córdoba Mosque

Date	Christian Rulers	Moslem Rulers	Events
1000		Nonentities	Battle of Calatañazor; death of Almansor
		End of Caliphate. Taifas (1031)	Destruction of Medina Azzahra
1050	Alfonso VI of León	Al Mutamid (Seville)	
		Almoravid invasion	El Cid (died 1099)
1100		Almoravids	Almohad invasion (1147)
1150	Alfonso VIII	Almohads	Giralda begun (1184)
1200		Second Taifas	Battle of Navas de Tolosa (1212)
	Ferdinand III, the Saint		Conquest of Guadalquivir Valley, Jaén,
		Mohamed Ibn Alahmar, first Nasrid Sultan of Granada (1238–72)	Úbeda, Murcia, Córdoba, Seville
1250	Alfonso X, the Learned (*el sabio*)	Mohamed II of Granada	
	Sancho IV, the Wild (*el bravo*)		Guzmán el Bueno at Tarifa (1294)
1300	Ferdinand IV, the Summoned (*el emplazado*)		The Carvajal brothers at Martos
		Yusuf I	The Alhambra Palaces built
1350	Pedro the Cruel (*el justiciero*)	Mohamed V	Alcázar of Seville rebuilt
		Mohamed VI, the Red King	Civil War. Defeat of Henry of Trastamara and Bertrand du Guesclin at Navarrete
	Henry II, of Trastamara		Return of Henry and killing of Pedro (1369)
1400	Juan II		Álvaro de Luna's expedition against Granada. Capture of Pinos Puente and Láchar
1450		Muley Hassan of Granada	Spanish Inquisition (1480)
	Isabel I, the Catholic		Spain united

Date	Christian Rulers	Moslem Rulers	Events
1450		Boabdil	Conquest of Granada
	Ferdinand II of Aragón, the Catholic		Discovery of America

Date	Christian Rulers	Artists Architects Writers	Events
			Life and achievements of Gonzalo de Córdoba, *el Gran Capitán*
1500	Juana the Mad (*la Loca*)	Berruguete, Alejo Fernández, Felipe Vigarni, Luis de Vargas, Pedro de	House of Pilatos, Seville ConquestsinAmerica
	Charles V, the Emperor (Charles 1 of Spain)	Campana, Luis Morales, Martínez Montañés, Sánchez	
1550	(first Hapsburg)	Cotán, Jacobo Florentino, El Greco, Torrigiani, Enrique	Victory of Lepanto (1571)
	Philip II	de Egas, Diego de Siloé, Andrés Vandaelvira	Drake and Essex raid Cádiz (1587, 1596) The Invincible Armada (1588)
1600	Philip III	Miguel de Cervantes Roelas, Ribera, Zurbarán, Murillo, Velázquez, Alonso Cano.	Seville School of Sculpture Granada School of Sculpture
	Philip IV	Vicente Espinel of Ronda, Luis de Góngora	
1650	Charles II, the Bewitched	Pedro de Mena, José de Mora Francisco Salzillo	
1700	Philip V (first Bourbon)		War of the Spanish Succession
1750	Charles III		An interlude of peace and reform
	Charles IV	Francisco de Goya	First modern corrida at Ronda (1786) Godoy favourite
1800			Peninsular War (1808-14).

Date	Christian Rulers	Artists Architects Writers	Events
	Joseph Bonaparte		Constitution of Cádiz (1812)
	Ferdinand VII		Insurrection of Colonel Riego. The 100,000 Sons of St. Louis (1823)
	Isabel II	George Borrow (1835–8) Richard Ford (1845)	Carlist Wars
1850		Pablo Piccasso (1881–)	Battle of Alcolea (1868)
	First Republic (1874–5) Alfonso XIII		
1900			Abdication of Alfonso XIII (1931) Civil War (1936–39)
	Generalísimo Francisco Franco		

Glossary

The following words, most of which occur in the text, may be encountered while sight-seeing.

Ajimez	Twin window with central column
Ajo	Garlic
Alameda	Promenade, originally under poplars
Alberca	Artificial pool
Albergue	Hotel, inn
Alcaide	Seneschal of castle
Alcalde	Mayor
Alcarraza	Clay jar
Alcazaba	Citadel (Ar. *kasba*)
Alcázar	Fortress (Lat. *castrum*)
Alfaqui	Moslem religious teacher
Alfarje	Decorative woodwork with geometric patterns
Alfiz (*alfices*)	Rectangular frame or 'label' of door or window
Aljibe	Cistern
Almenado	Castellated
Almenas	Merlons
Almohadillo	In quilted pattern
Almohads	Fanatical sect from Morocco; Spanish dynasty in twelfth–thirteenth century
Almoravids	Sect and dynasty preceding Almohads
Alternativa	Ceremony of admission as fully fledged matador
Arroz	Rice
Artesonado	Ceiling, often decorated with *alfarje*, shaped like an inverted trough
Atalaya	Watch tower
Atarazana	Shipyard (Ar. *Dar assinaa*, house of work)
Ataurique	A form of Arabesque, usually in stucco
Auto de fé	Formal reading of sentences passed on prisoners of the Inquisition
Ayuntamiento	(1) Town Council, (2) Town Hall
Azulejos	Coloured tiles
Banderilla	Dart used in the corrida
Banderillero	Torero who plants the *banderillas*
Bandolero	Brigand
Bandurria	Small instrument of guitar family

Barrio	District
Boquerón	Anchovy
Brasero	Brazier, usually placed under the table
Búcaro	Clay jar
Burladero	Safety screen in the bull ring
Burlador	Joker
Caballero	Gentleman
Cadí (Ar.)	Judge
Cala (Ar.)	Anchorage
Calañés	Hat of straw or palm fibre
Callado	Silent
Camilla	Long table cloth draped to retain warmth of *brasero*
Cancela	Wrought iron lattice screen
Cántaro	Water jar
Cante	Song, singing
Cante hondo	Deep song, variety of flamenco
Cantiga	Archaic poem
Caño	Conduit
Capa, capote	Bullfighter's cape
Capilla	Chapel
Caridad	Charity
Caseta	Hut, booth
Casino	Club
Castillo	Castle
Cerrado	Closed
Cerro	Hill
Ciudad	City
Claridad	Clearness
Cofradía	Religious association
Compás	Outside courtyard
Convidado	Guest
Copla	Popular song or verse
Coro	Choir of church
Corrida de toros	Bullfight
Cortijo	Complex of farm buildings
Cuadrilla	Matador's team
Cubierto	Covered
Cubilete	Dice box
Cuerda seca	Technique of tile making
Cueva	Cave
Cufic	Archaic Arabic lettering
Cuna	Cradle, foundling home
Chanquete	Whitebait
Churros	A kind of fritter
Darsena	See *atarazana*

Desamparado	Forsaken
Diez	Ten
Doce	Twelve
Duende	*Panache, espièglerie*. There is no adequate English term
Encierro	Herding of bulls into their pens
Enjuta	Upper corner of an *alfiz*
Enlacería	Reticulated wooden tracery
Espada	(1) Sword (2) Matador
Espontáneo	Unauthorised participant in bullfight
Estilo	Style
Fábrica	Factory
Facistol	Lectern
Farol	Street-lamp
Feria	Fair
Fiesta	Festival, holiday
Flamenco	(1) Flemish (2) Flamingo (3) A traditional form of song and/or dance
Fonda	Inn (Ar. *fonduk*)
Gaita	Bagpipes
Gallego	Galician
Garrocha	Goad
Gazpacho	Cold infusion of vegetables
Giraldillo	Weathercock
Guadamacilería	Ornate, often embossed leather work
Guiñapos	Rags, leavings
Hermandad	Brotherhood
Hidalgo	Nobleman
Hormigón	Concrete
Hueso	Bone
Kibla (Ar.)	Direction of Mecca
Lagartijo	Lizard
Lagarto	Crocodile, dragon
Lazo	Loop
Lidia	Bullfight
Lienzo	Canvas
Maestranza	Equestrian association
Majo	Plebeian dandy
Maksura (Ar.)	Lattice screen
Maravedí	Spanish coin, in use until last century, dating from and named after the Almoravids

Matador	Principal torero
Membrillo	Quince
Mezquita	Mosque
Mihrab (Ar.)	Niche meant to designate the *kibla*
Mimbar (Ar.)	Pulpit in mosque
Mina	Tunnel, mine
Mirador	Belvedere
Mocárabe	Wall or ceiling decoration of niches and stalactites
Morisco	Moslem convert to Christianity
Mozarab	Christian living under Moslem rule
Mozo	Youth, servant
Mudéjar	Moslem living under Christian rule
Muladí (*muwallad*)	Christian converted to Islam
Muleta	Crutch. Red cloth and batten used by matador
Mushrabiyyah (Ar.)	Screened window
Nacimiento	Nativity
Naranjo	Orange tree
Naskhi	Cursive Arabic script
Negro	Black
Niña	Girl
Noria, Ñora	Arabic water-wheel
Novia	Sweetheart, bride
Nuevo	New
Obispo	Bishop
Obras	Works, repairs
Olambrilla	Brick and tile floor patterns
Opus sectile (Lat.)	Inlaid marble surface
Oreja	Ear
Paella	Rice dish, whose home is the Kingdom of Valencia
Pantano	Reservoir
Párroco	Parish priest
Parroquia	Parish, parish church
Pasadizo	Corridor
Paso	(1) Step (2) Processional float carrying sacred images
Patillas	Side whiskers
Patio	Interior courtyard
Pesebre	Nativity set piece
Pica	Lance, goad, pike
Picador	Mounted torero
Piedra	Stone
Pilar	(1) Column (2) Ornamental fountain
Piquero	Herdsman using a goad

Plateresque	Ornamental Renaissance style, named after the work done by *plateros*
Platero	Silversmith
Plaza Mayor	Main square
Potro	Colt
Pronunciamento	Declaration of revolt
Puerta	Door, gate
Puerto	Port, mountain pass
Putti (Ital.)	Naked children used in decorative art
Rabo	Tail
Racimos	Clusters, bunches
Rambla	Sandy walk (Ar. *raml*—sand)
Razzia	Raid
Real	(1) A coin (2) Royal (3) encampment
Reja	Wrought iron grille
Rejoneo	Type of bullfight in which the matador is mounted
Retablo	Reredos, retablo
Romería	Pilgrimage, usually combined with a holiday and picnic
Rosetón	Rose- or wheel-window
Rueda	Wheel
Saeta	(1) Arrow (2) solo, unaccompanied song during Holy Week processions. Recently sung with accompaniment and commercialised
Sagrario	Church or chapel housing the Sacrament
Sala de Fiesta	Night-club
Salado	Salty
Salvador	Saviour
Sebka (Ar.)	Reticulated tracery
Sellía, subsellía	Rows of choir stalls
Semana Santa	Holy Week
Serrano	Of the sierra
Sierpe	Snake
Sierra	(1) Saw (2) Mountain range
Sillería	Choir stalls
Soga y Tizón	Masonry laid with alternate blocks sideways and end on
Soledad	Solitude
Sopa	Soup
Suerte	(1) Chance, luck (2) Phase of bullfight
Sufi (Ar.)	Religious mystic
Taifa	Splinter states after the fall of the Córdoba Caliphate
Tajo	Gorge

Tapas	Snacks
Tapia	Pisé *à* terre, cob, or wall thereof
Tenebrario	Fifteen-branched candelabrum
Tentadero	Miniature ring for testing fighting cows
Tesoro	Treasure
Tinaja	Large clay jar
Torero	Any bullfighter
Toril	Bull pen opening into the arena
Toro	Bull
Torre	Tower
Trascoro	Wall of the *coro* furthest from the high altar
Trumeau	Stone pillar between leaves of double door
Tympanum	Space above portal, usually bearing bas-reliefs
Vara	Lance
Vega	Cultivated plain
Vela	Vigil
Venta	Country inn
Verde	Green
Voussoirs	The stones that combine to form an arch
Walí (Ar.)	Governor
Yeso	Plaster
Zaguán	Passage leading to patio
Zancarrón	Foot bone of Mohamed
Zaragüelles	Baggy breeches (Ar. *sirwal*)
Zarzuela	Light opera

Books for Reference or Further Reading

Books for Reference or Further Reading

❧

Among the foreign books listed, those with the letters (G.A.) belong to the excellent series of *Guias Artísticas*, edited by Professor Gudiol

English

ARNOLD, T. & GUILLAUME, A. (Ed.) *The Legacy of Islam*, London, 1931
  A guide to the appreciation of Islamic culture
ATKINSON, W. C. *A History of Spain and Portugal*, Penguin Books, 1960
BEVAN, B. *History of Spanish Architecture*, London, 1938
BORROW, G. *The Bible in Spain*, London, 1906 (original edition 1842)
BRENAN, G. *The Literature of the Spanish People*, 2nd ed. Penguin Books, 1963
  The best English language compendium
Id. *South from Granada*, Penguin Books, 1963
  Daily life in the Alpujarras
CHASE, G. *The Music of Spain*, New York, 1941
CLEUGH, J. *Image of Spain*, London, 1961
CONDE, J. A. *History of the Dominion of the Arabs in Spain* (Trans. J. Foster), London, 1854
  Detailed but unreliable
DAIX, P. *Picasso*, London, 1965
DAVIES, R. TREVOR *The Golden Century of Spain*, London, 1964
  The sixteenth century; the zenith and beginning of the decline
DONALDSON, D. M. *Studies in Muslim Ethics*, London, 1963
DUMAS, A. *From Paris to Cadiz* (Trans. A. E. Murch), London, 1958
ELLIS, HAVELOCK *The Soul of Spain*, London, 1908
EPTON, NINA *Andalusia*, London, 1968
  An up-to-date account of people and customs
FORD, R. *A Handbook for Travellers in Spain*, London, 1966 (original ed. 1845)
Id. Murray's Handbook for Travellers in Spain, 6th ed., London, 1882
  The original account on which so many English travel books have relied. Spain has changed in the last century
GIMENAS REYNA, S. *The Dolmens of Antequera*, Antequera, 1967
GUDIOL RICART, J. *The Arts of Spain*, London, 1964
  The best summary of Spanish art in the English language
HARE, A. *Wanderings in Spain*, 5th ed. London, 1885
HARVEY, J. H. *The Cathedrals of Spain*, London, 1957
HINDE, T. *Spain*, London, 1963

IRVING, W. *The Conquest of Granada*, London, 1910 (first published 1829)
Id. *Tales of the Alhambra*, Granada, 1951 (first published 1832)
LANDAU, R. *Morocco*, London, 1967
LEWIS, D. B. WYNDHAM *The Shadow of Cervantes*, London, 1962
LIVERMORE, H. *A History of Spain*, London, 1958
MACAULAY, ROSE *Fabled Shore*, London, 1949
MICHENER, J. A. *Iberia*, New York, 1968
Another of the many books about people and customs
MILNE, J. LEES *Baroque In Spain and Portugal*, London, 1960
MORTON, H. V. *A Stranger in Spain*, London, 1955
MUIRHEAD'S *Southern Spain*, 2nd Ed., London, 1964
The standard guide book. Some details need revising
PILLEMENT, G. *Unknown Spain, Andalusia and Southern Spain* (Trans. A. Rosin), London, 1967
Some interesting routes
POLNAY, P. DE *A Queen of Spain*, London, 1962
The Life and Times of Isabel II (ruled 1833–1868)
PRESCOTT, W. H. *History of the Reign of Ferdinand and Isabella*, 2nd ed., London, 1883
ROMERO Y MURUBE *The Alcázar of Seville*, Madrid, 1966
SITWELL, S. *Spain*, 2nd ed., London, 1951
SORDO, E. *Moorish Spain*, London, 1963
STIRLING-MAXWELL, SIR W. *Annals of the Artists of Spain*, London, 1891
Id. *Stories of the Spanish Artists until Goya*, London, 1910
Largely excerpts from Cean Bermúdez (see below)
TREND, J. B. *The Civilization of Spain*, London, 1952
Id. *Spain from the South*, London, 1928
TSCHIFFELY, A. F. *Round and About Spain*, London, 1952
One of the few travel books by a writer who spoke Spanish
WILLIAMS, L. *The Arts and Crafts of Older Spain*, London, 1907
An essential guide to the minor arts

Foreign
ALCOLEA, S. *Granada* (G.A.), Barcelona, 1960
Id. *Córdoba* (G.A.), Barcelona, 1963
ARAMBURU, A. DE *La Ciudad de Hercules*, Cádiz, 1946
BALBINO SANTOS, D. *Guía ilustrada de la Cátedral de Sevilla*, Madrid, 1930
CABALLERO BONALD, J. M. *El Baile Andaluz*, Barcelona, 1957
CEAN BERMÚDEZ, J. A. *Diccionario histórico de los más ilustres profesores de las bellas artes en España*, Madrid, 1800
The source book for the lives of artists
CERVANTES, M. DE *Novelas Ejemplares* 5th ed., Madrid, 1961
ESTEVE GUERRERO, M. *Jerez de la Frontera* 2nd ed., Jerez, 1952.
FERNÁNDEZ DEL VALLE, A. B. *Visión de Andalucia*, Mexico, 1966
FERNÁNDEZ, F. *La Alhambra* 2nd ed., Barcelona, 1933

FUSTER, J. *Alicante y La Costa Blanca*, Barcelona, 1965
GALLEGO Y BURIN, A. *Granada*, Madrid, 1961
GARCÍA GÓMEZ, E. *Silla del Moro* 2nd ed., Buenos Aires, 1954
Id. *Cinco Poetas Musulmanes* 2nd ed., Madrid, 1959
Id. *Poemas Arabigoandaluces* 4th ed., Madrid, 1959
    One of today's leading authorities on Moslem Spain
GARCÍA MERCADAL, J. *Viajes de Extranjeros por España y Portugal*,
    Madrid, 1952
GAUTIER, T. *Viaje por Espana* (Spanish trans.), Madrid, 1920
GUERRERO LOVILLO, J. *Sevilla* (G.A.), 2nd ed., Barcelona, 1962
LATOUR, A. DE *Etudes sur L'Espagne. Seville et l'Andalousie*, Paris,
    1855
LAS CUEVAS, J. & J. *Los mil años del Castillo de Tarifa*, Cádiz, 1964
LÉVI-PROVENÇAL, E. *La Civilización Árabe en España* (Trans. from
    the French by Isidro de Cagigas), Buenos Aires, 1953
    This author's research work has thrown fresh light on many aspects
    of Spanish and Moroccan history
LOJENDIO, L. M. DE *Gonzalo de Córdoba*, Madrid, 1942
    The best biography of the Great Captain
MAIZ VIÑALS, A. *Guía histórico-turística de la Ciudad de Marbella*,
    Málaga, 1966
MARTOS LÓPEZ, R. *La Iglesia de El Salvador*, Úbeda, 1951
MENÉNDEZ PIDAL, R. *Historia de España*, Vol. III *España Visigoda*,
    by Manuel Torres López *et al*; Vols. IV & V *España Musulmana* by
    E. Lévi-Provençal
    A monumental history, compiled by leading authorities and profusely
    illustrated with ample bibliography
MOLINA HIPÓLITO, J. *Guía de Ubeda*, Madrid, 1962
Id. *Guia de Baeza*, Madrid, 1964
OROZCO DÍAZ, E. *Guía del Museo Provincial de Bellas Artes, Granada*,
    Madrid, 1966
PEMÁN, J. M. *Andalucia* 2nd ed., Barcelona, 1966
PÉREZ GALDÓS, B. *Trafalgar*, Madrid, 1949
Id. *Bailén*, Madrid, 1961
PIETRI, F. *Pierre le Cruel*, Paris, 1961
RAMÓN JIMÉNEZ, J. *Platero y Yo*, Madrid, 1959
SÁNCHEZ-ALBORNOZ, C. *La España Musulmana* 2nd ed., Buenos
    Aires, 1960
Id. & VINAS, A. *Lecutras Históricus Españolas* 2nd ed., Madrid, 1929
    Two volumes of excerpts illustrating life in Moslem Spain
SARAZÁ MURCIA, A. *Córdoba* (with English translation) 7th ed.,
    Córdoba, 1955
TIRSO DE MOLINA *El Vergonzoso en Palacio. El Burlador de Sevilla y
    Convidado de Piedra* 8th ed., Madrid, 1966
TORRES BALBÁS, L. *La Mezquita de Córdoba y Madinat Al-Zahra*
    6th ed., Madrid, 1965
    The last word on the Mosque of Córdoba and Medina Azzahra

Index

Index

B. PERSONS AND SUBJECTS